Malcolm Bradbury is a novelist, television
dramatist, literary critic, and part-time
Professor of American Studies at the
University of East Anglia, where h
runs a programm
His novels inclu
(1959), *Stepping*
Man (1975), *Rate*
Cuts (1987); a ne
His television dra
and the 'television ...., *Train*; he
has also written short stories, poems, and
parodies. Critical works include *Possibilities*
(1973), *Saul Bellow* (1982), *The Modern
American Novel* (1983), *No, Not Bloomsbury*
(1987) and most recently *From Puritanism to
Postmodernism: A History of American Literature*
(1991, with Richard Ruland). He has lectured
internationally, was Chairman of the Booker
Judges in 1981, and was awarded the CBE
in 1991.

Judy Cooke was born in Wiltshire in 1938
and educated at King's College, University of
London. She lectured in modern literature in
the Extra-Mural Department, University of
London, and in the USA, and became Head of
the English department at Richmond College,
Surrey. In 1981 she founded *The Fiction
Magazine* which she edited until its demise
in 1987, when she published a collection of
stories, essays and poems by its contributors,
The Best of the Fiction Magazine. She is now a
freelance editor and works in the literature
department of the British Council. She writes
critical articles, reviews fiction regularly for the
Guardian and has published short stories and a
novel, *New Road*.

New
Writing

edited by

MALCOLM BRADBURY
and JUDY COOKE

Minerva in association with the
British Council

A Minerva Paperback

NEW WRITING

First published in Great Britain 1992
by Minerva in association with the British Council
by Mandarin Paperbacks
Michelin House, 81 Fulham Road, London sw3 6rb

Minerva is an imprint of the Octopus Publishing Group,
a division of Reed International Books Limited

The British Council gratefully acknowledges
the support of the Arts Council of Great Britain
in the production of this anthology

A CIP catalogue record for this title is available from the British Library
ISBN 0 7493 9913 9

Printed and bound in Great Britain
by Cox & Wyman Ltd, Reading, Berks

CONTENTS

Introduction *Malcolm Bradbury*   I

Fiction

Ever After (extract from a novel) *Graham Swift*   13
Homeward Bound *Alasdair Gray*   22
At Hiruharama *Penelope Fitzgerald*   33
King Billy is a Gentleman *Hilary Mantel*   40
Tender *Philip MacCann*   50
Salvages *Marina Warner*   60
The Blaneys (work in progress) *Suzannah Dunn*   76
Sassia (work in progress) *Adam Zameenzad*   94

The Muse *Mel Calman*   113

Essays

The Europe of the Mind *Michael Ignatieff*   123
Anglo-English Attitudes *Geoff Dyer*   132
The Film Set *Gilbert Adair*   145
Of Poets and their Antagonists *Ben Okri*   151
Logical Conclusions *Lucy Ellman*   160

Interviews

Martin Amis *interviewed by Christopher Bigsby*   169
Angela Carter *interviewed by Lorna Sage*   185

Spring Gardens *Drawings by Paul Cox*   195

Overviews

The Novelist Today: Still at the Crossroads?
  David Lodge   203
British Fiction of the 1980s *Peter Kemp*   216
Facing the New *Valentine Cunningham*   229

Poems

History *Dannie Abse*   243
Dread *Fred D'Aguiar*   244
Poem Composed in Santa Barbara, Letter,
Reflections on a Royalty Statement *Wendy Cope*   245
Before You Were Mine, Away and See
Carol Ann Duffy   247
Tale of Robbing Wood, Poem in Blank Rhyme
Glyn Maxwell   249
Scrap *Craig Raine*   252
From 'Evagatory' *Peter Reading*   254
Above Ryotsu, The Rug *Anthony Thwaite*   256
Self-Portrait in Old Age, Standstill *Hugo Williams*   257

Fiction

Art Work *A. S. Byatt*   263
Over *Rose Tremain*   291
Serrusalmus *Lesley Glaister*   295
The Coat *James Lasdun*   302
DHSS *Doris Lessing*   317
L'Hotel des Grands Hommes *Clare Morgan*   323
Conspirators *Paul Bailey*   332
The Squire's Treasure *Adam Thorpe*   338
Habits *Georgina Hammick*   355

Biographical Notes on the Authors   382
Acknowledgements   390

Introduction

I

As I step forward to throw open the doors of this new anthology of contemporary British writing from the Nineties – the first volume, we hope, of many – the news has lately come in of two important literary deaths, firstly of Graham Greene, and then of Angus Wilson. No anthology of new writing should begin with obituaries, but this is an exception. The fact is that these are two of the most important writers of our recent literary past, and looking back across their work helps us to get a perspective on the task of new writing today.

There can be no doubt that, until 3 April 1991, Graham Greene was Britain's greatest living writer; the fact that he never won the Nobel Prize for Literature is more a comment on the sad politics of prizes than it is on his significance and excellence. And up to 31 May 1991, Angus Wilson was our most important *post-war* novelist. Wilson, who started writing late, in his mid-30s, published his first short story in 1946, just after the war ended. Thereafter his stories and his panoramic social novels offered one of the most complete fictional portraits we have of the end-of-empire, welfare state, secular and anxiously liberal age that we have passed through since.

Both Greene and Wilson were above all international writers, who cast their eyes over British life more from outside than from within. Like a good many British authors, Greene spent much of his life abroad, and his experience, his themes, his readership and his influence were to become worldwide. Indeed he was a world writer, a half-rootless wanderer who always saw his life as a journey without maps, and who travelled a good part of the landscape – moral and metaphysical, as well as geographical and political – of the troubled and anxious century which is just now coming to its no less troubled and anxious end.

Wilson was born in Bexhill, grew up partly in South Africa, and his snobbish, *déclassé* parents brought him up largely in the rootless world of hotels. He was homosexual, a constant traveller, and had both an observant and a highly satirical eye for British society and its Anglo-Saxon attitudes. *Anglo-Saxon Attitudes* was in fact the title of his second novel, published in 1956, about the decencies but also the hypocrisies of English public and private life. The title was taken from a scene in Lewis Carroll's _Through the Looking Glass_, where Alice observes the strange and curious contortions of the Anglo-Saxon messenger, and the White King explains, '. . . those are Anglo-Saxon attitudes. He only does them when he's happy.'

Between them, Greene and Wilson became the observant explorers of Anglo-Saxon attitudes, and of the wider world, for a significant part of the century. One thing about Greene that is striking in retrospect is the sheer scale and variety of his production – more than twenty-five novels, more than fifty books, several stage plays and a number of important film scripts which were to change the flavour and direction of modern cinema. And even more striking is the fact that he wrote – and with an authority that never flagged, right up to his death – across eight decades of the century, a century in which not simply the fundamental directions of history and ideology but the very forms of modern writing changed profoundly. His first book (a modest volume of poems) appeared in 1924, his notable first novel _The Man Within_ in 1929. So his career started just as the high point of the Modern movement was coming to an end, amid the disturbances of world economic depression, international political crisis, rising totalitarianism. Greene was influenced by some of the strands in Modernism; two of the writers he most admired were Joseph Conrad and Ford Madox Ford, whom he thought the British writer of the century most likely to live on. But his own work, with its spyings and treacheries, seedy landscapes and dangerous frontiers, its wastes of political and moral confusion and its religious anxieties, really belongs much closer to the mood of the Thirties. Some of his most vivid novels were written then, culminating in _Brighton Rock_, which came out in 1938 as the world was on the brink of the Second World War.

The war was not only a crisis for the world but for writing itself. In Britain the modern movement came effectively to its end in a sequence of deaths – of Ford himself, W. B. Yeats, Virginia Woolf, and James Joyce – which seemed to signal the end of an era. Many of the writers who survived found it difficult to write on through the war and into the uneasy peace that followed. Probably more successfully than any other British novelist of his generation, Greene negotiated the difficult passage from pre-war to post-war world, a time when modern history cracked open and the entire direction of the century changed, along with the role of the writer. In fact some of his very finest books are the work of this difficult and transitional period – *The Power and the Glory* in 1940, *The Heart of the Matter* in 1948, *The End of the Affair* in 1951, *The Quiet American* in 1955. They move us from the seedy era of pre-war political crisis through the wartime battlefronts and bombings to the no less seedy post-war world, with its shattered cities and its new climate of cold war superpower rivalry. Somehow Greene's themes and atmospheres grew ever more emblematic. His moral and metaphysical anxieties fitted the era of existentialism and absurdism, post-war stress, ideological conflict and division. His vision of spies and treacheries, urban wastelands and shattered lives suited the age of split and divided loyalties, and his traveller's curiosity took him by instinct to the key trouble spots of the times. There were those who found both his religion and his politics – he somehow merged an idiosyncratic Catholicism with a no less idiosyncratic sympathy for Marxism – and his ironic vision of western liberal intentions disturbing. Others were dismayed by his distinctive vision of a world where compassion often led to self-destruction, the survival of fundamental human values often seemed an arbitrary matter, and causes had strange effects.

But if post-war British writing could sometimes be accused (with some justice) of provincialism, Greene was never provincial. He was a writer never at home with the familiar. When he wrote of provincial life – seedy bedsitter Nottingham, the pre-war Brighton of the razor gangs – it was always as part of a larger world map of pain and compassion, guilt and sin, treachery and obscure redemption. Both a popular and a serious writer, a storyteller as well as, sometimes, an experimentalist, he saw the novel as a narrative for telling stories of heroes or, more often, anti-heroes who, in the dark and confusing passages of twentieth-century history, faced some difficult yet eternal trial, succeeded or, more probably, failed in some existential and metaphysical quest. This was the human adventure, which took place in that distinct social and moral landscape the critics called Greeneland. Here the cigarette end floated eternally in the lavatory bowl, the secret agent and the private detective, the spy and the traitor, stalked through the dark streets of an ill-lit world, kindness and compassion frequently led to self-betrayal and despair, and life was a gamble with a death that had its own obscure and radical theology of hell and redemption.

In some ways Greene may always have remained a writer of the Thirties, a voyager through a half-strange world where no maps were safe, and which was the political and historical landscape of the troubled twentieth century itself. But his vision stayed strong, and the second half of the century was when his influence was greatest. He has left his trace everywhere, in fiction and film, in popular and serious forms. His work bridged many different genres: the political novel and the religious novel, the spy novel and the crime novel, the thriller, the metaphysical novella, the novel *noir*. Writers who have little in common have a common influence in him – Malcolm Lowry and John Le Carré, Muriel Spark and P. D. James, Anthony Burgess and Ian McEwan, David Lodge and Martin Amis. He shaped the future of the spy novel, the genre that expressed with peculiar vividness the duplicities and conspiracies of the cold war age; he equally shaped the future of the experimental religious novel, as in the work of Muriel Spark, a writer who shared his sense of the paradoxical role of God as plotter and the implications of this on the paradoxical plots of literature. Not only did he keep alive the generic variety of twentieth-century fiction for British authors; no other writer has built a better bridge between the writing of the earlier part of the century and the task of writing in the Nineties.

II

The title of this new anthology contains a modest homage to the titles of several anthologies that were produced by John Lehmann over the pre-war, wartime and post-war years that some of Greene's best fiction explores for us. *New Writing*, *New Writing and Daylight* and *Penguin New Writing* were the names of several magazine anthologies where Lehmann presented the newer writers of those times of world crisis, war, fears of totalitarianism, and literary deaths, persecutions, and exiles. The 'new writing' Lehmann supported was the work of authors who were, as he put it, 'conscious of the great social, political and moral changes going on around them', and who saw the times not just from a British but from a European or an international viewpoint. His later, most brilliant venture, *Penguin New Writing*, built in its forty paperback issues a great bridge across the wartime years and into the post-war world. It was, alas, to die in 1950, just at the moment when post-war British writing was beginning to take on its character and shape.

Angus Wilson represented the writing that came after 'new writing'. His malicious, brilliant short stories – he collected them in *Such Darling Dodos* (1949) and *The Wrong Set* (1950) – exactly captured the post-war mood, portraying the ironies and oppositions of the quiet but real social revolution which had moved Britain from an age of middle-class snobberies and imperial confidence into the more egalitarian, and also more bureaucratic, age of the Labour government and the welfare state. It was a time when liberalism had grown anxious and self-questioning, and the problem of evil threatened liberal moral faiths. That was the theme of Wilson's first novel, *Hemlock and After* (1952), about a liberal writer, Bernard Sands, who discovers that the virtuous and progressive liberal principles his work embodies are built on, exactly, sand. With *Anglo-Saxon Attitudes* in 1956, Wilson began on the panoramic exploration of English social and moral life that was to be one of his main themes, drawing on the Dickensian sweep of nineteenth-century fiction and the parodic note of late twentieth-century writing. And with *The Middle Age of Mrs Eliot* (1958) Wilson confronts a safe and conventional English life with the experience of international terrorism and the disorder of modern identity.

Wilson indeed was the first voice of a whole new generation of post-war British writers who came to notice over the 1950s, and who now are some of our leading established writers; several of them will be appearing in this and later volumes. They included novelists like William Golding, Iris Murdoch, Doris Lessing, Anthony Burgess, Kingsley Amis, Muriel Spark, and David Storey, playwrights like John Osborne, John Arden, Harold Pinter, Edward Bond, and Tom Stoppard, and poets like Philip Larkin, Ted Hughes, Thom Gunn, R. S. Thomas and Anthony Thwaite. Because a number of their early books indeed dealt with the social changes of Britain in the post-war years – lower middle class and working class life, the rise of the meritocracy, scenes from provincial life, the rising tide of materialism and affluence – their work has often been read primarily in sociological terms, and seen as a reaction against modernism and a return to nineteenth-century realism. In retrospect this seems erroneous; a good many of these writers were to prove, like Wilson himself, significant explorers of and experimenters with the forms of late twentieth-century fiction. As David Lodge suggested in an influential essay called 'The Novelist at the Crossroads', the novel historically has usually oscillated between phases of realism and of experiment, and the late twentieth-century novelist has consistently been confronted with the choice in a time of social change and anxious history. Indeed the situation continues, as Lodge suggests in his reflections on his earlier essay in this present volume.

Certainly during the Sixties Wilson's own work grew far more complex and experimental. *The Old Men at the Zoo* in 1961 is a surreal and apocalyptic work of political crisis, and *No Laughing Matter* in 1967, probably his best book, is a mock version of the bourgeois epic Wilson had been associated with, using parody, pastiche and the methods of post-modernism to present in a funfair mirror the recent history of Britain. The critics were slow to see the point, though in fact Wilson's experiment was quite consistent with the direction of British fiction in a decade which began with the publication of Doris Lessing's experimental *The Golden Notebook* (1962) and ended with John Fowles's simultaneous reconstruction and deconstruction of the Victorian novel, *The French Lieutenant's Woman* (1969). These books, along with Wilson's own, seem to me some of the most important novels published in post-war Britain, and they show the critical and self-questioning impulse that went through the fiction of the Sixties, when the novel challenged its earlier realism and explored surrealism, fantasy, parody and fictional play.

In 1973 Wilson produced one of his most remarkable books, *As If By Magic*, an attempt at nothing less than a global novel, set worldwide and about the ambitious and in some ways dubious campaign to overcome third world poverty through biological science and miracle crops. It reflected his increasing impatience with British literary parochialism, and his desire to escape 'the homegrown and the immediate' that he spoke of when, as chairman of the Booker prize judges in 1975, he awarded the honour to Ruth Prawer Jhabvala's *Heat and Dust*. In fact by this date fiction in Britain was already growing vastly more plural and various. Another important new generation was emerging – it included Angela Carter, Beryl Bainbridge, Fay Weldon, Peter Ackroyd, Julian Barnes, William Boyd, Rose Tremain, Ian McEwan and Martin Amis – who no longer felt bound to realism, and who freely explored surrealism, fantasy and metafictional play.

The new fiction also reflected the ever widening cultural variety of British life; when I chaired the Booker Prize in 1981, it was awarded to *Midnight's Children*, Salman Rushdie's extraordinary, experimental endeavour to write a novel of international modern history which was also a vast post-modern construct of oral and written narratives from the multi-cultural tradition. Rushdie's serious and magnificent endeavour to write for a multi-cultural age was, alas, to end in his tragic exclusion by those he tried to draw into the world of fictions, but the widening of British fiction that both Greene and Wilson sought has come about, in an age when the novelists who publish from London not only have names like Drabble, Carter or Amis but Kazuo Ishiguro, Timothy Mo, Ben Okri, Hanif Kureishi, and David Dabydeen. It was a widening of culture that Wilson himself sought to shape, as novelist, critic, and influential teacher of younger writers. Like Greene, he has left his impact on the writing that was to follow.

III

Any new writing will owe something to the past and a good deal to the future. But one time when that is especially true is at the end of a century, when the sense that one order is about to close and another to open grows ever stronger. As that brilliant recorder of the last days of the nineteenth century, Holbrook Jackson, said in his book *The 1890s*, 'new' became the adjective of the decade: 'the range of the adjective spread until it embraced the ideas of the whole period, and we find innumerable references to the "New Spirit", the "New Humour", the "New Realism", the "New Hedonism", the "New Drama", the "New Unionism", the "New Party", and the "New Woman".' This is already very familiar, and so are some of the reasons for it. Like the writers of a hundred years ago, we are perhaps more than usually aware of the tensions and conflicts, the multiple directions, the reshaping of values and ideologies, of styles and roles, that belong to the dying and dawning not just of centuries but of the world orders they create and dissolve.

Since 1989, when the Berlin Wall came down, we have good reason to think that we no longer live in the modern or the post-modern, or indeed the post-war, world, but in an age that is in difficult transition into a changed world order. We too live in a time when the systems and ideologies a whole century has constructed are beginning to come apart, when two of the dominant ideologies – Marxism and liberal capitalism – are themselves showing, in their different ways, signs of crisis, when old systems are weakening and new ones are only just beginning to take shape. We too feel walls tumbling, connections fracturing, bridges being precariously crossed; we sense the familiar apocalyptic anxieties of such times about dusks and dawns, chaos and anarchy, the collapsing and the polluting of cities, the widening of the ozone hole, the threat less now of atomic than environmental annihilation. Our food, our water, our sex and our smoking threaten to injure us. As Martin Amis suitably put it in the prefatorial note to his novel *London Fields*, most books could be called *Millennium* just now.

The final years of centuries have usually contained more hunger for style than they have new style itself; the last decades are usually provisional, and that is the spirit in which we have edited this anthology. Clearly we are a long way away from the time when John Lehmann created his – not at the midpoint of a troubled century but at the end of it, when many of the issues, ideologies and artistic convictions that affected his new writing have changed fundamentally. Lehmann saw his volumes as European and international in emphasis; and so do we. But the shape of the European world changed irrevocably in 1989 and is in process of a further change that will continue through the Nineties, as new European ideals (and illusions) take shape. The literary scene generally – not only in Britain but also elsewhere – does little to help those critics who like their literature to come in the forms of clear movements, tendencies, and ideologies. In Britain as elsewhere, the dominant characteristic of new writing is its variety and pluralism, its multiplicity of expression, its breadth of voices, many of them challenging the realistic coherence or the themes of previous writing.

Thus the Eighties saw, in the work of writers like Angela Carter, Fay Weldon, Jeannette Winterson, and Marina Warner, as well as Caryl Churchill, Michelene Wandor and others in theatre, the rise of feminist writing, much of it challenging the representation of women in earlier literature. It saw, in the work of Scots writers like Alasdair Gray and James Kelman, or in drama Ian Heghie, of Irish writers like John Banville and John McGahern, as in the poetry of Seamus Heaney, Tom Paulin, Paul Muldoon, Michael Longley, and many more, the rise of a culturally various regionalized writing with similar intentions. The growth of bi-cultural writing (Kazuo Ishiguro, Timothy Mo) or multi-cultural writing (Salman Rushdie) has made phrases like 'the English novel' and 'English poetry' into misnomers. The current state of fiction in Britain is explored later in these pages by David Lodge, Peter Kemp and Valentine Cunningham, and I do not want to add to their portraits. But what is clear is that writing out of Britain today portrays a world far less coherent and easily definable than was true in the days of John Lehmann's anthologies. Sociologically it portrays a Britain that is placed in a larger human world, a land of late modern stagnating cities, cultural, ethnic and gender division, entrepreneurial adventurers and post-modern consumers of instant style, but with a strong sense of being in change. Aesthetically, it is equally plural, ranging freely from one genre to another, from the detective story to science fiction, the historical novel to the post-modern pastiche, reviving forms of writing from the past while experimenting with the often media-based forms of the future. It is a writing open less than ever to the classic distinctions between the 'serious' and the 'popular', or the 'experimental' and the conventional, and it is layered with many generations, especially a strong new generation that emerged during the course of the Eighties.

IV

So how does one select, construct and introduce the 'new writing' of the Nineties? In conceiving this anthology, our purposes were deliberately unprescriptive. We wanted to present writing from various different generations, tendencies and backgrounds that have been important in recent years and continue to be so into the Nineties. We wanted to range from work by well-known and established writers (in this volume, they include Doris Lessing, Penelope Fitzgerald, A.S. Byatt, David Lodge, Anthony Thwaite, and Danny Abse) to work by the new and in some cases the previously unpublished (like Suzannah Dunn and Philip MacCann). We share John Lehmann's belief in European and international writing, though less his conviction that important contemporary work reflects and addresses the political state of the world. With the room afforded by a book-sized magazine we want to be a showcase and a place of record for new developments, and to foreground what seems best and liveliest about writing from the British Isles, and further afield, in a given year. We have tried to give special attention to the short story, a form that is widely practised in Britain but less widely published; we will print a good deal of poetry, and contemporary drama where it benefits from print. One important aim is to publish extracts from novels in progress which are soon to appear. In this issue, there are sections from forthcoming novels of 1992 by Graham Swift, Adam Zameenzad and Suzannah Dunn.

It is also our belief that new writing always flourishes best when it is surrounded by a climate of good debate and discussion, something that has been rather lacking in a time when academic criticism has grown highly theoretical and the number of new literary reviews and magazines has severely diminished (we have recently, and sadly, lost *Encounter*). We wish to have new interviews with leading writers; there are two, with Martin Amis and Angela Carter, in this issue. We also wish to publish personal essays and statements, like those by Ben Okri and Lucy Ellmann here, as well as essays of literary and cultural criticism, for the general rather than the academic audience, by leading critics and commentators, and not solely from Britain. So we shall welcome essays that deal with literary and cultural affairs, especially in an international perspective, and hope in future numbers to address some of the important themes, issues and directions of the Nineties, from the state of contemporary drama and film to problems of literature in translation, from the development of multi-cultural writing to directions in such genres as spy, detective and science fiction. We wish to make British writing more internationally visible; we also wish to encourage the internationalisation of that writing. But the main aim is first to display, in quantity, variety and at length, the new writing of what seems to us an active, lively and exploratory time. Here, then, it is, in its first instalment. Do let us know how you like it.

Fiction

Ever After

The first chapter of a novel
to be published by Picador in 1992

These are, I should warn you, the words of a dead man.

Or they are at least – the warning stands – nothing more
than the ramblings of a prematurely aged one. I have been in
this place now barely a year, but I am fully aware from the
inside, as I think the public is from the outside, of its effect of
induced senescence. There are of course, these days, those sexy
young studs of academe who attempt to go against the grain.
But even they, it can be observed, when they reach a certain age
– roughly my age, a little past fifty – begin to settle rather quickly
into the lean and slippered pantaloon. They look about them at
their venerable surroundings, at the privileges they possess, they
take stock of their no longer galloping careers, and they decide,
consciously or not, that true donhood, like the quality of fine wine,
is inseparable from age.

It is something in the air here. Before they are sixty, they are
emulating one of the many varieties: the crusty and cantanker-
ous; the bald and bumbling; the silver-haired exquisite; the
bespectacled and tousled distrait; the free-wheeling eccentric;
the wide-eyed, latter-day infant, helpless in all mundane matters
but possessed of a profound understanding of Sanskrit. By seventy
or eighty – and there is no reason, given the pampering they get,
why they shouldn't go on for decades – they are convinced they
have reached their true flowering and that, whatever their status
in their particular fields (though eminence may be assumed) they
are, in themselves, rare birds, exceptional cases, worthy of living
enshrinement.

(Potter, by the way, is pushing forty-eight.)

We are, of course, an endangered and thus protected species.
If natural selection had had its nasty way, we should have been
wiped out long ago, a fragile, etiolated experiment (I have slipped
into the insidious 'we'). Once, no doubt, when we stepped, blinking, out of our cloisters, the new-fangled foibles of the modern city,
not to say of the world beyond, would have seemed specious and
temporary; our ancient walls would have seemed the true, real,

permanent thing. But now it is those ancient walls which have become artificial and implausible, like a painstakingly contrived film set. It is everything beyond that is real. If hardly reliable. Out there, we are given to believe (twelve months, did I say? It feels like twelve years), the world is falling apart; its social fabric is in tatters, its eco-system is near collapse. Real: that is, flimsy, perishing, stricken, doomed. Whereas here . . .

But shouldn't we dodos understand this?

The University, of course, takes its own shrewd steps, as it has always done, to ensure its survival. But survival of the fittest? A few dubiously nimble brains in a few desiccated, enfeebled bodies? I had hardly been here a few weeks when I began to have a dream which I am sure all my fellow Fellows dream. Out there in the dark, in the 'real world', is a prowling, snarling lout, all tattoos and bared teeth. He too, like us, is social scrap, but without our preservation order. No privileges, no prospects, no pride, no compunction. Like many who do not have these things, he has plenty of brawn and spite, and one day, with a horde of his brethren, he is going to break through our precious, time-honoured walls and beat our estimable brains out.

But this vision does not trouble me so much now. Not now. If the Vandals are coming, the Vandals are coming. Death in such a fashion, deserved or undeserved, would of course be appalling. But death itself is another matter. The deaths of others have lately punctuated – shattered, overturned – my life. No less than three – I shall come to them all – in eighteen months. But only very recently, despite this forced familiarity, have I looked the beast itself hard in the face. Not just looked it in the face but wanted it to devour me. I am talking of that experience, given to few, of being returned to life from almost-death. I am talking, in my case, of attempted self-slaughter.

This is the real reason why I say I am prematurely decrepit. My recipe, you see, was at fault. These things (I know from example) can be well executed or hopelessly botched. I was found. They rushed me away, pumped me, thumped me, jump-started me, wired me to the latest gadgets. And the net result of all this was that I opened again these eyes which I thought to have closed for ever and began breathing and thinking for myself (though that phrase begs questions) once more.

But you can imagine the shock to the system. It is not as though my hair has turned white or I have been reduced to a haggard and wasted spectre. I recognise the face in the mirror. Or rather, I recognise that I have never truly recognised it. But I have certainly slowed down a bit. I certainly need to take it easy. I have, for the time being at least, the pitiful gait, the sad posture and the low reserves of an old man. I look more *like* a don. But, more to the point, I feel as though I have *moved on*, in some critical but indefinable way, from what I was before. I have left my former self, whatever that was, behind. I am changed.

What I do not feel is pain – I mean spiritual pain. I do not groan and weep to be restored again to the consciousness I had hoped to forfeit, I do not regard the failure of my attempt as a twist of ineffable cruelty. I simply feel as though I have become someone else. And I am not sure if I accept or resent the process. One part of me seems to have occupied a place of serene detachment. I feel like the ghost of Troilus at the end of Chaucer's poem, which, ascending through the spheres of heaven (no, I did not have that famed experience of rising out of my own body and surveying it from the ceiling) looked down with dispassionate equanimity on the former scene of all his joy and sorrow. While another part of me – hence these ramblings – feels the forlorn urge to find and meet my former self again, while secretly wondering whether the meeting will be a happy or disastrous one.

I am not me. Therefore was I ever me? That is the gist of it. A proof of all this lies before your very eyes. Or at least before mine, since you have no means of comparison and only my word to go on. But that is the point: these *words*, or rather the tone, the pitch, the style of them and consequently of the thoughts that underlie them, are not mine. I have penned in my time – long ago – a thesis and an academic paper or two, but I have never begun to write anything as – personal – as this. Yet this way in which I write is surely not *me*. What would you call it? A little crabbed and sardonic? A little wry? A tendency to the flippant and cynical? Underneath it all, something careless, heartless? Is this how I am?

But these are minor matters, you say. What is important, what you are dying (excuse the phrase) to know, is what brought me to the pitch of staging my own death in the first place. I could get out of this by saying that since I am a different person now from what I was then (only three weeks ago), how can I possibly tell you? But it is not as simple as that. Perhaps these pages will eventually explain. Perhaps they will give *me* an explanation. I will only say, for the time being, that for a large part of my life, ever since my old English master, Tubby Baxter, made us read the play, I have imagined myself – surreptitiously, presumptuously, appropriately, perversely – as Hamlet. And you all know one of his tendencies.

Fifty-two, you will say, is a little old to be playing Hamlet, but the fads of adolescence die hard. If you knew me better, you might suppose that for much of my time, despite being for some years (things have come full circle) a professional exponent of English literature and having also a privileged link with the theatre, I would have had no use for this skulking, brooding figure. This is a roundabout way of saying that if happy men exist, I was for many years, for the best years of my life, a happy man. Yes, a happy man. But perhaps the pensive prince was always there, lurking in some morbid toy-box, a foil to the brightness of my days. And when the lights suddenly went out, less than two years ago, he popped up again with a vengeance – vengeance being another of his preoccupations.

It is strange that I never told Ruth about this secret affinity. After all, she more than once played Ophelia – the last time, you might say, for real. I don't like to think I had secrets from Ruth. But perhaps it was because she was an actress that I never confessed: she would have taken my fixation as the pretension of a would-be actor. And it was she, in any case, who made the image absurd. It was she who made me happy.

I shouldn't blame Tubby Baxter. Rather, I owe him infinite thanks for introducing me to Literature, which despite its failure to save lives, including, I suppose I must say, my own, and despite its being, in a place like this, for ever chopped up and flung into preservatives as if it were a subject for an autopsy, I still believe in. I still believe it is the speech, the voice of the heart. (Say things like that round here and see what happens.) Tubby Baxter was not to blame for the doleful but charismatic Renaissance protagonist who has somehow got under all our skins. Nor was he to blame for the circumstances which induced in me a particularly acute rapport.

Hamlet is actuated, or immobilised, by two questions: 1) is there or is there not any point to it all? 2) shall I kill Claudius? Or to put it another way: shall I kill Claudius or shall I kill myself? It was the vengeance theme that grabbed me from the start, just as much as the distraught meditations on the meaning of life, though I understood, even aged thirteen and a half, that the two questions were not inseparable.

For Claudius, read Sam Ellison. 'Uncle Sam', as he was inevitably known, since he hailed from Cleveland, Ohio. Otherwise my stepfather, and founding father of Ellison Plastics (UK). For forty years of my life I have conducted a theoretical vendetta against Sam, though I do not think real killing was ever on the cards. And the odd thing is I have always liked him. I have never been able to help liking him.

Now he is dead; and revenge is pre-empted, or has been satisfied. Or, if revenge is a two-sided game, it is Sam who in a posthumous but canny fashion has got his revenge on me. I rather think, in fact, that Sam's death, which occurred only six weeks ago, may not have been unconnected with my own adverted one. It is not the huge, primary things that push you over (I suppose I can speak now as an authority) but the odd, secondary things. He died, and I always really liked him. Furthermore, Ruth being already dead, his death removed, I have to admit it, absurd as it seems, one of the main shaping factors, one of the plots of my life.

What was left? Potter? Katherine? The strange, stray notebooks of an unknown man – another latter-day fixation – who lived over a century ago? But I will come to all this.

The manner of his death – death number three, chronologically speaking – was also significant, though to me it was neither as surprising nor as scandalous as it might be to a number of people who do not know about it or as it is to a number of people who are conspiring to hush it up. (I could get my posthumous revenge that way, but it would be cheap, low-down revenge.) He died of a heart attack in a Frankfurt hotel room, aged sixty-seven. His death was reported by the call-girl he was with at the time who, to give her her due, might simply have fled the scene. At the fatal moment either Sam was on top of her or she was on top of Sam. At any rate, it seems they were intimately connected when death occurred. An unsavoury business. But then if we could choose our deaths – and I tried to choose mine – I am not so sure that this wasn't exactly the kind of death Sam might have preferred. (You see what this new me is like.)

Under certain circumstances, generosity is one of the most effective and perhaps one of the sweetest means of revenge. If it were not for Sam, I would not be enjoying the mixed blessings of my present situation – I mean the sanctuary of these ancient walls, not my recent resurrection. I will come to this too in a moment. There is the more immediate question of Sam's will and my prominent inclusion in it. I must reveal that I find myself a rich man, and that had my attempted demise been successful, I would have immediately made the taxman the chief beneficiary of my short-lived wealth. I am a plastics heir, you might say, in the way that people talk of cocoa heirs or rubber barons.

But it is not just a question of the money. Is a plastic cup less real than a china one? Nylon stockings less real than silk? More to the point, is plastic any more fraudulent than a stage performance? Or a poem? Yet long ago when my former self refused my stepfather's offer of a future in plastic, it did so in the conviction that the real stuff of life lay elsewhere. And I am not alone, perhaps, in regarding plastic as the epitome of the false. Sam never saw it that way. In those days when it seemed to me that his goal was nothing less than the polymerisation of the world (this is when the spirit of Hamlet breathed newly and fiercely in me), his argument would have been roughly thus: 'You gotta accept it, pal,' (he called me pal, when he did not call me 'kid' or, scathingly, 'professor'), 'the real stuff is running out, it's used up, it's blown away, or it costs too much. You gotta have *substitoots*.'

Yet, as Ellison Plastics went from strength to strength (without my assistance), it would have been clear to anyone that Sam's appetite for the 'real stuff' developed in proportion to his capacity, with the money he made from substitutes, to purchase it: the new mansion in Berkshire – *real* Tudor (with a swimming-pool), as opposed to the mock Tudor in which I was raised; the affectation of fine tailoring and choice antiques; in its ultimate form, the apotheosis of Sam, a New World clone, into a Real English Gentleman. A plan preposterously conceived, doomed from the start by his indelible Cleveland accent, but earnestly and perseveringly undertaken: the genealogical investigations (why should these things have mattered to *him*?); the wondrous discovery, not that he had come over with the Normans or was of *Mayflower* stock, but that a former Ellison, John Elyson (d. 1623) had been a senior Fellow of this College, this place where I am now myself an inmate. Which gave him an hereditary stake in the hallowed ancient walls; and gave him the nerve, in his sixty-seventh year, to boost the College finances by a handsome endowment, the one (secret) condition of this munificent gesture being that it should provide for a new College fellowship, the Ellison Fellowship, whose first incumbent, whatever the outward form of selection, should be me.

And this is the Sam who once mocked and refused to fund my former yen to be a scholar.

Without knowing the full story – give me time – you may sniff here the bitter scent of retaliation. It was his way of coming to my rescue after Ruth's death. There was the question of my income. One way or the other, as he tenderly reminded me, I had lived off Ruth's earnings. And there was the question of my seemingly incurable paralysis in the face of Ruth's loss. Better to be somewhere where paralysis was generally accommodated. In other words, it was his way also of humiliating me and, after life-long resistance, rendering me entirely dependent upon him. The cloister was my real home all along, wasn't it? So much for my fugitive dream of a life with performers, show people. Back to your books, professor.

The trouble was I really liked him, and the trouble was I was desolate and he was being kind. In the event, anxious not to forgo its windfall, the College did not raise a squeak at the dubiousness of my candidature (a ten-year career, abandoned some fifteen years ago, as an unillustrious university lecturer). The embarrassments and resentments came later. Nor did the College seem to mind its revered fabric being underpinned by plastic.

Sam's death, leaving me in this utterly bogus position, with the duty of being a living testimony to his noble public gesture, was like the closing of a trap. 'One day, pal, you'll get the money, I'll see that you get the money!' This was how he threatened me when I went my own proud, penniless way, years ago – as if money were a penalty, an inescapable second-best.

You see, I think I found the real stuff, the true, real stuff. Now it seems, in this new life, I am turned to plastic. I am born again in plastic.

Four o'clock. Chimes float gently over the soft, historic air. What benign incarceration! What beguiling obsolescence! What agreeable trappings in which not to know who you are. The contemplative life! Sometimes even the most disgruntled inmate or sceptical visitor will be touched by a sentiment that is more than just picturesque nostalgia. Twilights full of bells and the pad of feet on old stones. Lights in study windows. Arches and towers. The whole absurd but cherished edifice rising like some fantastical lantern out of the miasmal Fens and out of the darkness of dark ages. The illusion of the illusion. It is civilisation that we are talking about, that we are saving, we dotty dons.

Here, in our exclusive asylum.

When I emerged from the hospital, a fully reconditioned if fragile specimen, a period of convalescence was ordained. What better convalescent home than the old College itself? With its immured peace, its quiet lawns and its long experience of catering to the frailties and follies of learning. It was the long vacation. The long vacation, indeed. I was considerately and spitefully relieved of my scant College duties. A mere charge to its budget. A mere token of a Fellow.

And so I sit in these College gardens, under the shade of an Indian bean tree (a fine, mature example), trying to recover my substance. The weather is warm and settled. All the tranquil delights of a lovingly tended garden in high summer greet my eyes. The gardeners give me a wide, respectful berth. It is not quite a case of the bath chair and the plaid rug. I can make my own way here from my rooms. On my knees is an inverted wooden tray and on it this notepad. The garden lies separate from the College buildings, across the river and, happily, some distance from it. At this time of the year, in weather like this, the river is a mêlée of mismanaged punts, splashes and squeals, with all the gentle charm of a wet T-shirt competition. Even here, in my arbour, the occasional scream or cackle of laughter reaches me; and more adventurous tourists, taking the path from the bridge, through the avenue of limes, and stopping at the gap in the high hedge and the little gate with its discreet, white-on-black sign, 'Fellows Only', might even be able to observe me, across the lawn. 'Look,' they must think, like visitors at a zoo, pausing by some cage of shy rarities, 'there is one of *them*.' And no doubt, seeing me scribble at this notepad, they take me to be immersed in some unfathomable and abstruse research.

But aren't I?

Why should I resent my situation? I am restored to life. The sun shines through a punkah of green, tender leaves. Life! Life! Does it matter, so long as you breathe, who the hell you are? Or where you are? Or what you remember? Or what you miss? Why should I hate the man – who is dead anyway, and whom I

liked – who has provided me with all this? Who has taken away
from me – good God! how life can change, how everything can
change in the space of less than two years – all worldly cares?
But I have not told you yet the nub of my hatred, the nub of my
forty years' vicarious habitation of Elsinore as my second home.
There is nothing worse than Revenge Refuted. You see, I thought
Sam killed my father. So to speak. But now I know he didn't. My
father killed my father. And this in more ways than one.

Homeward Bound

This thirty-year-old college lecturer is big, stout, handsome, with the innocent baby-face of a man used to being served by women, the sulky underlip of one who has never been served as much as he wants. It is Sunday afternoon. He compares the dial of his wristwatch with that of small ornate clock under glass dome on mantelpiece. Both indicate 2.49. He sighs and looks critically round his apartment like a mechanic surveying a machine that has stopped working for him. Walls are pale grey, woodwork white, the moss-green fitted carpet harmonises (not too obviously) with his immaculate dark green sweater. A large low bed lacks foot and headboard, has big blue cushions strewn on it, derives an air of invitation from a nearby coffee table on which lie a board supporting cold roast chicken, oatcakes, pat of butter, knife, salt-cellar; a salver of apples, peaches, grapes; a dish of small bright cakes and sweets. A few stones in the marble fireplace look nothing like coal, but bright flames among them give the air warmth which would make undressing easy, without making clothed people sweat. Through an oriel window a view of sunlit treetops can be blotted out (when wished) by smoothly running floor-length curtains, curtains with the light tone of his finely creased flannel trousers. Yet he sighs again, not feeling truly at home. Maybe an apple will help. He goes determinedly to the table but hesitates to disturb his arrangement of the fruit. A bell chimes softly. Smiling with relief he leaves the room, crosses a lobby, opens the front door and says, 'Vlasta.'

A bitterly sobbing woman runs in past him. He looks out into corridor, sees nobody else, closes door.

Returning to the main room he stands, watching the woman and thoughtfully rubbing his chin. She crouches on an easy chair, handbag on lap, sobbing into handkerchief. She is bony and fortyish with wild black hair flowing over the shoulders of her fur coat, a long black skirt and histrionic earrings. The sobs lessen. He tiptoes to the coffee table, lifts and places it softly near her right elbow, selects an apple and sits on a chaise-longue facing her. Cautiously he bites the apple. Her sobbing stops. She removes mirror from handbag and blots off tears, taking care not to damage make-up. He says softly, 'I'm glad you came. Eat something. It sometimes helps.'

She says hoarsely, 'You are always so sweet to me, Alan.'

She restores mirror and hanky to handbag, tears a wing from the chicken, bites, swallows and says, 'Half an hour ago I threw out Arnold. He did not want to go. I had to call the police. He was drunk and violent. He cracked my tortoise, Alan.'

'You were right to call the police.'

'He was sweet to begin with – just like you. And then he went bad on me. Eventually they all go bad on me – except you.'

She bites and swallows more chicken.

Then looks around and says, 'Are you expecting someone?'

He smiles sadly, says, 'Expecting someone? I only wish I was.'

'But this food! . . . And the room. You did not always keep it so spick and span.'

'I do nowadays. I've become a real old woman since you left me, Vlasta, hoovering the carpet, dusting the clock – I've even grown cranky about food. I don't eat regular meals any longer. I keep plates of fruit and cold chicken beside me and have a nibble whenever I feel like it.'

'How odd! But have you no little girlfriend? No mistress?'

A brass coal-scuttle on the hearth is used as a waste basket. With a harsh laugh Alan throws in the apple core and says, 'None! None! I know plenty of women. I've invited some of them up here, and they've come. A few stayed the night. But (I don't know why) they all bored me. After you they were all so insipid.'

'I knew it!' cries Vlasta exultantly. 'Yes I knew it! When I left you I told myself, You are destroying this man. You have taught him all he knows and now that you leave him his confidence will vanish also. In fact you are castrating him! But I had to do it. You were sweet but . . . oh so deadly dull. No imagination. And so I had to leave.'

'It was agony,' he assures her.

'I knew. I was sorry for you but I needed excitement. I will take my coat off, this room is far too warm, how can you bear it?'

She stands and flings her chicken bone into the scuttle.

But Alan has risen first. Slipping behind her he helps remove the coat murmuring, 'Perhaps you'll remove more before you leave.'

'What a fool you are Alan – you still know *nothing* about women. It was four years ago, not last week we ceased to be lovers. I came here for peace, not erotic excitement. In the last three hours I have had more excitement than many of the bourgeoisie experience in a lifetime.'

'Sorry!' murmurs Alan, and carries coat to bed. He lays it there then sits on bedfoot, right elbow on knee, right hand supporting chin like Rodin's *Thinker*.

'I am a dreadful woman, I destroy men!' says Vlasta, yawning and stretching her arms. 'Arnold kept shouting that while the policemen dragged him away.'

'Please sit beside me. I'm very lonely.'

She sits beside him saying, 'Think of Mick McTeague, old before his time and drinking like a fish.'

'He was a sixty-year-old alcoholic when you first met him.'

'He's worse now. Last week I saw Angus pushing his baby in a pram in the park, a slave to a woman too foolish to understand him.'

'He seems perfectly happy to me,' says Alan, sitting up and facing her. 'We play snooker sometimes.'

She laughs aloud at his naiveté.

'Oh Alan, have you forgotten *everything* I taught you? Beneath the calmest of lives all sorts of dreadful things are happening: spiritual rapes, murders, incests, tortures, suicides. And the calmer the surface the worse what is hidden beneath.'

Her perfume fills his nostrils, her body is an inch away, with real excitement he declares, 'I love the way you turn life into an adventure, an exciting, idiotic adventure.'

'*IDIOTIC?*'

She glares at him.

'No no no no!' he explains hastily, 'That was a slip of the tongue, a device by which my conventional bourgeois hypocrisy attempted to defend itself.'

'Hm!' she says, only slightly placated, 'I see you remember *some* of the things I taught you.'

She sits beside him again, yawns and says, 'Ahoo, I am very tired. It is exhausting work, explaining life to thick policemen.'

She lies back on the bed with her face upward and eyes closed.

A minute passes in silence. He stealthily pulls off his shoes, lies beside her and unfastens the top button of her blouse. Without opening her eyes she says in a small voice, 'I told you I was in no mood.'

'Sorry.'

He sighs and resumes the Rodin's *Thinker* pose.

After a while she says lazily, 'I love you for being so easily discouraged.'

He looks hopefully round. Her eyes are open, she is smiling, then laughing and sitting up and embracing him.

'Oh Alan, I can refuse you nothing! You are like an ugly old comfortable sofa I must always fall back upon.'

'Always at your service!' he assures her. They stand up. He pulls off his sweater, she starts removing her blouse, and the bell chimes.

The doorbell chimes. He stands as if paralysed and whispers, 'Fuck.'

She cries, 'You WERE expecting someone!'

'No. Nonsense. Ignore it. Please speak more quietly Vlasta!'

The bell chimes.

'Do you tell me you do not know who is there?'

'I swear it.'

'Then go to the door and send them away,' cries Vlasta, rapidly fastening her blouse, 'Or I will!'

The bell chimes. She strides to the lobby, he dodges before her and stands with his back to the front door hissing, 'Be sensible, Vlasta.'

'Open that door or I will scream!'

Through clenched teeth he mutters, 'Listen! This might be, just might be, a young woman I greatly admire and respect. She must not be upset, you hear? She must not be upset!'

The bell chimes. Vlasta smiles coolly, folds her arms, says, 'So open the door.'

He does. A stout man wearing a raincoat and trilby hat stands outside. He says, 'Scottish Power. Can I read your meter sir?'

'Yes,' says Alan. He opens a cupboard (Vlasta has strolled back to the main room) and the man directs a torch beam on the dials of a squat black box.

'Sorry I'm late Alan,' says a small pretty girl of perhaps eighteen.

'Hullo,' says Alan. She goes into the big room and Alan hears her say brightly, 'Hullo – my name is Lillian Piper.'

He hears Vlasta say, 'You are one of his students, of course.'

'Yes!'

'What a *coward* he is.'

'In Australia,' says the stout man writing figures on a pad, 'all meters have dials which can be read from outside the main door. I wish we had that system here, sir.'

'Yes. Goodbye,' says Alan shutting the stout man out. Then he sighs and joins the ladies.

Vlasta (grim faced, arms folded, legs astride) stands in the middle of the room. Lillian stands near the fire looking thoughtfully at the rumpled bed-cover and his sweater on the floor beside it.

'Lillian,' says Alan, 'this is Vlasta – Vlasta Tchernik, old friend I haven't seen for years. She called in unexpectedly fifteen or twenty minutes ago.'

'He was seducing me when the meter man called,' explains Vlasta. 'He had my blouse off.'

'Is that true?' asks Lillian.

'Yes.'

'Oh Alan.'

Lillian sits down on the chaise-longue, Alan on the easy chair. They seem equally depressed. Vlasta, glaring from one to the other, feels excluded, awaits an opening.

At last Alan tells Lillian, 'I wish you had come when you said you would. I'd given you up.'

'I was only forty minutes late! I've been very punctual till now.'

'I know. So I thought . . . since you didn't even phone . . . that you'd suddenly tired of me.'

'Why did you think that? We got on so well the last time we met . . . Didn't we?'

'Oh I enjoyed myself. But did you?'

'Of course! I told you so.'

'Maybe you were just being polite. A lot of women are polite at those times. After I'd waited fifteen minutes I thought, She was being polite when she said she enjoyed herself. And after twenty minutes I thought, She's not coming. She's met someone more interesting.'

Lillian stares at him.

'He has NO self-confidence!' cries Vlasta triumphantly. 'He is a weakling, a coward, a liar, a cheat, and DULL! Oh, so deadly dull.'

'Nonsense,' says Lillian, but without much force, 'he says very clever things sometimes.'

'Can you give me an example?'

Lillian thinks hard and eventually says, 'We went for a walk last Sunday and he said, The countryside looks very green today but I suppose that's what it's there for.'

'He was quoting me,' says Vlasta with satisfaction, 'and I got it from a book.'

'*Were* you quoting her?' Lillian asks Alan. He nods. She sighs then tells Vlasta that cleverness isn't important – that Alan says very sweet sincere things which matter a lot more.

'Oho!' cries Vlasta, inhaling deeply like a war-horse scenting blood. 'This really interests me – tell me about these sweet sincere things.' She strides to the chaise-longue and sits beside Lillian.

'Would either of you like a glass of sherry?' asks Alan loudly. He has gone to the fireplace, unstoppered a heavy cut-glass decanter and now tilts it enquiringly above a row of frail glasses on the mantelpiece. The ladies ignore him. He fills a glass, swigs it, then fills and swigs a second.

Vlasta says, 'Tell me just one of his sweet, tender remarks.'

'I'd rather not,' says Lillian shortly.

'Then I will tell one to you. Let me think . . . yes. When you get in bed together, does he stretch himself and say in a tone of oh such heartfelt gratitude, *Thank God I'm home again*?'

Lillian is too depressed to speak but nods once or twice. Vlasta notices Alan swallow a third sherry and says, 'You are trying to give yourself Dutch courage.'

'I'm trying to anaesthetise myself,' he tells her sulkily. Lillian goes to him saying, 'Give me the sherry, Alan.'

She reaches for the decanter. He gives it to her. She drops it to smash on the hearth tiles and says, 'You don't deserve anaesthetic,' and wanders away from him, clenching her hands and trying not to weep. He stares aghast saying, 'Lillian! Lillian!'

Then sighs, kneels, takes a brass-handled shovel and broom from a stand of fire-irons and starts sweeping up the mess.

But Vlasta is more impressed than he is. She cries, 'That was magnificent! You are wonderful, little Lillian! People think I am very fierce and violent because I always tell the truth, but believe me I am too timid to smash furniture.'

Lillian asks harshly, 'What other sweet things did he say to you?'

'Stop!' cries Alan. He pitches broom, shovel, broken glass into the scuttle and says firmly, 'Leave us, Vlasta, we're as miserable as you could want us to be.'

He is head and neck taller than Lillian, half a head taller than Vlasta, and for the first time today his bulk suggests dignity. But Vlasta says, 'I enjoy myself! I shall not leave,' and answers his stare with a hard bright smile, so he says quietly to Lillian, 'Lillian, I have been stupid, very stupid. Maybe in a week or two you'll be able to forgive me, or even sooner, I hope so. I hope so. But this is an indecent situation. Please clear out before she hurts you any more.'

'She didn't hurt me,' says Lillian. 'You did. And I have no intention of being hurt any more. Vlasta! *Thank God I'm home again*. What other things did he say?'

'I get no pleasure from this conversation!' says Alan loudly. 'You two may, I do not. Vivisect me all you like – behind my back. I'm going to my mother's house. Feel free to use the kitchen if you want a cup of tea. The front door will lock itself when you leave. Have a nice day.'

By now he is in the lobby taking a coat from the cupboard. He hears Lillian say, 'He's very house-proud, isn't he? How much do you think this cost?'

'Oh a great deal of money,' says Vlasta. 'Will you smash it too?'

Through the doorway he sees Lillian standing with her hand on the glass dome over his clock. He drops the coat and goes to her with arms outstretched like a fast sleepwalker saying, 'Lillian, that has a Mudge pirouette triple escapement please, *please* don't jar the movement!'

Lillian retreats from the clock but grabs a slender clay ornament from the top of a bookcase. She holds it straight above her head like a flagstaff saying, 'What about this?'

'That is a terracotta by Shanks!' cries Alan in an agony of dread. 'By *Archibald* Shanks, for God's sake be *careful*, Lillian!'

'Strange how much he cares about things being hurt and how little about feelings being hurt,' says Vlasta. Alan tries to master the situation with college lecturer's logic.

'In the first place I haven't tried to hurt people's feelings, I've simply tried to, to, to enjoy myself. In the second place of *course* things are more important than feelings. Everybody recovers from hurt feelings, if they aren't children, but damage a well-made clock or ceramic and a certain piece of human labour and skill and talent leaves the world for ever. Please Lillian – put that figurine down.'

'Smash it!' hisses Vlasta.

Lillian has never before had two adult people so interested in what she will do next. It makes her playful. She has also been slightly impressed by the last part of Alan's speech. The figurine, though too simplified to suggest a personality, is obviously female. Lillian cradles it in her arms, pats the head and says, 'Don't worry little statue, I won't hurt you if your owner acts like a sensible boy and doesn't run away to his mummy whenever life gets tough for him. Sit down Alan. What were you going to say about him, Vlasta?'

She sits beside Vlasta on the sofa. Alan, after a pause, slumps down in the easy chair, notices the chicken, wrenches off a leg and tries to comfort himself by chewing it.

'Have you noticed,' says Vlasta, 'how he always plans his seductions with food nearby? Obviously sex and eating are very mixed up inside his brain. I have not yet worked out what that means yet, but something nasty anyway.'

Alan stares haggardly at the bone in his hand then lays it down.

'Then again,' says Vlasta, 'he is not a very passionate lover physically.'

'Isn't he?' asks Lillian, surprised.

'Oh I do not say that he gives us no pleasure, but he depends upon words too much. He keeps whispering these little monologues, erotic fantasies, you know what I mean ...?' (Lillian nods and Alan sticks his fingers in his ears.) '... He can get you very excited by mixing this into his foreplay but when he nears the climax he just lies back and leaves all the work to the woman. Eventually this becomes dull. How long have you known him?'

'A fortnight.'

Vlasta looks at Alan and shouts, 'Take your fingers out of your ears!'

Lillian holds out the figurine by its feet at the angle of a Nazi salute. Vlasta shouts, 'Remember the talent and skill which made this statue! Will you see them leave the world forever because you are ashamed of hearing a few simple facts?'

Alan withdraws fingers from ears and covers his face with them. The women contemplate him for a minute, then Vlasta says, 'What monologues has he used on you?'

'The king and queen one.'

'That is new to me.'

'He pretends we are a king and queen making love on top of a tower in the sunlight. There is a little city below with red roofs and a harbour with sailing ships going in and out. The sailors on the sea and farmers on the hills round about can see us from miles away. They're very glad we're doing that.'

'Very poetic! Yet the scene is strangely familiar ... Ah, I remember now! It is a picture in a book I lent him, Jung's *Psychology and Alchemy*. But have you never had to be Miss Blandish?'

Alan stands up looking dazed and walks across, snapping his fingers, to the bed, on which he flings himself flat with his face pressed deep into the coverlet. The women arise and follow him, Lillian with the figurine still cradled in her arms. They sit down primly on the foot of the bed with Alan's heels between them.

'No,' says Lillian, 'I have never had to be Miss Blandish.'

'He would have made you that eventually. *No Orchids for Miss Blandish* was a sadistic American thriller which made a great impression on him when he was ten or eleven. It is a pity Britain has no respectable state-inspected brothels, male adolescents here get initiated into sex through books and films which leave them with very strange ideas. Alan is such a milksop that I expected his intimate fantasies to be masochistic – no such luck! I had to be Miss Blandish while he raved like a madman in a phoney Chicago accent. Does that connect with his feelings for food? Yes of course! Too little breast-feeding in infancy has made him an oral sadist. At the same time his clinging attitude to objects is a transference from the oral *and* anal retention syndrome.'

Alan, without moving, emits a small but sincere scream.

'End of round two,' says Vlasta happily. 'Enemy flat on canvas.'

But Lillian is not happy. She lays the figurine carefully on the floor and says sadly, 'You know, when he spoke to me at these times I felt so special . . .'

'And now you find you have been to bed with a second-hand record player.'

Speaking with difficulty, Alan turns his head sideways and says, 'If I – sometimes – said the same thing to both of you – it was only because you both – sometimes – made me feel the same way.'

'How many women have made you feel the same way?' demands

Vlasta, then sees Lillian is sobbing. Vlasta places a hand on her shoulder and says hoarsely, 'Yes weep, weep little Lillian. I wept when I came here. *YOU* have not wept yet!' she tells Alan accusingly.

'And I'm not going to,' he declares, sitting up and wriggling down to the bed-foot on Lillian's side. He hesitates then says awkwardly, 'Lillian, I haven't had time to tell you this before, but I love you. I love you.' He looks at Vlasta and says, 'I don't love you at all. Not one bit. But since you don't love me either I don't know why you're so keen to crush me.'

'You deserve to be crushed, Alan,' says Lillian in a sad remote voice.

He wriggles close to her pleading, 'I honestly don't think so! I've been selfish, greedy, stupid and I told Vlasta a lot of lies but I never tried to hurt anyone – not even for fun. My main fault was trying to please too many people at the same time, and believe me it would never have happened if only you had been *punctual*, Lillian . . .'

In order to see her face he stands up and shatters the figurine under foot. The women also stand and look down at the fragments.

Slowly he kneels, lifts the two biggest fragments and holds them unbelievingly at eyelevel. He places them carefully on the floor again, his mouth turning down sharply at the corners, then lies flat again on the bed. Lillian sits beside him, supporting herself with an arm across his body. She says sadly, 'I'm sorry that happened, Alan.'

'Are you *sympathizing*?' cries Vlasta scornfully.

'I'm afraid so. He's crying, you see.'

'You do not think these tears are *real*?'

Lillian touches his cheek with a fingertip, licks the tip, touches the cheek again and holds out the finger to Vlasta saying, 'Yes, they are. Taste one.'

Vlasta sits down too, presses Lillian's hand to her lips but does not let it go. Vlasta says, 'What beautiful fingers you have – soft and small and shapely.'

'Oh?'

'Yes. I'm more than a little butch, you know. How else could I have given myself to a thing like *THAT*?'

But Lillian is tired of this game and pulls her fingers away.

And leans closer to Alan, lays her hand gently on his neck and murmurs, 'I'm sure Archibald Shanks has made hundreds of little statues. You can always get another.'

In a muffled voice he says, ''Snot just that. I've ruined everything between you and me, you and me.'

Lillian says, 'I don't hate you, Alan,' and snuggles closer. Vlasta, watching them, feels excluded again, but knows anger and denunciation will exclude her even more. She also feels a softening toward Alan. Is it pity? No, it is certainly not pity, she has no pity for men and enjoys destroying them, especially smart manipulators like Alan. But when you have knocked such a man down, and don't want to go away and be lonely, what can you do but help set him up again, like a skittle?

'I too cannot exactly hate you Alan,' she says, snuggling close to his other side. And he, feeling heartfelt gratitude, thanks God he is home again.

At Hiruharama

Mr Tanner was anxious to explain how it was that he had a lawyer in the family, so that when they all decided to sell up and quit New Zealand there had been someone they could absolutely trust with the legal business. That meant that he had to say something about his grandfather, who had been an orphan from Stamford in Lincolnshire and was sent out to a well-to-do family north of Auckland, supposedly as an apprentice, but it turned out that he was to be more or less of a servant. He cleaned the knives, saw to the horses, waited at table and chopped the wood. On an errand to a dry goods store in Auckland he met Kitty, Mr Tanner's grandmother. She had come out from England as a governess, and she too found she was really wanted as a servant. She was sixteen, and Tanner asked her to wait for three years while he saved his wages, and then to marry him. All this was at a Methodist social, say a couple of weeks later. 'What family have you got back home?' Kitty asked him. Tanner replied just the one sister. Younger or older? Older. She probably thinks I'm a skilled craftsman by now. She probably reckons I'm made. – Haven't you sent word to her lately? – Not lately. – Best write to her now, anyway, said Kitty, and tell her how it is between us. I should be glad to have a new relation, I haven't many – I'll think it over, he said. Kitty realised then that he could neither read nor write.

They had to start in a remote country place. The land round Auckland at that time was ten shillings an acre, a third of the price going to build the new churches and schools, but where Tanner and Kitty went, north of Awanui, there weren't any churches and schools, and it was considerably cheaper. They didn't have to buy their place, it had been left deserted, and yet it had something you could give a thousand pounds for and not get, and that was a standpipe giving constant clear water from an underground well. But whoever lived there had given up, because of the loneliness and because it was such poor country. Don't picture a shack, though. There were two rooms, one with a stove and one with a bedstead, and a third one at the back for a vegetable store. Tanner grew root vegetables and went into Awanui twice a week with the horse and dray. Kitty stayed behind, because they'd taken on two hundred chickens and a good few pigs.

Tanner turned over in his mind what he'd say to his wife when she told him she was going to have a child. When she did tell him, which wasn't for another two years or so, by the way, he didn't hear her at first, because a northerly was blowing and neither of them could expect to hear each other. When he did catch what she was saying, he hitched up and drove into Awanui. The doctor was at his midday dinner, which he took at a boarding-house higher up the main street. When he got back and into his consulting-room Tanner asked him what were the life statistics of the North Island.

'Do you mean the death statistics?' the doctor asked.

'They'll do just as well,' said Tanner.

'No one dies here except from drink or drowning. Out of three thousand people in Taranaki Province there hasn't been a single funeral in the last sixteen months and only twenty-four sick and infirm. You may look upon me as a poor man.'

'What about women in childbirth?' asked Tanner.

The doctor didn't have any figures for women dying in childbirth, but he looked sharply at Tanner and asked him when his child was due.

'You don't know, of course. Well, don't ask me if it's going to be twins. Nature didn't intend us to know that.' He began to write in his notebook. 'Where are you living?'

'It's off the road to Houhora, you turn off to the right after twelve miles.'

'What's it called?'

'Hiruharama.'

'Don't know it. That's not a Maori name.'

'I think it means Jerusalem,' said Tanner.

'Are there any other women about the place?'

'No.'

'I mean someone who could come in and look after things while your wife's laid up. Who's your nearest neighbour?' Tanner told him there was no one except a man called Brinkman, who came over sometimes. He was about nine or ten miles off at Stony Loaf.

'And he has a wife?'

'No, he hasn't, that's what he complains about. You couldn't ask a woman to live out there.'

'You can ask a woman to live anywhere,' said the doctor. 'He's a crank, I dare say.'

'He's a dreamer,' Tanner replied. 'I should term Brinkman a dreamer.'

'I was thinking in terms of washing the sheets, that sort of thing. If there's no one else, can you manage about the house yourself for a few days?'

'I can do anything about the house,' said Tanner.

'You don't drink?'

Tanner shook his head, wondering if the doctor did. He asked if he shouldn't bring his wife with him for a consultation next time he drove over to Anawui. The doctor looked out of his window at the bone-shaking old dray with its iron-rimmed wheels. 'Don't.'

He tore the prescription out of his notebook. 'Get this for your wife. It's calcium water. When you want me to come, you'll have to send for me. But don't let that worry you. Often by the time I arrive I'm not needed.'

Other patients had arrived and were sitting on the wooden benches on the verandah. Some had empty medicine bottles for a refill. There was a man with his right arm strapped up, several kids with their mothers, and a woman who looked well enough but seemed to be in tears for some reason or other. – Well, you see life in the townships.

Tanner went over to the post office, where there was free pen and ink if you wanted it, and wrote a letter to his sister. – But wait a minute, surely he couldn't read or write? Evidently by that time he could. Mr Tanner's guess was that although Kitty was a quiet girl, very quiet, she'd refused to marry him until he'd got the hang of it. – Tanner wrote: My darling old sister. Well, it's come to pass and either a girl or a boy will be added unto us. It would be a help if you could send us a book on the subject. We have now a hundred full-grown hens and a further hundred at point of lay, and a good stand of potatoes. – After mailing the letter he bought soap, thread, needles, canned fish, tea and sugar. When he drove out of Anawui he stopped at the last homestead, where he knew a man called Parrish who kept racing-pigeons. Some of them, in fact were just arriving back at their loft. Parrish had cut the entrances to the nests down very small, and every time a bird got home it had to squeeze past a bell on a string so that the tinkling sound gave warning. They were all Blue Chequers, the only kind, Parrish declared, that a sane man would want to keep. Tanner explained his predicament and asked for the loan of two birds. Parrish didn't mind, because Hiruharama, Tanner's place, was on a more or less direct line from Awanui to Te Paki station, and that was the line his pigeons flew.

'If you'd have lived over the other way I couldn't have helped you,' Parrish said.

A Maori boy took the young birds out as soon as they were four months old and tossed them at three miles, ten miles, twenty miles, always in the same direction, north-north-west of Anawui.

'As long as they can do fifteen miles,' said Tanner.

'They can do two hundred and fifty.'

'How long will it take them to do fifteen miles?'

'Twenty minutes in clear weather,' said Parrish.

The Maori boy chose out two birds and packed them into a wicker hamper, which Tanner wedged into the driver's seat of the dray.

'Have you got them numbered in some way?' Tanner asked.

'I don't need to. I know them all,' said Parrish.

He added that they would need rock salt, so Tanner drove back into the town once more to buy the rock salt and a sack of millet. By the time he got to Hiruharama the dark clear night sky was pressing in on every side. I ought to have taken you with me, he told Kitty. She said she had been all right. He hadn't, though, he'd been worried. You mean you've forgotten something at the stores, said Kitty. Tanner went out to the dray and fetched the pigeons, still shifting about and conferring quietly in their wicker basket.

'Here's one thing more than you asked for,' he said. They found room for them in the loft above the vegetable store. The Blue Chequers were the prettiest things about the place.

The sister in England did send a book, although it didn't arrive for almost a year. In any case, it only had one chapter of a practical nature. Otherwise, it was religious in tone. But meanwhile Kitty's calculations couldn't have been far out, because more or less when they expected it the pains came on strong enough for Tanner to send for the doctor.

He had made the pigeon's nests out of packing-cases. They ought to have flown out daily for exercise, but he hadn't been able to manage that. Still, they looked fair enough, a bit dishevelled, but not so that you'd notice. It was four o'clock, breezy, but not

windy. He took them out into the bright air which, even that far
from the coast, was full of the salt of the ocean. How to toss
a pigeon he had no idea. He opened the basket, and before he
could think what to do next they were out and up into the blue.
He watched in terror as after reaching a certain height they began
turning round in tight circles as though puzzled or lost. Then,
apparently sighting something on the horizon that they knew, they
set off strongly towards Anawui. – Say twenty minutes for them to
get to Parrish's loft. Ten minutes for Parrish or the Maori boy to
walk up the street to the doctor's. Two and a half hours for the doctor to drive over, even allowing for his losing the way once. Thirty
seconds for him to get down from his trap and open his bag. –

At five o'clock Tanner went out to see to the pigs and hens.
At six Kitty was no better and no worse. She lay there quietly,
sweating from head to foot. 'I can hear someone coming,' she
said, not from Anawui, though, it was along the top road.
Tanner thought it must be Brinkman. 'Why, yes, it must be
six months since he came,' said Kitty, as though she was making
conversation. Who else, after all, could it have been on the top
road? The track up there had a deep rounded gutter each side
which made it awkward to drive along. They could hear the
screeching and rattling of his old buggy, two wheels in the gutter,
two out. 'He's stopped at the gully now to let his horse drink,'
said Kitty. 'He'll have to let it walk the rest of the way.' – 'He'll
have to turn round when he gets here and start right back,' said
Tanner.

There used to be a photograph of Brinkman somewhere, but
Mr Tanner didn't know what had become of it, and he believed
it hadn't been a good likeness in any case. – Of course, in the
circumstances, as he'd come eight miles over a rough road, he
had to be asked to put up his horse for a while, and come
in.

Like most people who live on their own Brinkman continued
with the course of his thoughts, which were more real to him
than the outside world's commotion. Walking straight into the
front room he stopped in front of the piece of mirror-glass tacked
over the sink and looked fixedly into it.

'I'll tell you something, Tanner, I thought I caught sight of my
first grey hairs this morning.'

'I'm sorry to hear that.'

Brinkman looked round. 'I see the table isn't set.'

'I don't want you to feel that you're not welcome,' said Tanner, 'but Kitty's not well. She told me to be sure that you came in and rested a while, but she's not well. Truth is, she's in labour.'

'Then she won't be cooking dinner this evening, then?'

'You mean you were counting on having it here?'

'My half-yearly dinner with you and Mrs Tanner, yis, that's about it.'

'What day is it, then?' asked Tanner, somewhat at random. It was almost too much for him at that moment to realise that Brinkman existed. He seemed like a stranger, perhaps from a foreign country, not understanding how ordinary things were done or said.

Brinkman made no attempt to leave, but said; 'Last time I came here we started with canned toheroas. Your wife set them in front of me. I'm not sure that they had an entirely good effect on the intestines. Then we had fried eggs and excellent jellied beetroot, a choice between tea or Bovo, bread and butter and unlimited quantities of treacle. I have a note of all this in my daily journal. That's not to say, however, that I came over here simply to take dinner with you. It wasn't for the drive, either, although I'm always glad to have the opportunity of a change of scene and to read a little in Nature's book. No, I've come today, as I came formerly, for the sake of hearing a woman's voice.'

Had Tanner noticed, he went on, that there were no native songbirds in the territory? At that moment there was a crying, or a calling, from the next room such as Tanner had never heard before, not in a shipwreck – and he had been in a wreck – not in a slaughterhouse.

'Don't put yourself out on my account,' said Brinkman. 'I'm going to sit here until you come back and have a quiet smoko.'

The doctor drove up bringing with him his wife's widowed sister, who lived with them and was a nurse, or had been a nurse. Tanner came out of the bedroom covered with blood, something like a butcher. He told the doctor he'd managed to deliver the child, a girl, in fact he'd wrapped it in a towel and tucked it up in the washbasket. The doctor took him back into the bedroom and made him sit down. The nurse put down the things she'd brought with her and looked round for the tea-tin. Brinkman sat there, as solid as his chair. 'You may be wondering who I am,' he said. 'I'm a neighbour, come over for dinner. I think of myself as one of the perpetually welcome.' 'Suit yourself,' said the sister-in-law. The doctor emerged, moving rather faster than he usually did. 'Please to go in there and wash the patient. I'm going to take a look at the afterbirth. The father put it out with the waste.'

There Tanner had made his one oversight. It wasn't the afterbirth, it was a second daughter, smaller, but a twin. – But how come, if both of them were girls, that Mr Tanner himself still had the name of Tanner? Well, the Tanners went on to have nine more children, some of them boys, and one of those boys was Mr Tanner's father. That evening, when the doctor came in from the yard with the messy scrap, he squeezed it as though he was wringing it out to dry, and it opened its mouth and the colder air of the kitchen rushed in and she'd got her start in life. After that the Tanners always had one of those tinplate mottoes hung up on the wall – Throw Nothing Away. You could get them then at the hardware store. – And this was the point that Mr Tanner had wanting to make all along – whereas the first daughter never got to be anything in particular, this second little girl grew up to be a lawyer with a firm in Wellington, and she did very well.

All the time Brinkman continued to sit there by the table and smoke his pipe. Two more women born into the world! It must have seemed to him that if this sort of thing went on there should be a good chance, in the end, for him to acquire one for himself. Meanwhile, they would have to serve dinner sometime.

King Billy is a Gentleman

I cannot get out of my mind, now, the village where I was born, just out of the curl of the city's tentacles. We were too close to the city for a life of our own. There was a regular train service – not one of those where you have to lie in wait and study its habits. But we did not like the Mancunians. 'Urban, squat and packed with guile' I suppose was our attitude; we sneered at their back-to-back accents and pitied their physiques. My mother, a staunch Lamarckian, is convinced that Mancunians have disproportionately long arms, as a result of generations of labour at the loom. Until (but this was later) a pink housing estate was slammed up, and they were transplanted in their hundreds, like those trees plucked up for Christmas whose roots are dipped in boiling water – well, until then we did not have much to do with people from town. And yet if you ask me if I was a country boy – no, I wasn't that. Our huddle of stones and slates, scoured by bitter winds and rough gossip tongues, had no claim on rural England, where there is morris dancing and fellowship and olde ale flowing. It was a broken, sterile place, devoid of trees, like a transit camp: and yet with the hopeless permanence that transit camps tend to assume. Snow stood on the hills till April.

We lived at the top of the village, in a house which I considered to be haunted. My father had disappeared. Perhaps it was his presence, long and pallid, which slid behind the door in sweeps of draught, and raised the hackles on the terrier's neck. He had been a clerk by profession; crosswords were his hobby, and a little angling: simple card-games, and a cigarette card collection. He left at ten o'clock one blustery March morning, taking his albums and his tweed overcoat and leaving all his underwear; my mother washed it and gave it to a jumble sale. We didn't miss him much, only the little tunes which he used to play on the piano: over and over, 'Pineapple Rag'.

Then came the lodger. He was from further north, a man with long slow vowels, making a meal out of words we got through quite quickly. The lodger was choleric; his flashpoint was low. He was very, very unpredictable; if you were going to see the shape of the future, you had to watch him very carefully, quiet and still, with all your intuitions bristling. When I was older I became interested in ornithology, and I brought into play the expertise I had picked up. Again, that was later; there were no birds in the village, only sparrows and starlings, and a disreputable tribe of pigeons strutting in the narrow streets.

The lodger took an interest in me, getting me outside to kick a football around. But I wasn't a robust child, and though I wanted to please him I hadn't the skill. The ball slipped between my feet as if it were a small animal. He grew alarmed by my bouts of breathless coughing; mollycoddle, he said, but he said it with fright in his face.

Soon he seemed to write me off. I began to feel I was a nuisance. I went to bed early, and lay awake, listening to the banging and shouting downstairs; for the lodger must have quarrels, just as he must have his breakfast. The terrier would begin yelping and grizzling, to keep them company, and then later I would hear my mother run upstairs, sniffling quietly to herself. She would not let the lodger go, I knew, she had set her mind on him. He brought home in his pay packets more money than we had ever had in the house, and whereas when he came at first he would hand over his rent money, now he dropped the whole packet on the table, and my mother would open it with her small pointed fingers, and give him back a few shillings for beer and whatever she thought men needed. He was getting a bonus, she told me, he was getting made up to foreman. He was our chance in life.

If I had been a girl she would have confided in me more; but I caught the drift of things. I lay awake still, after the footfalls had stopped, and the dog was quiet, and the shadows crept back into the corners of the room; I dozed, and wished I were unhaunted, and wished for the years to pass in a night so that when I woke up I would be a man. As I began to doze, I dreamed that one day a door would open in the wall; and I would walk through it, and in that land I would be the asthmatic little king. There would be a law against quarrelling in the land where I was king. But then, in real life, daylight would come, a Saturday perhaps, and I would have to play in the garden.

The gardens at the back of the houses were long narrow strips, fading by way of ramshackle fences into grey cow-pat fields. Beyond the fields were the moors, calm steel-surfaced reservoirs and the neat stripes of light and dark green conifers which mark

out the good offices of the Forestry Commission. Little grew in
these gardens; scrub grass, tangles of stunted bush, ant-eaten
fence poles and lonely strands of wire. I used to go down to the
bottom of the garden and pull long rusty nails out of our rotting
fence; I used to pull the leaves off the lilac tree, and smell the
green blood on my hands, and think about my situation, which
was a peculiar one.

Bob and his family had come to live next door to us in
some early, singular transplantation from the city. Perhaps this
accounted for his attitude to his land. We viewed with distrust
the handful of wormy raspberries the garden produced by itself,
the miserable lupins running to seed; the straggling rhubarb was
never cut and stewed. But Bob had fenced in his garden like the
propositions central to a man's soul; as if he had the Holy Grail
in his greenhouse, and the Vandals were howling and barracking
in the cow-pat fields. Bob's garden was military, it was crisp; it
knew its master. Life grew in rows; things went into the ground
out of packets and came up on the dot and stood straight and
tall for Bobby's inspection. Unused flowerpots were stacked up
like helmets, canes bristled like bayonets. He had possessed and
secured every inch of the ground. He was a gaunt man, with a
large chin and a vacant blue eye; he never ate white sugar, only
brown.

One day over the fence erupted Myra his wife, about my mother's immoral way of life; twittering in incoherent and long-bottled
rage about the example set to her children, to the children of the
gardens around. I was eight years old. I fixed her with my very
gimlet eye, words of violence bursting into my mouth, contained
there swilling and bloody, like loose teeth. I wanted to say that the
children of these tracts of ground – her own in particular – were
beyond example. My mother, at whom the tirade was directed, got
up slowly from the chair where she had been taking the sun; she
gave Myra one cursory unregarding glance, and walked silently
into the house, leaving her neighbour to hurl herself like a crazed
budgerigar at Bob's good fences. Myra was little, she was mere,
rat-faced and meagre, like a nameless cut in a butcher's window
in a demolition area. In my mother's view, her arms hung below
her knees.

I think that before this the two households had been quite
friendly. Increasingly, then, Bob and his preoccupations (nine
bean-rows will I have there, a hive for the honey bee) became

the butt of our secret sniggers. Bob slunk nightly into the garden, to be away from the stewing-cut his wife. When his mysterious grubbings were done, his drillings and ploughings, he stood by the fence and lifted lacklustre eyes to the hills, his hands in his pockets; he whistled an air, tuneless and plaintive. From our kitchen he could just be seen, through the clammy evening mists that were the climate of those years. Then my mother would draw the curtains and put the kettle on the gas, and bemoan her life; and she would laugh at Bobby boy, and wonder what damage would be done before he stood there again next day.

For Bob's fences were not secure. They were elaborate, they were refined, you might say they were highly strung, though that is a strange word to apply to a fence. They were like Stendhal on the shelves of the village library: impressive, but not adapted for any purpose we could discern. The cows would get in; we would watch them nosing softly in the dawn or dusk, lifting Bobby's neat catches with their heads; and trample, they came, slurping and crunching on his succulent produce, satisfying each of their four stomachs, their ruminant eyes mildly joyous with the righteousness of it all, like the Meek come into their kingdom.

But Bob had a low opinion of bovine intelligence. For leaving the gates open, he would thrash his son Philip. From behind our own stone walls we would hear Bobby's demented passions pouring out, his great explosions of grief and despair at the loss of his cucumber frames, wails torn out of his gut. This state of affairs afforded some satisfaction to me.

I had some friends; or rather, there were children of my own age. But because my mother kept me away from school so often – I was sick with this and I was sick with that – I was a strange object to them, and my name, which was Liam, they said was ridiculous. They were wild children, with scabbed knees, and hearts full of fervour, and intolerant mouths and hard eyes; they had rites, they had rules, and they made me an outsider in the tribe. Being ill was almost better; it is something you must do alone.

When I did appear at school, it was seen that I had fallen behind with the lessons. Mrs Burbage was our teacher, a woman of perhaps fifty, with sparse reddish hair, and fingertips yellow from cigarettes. She told me to stand up and explain the proverb 'Never spoil the ship for a ha'pennyworth of tar'. In those days that was how children were educated. She carried a bulging tartan bag with her, and each morning deposited it, with a plump thud, on the floor by her desk; then in no time at all the shouting and hitting would begin. It was a tyranny, under which we laboured, and while we dreamt of retaliation a year of our childhood slid by, unnoticed. Some of the children were planning to kill her.

There was nature study; while we sat with our arms folded behind our back, she read to us about the habits of the greenfinch. In spring there was pussy willow, which is thought to be of interest to children everywhere. But it is not spring that I remember: rather those days when the lights were on by eleven o'clock, and wet roofs and the mill chimneys shivered behind a curtain of water. At four o'clock the daylight would almost have vanished, sucked away into the sky; our wellingtons squelched in the mud and dead leaves, and breath hung like disaster on the raw air.

The children had been listening in to their parent's gossip. They asked me – the girls especially – searching questions about the sleeping arrangements in our house. I did not see the point of these questions, but I knew better than to answer them. There were fights – scrapping and scratching, nothing serious. 'I'll show you how to fight,' the lodger said. When I put his advice into practice I left tears and bloody noses. It was the triumph of science over brutality, but it left a sick taste in my mouth, a fear of the future. I would rather run than fight, and when I ran the steep streets turned misty and liquid before my eyes, and the marching fence of my ribs entrapped my heart like a lobster in its pot.

My relations with Bob's children had little to commend them. Quite often when I was playing outside Philip and Suzy would come into their own garden and throw stones at me. Looking back, I don't know how there could have been stones in Bobby's garden: not stones just lying about, for use as casual missiles. I suppose if they found any they thought they were doing their father a favour by lobbing them over at me. And as he got stranger, and more persecuted, and ate ever more peculiar foods, no doubt they had to jump at the chance to do him a favour.

Suzy was a hard little madam, with an iron wide mouth like a postbox; she hung on the gate and taunted. Philip was older than me, perhaps by three years. He had a modified coconut head and a puzzled narrow grey eye, and a sort of sideways motion to his neck, as if constantly in training to avoid the blows he got on account of the cows; perhaps he was concussed. As for the missiles, it didn't give me much trouble to stay out of the small range of his accuracy; but when I evaded him once too often, when I saw I was making him look a fool, I would get myself indoors, because I saw in his face a sort of low destructive rage, as if he might break out into some other sort of creature, a wilder beast; and it is true that I have seen this look since, on the faces of large intelligent dogs that are kept tied up. And by saying this I do not mean that I thought Philip was an animal, then or now; what I thought was that we all have a buried nature, a secret violence, and I envied the evident power of his skinny sinewy arms, veined and knotted like the arms of a grown man. I envied him, and loathed his subject nature, and I hoped it was not my own. Once I scrabbled for clods of earth and sticks and hurled them back howling like a demon, with all the invective I had at my command from the books I had read: varlet, cuckold, base knave and cur.

As the months passed, Bob grew more vacant in his expression, more dangerous in his rages; his clothes, even, seemed to share his lack of coherence, flapping after him dementedly as if trying to regain the security of the wardrobe. He bought a motor scooter, which broke down every day at the top of the hill, in front of the bus queue. The queue was for the bus to the next village; it was the same people every day. Each morning they were eager for the spectacle.

At this stage Philip used to approach the fence and talk to me. Our conversations were wary and elliptical. Did I, he asked, know the names of all the nine planets? Yes, I knew them. He betted, Philip said, I only knew Venus, Mars. I recited them, all nine. The planets have satellites, I told him. Satellites are small things that revolve round big things, I said, held in an orbit by forces beyond themselves; thus Saturn has amongst others Dione, Titan, Phoebe, and Mars has Deimos, Phobos. And as I said 'Phobos' I felt a catch in my throat, for I knew that the word meant 'fear'; and even to speak it was to feel it, and summon up the awkward questions, the lodger, the door in the wall and the shadows of encroaching night.

Then Philip threw stones at me. I went inside and drew pictures sitting at the kitchen table, watching the clock in case the lodger came home.

Now, Philip and I did not attend the same school. Our village had its division, and while the grown-ups were tolerant, or perhaps contemptuous of religion, immersed in football pools and hire-purchase agreements, the children kept up the slanging matches and the chants, the kind of thing you might have heard on Belfast streets, or in Glasgow. Suzy sang out in her tuneless cackle:

> King Billy is a gentleman
> He wears a watch and chain
> The dirty Pope's a beggar
> And he begs down our lane.

Irish pigs, Philip said. Bog-hogs. Petrol ran in my veins; my fingers itched for triggers; post offices were fortified behind my eyes. Philip threw stones at me.

My territory was shrinking: not the house, not the garden, not home and not school. All I owned was the space behind my ribs, and that too was a scarred battleground, the site of sudden debouchements and winter campaigns. I did not tell my mother about the external persecutions. Partly it was because she had enough to bear on her own account; partly because of a sneaking pity invading even my own hard heart, as the misunderstanding about the cows grew keener, and Philip's head shrunk more defensively onto his neck. We might call the NSPCC, my mother said. For Philip? We might, I said, call the RSPCA. Bobby took the motor scooter behind the house and kicked it savagely; we no longer knew where our duty lay.

Our neighbour then ceased to keep regular hours. He paced the length of his plot, furrowed, harrowed. He lay in wait: for Philip, for the beasts, for Revelations. He crouched by his fence in a corner, skeletal in his blue overalls. The cows never came, when he watched for them. My mother looked out of the window. Her lips curled. You make your own luck, she said. The neighbours discussed Bobby now. They no longer watched for my father's return; by comparison he lacked interest. Bobby weeded and hoed with one eye over his shoulder. Our circumstances are improving, my mother said: with application, you will go to the grammar school. Her dark shiny hair bounced on her shoulders. We can pay for your uniform, she said; once we couldn't have managed. I thought, they will ask more probing questions at the grammar school. 'Where is my Dad?' I asked her. 'Where did he go? Did he write you a letter?'

'He may be dead, for all I know,' she said. 'He may be in purgatory, where they don't have postage stamps.'

The year I took my exam for the grammar school Bobby was growing cress in pots. He stood at the front gate, trying to sell it to the neighbours, pressing it upon them as very nutritious. Myra, now, had not even the status of the scrag from the slum carvery; she became like one of the shrivelled pods or husks, from dusty glass jars, on which Bob eked out his existence.

The priest came, for the annual Religious Examination; the last time for me. He sat on the headmistress's high chair, his broad feet in their brogues set deliberately on the wooden step. He was old, and his breath laboured; there was a faint smell about him, of damp wool, of poultices, of cough linctus and piety. The priest liked trick questions. Draw me a soul, he said. A dim-witted child took the proffered chalk, and marked out on the blackboard a vague kidney-shape, or perhaps the sole of a shoe. Ah no, Father said, wheezing gently; ah no, little one, that is the heart.

That year, when I was ten years old, our situation changed. My mother had been right to bank on the choleric lodger; he was an upwardly mobile man. We departed with him to a neat town where spring came early and cloyed with cherry blossom, and thrushes darted softly on trim lawns. When it rained, these people said, lovely for the gardens; in the village they had taken it as one more bleak affront in the series life offered them. I never doubted that Bob had dwindled away entirely among his mauled lettuce rows, out of grief and bewilderment and iron-deficiency, his bones rattled by our departing laughter. About Philip I never thought at all. I wiped him from my mind, as if he had never been.

'You must never tell anyone we are not married,' my mother said, blithe in her double-life. 'You must never talk to anyone about your family. It's not their business.' You must not taunt over the garden fence, I thought. And the word *phobos* you must never say.

It was only later, when I left home, that I understood the blithe carelessness of the average life – how freely people speak, how freely they live. There are no secrets in their lives, there is no poison at the root. People I met had an innocence, an openness, that was quite foreign to my own nature; or if once it had been native to me, then I had lost it long ago in the evening fogs, in the four o'clock darks, abandoned it in the gardens between the straggling fences and tussocks of grass.

I became a lawyer; one must live, as they say, *il faut que je vive* but then sometimes I think of d'Argenson's reply: 'I do not see the necessity.'

The whole decade of the Sixties went by, and my childhood seemed to belong to some much earlier, greyer world. It was my inner country, visited sometimes in dreams that shadowed my day. The troubles in Northern Ireland began, and my family fell to quarrelling about them, and the newspapers were full of pictures of burned-out shopkeepers, with faces like ours.

I was grown up, qualified, long gone from home, when Philip came back into my life. It was Easter, a sunny morning. The windows were open in the dining-room, which overlooked the garden with its striped lawn and rockery; and I was a visitor in my own home, eating breakfast, the toast put into a rack and the marmalade into a dish. How life had altered, altered beyond the power of imagination! Even the lodger had become civilised, in his fashion; he wore a suit, and attended the meetings of the Rotary Club.

My mother, who had grown plump, sat down opposite me and handed me the local newspaper, folded to display a photograph.

'Look,' she said, 'that Suzy's got married.'

I took the newspaper and put down my piece of toast. I examined this face and figure from my childhood. There she stood, a brassy girl with a bouquet that she held like a cosh. Her big jaw was set in a smile. At her side stood her new husband; a little behind, like tricks of the light, were the bowed, insubstantial forms of her parents.

'Where's Philip?' I said.

'Philip?' My mother looked up. She sat for a moment with her lips parted, a picture of uncertainty, crumbling a bit of toast under her fingers. 'Did nobody tell you? About the accident? Did I not write to you and let you know?' She pushed her small breakfast aside, and sat frowning at me, as if I had disappointed her.

'He's dead,' she said. 'Let me think . . .'

'Dead how?'

'Killed himself.' She dabbed a crumb from the corner of her mouth. She got up, went to the sideboard, opened a drawer, rummaged under table mats and photographs. 'I kept the paper. I thought I'd sent it you.'

I knew I had been pulling away; I knew I had been extracting myself bodily, piece by piece, from my early life. I had missed so much, naturally, and yet I thought I had missed nothing of consequence. But Philip, dead. I thought of the stones he threw, of the puzzled squint of his eye, of the bruises on his gangling legs below his short trousers. 'It's *years* now,' my mother said.

She sat down again, opposite me at the table, and handed me the paper she had preserved. How quickly newsprint goes yellow; it might have come from a Victorian public library. I turned to read, and read how Philip had blown himself up. All the details from the coroner's court: and the verdict, death by misadventure.

Philip had constructed, in Bobby's garden shed, a sugar and weedkiller bomb. It was a fad of the time, making bombs at home; it had been popularised by events in Belfast. Philip's bomb – the use he had for it was unknown – had blown up in his face. I wondered what he had taken with him in the blast: I pictured the shed splintered, the stacked flower pots reduced to dust, even the cows in their field lifting bemused heads at the noise. An irrelevant thought slid into my mind, that Ireland had undone him at last; and here I was still alive, one of life's Provisionals, one of the men in the black berets.

Philip was the first of my contemporaries to die. I think about him often now. *Weedkiller*, my brain says back to me: as if it needed replication. I am burning on a slower fuse.

Tender

I have just recently cut in through Hardwicke Street. A person can't forget this inner city. I was on my way to my pal's place and I cut in. Stay with me. A person in the first place says what comes to them, those things that make up their lifestyle, like walking down Hardwicke Street one evening for a thing to do. Don't get me wrong. I wasn't looking for something to love. That's not me.

This slum was wearing the blue-black punched out by the lamps, but with a dignity that I can believe is the start of poems. Pearliness. I was coming up to some tiny kids. This is a broad concrete street, Catholic, there are toys on the ground. Darkish, brightish, not gaudy, sort of classy mizzle was lapping against these Georgian grim hard houses like sick water. I was being stared at. One of those fucking babies shouted out towards me. My skin crept tighter over my bones. For some reason I wanted to write the word 'pearliness', even if it is a lie, and even if there is nothing to make this place worth more than a bit of its own dogshit. This is the poorest place you've ever seen. This is a poor city I walk around in. Still, there is something down here that gets me thinking of a feeling like pearliness. I walked brisk past these kids. But one of them started to stroll along beside me. A baby. My chest had become a toy drum. My legs were lumpish and truculent, they wanted to turn around and waddle back. 'Hey, mister!' the kid said. I looked down. He was far down. His face was light. I am surprised that such faces don't get bruised on the dark. 'What're you lookin' for?' There was glass under my feet, crushing deliciously. I wanted, you know, to be out of this electricity at once, this gorgeous blue sparkle, caustic, and the smell of wild light, distracted, fresh and smoky. I wanted to be elsewhere. Perhaps I belong in this air. I belong in that bunched up bit of messy cloud, it's free. Cloud, I think, you and I have something in common. 'Are you lookin' for somethin'?' that kid asked. His jeans were falling low, he was poor, his brown back was showing. I like that cloud. We've taken to each other so fast. I like it because it crosses my mind to tell me I understand nothing.

Where is this infant's mother? Some old tart, nowhere, I can't imagine who she is, she's tumbling by with the stars, anyway. But I know nothing, right? I don't care what I want, do I? I don't know what I'm looking for, do I? And everything I feel and everything that eats into me, they mean spit, don't they? Added up together and with the compound interest of my screams, they all amount to as much as a wisp. That kid stopped his walking beside me so I breathed a fat relief. Now you see it doesn't have any more importance than the wisp I mentioned, let me continue to tell you what I got from this here Hardwicke Street.

Make sure you can picture the air. It had flung on a moody shirt. It had struck a pose that it knew well was both a pose and seductive, and guaranteed to buzz through you if you were new to this place or didn't know a thing or two about air. Air can be treacherous. But take it easy, it has a lot of business to see to, a lot on its mind, a lot of houses to prop up and such like. Now there were young men doing their bit to hold a wall in place up ahead. Mere boys. But listen, that wall needed them. I was getting near when a stone hit my back. Those babies were still messing about with my discarded footsteps. They began shouting out. 'You fuckin' rapist.' That's what they shouted out. I got tense. Tense. We were all together inside a drizzle. And clinging to the drizzle was opalescence. I recognised it. 'Opalescence,' I wanted to yell to test it very loud. Interesting that so delicate a word should refer here to no more than needles and pins which have learned to fly. 'What's he want?' a mouth somewhere behind me said. I kept walking towards the boys. I learned then I have hackles. The shortest of them could bolt right through you if you itched in the wrong direction. I had to concentrate. For me, broken bottle glass and corner walls and the accent of the kids had already begun to tap infinity. It only takes the wink of that sharp corner, you could tell yourself, less, the mere sight of a broken flagstone, that puddle of oily sky, for you to get tangled up for ever in these images. Your foot will get caught up inside one. The darkening appeal of all this wants to trick us, it's got me by the hand now and is telling me now that I belong here in this gentle hardness. Better be careful if you're down here. Act right.

'Right?'

'Right.'

Together these boys had all the different faces necessary to

protect a wall. I won't deny that around these slum streets you can
see the diverse novelty of the animal and how dirty it is. There are
too many details down here to carry away on your shoulders. I still
had the words 'What's he want' sticking to me like tape. I looked
back at the boys. Oddly, I caught sight of two souvenirs: eyes,
crude things, like trinkets of eyes. Two unmistakables, impudent
and patient, got themselves half-hooked on my glimpse. They
wanted to be in my collection of reality. The night was a wall and
these were two stones in it. But they were malevolent pieces, eyelashes of light. I tramped on with my collection dead slow. Follow
this: I'm weak anyway with feeling what a zonked out stone we're
living on. Now I was obliging all those broken bottles and an inva-
lid flagstone which had attached themselves to me, as well as two
children's severed voices, as well as the cloud, wetly pestering my
back for a ride. So now I've got these additional two curios and it's
all just enough to make my neck lapse. I looked round again. This
blond idiot was snuggling his back up against the kind wall.

'Right?'

'Yeah.'

'What's he lookin' at?'

'Cool down, kid.' Here I caught another flash of that tarty
deliberate look. I walked on.

I was coming to the square. The babies had melted probably
now, or become brick. All around, sight was getting soupy and
eye-level ink leaves were twitching. This body of mine was angry
now. I climbed my angry way up the city along the square,
through sparkling chimney smoke, under the dusty spread of
trees, vandalised trunks. I strolled through where it all tumbles
down in sliced houses, wallpaper, fireplaces overhanging you. It's
not a good town, this big town. I don't recommend it. If things
were my way you would never get these mere teenagers standing
about arsechatting to the breeze anyway. I was turning over the
pieces I'd taken away and trying to comprehend them. That kid
had got something seriously wrong. This is a sick place. It's
imploring you to set it on fire. In the general run of most things
that look had only one meaning. Somebody ought to rub us out. If
I could get my hands on a fat city-size, colossal-size rubbing-out
instrument I'd just nicely rub out the whole bad picture. I don't
belong here. It's only out to trick you, the charm of this sketchy
city, it's a real photogenic grainy type of limbo, built brick for
brick out of dark light. I'd like to start again on a new picture.

I can redesign a better place. Don't doubt it. I'd use buckets of
colour. Pure blood purple. Tear white. I'd spring clean the secrets
out of those dark trees in Denmark Street and Hardwicke Street
too. Now I was coming near where I aimed to be, a house on
Dominick Street. I tell you, this was a poor situation. My pal, I
thought, better have some money. He better have some money, I
thought. So we could get ourselves pissed, I hoped. I felt like a
wild row could start, by me. Maybe I had a little short circuit.
I came to the house on Dominick Street.

I threw open the door. I walked straight up the stairs to where my
pal has his little home. 'Hi,' I said. 'Look who it is. My fucking self,'
I said. I was expecting him to trumpet, 'No problem' as I entered
and fly a flag made of money. This is what he would say and how
he would accompany his speech. But he didn't say anything, just
hugged his knees up on the bed and resembled a bald neckless piece
of pond life. I looked to the window at an oblong of pure lead air.

'Did you score?' I asked him. This pal was leaning back against
the wall in his black plastic jacket, looking like some activity was
going on behind his eyes of the level of a huff.

'No,' he said. 'There's been some shit.'

Well, that's a way of my understanding we've sweet nothing to
do with ourselves.

'What'll we do?' I said.

'Kill time,' he said.

'How?'

One thing we've been known to do when life gets this degree
of tedious is this: we connect up to the gas. Gas doesn't cost
any inconvenience and nothing in hard currency beyond the
cost of life. But gas can make you sleep on whiskery laughs,
soft thumps, threadlike things. He was into the idea. He went
over to his makeshift box room toilet and rolled out a pig-headed
canister from its sleep. He had a tube in his hand and he rammed
it onto the snout. In that state of mind right then I would either
sniff gas or else not know what to do with my particular self. I got
down on my knees. 'I'll go first,' I said. I stuffed the end of that
tube between my teeth and released the knob on the canister top.
I fear the smell, you know. The smell is the boss, you obey him,
he doesn't mess around. I would say gas is a bossy drink of petrol,
where colours hide, magenta and green, coin white, budgerigar,
as far as smell is concerned. But take my word for it, the taste is
a fast boot to the head straightaway. When you sniff gas you're

looking up the definition of a complicated word: brain. You find out whereabouts in life that idea hides itself and what it should do that it isn't doing right then. I fumbled with one big palm-size toe to turn off, then floated back in a blind blue. This is where I belong, I think: in gas, outside of everything, in nowhere.

When I came round I recollected one of my beliefs. I think gas is made for us. Gas slots into the spaces in your brain. Brain and gas. They both have the same deep structure from the point of view of the chemistry of peace. I believe a better person is in that gas and when you come round you're not yourself so much as maybe half or lots of fractions of a self that add up to a half. Don't be too mathematical about it. This issue here is achievement. Coming round to this pokey room in Dominick Street in that gas after-glow is like you've left half yourself behind in the black, your happier half. I asked my pal, 'Did you get a hit?' He answered, 'It was all right. Did you?' I told him, 'I fell asleep.' We lay about. There was a darkness more ultramarine now, real gloom now with cartoons fleeting in it, purples swelling. My pal was just a shadow against the wall above his bed. I let my underground gaspipe mind put my own choice of eyes and mouth on him and plenty of sequins. Already that image of eyes from earlier was returning, in soft focus, a kind of pillow of sleep over it, seemingly, thankfully not trying to worry my numb limbs. I lay relaxed. Then, soon I spoke. My voice was big in the room, loud, the corners woke up with sore ears.

'What'll we do now?' I didn't expect an answer. I didn't mean it. Being frank about it, I mean one word just as little as another. But just as passionately too. So I repeated it. 'What'll we do now?' The shadow of my pal moved, got up and slugged some milk from a carton, looking out of the window.

'Do something,' he said.

'What?'

When he sat down again he was not so much his own shadow any longer. He shook his fat slow head, but I was still messing about with it and the darkness, putting on him extraterrestial features, fish lips, swollen moony cranium. He was now one of those superior beings who ought to teach us one or two things when they drop by.

'Come on and we'll call into Maureen,' he said. He hoisted himself tall. He was really simply jealous of my image of that rich flag. 'C'mon.'

It wasn't easy standing up. The way I got into my coat was like he was forcing me to shake its hand. 'I can pay her back tomorrow when I get some stuff,' he said. 'Come on, she'll give us a suck. You know Maureen.' He gave the door of his cardboard room a sharp flap behind him to close it and we headed on out the door and down Dominick Street for a suck. I was still mildly high. I had a headache. The air reminded my head of its swollen importance. Don't underestimate the regrets of ingesting fuel of an evening. My innards were quivering under my raincoat. We climbed up towards 63b where Maureen is on that stinking old street that leads out of the city. It's a sewer of all-night shops and rubbish piles, bins. We were walking back up the way I had come down, past the half houses, the doors ajar overhead, billboard pictures of our earth or babies, all that stuff. The important point now is light. The light in this town is quite particular to this town, I suspect. There's a certain way it's dark here. In fact, I know the precise word which describes the property of this town's light. The light in this town is oleaginous.

'Come on,' said my pal. I was slacking. A crisp packet had begun to heel along beside me. Amazingly. It was loyal. When it panted on ahead of me it waited for me to catch up, then we carried on at the same pace more or less. Me and this crisp packet. But I was lagging behind my pal. We were just passing the turn for Denmark Street. I got a pang. The misted far end of the street ebbed inside me like a violet ocean. My head was sore, it was about to become a mouth and a shriek. I stopped. He stopped and looked round at me. The crisp packet went off for its own life.

'I've something to do,' I said. 'I'll come along to Maureen's in five minutes.'

'What?'

'I'll see you there,' I said.

'What?'

'Fuck off,' I said.

He walked away. I cut up the side street on my own into the inner city again.

I can re-emphasise a few points. Concerning this inner city, oleaginous is a key word. As you proceed through this town the buildings slide past in oil. It's a deep sea town, submerged. You don't live in this shit place. You pass. You have a pass-style, but without the style. You slip along in a kind of semi-swim posture with redundant eyes because light doesn't filter down, slip along dim-sightedly, weightily. Oleaginously. We don't belong to our eyes, we don't need them. There was some evil, real oily mist on the street. I came to a corner and turned it. Here was the street along the square. This wasn't far from that wall at the end of Hardwicke Street. A scream sounded far away. I could only just distinguish from the conspiratorial mist camouflaged as street, a huddle of kids along the railing under the million dry twigs and involute-type leaves poking out. Track suits, dulled red and dulled green, and little pale faces watching me pass. I saw tiny little soft movements. This is a palace of dirty necks. I was coming up to that wall now. I looked round at the kids to see if they were watching me now. But they were too well cloaked. Any second the wall would come up now. I was expecting a stone in my back. The wall was coming marginally too fast forward. Inside me things hugged together, kidney coloured stones, lung-shaped edges, whatever was down there in my submarine unknown inside bits. I was expecting to be pounced on. My legs were weak. I was dissolving. I reached the corner where those young yobs had their wall, the corner round which that little guy's image was leaning like a kink in the brick. My chest had already been hypnotised by the ritual of a tom-tom. As I walked round I kept my head low. When I had passed it I glanced back casually. Then I was surprised. I thought I might see that picture from earlier, that artful statuesque ease. I wanted to check something against my knowledge of life. I wanted to check I had seen those eyes right. But there was no one there. I walked on. I walked up towards Hardwicke Street, towards Maureen's place, 63b. My body was getting heavy. A sidelong block of flats peeped over the Georgian houses. I was hard to carry. There was an alley with smoke in it that led to those scarred flats. My body was in a sulk. As I walked towards the high street I glanced up that alley that lead to the flats. Then, all at once, this body of mine turned up that alley. It had a feeling about those flats. It wanted to see those eyes again, I believe.

I walked slowly, carefully. There was no sound. This body wasn't brave, it was tense to shuddering point, it was ready to sprint back at the softest signal. The smell of smoke pulled a gentle commotion right up to the outside edge of me, it was swirling like filthy milk through me, a blond grime. The courtyard of these flats was quiet and wide, but it wasn't easy to see things. Maybe I would love to belong here, I think. But I can't get my head round that idea. An invisible dog was trotting. It emerged. Behind the blocks a taller tower stood. I know this, not because it could be seen, but because of a few dim lights hooked up on the fog. Suddenly I heard a scraping sound. My body jumped an inch out of me. There was a child on a skateboard. He skated up to me. He was a small kid.

I looked around to see if anyone was watching me. My pulse was going crazy. I know nothing about the young. I can't imagine their lives. I tried to as I looked at this kid. He had a loud track suit, beginnings of a downy moustache on a baby face. I couldn't. I couldn't push my imagination out far enough to include a detail like, for example, this child eating, or that boy's legs from earlier walking away from the wall. I was rigid all over. My dreams only go so far. A flaxen image had got caught in the machinery of my day-to-day thinking. It had damaged some of my equipment. I needed to understand that image. I needed to be rid of it. I needed to pacify it. This is what happened next.

'Are you a doctor?' the kid said to me through a reed of a voice. I whispered, 'No' and carried on walking. He was short even on his skateboard. I tried to ignore him, looking around. 'Are you?' he said. I stopped. I was juddering. His blackberry hair was a wild clump. While he looked up at me he was persisting at a sore on his hand. That pale hand glowed. It was time for me to get out of here. If I was patient I would forget in time the idea of complicated eyes. I'd see how crude they are in the reality outside of my head. 'What're you doin' round here?' the kid said. My dreams had already given that picture from earlier a good smash, had shattered it, so it wasn't throwing up details other than the eyes. I was recovering. I couldn't any longer properly invoke the figure which had totally buckled the twilight. That is how it should be. That is how I want it.

'I . . .' My voice was stammering. 'I'm looking . . .' The kid narrowed his eyes. I said, 'Where's the street?' It would just take a specific time period to put images like these through the erasing process.

'Give us your money, mister,' the kid said. 'Would you?'

I came out with: 'I thought . . .' His tiny eyebrows got cross.

'I'll scream,' he said. He looked right up at me. 'And then you'll be for it.'

I was nervous. 'Look,' I said. The distance let out a yell. I started to walk back towards the alley. He picked up his skateboard and walked with me.

'Go on,' he said. I stopped again and turned. His finger was still at that sore. I was looking all around. I took out my wallet. 'Would you?' The only money I had was emergency stuff.

'I don't have much,' I whispered and I handed him these two colourful tiny flags. This was special money, money for dreams. His miniature hand touched my fingers. It was a warm mouse.

'You're fuckin' rich,' he laughed with his eyes bright.

'I'm not.' There was still nobody in the dark. He folded the money away tightly into his jeans pocket. 'I don't work,' I told him. He dropped his jaw in a playful way. 'How do I get out of here?' I said. I started walking.

'Through there.' He waved his hand lazily at the alley.

'Thanks,' I said. I stopped again. I nodded at him. 'Thanks for showing me the way out,' I told him and backed away.

'It's all right,' he smiled. He skated a little towards me. 'Do you live round here?' he asked.

I wanted to thank him. I just said, 'I really appreciate it.' He giggled nervously. Then I turned quickly away down the alley. 'Thanks, mister!' he shouted out. I walked rapidly up Hardwicke Street. A burglar alarm started up, wrapping an everlasting steel chain round the streets. This earth we live on was right then unstable, I wanted to get indoors, away from the stars. I came up towards the high street where this Maureen is. Smoke was rising from a rubbish pile, it was sighing, the street was trying to enchant itself. It would just take time, I was thinking to myself. I can't cope until I can grasp what those eyes earlier signified for sure. Soon I will understand what it's all about. My inside dream mechanism had done its best with them. It was even now working, I knew, to crush that image, to grind it right down to a substance as tender as petals. But it needed time. It would keep on at it till there was fat and blood on the cogwheels, till the boy at the wall with milky hair and long eyelashes was mangled to pure tears. I'll be able to cope with it soon, when piss and juice and the sweat between his sweet dirty arse have cooled off the situation here inside me. It just needs patience.

Salvages
(After seeing Tiepolo's The Finding of Moses in the National Gallery of Scotland.)

The only other woman living in the hotel besides Kate was not a guest; she was the companion of the hôtelier. He was a Pied Noir who had come out to this corner of the colonies with a strangers' army a long time ago; he had the flowery manners of the past, and a formal mode of speech, and she waited on him with delicate ceremony each night, as he presided over the restaurant from the corner of the dark inner room behind the bar. She never sat down with him, but disappeared behind a curtain, where, it was said, she fixed his pipes for him.

There were other women, younger than Kate, who frequented the verandah of the hotel; they were not admitted into the dining-room, or to the hotel's inner courtyard, where it was easy to forget that a war was going on, as a broad-leaved frangipani tree spread scented shade beneath its branches and dropped waxy flowers onto the undiminished fine linen of earlier days, while croissants were brought warm from the oven by the cook who had also learned his trade from the former power. The other women waited for customers at the guéridons on the verandah, with fizzy drinks from bottles with famous American brandnames. But you could tell from the cap, which was stamped off-register by hand, that they weren't the real thing.

Kate was shown the difference during the first days of her stay in the city, and she soon learned on her own account how everything was used more than once, passed from hand to hand, leaving a tiny doit of wealth behind as it went. Imitation wasn't really the word. Nor was fake, or cheat. It was more that things were adapted. Taken, named, made to resemble, to belong to a family of other things that offered them hospitality and added value. Salvaged. She had arrived in the city in the final spasm of the counter-insurgents' offensive and she was to stay to within a few days of their success; she had come because the man she had recently married was reporting there, and seeing the news of mounting catastrophe after he had gone frightened her so much for his safety, she chose to join him rather than live in helpless anguish. It had been a risk, less on account of the danger the war presented than the nuisance she might become to him, the assault her company made on his heroic witness to the savagery of the régime's reprisals, the horror of the rebels' attacks. Though the city would fall, it was at that time still the most protected fortress of the whole country, out of range of the rebel army's artillery, under strict curfew from dusk to dawn and seething with soldiers of the allied armies come to help save the incumbent government. Kate loved her husband more than he requited, and because she was young and girlish with it, and felt that life had dealt her a hand with undue generosity, she liked to provoke his cold impatience and prove her devotion by forgiving it and loving him the more.

One of the other journalists in the hotel played go-between with a few of the whores; after that, Kate befriended two of them, learned their first names, Solange and Noëlle, and went to eat with them off formica and steel tables, feasting on spicy soup and fried fish after – sometimes, for it was the rainy season – plunging knee deep through the monsoon flood that swelled with tidal power in the streets every evening, to reach the place down some alley the girls knew was cheap and good. Kate paid, it was the least she could do. She saw Solange and Noëlle separately, and she never sat on the verandah with them for fear of causing embarrassment if a soldier thought she was turning a trick too; and as she was white, she offered unfair competition, even though in her own country, she was a young woman with pleasant features, but no siren. Solange giggled when they walked side by side, for Kate soon outstripped her and then had to stop to draw level again; Kate wore cotton trousers and sandals in the heat, and her usual gait was a stride. Whereas Solange was in the country's traditional costume, silk, tight-fitting, and she wore tiny beaded high heels, so that she furled and unfurled when she moved like the kite-tails that streamed from some of the yards in the city where a child cut out relief agency rice-bags and stitched them to a frame of jetsam. This was another of the retrievals Kate admired, another secondary use, another salvage, transforming the foreign into the native. The journalist who had effected Kate's introduction to Solange – it was necessary because she could have been an official, a medical worker, a missionary, intent on stopping her practise her trade – pointed out to her that the bras in vogue in the country were relics of the colonial past. 'They're all uplift and points like the nose of mortar shells – the style that went out at home with hula hoops!'

When she went to the room where Solange lived, she expected
something like the brothels in Amsterdam: a pallet spread with
a white sheet, a bidet on a stand, a towel, a mirror, a curtain, a
calendar with a photograph of a Swiss chalet or a Cotswold lane.
She travelled alongside the prostitute in another cyclo; through the
swirling putty water her wrinkled old driver pedalled. The cyclo
drivers were either too old or too young to be conscripted, and as
this meant a pensioner or a child, Kate sat back helplessly pricked
by the sight of the man's chicken calves as she was drawn through
the muddy torrent and the hooting, kerosene fog of traffic someone
for whom she would give up her seat on the tube in her own native
place. 'What can you do?' Richard said to her when she moped
about it. 'Don't be silly. They need the money, your hire is what
puts bread on their plate, rice in their ricebowl. There are quite
enough beggars round the place without your helping to create
more by refusing to ride the cyclos. Come on.'

It turned out that Solange lived in a small wooden cabin, polished
and plain and flat-bottomed on legs like a coble built for easy
beaching, under a canopy of banana and some flowering tree,
with her mother and two children, one who looked about five,
the other a baby, an infant, but mute with the slate blank eyes
Kate knew from other children in the city streets. Solange showed
Kate a photograph of the elder child's father, resorted to bargirl
slang to describe their sweet and eternal love, 'You are my number
one baby, my oochy poochy sweetypie', she chanted, quoting him.
'Solange, you're good enough to eat. I love you.' He was about
twenty in the army snapshot, with a moustache, a white GI with
an Italian name. He had been going to volunteer for a second
tour; he'd promised to send money, for Tony Junior, she was still
waiting, still hoping, though it had clearly been years. Oh, it was
so bloody typical, such utter stale buns, Kate could have slapped
Solange. She hoped that she was making it up, that she didn't
know who the father was, she'd rather her life was a racket,
wanton anarchy, ferocious, cynical chaos, than have her duped
and asking for more. Hitting her, Kate saw, was the invitation
her swaying sweet baby-talking presence issued, her jump leads,
the only certain seductive powers she had learned.

Meanwhile, Solange's mother in black pyjamas squealed and
flapped at the child until he went outside again holding the baby

and stopped looking at the roundeye woman with their mother. When had she started work again after this infant? Kate saw a gash, imagined tender walls, sore breasts, and firmly set such thoughts aside.

'I no want em fight. Not like other kids,' said Solange. 'Soon he go to army, get killed.' She pointed at the child who was now holding the baby in his arms. 'Junior eight years old now.' It was less hot in her hutment than outside, but her lip was beaded, and she wiped her face with a towel, then handed the aluminium waterpot to her mother to fill from the standpipe in the street outside.

Kate was large for the room; she became aware of her heft as she sat on the stool Solange indicated, and waited while the pot began to rattle on the primus lit on the step outside. The boy was now playing under the eave of the hut's floor; looking for ants, for spiders. He'd left the baby lying on the ground on a mat in the shade of the wall. Solange said, 'She sleep now.'

The bed was in the corner; there was a curtain, a picture, of a Filippino Lippi Madonna. Solange was clearly better off than some of the bargirls who worked the alleys and weren't even allowed on the verandah of the hotel. She still had her teeth, for one thing. 'The blowjob experts have them pulled,' one of the other guests in the hotel told her. 'When they're kids. The earlier the better. Soldiers don't like taking those kind of risks.'

There were always stories in the hotel at night, when Richard was away, at the front, gathering material, doing his job. She was so outnumbered they did not count her as female, they spoke quite freely, she eavesdropped on the folklore of the jon, the mysteries of the locker-room. 'This guy'd been doing something he shouldn't have been doing, and this little lady she goes right ahead and bites him — bites right through it. What does he get?' (Slap, guffaw, slap.) 'A Purple Heart for valour in the field!'

Kate was drinking tea from a cup with a pattern on it like the set her parents had in Guildford; it was a different shape, however, more like an egg-cup. She wondered what Solange did on the bed in the corner; she thought about her mother and the children in the room with her, she had seen families, all curled up together, kindle-like, using one another's legs and backs for pillows, sometimes out by the traffic on the pavement where it was cooler than under the tin roofs of the shanties. They

could sleep through a lot; they had learned to sleep through
the mortar explosions since the shelters had been flooded out
and the attacks were closing in, the centre of the city gradually
coming into range.

'You take him home with you, Kate. You call up Tony, Tony
Junior go to college, go with you.'

'I live in England.'

'England, America, same, same. Yes? You rich. You take him
when you go England. Him learn quick.'

Tony Junior had come in again, encumbered by the baby, who
clung to him like a growth.

Kate nodded, but said, 'I can't Solange. It isn't possible.
I'm sorry.'

She gave her twenty dollars, two, three tricks' worth, maybe
more. The boy ran for a cyclo. Solange smoothed the note between
her pale slender fingers and smiled. She tapped a tooth, gold, as
was fashionable.

'I sell this, bribe officials, stop him go army.'

The city was full of business; though there were shortages,
there was also surplus, and bartering was brisk on the pavements.
Medicines beyond their due date lay on rush mats in neat piles
like towers of toy bricks beside varied anatomies of hardware and
dead soldiers' paraphernalia – contraband watches, radios, hi-fis,
compasses, electrical parts and bicycle parts, recharged batteries,
boots, coats, wallets, belts – as well as rebottled Dewar's and Black
Label and Kentucky Sour Mash with the wrong screwtops. Their
minders were children mostly, boys. With small, lithe hands, the
vendor would clutch at Kate's arm, and screech at her, begging
her to buy. If she didn't want what she could see spread out,
they had plenty more things elsewhere they could fetch, they
had anything she might want. This was the world of the jokes
she overheard, 'You want my little sister? No? You want my
little brother? You want nice big smack – cheap, cheap? You like
sucky-sucky?'

Girl children were not so visible; they were indoors, Kate
supposed, under protection or already conducting the curtained
business of their own. In the market, the slimy, fetid, sprawling
downtown market in the Chinese quarter of the city, there was still
plenty of food for sale, much strangling of various fowl and gutting
of fish, crabs lumbering in wicker cages and jackfruit splitting
at the seams and ripely adding to the mixed perfumes in the

contrived darkness. Her first wander there, Kate was attracted by the toys, the heaps of paper boats and houses, horses and mobiles, figures of men and women made of indigo- and cochineal-dyed rice paper stitched by hand. She bought a rider on his steed, a pagoda, and a bundle of paper money in brilliant scarlet with gold leaf stamps on it, while the market women roared with laughter at her, calling out names. Later she was told, 'They were shouting "Peasant" because of your hat.' (She had taken to wearing a tribal straw hat against the sun.) She also learned from another informant that her toys were funerary offerings: 'The gooks burn them on the pyre, so that the dead can take that stuff to heaven with them. It's symbolism, far out Booudhist symbolism.' She took them up to her hotel room, unswerving from her pleasure in their craft, though they would not travel well.

Solange's boy was the first child she was offered. There were no babies arranged on the rush mats and no booths at the market which dangled them for sale. But the goods came her way, like the other things she could have tried if she had a fancy to. (She did try everything she had the nerve to try.) She was never offered a girl baby, however. Her own singularity remained intact, if anything became deeper. When she commented to Richard, after the third child she was asked to take, that she was surprised they were all boys, he said, 'It stands to reason. They don't want them to be called up. It's a good story. I should write it. But it's Human Interest, and they want War Games from me, the Allied Strategy, the Body Count, the Weapon Stockpile, the odds on a ceasefire, etc. Why don't you do it? Keep you busy.'

'I've never written an article,' said Kate.

'You write law reports, you brief barristers. You know how to string your thoughts together on paper. Which is more than most of the poor fuckers here. Use your education, you've had the luck to have one.'

She began to listen to the diners in the hotel with more care.

'Where can you get contraception in the city?' she asked.

After an outburst of obligatory fun, one of the wire men answered, 'Anywhere and everywhere. They're free at the PX; they're in every bar that's got a jon, and the girls have got them on them.'

'So why is the birth rate so high?'

Then Kate met Jinty, and found comfort in the company of

another woman. Jinty was short and plump and solid like a riding mistress; she gave the impression from her carriage that she'd keep a good seat on a horse, and her hair clasped her head closely as if used to a hard hat. She also came from Surrey, and lived in Cobham when she was at home, among gorse bushes and pines. But she specialised in children in crisis, famine relief, and the administration of foreign aid. The charity organisation called Sangrail had sent her to this war, to see if there was any way through the political deadlock; the charities' money to the government was routinely siphoned off, money to the rebels was against UN rules; the counter-insurgents were holed up in villages badly needing supplies of all kinds, but officially they did not exist, so it was not possible even to put into gear any means of helping civilians in the territory they held. After a month of impasse with officials, when Kate met her at a function in the Canadian envoy's villa, Jinty was concentrating her attention on the city's orphanages. 'I'm practical,' she told Kate. 'Wrangling with colonels isn't my cup of tea at all. I don't want to waste time wittering, though the Lord knows I still have to do a heck of a lot of it.'

The next day, Kate went with her to a children's hospital, down sidestreets heavy with kerosene and churning with cyclos, to the old European quarter of the city, where three Belgian nuns in a convent founded in the last century were nursing foundlings, some of whom had been left on their doorstep, while others had been brought in from the war, from burned villages, from the evacuated rebel-held countryside.

'The situation's worsening as the war is being lost,' Jinty went on. 'And in the meantime, orphanages like this one are filling up to bursting point, and still more refugees are entering the city every night. They wade the irrigation ditches, in spite of the mines, they duck the sentries. Because this is the only safe place to be. There's still food here. Brought in by villagers, sold off into the topsy-turvy economy they don't understand. The supplies won't last, of course, and there'll be thousands more people pouring in, and then, when the end comes, they might all start streaming the other way, who knows, back into the countryside. Depends on what shape the end takes. Doesn't interest me, who wins. Does it you? No? Good. Let the generals argue the toss with one another. There's plenty to be done while they chinwag.'

*

They were at the door of the infirmary. In Italy, at the Innocenti hospital in one of the northern towns, Kate had once seen the special compartment in the door, where the babies were to be put; like the night safe in a bank's outer wall, it allowed the packet to be passed through without either side seeing the other. But here, there was no sign of the place's purpose, of the bundled children delivered to the step, as Kate had half expected. The nun who came to open to them was not a stranger, but a native, wearing a grey veil, and pearl-headed pins to secure it to the white wimple which covered her ears and neck. She kissed Jinty, and left one hand on her shoulder with lingering tenderness; they exchanged words in French, which Jinty spoke with a West African accent Kate recognised from students she had known when she was studying law at one of the Inns of Court in London.

'Soeur Philippe,' the nun introduced herself to Kate. The skin of her palm was dry and hard. 'Come and see our children.' She had that way of smiling nuns catch from statues, beatific, and without a trace of laughter.

This first infirmary gave model treatment, compared to other establishments Kate was to visit. At first she thought she was doing as Richard said, and gathering material for an article on the plight of the abandoned children and orphans of the war, but soon she found that without consciously embarking on helping Jinty, she was running errands for her and carrying out certain tasks for her. There was, as Jinty had said, plenty to do. In the Belgian nuns' hospital the children lay two to a cot, one at each end, on a sheet, with a nappy on and a bottle each tied to a strut in the cot's side near their mouth; most of them were far too weak to reach the teat even if they were developed enough to roll or otherwise make a move towards it. So someone was needed just to go round and try and fit the babies' mouths to their feed and stimulate them to suck. There wasn't time to pick them up and nurse them individually, there were far too many of them. Starvation had turned their clocks back; they looked like medical photographs of gestating embryos, with huge frontal lobes and tiny sperm-like limbs. In some cases, Kate could have scooped them into the palms of her hands.

'You see, they are frequently born premature. The mothers are not eating enough, in their bodies they are . . . how shall I say . . . not healthy . . . Their way of life . . .' Soeur Philippe joined hands over her habit as if praying. 'They do not leave their children to die. No, they abandon them so that they have a chance to survive. Somewhere else. Here, or, if possible, in Europe, America. They dream . . . but, you know . . .' She put out her hand and touched a baby's face; the open eyes, huge as an owl's, did not flicker. '*On fait de son mieux.*'

Jinty was examining the register: 'I need to make a copy of the figures, to send to London. We must have facts. It's not to be believed otherwise.'

The nun shook her head. 'The register is out of date, it is hard to keep it up. We pray at the burials, of course, we remember all of them in our prayers. But the record – we don't have time for the record.' Jinty handed Kate the book, where in theory each child was to be entered, with a case history, weight, race, symptoms, treatment, outcome – discharge to another orphanage, or, death. 'Make a few copies anyway – and come back.'

Kate took the ledger; she tried various shops with photocopiers, but none was working, contraband toner was harder to fake than bourbon and Coke. So eventually she went round to the daily briefing centre and used the journalists' office facilities, thinking how stupid she was not to have thought of that immediately. She was confused, the children had confused her, they made her feel lewd in her healthiness and her strength. The smell of them was still in her nostrils, the leaky milk-and-piss sickliness of their feeble hold on life.

That night in the hotel, she spoke up, from her table where she sat on her own, over the head of the Agence France Presse rep who was also on his own, to the room where a group of wire service journalists and other papers' stringers were eating together. 'I saw about two hundred babies today who had been abandoned in the last few months, since the offensive started.' She was eating alone because Richard had gone up country with a general to write up the régime's supposed progress. 'Most of them looked as if they were dying. They're mostly half-black and half-white. The mothers are all bargirls, apparently.'

'Yeah,' said one newspaperman, 'The whole fucking country's one big brothel. That's our present to the people: we teach the women how to fuck. That's freedom. That's a law of the free market.'

'I guess, who's going to use a rubber when his life is on the line?' This was another man, joining the conversation. 'Those guys, they want to leave something of themselves behind, you know.' The veteran newspaperman, famous for hard-hitting coverage, spread his hands and shrugged.

Another put in, 'Two hundred? That's a lot of children. I reckon, they're telling us something about what's happening out there. Nobody wants to get caught with anything incriminating on them when the end comes, now do they? And what would be more incriminating than a little roundeye babba with funny coloured skin?'

The most famous reporter of all nodded at Kate and called out, 'It's like we wrote at the start of the war, it's still the same story. "You gotta destroy the village in order to save it." You gotta leave your fucking child if you want him to stay alive. The only safe place to be is elsewhere.'

The next day, Kate joined Jinty in a different orphanage; this one for babies and children who could feed themselves and obey their minder's order to sit in line on potties and perform. Many of these did not have foreign fathers, but had lost their parents, either through death during a raid, or dispersal, as they took flight from a village under attack, or were scattered as they stole into the city at night for safety. The authorities in this establishment were secular, and local; The Good Fortune and Long Life Prudential Society.

This time, the reactions in the hotel afterwards to Kate's report were less jock-like, more informed. 'You should watch out, they'll bleed you for all you're worth, that little lot. It's Mme. So-and-So's outfit, isn't it? Her good works my ass. It's just a cover for far more important business. She's using it to launder – you take a little look at the books, my dear, and see if you can make head or tail of the finances of the Good Fortune and Long Life Prudential Society – if they've got any books they'll let you see.'

When she brought it up with Jinty, the older woman replied, 'Journalists like plots. I'm not interested in plots, and the people aren't characters to me, they're not pieces on some almighty chessboard. Close your mind to them. If you think about who you're helping you'll never do anything. There'll always be a good reason to sit on your bottom and do nothing.'

That day they went to a city shelter for disabled children. These were orphans of all ages, and their handicaps were in some cases the results of wounds from bombs, shrapnel and gas, in others congenital. When they arrived in the former warehouse, the reek of disinfectant was overwhelming. It was dark inside, which helped to keep down the temperature under the metal roof, though the absence of windows made the interior atmosphere asphyxiating. First Kate noticed that the walls were dripping and the dirt floor was covered in a film of water tinged with the blue-grey bubbles of some toilet cleansing fluid; then she saw that the children were soaking too, lying nappy-less on rubber sheets draped on iron bedsteads or on the floor, where ammoniac puddles had also collected.

'They hose them down in the morning,' Jinty told her. 'It's the quickest way to clean up the ones who are incontinent, and restore some level of hygiene to the room.' She looked at the room, as Kate beside her swallowed, and went on, 'As boys and girls are all mixed in together, so we can't vouch for another sort of hygiene.'

Jinty had commandeered a team of allied soldiers to plumb in showers and basins, linked to the standpipe in the street outside; Kate had accompanied her to the army depot and watched her rustling the equipment, the parts and the fittings from the sergeant on duty. She helped move the children from one side of their dark quarters to the other, and separate the boys from the girls. To the ones with power in their arms, she gave piggy backs; their heads on her shoulders like stones, their breath sour with the sour juices of malnutrition. One girl patted her hair, and said something softly, twisting her head around to smile in Kate's eyes. She was admiring it, Kate realised, admiring it for its difference from her own in lightness of colour and fluffiness of texture.

She helped put up a partition, to give some privacy to the older girls who had started to menstruate. It was built of tough cartons that had delivered something marked Fragile to the assisting army; they'd been salvaged from one of the many public dumps before someone else had taken them to turn them into a street cabin (there were families living in shipping containers discarded by the supporting foreigners); she helped Jinty and a male army nurse Jinty had also borrowed to wash some of the children and cover them in clothing they had brought. On examination close up, many of the bodies were terribly damaged; but there were no dressings available and only bleach for disinfectant. A softish, wadded parcel from England had miraculously passed through the thieving hands of customs and other authorities; it proved to be full of teddy bears.

Attending to the children, Kate was reminded of the heaps of rubbish behind the foreigners' haunts, and near other places of abundance, like the market, where the natives swarmed to pick over the fruit and vegetables, the burst packaging, the rags and débris. The child prone on the rubber sheeting whom she was swabbing looked as if he had fallen from a tree onto stones where wasps and worms had feasted on the tears in his flesh. Kate clenched her teeth to stop herself gagging, her repugnance increased by shame that she should feel disgust at all. Jinty noticed, and told her, kindly, 'Listen, old girl, no need to linger. You need time to get used to this sort of thing. Go on, have a breath of fresh air outside. If you can find some.'

Richard came back from his expedition to the counter-insurgents' territory. He was frustrated in his attempts to file, because the government censors had picked up his denunciations of the three-cornered civil war; he was furious. In the hotel, the number of pressmen had grown; from the corner of the dining-room where he was waited on by his companion, the proprietor now rewrote the hotel charges on a nightly basis as prices rose; the wines drunk improved in labels and vintage as he dug deeper into the last of the cellar. There was a trade in passports and visas at the bar; in other things as well. Contractors arrived and were busy; the beggars at the hotel door grew bolder, as did the rats, sometimes making an appearance before the dining-room was empty to snatch at fallen scraps. The embassies notified their nationals to leave. 'You're to get out, Kate, there's no two ways about it,' said Richard. 'It's the end, and I've got to stay as long as I can. But you . . .'

Kate tried to make love to him that night. She saw the children's bodies in her mind's eye, their own gaze shadowless, like the moon in eclipse. She wanted the sap and the kick of sex to move the darkness and lift the heavy bodies of the orphans where they were lodged in her, torpid and undigested. But Richard wouldn't, he too lay leaden, a reproach to her, as if he were saying in his unresponsiveness, How could you at a time like this? She was half thinking to herself, We should have a child ourselves, a strapping, crowing, pink and white child who knows how to express hunger and discomfort and ask for everything, not like these inert lumps of flesh in their silence and their stink. All the time she'd been with Jinty trying to help with the orphans she'd never shed a tear. It had left her as numb and cold as if she were made of ten-day-old suet, and she hated herself for it and for not being able to get through to Richard: he was out there on the front line, fighting, even when he was in bed with her, and women had no place there, no, nor love neither. So she wept now for herself, lying naked in the stifling room, hearing the distant boom and crackle of the mortars and the scritch of the rats in the walls.

*   *   *

I watch the big English who come one day see my mother drink tea with her I follow her offer her cigarettes the man gave me sell sell. She say no cigarettes but she give me two quarters an tell me no smoke myself have something eat she no recognise me I go with her she go to Sisters' infirmary where they take babies she ask why you follow me I tell her you pretty woman you kind woman she laugh she say go away home I say please I come see you again tomorrow she say no no I say please again she gets angry shoo shoo little boy I no have more money I say please she no say name of hotel but I know where she stay (she no realise I know of course) but she say tomorrow she come one more time say goodbye she leaving she sad this country number one people in it so sweet and never complain she say. I find my mother home she sick now an I tell her and she say Take Theresa so I take my sister mother give us money for cyclo I only ride cyclo one time before and I tell driver go Sisters' infirmary, he go and I leave Theresa in basket with blanket and other things on the step

first nobody come and I hidin by door nearby an waitin an watchin hopin big English come like she say an then I see her she hot she puff she stop an make little cry when she see basket and baby then she pick up Theresa and hug Theresa an look in basket I wait see what she do then if she ring bell give Theresa to door Sister she do she go in with Sister they talk talk high voices big English I hear she cry again

my mother burn many offering she light candle though she sick she walk to church to make special prayer for Theresa the big English no want to take me I too grownup take care of things here now so mother pray she take Theresa and we all be leaving soon soon for to find Tony

*   *   *

After the fall of the city and the establishment of the new régime, Kate returned to the city to join Jinty, who had remained throughout, and to complete the adoption process of the child she had chosen when she found her lying on the steps of the Belgian nuns' infirmary. Jinty had helped her with the paperwork; by completion, Kate spent about ten thousand pounds, she reckoned, buying her baby. But it was a small price for Theresa (that was her name; it had been written on a bracelet left in the basket, alongside one or two other tokens, just like in a fairytale), Theresa who had lain there in her path as if destined for her, and who had put her arms around her neck confidingly when she picked her up that first time as if she knew Kate and understood that she could care for her. Kate had turned over inside at her touch; Theresa was like the spark in flint and she had lit Kate back to life.

Jinty said, 'A lot of people bleat about uprooting children from their culture and whatever. Culture? When you haven't got enough to eat? When you'll be on the streets by the age of ten? Oh, they're dear, clever little things, and they might manage to survive, but what kind of a life will it be? Don't let the doubters and the purists torment you, you go ahead, Kate, give Theresa an English life, give her pony clubs, ballet classes, meat and two veg; Jeeves. Hell's bells, one has to believe in something. Besides, she's half-and-half anyway – her father could have been God knows what.'

When Theresa was six and began going to school all day, Kate took on full time work for Sangrail as an expert on refugees, specialising in adoption and immigration law. As Richard was often travelling, still covering the hot spots, but for another paper now (his old one had been taken over and used news agencies in the interest of profits), Kate had always employed a housekeeper. She drew them from the large population of boat people; she was good at helping them get the right papers for the country of their choice. Canada was very popular, so were some of the Caribbean countries. This was Kate's field, and a trickle of women – and sometimes their husbands – from Theresa's birthplace had passed through the Georgian house on the Hackney/Islington border to live in the basement flat and work for the family before they settled elsewhere.

One day, a refugee liaison centre telephoned Kate about a case: an economist exchange student in Paris had applied for his mother to leave and join him, but she wanted to work in England, she had a little English she had learned in the war. He was making approaches to transfer his scholarship to LSE, in order to continue his studies. He was bright, and he was resolved, at present, to return to his country; he had prospects and he was not seeking residency or citizenship for himself. As for his mother, he had specifically given them Kate's name as a possible sponsor; her name was Solange Ngu. Did Kate want to take the matter up?

Solange arrived to start her post as housekeeper in the summer holidays of Theresa's eleventh year (or what was thought to be her eleventh year, on the basis of a conjectured age of three months when she was found). Kate interviewed Solange beforehand; after all, she had been a bargirl, and a mother doesn't want her only daughter coming under a bad influence. But Kate had also known several other women from the city who had worked the streets in those days, and she knew that after what they had been through, they were more likely to be strict, even over-zealous guardians of morality. She would not have recognised Solange, though for her own part, Solange laughed and said she would have recognised Kate anywhere anytime; but Solange looked much older, with her hair cut short and straight and her torso slightly bent – an abdominal operation had left a lumpy scar, and she leaned forward as if to shield it. She was proud of her son, and she no longer called him Junior; also, the new régime's debriefing about America seemed to have impressed her. She did not want to emigrate there, unlike some of her predecessors, but to stay in London. This was harder, but Kate promised to do her best.

Theresa was the same height as Solange, for, in spite of her puny size in the first year of life, she had been fed on muesli and kiwi and other vitamin-rich foodstuffs and grown rangy in limb, with a light sheen on her skin like amboyna wood. She had the quicksilver energy of childhood, and so tended to be impatient with her refugee minders, especially with their lack of English and their timorous ways negotiating London transport systems, until Kate – or Richard – had to scold her and teach her to make allowances for newcomers. But Solange seemed to dust off the little girl's prickliness. 'I love Mummy best, this much,' – the child stretched her arms wide – 'Then Daddy, this much,' – she brought her arms in a little – 'And then you, Solange, this much!' She stretched them out again, hooting, her mouth full of spring rolls Solange had cooked for her. Kate stood in the doorway, watching her at the kitchen table as Solange dished up another; these rolls had become favourite food. 'You eat now, Theresa, and don't chit-chat so much,' responded Solange, already busy scouring the pan at the sink.

Kate felt a tweak of jealousy, but she quelled it. It would be stupid to mind that Theresa had a nanny she liked; she had always wanted her to feel something in common with the people she came from, and after all, it was every working woman's dream to find someone who would be a substitute mother to her children when, for one reason or another, she couldn't be there all the time to take care of them herself.

The Blaneys

From a novel in progress

I walk towards the front door. The driveway is bright with the crazy paving of bald pink stones. It was left by the people who lived here before us. They also planted a rockery of sparkling silvery rocks. Dad prefers tarmac. Tarmac is burning like molasses in the sunshine on the driveway next door. I walk across our pink stones and open the front door. Then I hurry through the hallway towards the kitchen, dropping my schoolbag at the foot of the stairs. The kitchen is shaded. The blind hangs listlessly at the open window. In the glass bowl on the sill the goldfish sinks in a steamy swamp of water and weeds. I hurry to the bread bin. My sister, Jane, is sitting at the table, doing nothing.

She's at that age, says Mum: the age of doing nothing; nothing except sitting, chin in hand, and glaring. Jane glares at me as I reach into the bread bin.

'What?' I challenge.

She continues to glare.

'*What?*'

Mum appears at the back door, leaving the garden to a fanfare of shrieks and splashes from my little brother and sister in the paddling pool. On the doorstep she is taller than usual. She stares down at us. 'Stop it, you two,' she warns before she descends.

'It was Jane,' I protest.

Jane widens her glaring eyes. 'I wasn't doing anything.'

Mum sighs and rakes her fingers through her hair as she crosses to the fridge. 'I don't care *who*. Just *stop*.'

Jane pouts. 'I wasn't saying anything.'

I protest to Mum: 'She was looking at me.'

Mum's bright head glows at the open door of the fridge. 'Oh stop it,' she garbles, probing the freezer box, 'both of you. Now.'

Jane transfers her chin from one hand to the other. 'Pardon me for breathing,' she hisses.

'No,' I reply.

Mum straightens and turns towards me. 'Now, that's enough,' she commands, blonde curls bouncing around her face.

I return my attention to the bread bin. 'Is there any brown?' I push around the packets and bags of white bread.

Mum snarls again into the fridge: 'Have I had time today to worry about bloody brown bread?'

I grimace as rudely as possible at her back. 'Just asking.'

She sighs heavily and closes the fridge, turning towards me with a packet of frozen sausages in her hands. 'No,' she admits, 'there's no brown.'

She crosses to the cooker. 'Anyway, it's nearly teatime. We're having an early tea because Erin has Brownies at six o'clock.'

'Tea? Now?'

She opens the cupboard and selects a tin of baked beans.

'Tea? Now?' I sigh emphatically. 'It's too hot for tea.'

Mum slams the tin onto the table. 'Oh stop complaining. I'm sick of it. Do you imagine that I want to stand here in this heat and cook your tea?'

I draw two slices from a packet of bread and drop them onto the breadboard. I want to suggest salad, but do not dare.

'And don't mention salad,' she says suddenly. 'You can't live on salad, not all the time.'

I butter the slices of bread and lift them onto a plate.

'Don't spoil your appetite,' Mum says as I leave the table. She begins to prick the sausages, thudding the prongs of the fork into the slushy grey flesh.

I shut the door behind me and walk through the dining area to the living room. Sitting down on the settee, I tear a piece from one of the slices of bread and squash it into a buttery ball. A cloud of net curtain hangs at the open windows: visibility, nil; and just the sound of a pushchair somewhere, of small hard wheels skipping over the uneven surface of the pavement, moving away. I press the buttery ball against the roof of my mouth. The room is scented with dust baking slowly in sunshine. *That's the one thing that I hate about summer*, says Mum: *the spring-cleaning waiting to be done.*

The room divider no longer divides the room but stands as shelves against a wall: caramel brown in the sunshine; sticky with fingerprints and dredged with a pale dust. Spider plants flop from shelf to shelf and tangle with the ornaments. On the middle shelf there is a row of books: Reader's Digest, cities and monuments photographed against enamel blue skies. I am supposed to want to visit the cities and monuments when I am older: the Parthenon, the Eiffel Tower, the Sistine Chapel. There is also a book of health, the cover black with the silhouette of a woman with childbearing hips.

I notice Erin's scrapbooks on the floor as Mum opens the door, strides across the dining area and stares at the debris. She jabs the tip of her tongue against the roof of her mouth in irritation. 'Look at that,' she says to me, pointing at the pile. She hurries across the living room, through the door, and halts in the hallway at the foot of the stairs. 'Erin,' she yaps, 'Erin. Erin. Erin.'

I despair, dumping the plate of bread beside me on the settee. 'Perhaps she can't hear you.'

Mum turns briefly towards me. 'I'll be the judge of that.' She turns again to the stairs. 'Erin. Erin.'

'*All right*:' the voice at the top of the stairs is faint but indignant.

Mum sighs. 'It is *not* all right. Don't talk to me like that. Get down here and tidy your things.'

'In a minute.'

'Not in a minute. Now.'

Erin comes down the stairs so slowly that it must be difficult to balance. 'Take your stuff to your room,' demands Mum: Jane-and-Erin's room. Mum insists that they share a room: *Your sister is a teenager now, she needs privacy, she has bosoms.*

Erin kneels on the floor and gathers pens and books into her arms. She drops more with each movement than she gathers.

Mum winces. 'Will you look at this?' she says to me, indicating Erin. Erin rises, stumbles, and drops a pencil case.

Mum turns to me. 'Are you around on Saturday night?' she asks, changing the subject.

I shrug, affecting nonchalance: 'Yes, probably.' I hope that she will ask me to babysit. I like babysitting because my boyfriend visits me.

'Oh, good. Can you babysit?'

I shrug again: I will not babysit for Jane; Mum knows that I will not babysit for Jane. I will babysit for the others, and Jane can stay with them, but I will not babysit for Jane. Sometimes on

Saturday mornings Mum persuades me to take Jane-and-Erin to the shops or the pool, and I walk with Erin on one side of the street whilst Jane walks on the other.

'Oh, good,' says Mum. 'I was wondering whether I could possibly borrow that little white top of yours?'

Erin shuffles from the room. I fold a piece of bread between my fingertips. 'Mmmm.'

'Because it'll go so nicely with that skirt of mine.' She leans towards the window and lifts the corner of the net curtain. She peers through the window, squinting into the sunlight, and seems surprised to see nothing at all of interest. 'That green skirt,' she finishes, dropping the net curtain from her fingers. She turns from the window. 'We're off out for a meal with Jenny and Graham.' She walks across the room into the dining area.

I tear a corner from the last slice of bread.

'Poor Jenny,' she says, 'she hasn't been at all well lately.'

'No?' I slur through a mouthful of bread.

'No. Back trouble.' She opens the kitchen door. Sausage smoke billows into the room. 'Mind you,' she calls cheerfully to me as she leaves the room, 'who would feel well, living with Graham?'

I finish the bread and take the plate to the kitchen. Jane does not glare at me because she is reading a magazine: *nineteen*, although she is thirteen. She reaches blindly across the table into an open packet of peanuts.

'Peanuts are fattening,' mutters Mum at the cooker. She glances over her shoulder at Jane. 'And stop reading that bloody rubbish.'

Jane turns the page and crams some more peanuts into her mouth.

Mum is standing on tiptoe and poking a fork into the eyelevel grill: *An eyelevel grill for giants*, she joked after the kitchen was refitted. The sausages spit and roll, their blistering skins burnt with thin deep scars.

'Bloody Brownies,' says Mum as I step past her to put my plate into the sink. 'Tea at five-thirty because of Brownies. For how many years have my evenings revolved around Brownies?'

'Perhaps it'll be cancelled,' I suggest.

'No chance,' says Mum, fending sausages from the edge of the grill pan. 'There's Brown Owl, Snowy Owl, and all those other owls. If one of the Owls is indisposed, there's always another species around to take control.' She turns to the saucepan of baked beans. 'Brownies are invincible: Baden Powell, BP, Be Prepared.'

I am amused by the mention of Baden Powell: I remember pale photographs of a man in flappy shorts.

'Never mind,' I remind her: 'Erin's ten, she will have to leave at the end of term.'

Mum inclines her head towards the back door: my little brother is trundling across the crazy pink patio in his red plastic Rolls-Royce, the pedals churning under the bonnet. 'And then it's Cubs,' she says. We crane our necks: on the lawn, my baby sister is emerging from the paddling pool; fat fists seizing the sides, terry towelling knickers sagging to her knees. Mum sighs. 'And then Brownies again.' She reaches into the cupboard for plates. 'And then retirement, and peace, and oblivion.'

'Jane,' she says, 'would you go and tell Erin that it's time for tea?' She places a bottle of ketchup on the table. 'If you tell her now, she might come down in time for Brownies next week. And if you remind her that it's Brownies, she might not try to come down in a tutu for ballet class or a toga for a fancy dress party or whatever.'

Jane continues reading. 'I'm reading.'

Mum snatches the magazine and throws it on top of the fridge. 'Not any more.'

Jane sighs noisily and leaves the table with maximum indignation.

I fetch the magazine from the fridge and sit at the table to flick through the pages. Mum lays the plates on the table, peering over my shoulder. 'My best friend's boyfriend,' she announces, quoting a headline. She shrugs. '*My* best friend's boyfriend had a glass eye.' She reaches for the grill pan and lowers the mass of sausages to the table. 'So I wouldn't have wanted to kiss him, even if he had been the most gorgeous boy in the school.' She flicks two sausages onto a plate. 'Which he wasn't.' She flicks another pair of sausages onto another plate.

'That's an awful thing to say,' I protest, laughing quietly, 'about the eye. It wasn't his fault.'

'No, I know it wasn't his fault,' she replies, dicing a sausage for the baby, 'and I know that it was an awful thing to say, but it's true. A glass eye is somehow worse than a wooden leg.'

'Your boyfriend had a wooden leg?'

She glances at me in surprise and lowers the knife and fork onto the messy plate. 'Did I say that my boyfriend had a wooden leg? No, no wooden leg, or not that I noticed.'

She fetches the saucepan of beans. 'No, my boyfriend was fully ambulant.' She relishes the word *ambulant*. 'Mind you, his father was in the RAF during the war, he was a navigator. And Douglas Bader lost his legs.'

I smirk. 'Douglas Bader lost your boyfriend's father's legs?'

The wooden spoon drips beans onto one of the plates. Mum raises her eyebrows. 'Douglas Bader lost his own legs; or what used to be his own legs, before he lost them, if you see what I mean.'

Beans pool on the remaining plates.

In the distance, in the hallway, Jane is shouting: 'Erin! Erin!'

Mum lifts the plates in pairs to the oven and loads them onto the shelves.

'Did you get a lift home from school today?'

'Yes.'

'Who?'

'Lucy.'

'Oh, Lucy.' She closes the oven door. 'Weird and wonderful Lucy.' Her voice is brittle with sarcasm.

I refuse to rise to the bait. I turn a page and glance at *Holiday Reading, Books For The Beach*.

'And is she still driving around in her mother's car?' Mum leans over the sink to scrub the grill pan with a scourer. The scourer skids on the layer of fat.

Does she disapprove of the driving around? or is this an in-my-day story, a story of trams? Does she disapprove of Lucy, or Lucy's mother, or both? I know that she regards Lucy as feckless, and she believes that character traits belong to families: there are good families and bad families.

So, what does that mean for us, for our family? Apparently, I am *uncommunicative, uncooperative, defiant*; whilst Jane is on probation at school for stealing a packet of cigarettes from Matron's handbag in Sick Bay, and Erin cannot find her own way home from the bus stop. Mum despairs of us, but she despairs even more of Dad's family: *The Blaneys*. The Blaneys live in a row of tied cottages on a local farm: Dad's Gran; Dad's Dad; and his brother and sister-in-law, Uncle Tom and Aunty Mo. Dad's Mum left more than thirty years ago:

She was a GI bride, says Mum, *the second time around*.

Whenever she tells the story, she whispers *Scandal*: an unnecessary emphasis.

And who can blame her? she asks rhetorically: *Manhattan skyline, or Cold Comfort Farm?*

But there was plenty of blame, of course: Mum tells us that Gran never liked the daughter-in-law, and advised the Blaneys to *never trust a blonde*. *Well*, concludes Mum, *as far as I'm concerned, all hope for the Blaneys went to the New World with Blondie Brenda*.

The hopelessness is a reference to Aunty Mo, who is fat with metabolism. *Childless*, says Mum of Uncle Tom and Aunty Mo; breathing the word as if it is a curse.

The Blaney cottages are fenced with rusty machinery.

Motorbikes, explains Dad, uncomfortably: *The Blaneys have an interest in machines*.

They're tinkers, says Mum.

They're mechanics, corrects Dad, half-heartedly: a reluctant defender.

They're Irish, says Mum; and there is no answer, because it is true.

Gran Blaney has an interest in clothes.

Finery, sneers Mum.

When worn, Gran's silk blouses and linen suits echo the rustle of the tissue paper in which they are stored.

But where does she find the money? mutters Mum, voicing everyone's thoughts. *I'll tell you where she finds the money, she finds the money by hook or by crook*. When she says *by hook or by crook*, she fixes us with a knowing stare; but we do not know what she means, and nor does she know what she means. No one knows. Gran has a vast selection of wide-brimmed hats. She skewers them to her dark hair with ornate pins. One of the pinheads is a small silver skull.

*

The Blaneys give me the creeps, says Mum.

She sends me to the cottages with birthday and Christmas gifts. She believes that gifts within families are an obligation.

Why me? I ask before each trip.

Because I can't send your Dad because men are no good with gifts; and, besides, they'll want to see one of you kids, and you're the eldest, and you're one of them.

I am one of them because, unlike my sisters and my brother, I am tall and thin and I have straight dark hair. My sisters and my brother resemble Mum: short, with fair curls; Blondie Brendas.

Whenever I visit Gran I drink dark tea and stare at the stuffed monkey on the mantelpiece.

A stuffed monkey, shrieks Mum: *how unhygienic*.

I have not told her about the shrunken heads pinned by their pigtails to the wall above the fireplace. Gran describes them as heirlooms.

Gran serves Jaffa Cakes and asks me about my school reports. Sometimes she suggests that I come along when she is working at one of the local fayres. She trades in a small ivory tent as *NostraMadamus*.

Mum is leaning across the table, staring at me: 'Eh?'

I blink thoroughly: *is* Lucy still driving around in her mother's car? 'No,' I answer, 'she swapped a book of Green Shield stamps for an E-type Jag.'

Mum turns away in a flamboyant gesture of disgust. 'If you can't answer sensibly, then don't answer at all.' She switches off the oven. 'Fetch the little ones from the garden, will you. It's time for tea.'

I lean from my chair and look into the garden. My little brother is disembarking gravely from the Rolls-Royce, which is not well parked. He is searching for a foothold on the grass.

'Lynd,' I call to him, reorientating him, 'it's time for tea.'

My brother's name is Lyndsay, which horrifies Dad. It was Mum's choice after Dad pleaded for *anything, anything but Ashley*.

Mum relinquished Ashley, and enjoyed the search for a name. The sole stipulation was *no royalty*. She did not want a George, a Charles, an Edward, a William, a Henry: *Stuffed shirts*, she says. She was almost prepared to make an exception for Richard, but was troubled by the notion of Richard the Third: 'No one thinks of Richard the Lionheart,' she said, 'but everyone remembers Richard the Third.'

'Richard the Third, turd,' said Jane.

I pointed out that there had been a Queen Jane.

Mum explained that Jane Grey was Queen for nine days, before she was beheaded by the next one: 'It seems unlikely that she was regarded by them as one of their own.'

Mum likes dissenters, outsiders; and she is not bothered by Queens: Queens are not stuffed shirts, and they have nice names like Victoria and Elizabeth.

For a while, Mum favoured *Corin*.

'Corin?' Jane and I crowed.

'After Corin Redgrave,' Mum informed us. 'Well, not after Corin Redgrave, but that's how I know the name.'

Jane wondered whether babies continue to be named Adolf.

I pointed out that *Corin* might be mistaken for *Colin*, and the option was dropped.

Then Mum wanted *Linus*.

'Snoopy,' we said: Linus was a character in the Snoopy cartoon, the small one with a blanket as a comforter. In retrospect, Linus would have suited my brother.

In the end, she chose *Lyndsay*.

'It's a girl's name,' we said.

'No,' said Mum, 'you're wrong: it's like Lesley, it's unisex.'

'Lesley's vile,' I breathed; 'it's the worse name in the world.'

'Says who?' challenged Mum.

I knew that Lyndsay was a better option than Lesley.

Mum told us that it is a unisex name like Hilary and Shirley: 'Yes,' she insisted, 'there are men called Shirley.'

'You're joking,' we said.

'No,' she said, 'I'm not, I promise.'

I was persuaded when Mum explained that Lyndsay is Bohemian.

'What's Bohemian?' puzzled Jane.

Mum shrugged. 'Different,' she said eventually, 'unusual, wild.'

She tried to soothe Dad by explaining that Lyn is a man's name in Wales. 'Lyn for short,' she said cheerfully, 'if you like: in Welsh, it means lake, so it's a lovely lyrical name.'

Dad said that we were not Welsh and that he did not want a son named Lake.

'Lyn is a girl's name,' he insisted morosely.

We were worried that Lyndsay would be teased at school, but this was not one of Mum's considerations. She believes that there are more worrying things in life than teasing.

Lyndsay picks his way across the garden towards me. He is followed by the baby, Lauren. She slinks past him. At three years old, she is half his age and half his size but twice as bright. The last of the line, Mum decrees of Lauren. The five of us were born at regular intervals of three years so that no one would mistake us for Catholics.

I don't want anyone to think that some old goat of a Pope dealt with my family planning for me, says Mum. Then she begins to muse: *Come to think of it, there are more than a few similarities between the Pope and my GP; two sanctimonious old gits in white coats.*

There was no difficulty in naming Lauren: Mum continued the theme that began with Erin, the American theme. American names, for Mum, evoke a pioneering spirit. There is nothing pioneering about Erin: she looks like something out of Sesame Street. It is too soon to know about Lauren.

I'm surprised that she isn't Laurence, says Dad, sarcastically. He calls Erin *Eric*; and Erin has only recently learned not to look puzzled and hurt, not to whine *but my name's Erin*.

Mum assured us that Dad was secretly pleased by the decision to name the baby Lauren because he fancies Lauren Bacall. She was changing Lauren's nappy when she told us.

'Isn't Lauren Bacall dead?' asked Jane, peering into the dirty nappy.

'I don't know,' replied Mum, folding a clean square of terry towelling into a triangle, 'and, anyway, it doesn't matter.'

'Doesn't matter?' echoed Jane; 'doesn't matter if Dad fancies a dead person?'

Mum's teeth were bared, clenched on a safety pin: 'It's different for film stars.'

'I'm sure she's dead,' muttered Jane, searching through the basket of baby lotions. She span the lid from the jar of Vick and inhaled the fumes. 'Who is dead, then?'

Mum forced the safety pin into a wedge of terry towelling. 'What?'

'Who is dead?'

'What do you mean, who is dead? Lots of people are dead. Don't be silly, Jane.'

I lifted a bottle of gripe water from the basket. 'Carole Lombard,' I said, 'in a plane crash.'

Jane seemed satisfied with my answer. She replaced the lid on the jar of Vick and dropped it into the basket before leaving us alone.

The meal has been hurried and noisy, the cutlery spinning through the soft food and ringing against the plates. Now there is pudding: at school, it is *afters*; at my friends' houses, it is *sweet*; in restaurants, it is *dessert*. For Mum, it is *pudding*:

Hurry up, eat your pudding.

She believes in pudding. This evening we are having ice-cream, American flavoured: pecan or praline or butter or something. Mum levers shards from the tub into our bowls with a large flat spoon. I think fondly of the scoops at school that extract smooth balls of mashed potato as the shards of ice-cream slither around my bowl, escaping my spoon and leaving thick buttery trails.

Mum takes the plates from the table and dumps them into the sink.

'Come on, Erin,' she complains, 'finish your ice-cream.'

Erin has to be accompanied to Brownies. Mum says that Erin has as much road sense as a hedgehog. Jane and I learned to cross roads with the help of Tufty. We were introduced to Tufty at school by the policeman who came each year to the infant class and left his big black bicycle chained to the railings in the playground.

'A policeman came to school today,' Jane told Mum.

'At least it wasn't the nit nurse,' said Mum.

'Nit?' repeated Jane, amused. 'Nit nurse? Nit policeman. The policeman was a nit.'

The policeman bribed us with books and badges to cross roads with care: *Look both ways*. My badge proclaimed that I was a member of the Tufty Club. I had done nothing to qualify for membership, and there was no hint of exclusivity; although I was only five years old, I had a strong suspicion that this was a contradiction in terms. Besides, I did not want to be a member of the same club as Jane. When she obtained a badge, I relinquished mine. For Erin, three years after Jane, there was no club or badge; there were no furry animals. Instead, there was someone resembling Superman, who favoured the Green Cross Code: *Right, left and right again.* Erin did not benefit from this: she was uninterested in supermen, and confused by the mention of left and right.

Erin struggles from the table, squeezing behind Lyndsay. Her bowl, wet with uncaptured ice-cream, tilts precariously above his head. Mum mutters and snatches it away.

'Come on, Erin,' she insists loudly, hurrying to the sink, 'we're late.' She turns to Jane and me: 'I want this table cleared and wiped before I return.' Then she ushers Erin through the door.

Jane glares into an empty bowl.

I reach for Lyndsay's and Lauren's sticky bowls and stack them with mine. 'Off you go,' I command.

They slide from their chairs and scurry from the kitchen to the garden. I take the bowls to the sink and return with a damp cloth to wipe across the table. 'Don't forget to clear your place,' I say to Jane.

She sighs wearily and raises her eyes to mine: 'Fuck off.'

I slap the cloth onto the table and turn towards the door. 'Mum?' I turn back to Jane. 'I'll tell Mum.' I will not tell Mum because Mum has gone. Also, I do not want to repeat the *fuck off*, and Mum will demand a full account. She will not accept *Jane swore*. She is unperturbed by swearing in general, by *bloody* and *bugger*, but tormented by four-letter words: it is a rule, *no four-letter words*.

Four-letter words, I taunt, *like shed or song, perhaps? or town or long?*

Her eyes are narrow when she replies: *four-letter nasty words*.

Nasty words? I goad. *How can a word be nasty?*

It is not clear whether *crap* is included in this category.

Mum's zeal is awesome: punishment of offenders is indiscriminate. Whenever I repeat Jane's *fuck off*, I am in trouble; and whenever I protest, Mum becomes indignant and frantic with insinuations. *Who taught Jane to say something like that? You're the eldest.*

Mum's own swear word is *git*, because she is a Londoner.

Nothing nasty, she says: *I might come from Wandsworth, but I'm not common. No pun intended.*

Dad says an occasional *sod*. At Primary School I was delighted to discover *sod* in the Bible.

I suspect that Jane knows that I will not tell Mum, but I call her bluff: 'Mum!'

Jane shrugs. 'You can tell Mum whatever you like.'

I leave Jane and go into the living room. I kneel at the cabinet, and coax open one of the small doors. Mum refers to the cabinet as *the unit: be careful with the unit*, she says. I pull gently on the flat white knob, and the door drops forward. I take the large black bag of photos from the cupboard and then close the door by lifting and jamming it into the frame. The units came from a warehouse in a box marked *self-assembly*. They require constant re-assembly. I drag the black bag onto my lap. The photos remain in packets in a dustbin liner despite Dad's insistence that they should be in albums.

I delve into the bag. There are too many photos for albums; there are too many children: our dustbin liner is constantly refilled with recent photographs of first smiles, first birthday parties, first days at school. I lift the shiny yellow wallets, and strips of negatives scatter into my lap, the large dark smooth seeds of photographs. Most of the wallets bear a bright motif: on the new wallets it is discreet, an identifying mark, but on the older wallets it blazes as an advertisement for colour, a celebration of technological achievement. It seems that colour photography was once a cause for celebration.

Black and white? gasps Mum in horror whenever she sees me with my camera. For Mum, my black and white photographs are reminiscent of the dark ages: they cannot be included in the category of old-fashioned things such as natural childbirth, herbal shampoo and pine dressers, but belong instead with outside toilets.

On the older wallets there is a picture of a woman in a bikini on a beach. She is holding a beach ball and looking delighted.

The pieces of the bikini are too large, and the colour is too light. Nowadays, bikinis are black, or magenta, but not sky blue. Nurses' uniforms are sky blue. Also, the woman is too pale. Nowadays, beach belles roast in coconut oil. They do not smile, but squint and leer. Nor do they leap after beach balls, but recline instead on burning sand. Today's beach belles are indolent. The woman in the picture is healthy. I can see her tummy button: a firm thumbprint in the pale flesh. She looms: the smile wide, the arms open. Prancing on the sand, bleached by sunlight, she is a Slimcea or Nimble woman: extra light, no mystery, no promise.

On some of the newer wallets there is a picture of a happy family: they are happy because they are smiling. In real life, people smile because they are happy; but the wallets do not contain real life, they contain photography: a gift of smiles in darkness. Inside our dustbin liner we are a happy family, we are smiling, smiling throughout our colour lives; our lives of parties and holidays. Would the parties and holidays have taken place without a camera? The photographs in the dustbin liner are presumably more important to Mum and Dad than our birth certificates, which are stored in the loft in a Sealink sickbag.

I sift the photographs. In some of them we have food in our mouths: Mum regards these photographs as failures because the food interferes with our smiles. *Cake-hole*, she says, distressed. Also, eating is personal: Mum complains that *we might as well have a photo of you picking your nose.* Food in our photographs is usually decorative: birthday or Christmas cake. In most of the photographs we are foodless and standing to attention, instructed to smile. These group photographs exhibit the striking resemblance of my sisters and brother to Mum. Indistinct blonde babies in individual portraits carry clues: Jane in the old armchair which was replaced by a brown corduroy bean bag; Erin and the eyeless teddy bear; Lyndsay in the red Rolls-Royce; Lauren in the shiny new buggy which disappeared one day without her in Mothercare. In all the photographs Mum is not unlike the woman with the beach ball. She smiles strenuously. Dad is invisible: he owns the camera, he takes the pictures. Alongside my sisters and my brother I am the eldest, tallest, darkest; the shadow at the end of the line.

*

I continue to sift the photographs. I am not interested in these
lifestories. I do not need to be reminded that Jane wanted to
be a showjumper, that she went with friends every weekend to
gymkhanas; that she stood solid in black boots with a riding hat
frown on her face. I have not forgotten that I once wanted to be
a ballet dancer: I do not need to see the marshmallow coloured
tights flopping into creamy folds around my ankles, stemmed by
whorls of pink silk ribbon. I am searching for photographs of the
Blaneys. At the bottom of the dustbin liner I run my fingertips
over several small pieces of board and some large silky squares.
I pull them to the surface and spread them around me on the
floor. The faces glow: The Blaneys. There is no pretence of
spontaneity in these photographs; they are portraits. In one
photograph Grandad is a young man with a motorbike, framed
by protruding pedals and pipes; in another, he stands beside a
car. Dad once told me that the Blaneys were the first family in
the village to have a car. They still have the car; it is kept in
a barn on the farm. Among the photographs of motorbikes and
cars there is a photograph of Gran. She is close to the camera,
her smile encircled by the brim of a hat.

The photographs are old: dark colours, papery smells, odd shapes
and sizes that do not slot into yellow wallets. In the dustbin liner
they sink below the technicolour celebrations. In each photograph
the props are familiar: in a photograph of Gran I recognise the
tumbling shadows of a silk-wrapped, fruit-topped sundae hat;
the medallion glint of a brooch; the chaos of a charm bracelet.
Other photographs show two loose black suits: Grandad and
Uncle Tom, the magpies at our family weddings and funerals.
The waddings of waistcoat are hidden from view, along with the
scarlet braces, hard white cuffs and shiny gold cufflinks. In most
of the photographs there are engines snarling oil: cars, tractors,
motorbikes. I search in vain for the monkey.

The inky gazes of the Blaney faces are as familiar to me as the
baby blonde smiles festooning the newer photographs. There have
been very few changes in their appearances: Grandad's greased
dark head is now a wild white cloud; Gran's smooth skin is now
shattered by wrinkles, and the smile is less spry. Mum used to say
that *we should all bow out at sixty*, but recently she has revised this
to sixty-five. Gran was seventy when I was born: an old woman.

She is not old in these photographs. Is she younger than Mum?
I take the photograph of the hat and turn it towards the light. Is
she thirty, perhaps? By the time she was thirty, she was married.
Her husband died before I was born. She was a widow when I
was born. It is difficult for me to imagine Gran as a wife. Did she
ever cook his tea? It is difficult for me to imagine Gran cooking
anyone's tea.

I lay the photograph with the others and delve again into the
dustbin liner. I pull a handful of wallets to the surface and lift
the flaps. I am looking for a photograph of myself. Presumably I
have at least a one-in-five chance of success: I was the first born,
posing alone; and subsequently I am present in the snapshots of
the others. But unlike the others, the blonde babies, I am not
photogenic. In one of the solo photographs I glower underexposed
from the saddle of a seaside donkey. I discard the dim seasides
and continue to search until I find my most recent school photo.
At school we are photographed individually: most recently, I am
thirteen and under duress; but I am visible, I am not a shadow
at the end of a line of blondes. I take the photograph, which has
never been removed from its brown plastic presentation wallet,
to the window; and I examine the reluctant smile. *You're a Blaney*,
says Mum; and she is right, I can see what she means: the Blaney
eyes are burning like stigmata on the glossy surface of the paper.
In the searchlight of sunshine at the window they are wounded
stars. I stare into their startling darkness and I realise that there
is no escape for me: I am a Blaney, a black-eyed Blaney.

I move away from the light and return the photo to the bag. I
recall Mum's theory: the Blaneys have black eyes because they
are the descendants of Spanish pirates shipwrecked on the coast of
County Cork. Thus, for Mum, the Blaneys are even more foreign
than Irish, and spectacularly untrustworthy. Piracy suggests
rampant opportunism and excessive cruelty: gangplanks; press
gangs. Pirates preyed on the vulnerable; they did not steal from
the rich to give to the poor: they were not Robin Hoods; not part
of an English tradition of lovable rogues and likeable eccentrics,
of monks and kings and twenty-four blackbirds baked in a pie.
Pirates did not turn aristocrats topsy-turvy in leafy glades as
comeuppance; nor did they tumble in true love with Maid
Marian. There were no Maid Marians at sea. 'You never hear of
a woman pirate,' said Mum, when she had told me the theory.

'You never hear of a woman anything,' I replied; meaning that they might have existed nevertheless.

Mum remained unconvinced, muttering about the problems of babies and sanitary towels at sea.

Pirates lived on the high seas: *high*; dangerous, unpredictable, not-quite-right, not-all-there, you-never-knew-where-you-were-with-a-pirate. Mum is similarly wary of the Blaneys. I like the theory but remain sceptical: what were Spanish pirates doing in the Irish sea? I am entranced by the idea of County Cork: *Cork*, a strange name for a County. 'What I remember about Cork,' said Mum, who once went on holiday to Ireland, 'is the stink of fish.' Then, seeing my disappointment, she conceded reluctantly: 'But that was years ago, and things change, I suppose.'

I hear footsteps and turn to the window to see Mum and Erin outside on the tarmac. Why Erin? Erin should be in the village hall with the Brownies: socks flaccid around ankles, plimsolls punching softly into wooden floorboards. Mum stops at the door and grinds the key into the keyhole. Her face is hidden from me in a haze of bright curls. Erin stands at her side; dimmer, duller; frowning, puzzled. The Brownie beret is askew. In the uniform in the sunshine she is yellow and brown like a soft bruised fruit.

Erin follows Mum over the doorstep into the house. Mum rustles in the hallway and then comes into the living room: she does not pause as usual in the doorway to survey the scene and identify the perpetrators; she does not stare at me and demand *What are you doing?* Instead, she hurries towards me, taut with excitement. 'Guess what?'

I cannot guess, of course. I lower the dustbin liner, and it sags noisily at my feet.

'There was a car accident, just now,' she waves towards the window, 'outside the village hall, just before we arrived.'

Erin follows, eddying in the doorway.

'All the owls,' continues Mum, anguished, 'in one car.'

Erin's beret flops across her eyes.

'All in one car, turning into the car park, when some stupid old sod from the Over-65s Bring And Buy comes out in his Range Rover without looking: slam!' Mum shrugs in despair. 'There was an ambulance and everything; a policeman. One whiplash injury, they reckon: Snowy Owl. With any luck, it's just cuts and bruises for the others.' She pauses and shrugs again. 'There was talk of cracked ribs.' She steps closer to me. 'But what worries me,' she confides, 'is Brown Owl's palpitations: she told me that she went to see the doctor last week. She's no spring chicken.'

Dismayed, I murmur my sympathies.

Mum sighs. 'Cars all over the road.' Suddenly she remembers Erin, and turns to smile. 'What a mess, eh?' she cajoles. There is no response from Erin. 'So,' she says, returning to me, 'Brownies is cancelled, and we need a cup of tea.' She moves towards the door. 'Perhaps they should avoid travelling in the same car, like royalty.' When she reaches the door she turns to face me, sparkling with suspicion. 'You *said* it would be cancelled.'

'No . . .' I reply hurriedly.

'Yes,' she muses.

'No,' I refute, 'I said it *might* be cancelled.'

She is unconvinced. 'Same thing.'

'It is not the same thing.' I was aware of the possibility of cancellation; I did not expect it, I did not foresee it.

She opens the door. 'Blaney blood,' she mutters as she disappears. 'You give me the creeps.'

Sassia
the legend and the woman

From *The River and the Road*, a novel in progress

AUTHOR'S NOTE The story that follows is based on facts, although I have tried to avoid them wherever possible.

After the mysterious death of Sassia's third husband Oppianicus, her son Cluentius by her first husband Habitus was tried for murder in the Court of Poison Cases. The renowned Cicero, speaking for the defence, turned the case round and indirectly blamed the 'unnatural mother', while at the same time accusing her of many other crimes of a peculiarly hideous nature. The result was acquittal for Cluentius and a resounding public humiliation for Sassia. The case acquired wonderful notoriety and has since been declared by legal historians as 'the most singular *cause célèbre* that has come down to us from antiquity'.

There is little evidence of what actually took place except the text of the deceptively convoluted defence speech left to us by Cicero – he himself later claimed to have 'blinded the eyes' of the jurors. I have elected to put my own interpretation upon events which scandalised even the most scandalous echelons of Roman high society.

What happened before and after is the stuff of impure fiction. As is the account of Sassia's early life, her later marriages, and the details of her spectacular funeral, unprecedented and unrivalled in its concept and splendour to this very day. The burial that followed turned out to be not hers, but that of her aforementioned son Cluentius for whom she nurtured the most passionate hatred even before his misplaced obstructions in her scheme to break up her daughter's marriage and wed her son-in-law, Melinus, whose company and bed he enjoyed as much as she. This hatred of her son was later matched by her reciprocal contempt for Cicero. I have worked on the assumption that she lived to rejoice in both their awesome deaths.

Not merely that, in my reconstruction of her larger-than-life life, she survives her apocryphal rite of ultimate passage to carry on carrying on for many more years, the last of her great family, happy in the knowledge that she had had the pleasure of poking her fingers through every single one of her relatives' ashes, man woman and child; and that none of those grasping leeches or their progeny was in a position to pocket one sestertius of her considerable fortune upon her passing on to wherever one passes on to, if anywhere.

I have taken the aftermath of Cicero's murder, when Sassia the legend plans her own funeral to celebrate the event, as the starting point of my exploration of Sassia the woman.

PART I: EXORDIUM
FEBRUARY 712* AB URBE CONDITA

I

'I have no intention of being dead at my funeral; son, dear' said Sassia spreading out her long thin arms in a carelessly loose gesture, at odds with the carefully controlled note of the tease in her voice. 'In fact I aim to be hideously alive, as ever, to savour every joyous moment of it to the full; son, dear. I only hope you will be there to enjoy it too, and be glad for my sake, as ever?!' The last sentence managed to combine a question, a request and a command in a way only Sassia could, without even appearing to try.

Cluentius looked up to the heavens for a brief moment, then eyed his left shoulder before going back to gazing at his feet. Anything to avoid meeting his mother's twinkling stare. Although for once he was filled with a great urge to study her face and see if she was finally cracking up, showing signs of madness or senility. After all she was an old woman now, a very old woman, and these last few days – ever since she heard of what befell that Cicero – beginning to behave and act in a manner somewhat too unstable even for her; and this particular morning seemed mad enough to be worthy of a seat in the Senate. Still, he dared not look; what's more, he dared not hope. Sassia had a way of raising hopes. He was not going to let her have the pleasure of thinking that he

* 42 BC.
Cicero was murdered on 4 December 43 BC.

was hoping. He would much rather be planning. If she really was arranging a grandiose mock funeral for herself, could it not, with a little ingenuity, be turned into a real one? He was hoping again. He would have to do better than hope.

In the meantime he must keep his nerve, and his cool, and his wits. That was the only way to survive with her around.

'Not for all the gold in a Pharaonic tomb would I miss the joy of seeing your soul turn into fire with the help of fire, even if your body happens to be alive and well at the time, Mother darling. I will gladly light the flame myself, in your eternal honour,' responded Cluentius with as straight a face and voice as he could muster.

'*That* you'd do for half the snot up a Samnite nose. But I suspect the honour to honour my bones will not be yours. However, I am happy to see there's still some fire left in you, Cluentius. No fun nor point in putting out a light that no longer burns with heat or passion. Show my son the door, Lucia, my beloved one; I have preparations to make. The day is still young and I am not. I need more and more time every time.'

Cluentius rose to leave, forcing his eyes into his mother's eyes, if only for a momentary encounter, his thoughts lingering on the tight little mole at the lobe of her left ear above the pearl earring; it reminded him of Melinus. He used to love biting at it while giving Cluentius a come-on look at the same time, extending his left hand to . . . Embarrassed, he looked away from Sassia and out, out into the long-distant past.

I hobbled up to let him out into the present, with pleasure. I hated him more than their combined hatred for each other. There was still a nugget of love buried somewhere in their battlegrounds. I was sure of that. That alone would have been reason enough for my hatred. There were others too.

But I also felt sorry for him, for I could read his soul, and it was a soul well-inscribed with pain. I have this ability to read the souls of all who have eyes, better than the best augurs can read the birds and the skies. Not for nothing do they call me the evil one, and a lot worse beside: they who fear my one sharp eye and my many sharp tongues, they who recoil at the dried-up map of wrinkles etched deep as life on my deathless face, they who scuttle at the croaking of my raven voice and the hissing of my toothless words, they who are jealous of my mistress's love for one so ugly and old and wretched and unbalanced as I.

I wasn't always like that. There was a time I was more beautiful than the summer dawn, more gentle than the morning breeze, and young. I had both my eyes, my legs were straight and unbroken, and I knew how to laugh with happiness. My mistress loved me then. She loves me even more now.

When I was seven and her mother died as she was born, I was like a mother to her. When I was seventeen we were as sisters. When I was twenty she was like a mother to me. I was also her confidante, her go-between, her friend and adviser, the chosen one to execute her plans and her enemies, her comforter and her footstool. Now I was her mother again. But I have always been her slave, then as now, even though I was made a freedwoman over thirty years ago.

There I go, limping back to the past, like Cluentius. Sassia does not, unless it lends an edge to the here and now. She revels in the present and dances to the future. In that lies her strength, and in that her victories. She was planning one now. The biggest of her life. Victory over death itself.

II

Sassia bathed, kissed the soil, sent her breath to the skies, gave thanks to and made peace with the elements of the flesh; the earth, the air and water, and now awaited the glorification of the soul. She lay on the *lectus funebris* in the atrium of her villa, feet to the door, receiving clients and visitors for the seven days appointed before being taken to the Forum for eulogies; and thence to the chosen Necropolis, the touch of fire, the freedom of the spirit, the entombment of the ashes. And what a tomb it was that awaited to protect her remains for eternity! When *she* was good and ready for it, of course.

Her bed of rest was carved out of African ivory and draped in silk of the brightest purple hue. Around it burnt seventy-three lamps and seventy-three candles. Red flowers lay strewn all across the black and white mosaic of the floor. A trio of cypresses stood outside in mournful obeisance. The scent of perfumes and incense misted the atmosphere, intoxicating the senses with the magical illusion of life in death.

The Forum where she would eventually be laid out in all her splendour would not be that of Larinum – the place of her birth and where her family held sway for as long as the memory of man – but that of Rome itself, well over two hundred miles away. Her bier would be placed before the *rostra*, the *rostra* upon which Cicero's mortal head and hands were displayed in immortal disgrace; and there, in front of whatever iota or morsel or mark or smear or sign was left of his eyes and mouth and finger, nail or hair, there! there her praises would be spoken and sung.

There the dancers would dance, the *imagines* of the ancestors assemble and the mummers mime; the trumpeters trumpet, the flautists play, the drummers drum. There the mourners would weep and beat their breasts and proclaim her departure from the world of men. There the rejoicers would laugh and be happy and feast and tell stories and make love and announce her assumption to the world of gods. There the slaves would be freed and the poor fed. There torches would burn and games evolve and gladiators fight and kill and triumph and die. Same as all of this would have happened all through the two hundred and fifty miles of the roads to Rome, but topping what had gone before in a climactic crescendo.

No god nor mortal would have had, or witnessed, or heard of a funeral such as the funeral of Sassia. All those who burned with jealousy and hatred at the excesses of her life would burn more than ever at the extravagance of her death. And she'd be there, alive, to see them burn.

III

SASSIA IS DEAD! spread the news as news does.

SASSIA IS ALIVE! spread the rumour as rumours do.

SASSIA HAS COME BACK FROM THE DEAD!

SASSIA HAS BECOME AN IMMORTAL OF MARS! and no wonder, after all her devotion to him!

COME BACK FROM THE DEAD! Your buttocks. IMMORTAL OF MARS! Your cock. What IS she trying to pull now? DEVO-TION TO MARS! Your balls. The only devotion she has is to her-self.

And to lucre.

And to that one-eyed monster.

DEAD! Go on, tell me another. SHE is not going to let go of life unless somebody sticks a knife through her guts seven and twenty times, and even then she will not go before she has scratched out the eyes and torn out the heart of her murderer.

YOU tell me another! She has to die same as anybody else. Even she can't go on forever. No one can cut off the cold hand of death.

She can!

Your anus.

You can hope.

No thank you. I don't go near open gutters.

With your limp you can hardly get anywhere.

I'd give her the seeds of choke cherry ground with vinegar in her morning wine.

She has that the second hour of every night, to perk up her shameless desires. Besides, she's taken enough poisons to immune herself. She wasn't born yesterday, nor schooled with fools like yourself.

I know, she prefers knaves like yourself.

You watch out, asshead.

No, you watch out, cuntlip.

Break it up, break it up, you two. Let's go see Sassia's body: alive or dead. It's open house they say. Anyone is allowed, enemies and all, not just friends and slaves and clients. Come, let's go. Come, come, come.

IV

The seven days of lying in state were over. Early next morning we were to hit the road. I was as relieved as agitated. More agitated, I should say.

However, despite all my fears we did have fun, I must admit to that.

Whenever she felt another attack of death would be amusing she'd send for Cluentius to catch her 'last' breath, usually during the second watch of the night or before the first hour of the morning when he was fast asleep. It was more than amusing, it was hilarious. Each time he brought his mouth down to hers, she'd wet-kiss him or bite his lip and make him place a piece of gold or a precious jewel in her mouth. 'You wouldn't let your poor mother go for a mere *as*? would you now? son dear,' she'd say, knowing that even the faintest hope of laying hands on her gold and assets would make him give up the last of his.

Surrounded by mourners Sassia could suspend breathing, half shut her eyes and drop her jaw while at the same time clenching her cheek and neck muscles and making her entire body go rigid to act the perfect stiff corpse; or let every bit of her flesh hang loose to be the genuine limp cadaver. She even managed to drain the blood out of her face and go ashen pale. Then, when a particularly unwelcome client or a peculiarly ghoulish neighbour came near her and began uttering long-winded words of praise and grief, she would squint her eyes open and give a wink like only she knew how; or let out a rasping chuckle; or raise a quivering hand with the flicker of a wrist and croak a curse. Unlike the grief and the praise, the screams and moans that followed were for real. More than a few old bats fainted. One young man wet himself and the floor. It wasn't very pleasant. Luckily he missed the corpse, who from her prostrate position could often see more than was good for a good corpse to see in that position, and witnessed the hosing from an alarming perspective, almost losing her nerve for the first time during the whole charade. He was a big strong fellow, a magistrate's son who had just come back from Rome after training in high oratory, ready for a political career. Not best pleased at this betrayal by his own kidneys and to hide his embarrassment, he began to shout and scream obscenities. Eventually he had to be dragged out naked as two slaves removed his dandy cucullus and high tunic to stop the foul dripping. It was a cold evening too, ten days before the Calends of March! I felt sorry for the poor turd. Anyway, somebody covered him up, I believe. Couldn't stop laughing though, and that in a house of death! Once over her initial panic, Sassia herself fell into gurgling spasms of glee causing further uproar as the hall was cleared for cleaning up.

Once there was so much commotion when she spat in a face that dared to bend over too close to hers that two of the gladiators hired for the procession were called in to restore order. One, a Gaul: a retinarius with his net, and one a Thracian, gathered in the inoffensive offender and his companions like so many beetles and nearly choked the life out of them.

Greater fun was yet to come, though not unalloyed with tensions and aggravations and some real dangers too. Times were difficult. Symbols and signs of civil and political unrest, both covert and overt, were manifest all around for the eye to see, the ear to hear and the heart to feel. Turmoil was everywhere, violence could be anywhere. Trust Sassia not to care.

There she lay, as serene and peaceful as your newborn asleep. But I couldn't help being worried. Would she be able to stand the strain of it all, despite her strength and strengths?

I should have known better.

I should have known that her passion alone would be enough

to carry her through anything that even the Fates thought fit
to impose on her, not to speak of something she had devised
herself.

But I worried.

She looked so frail, so delicate, so *gentle*. Just like your newborn
asleep. Just like she was when I picked her up in my arms, hugging
her close to the bones of my chest, grateful to Vesta for not letting
her father throw her out on the streets for causing the death of her
mother.

So grateful.

And so happy.

I had something I could call my own. At least in secret, in my
soul, to myself. And a living breathing dark-eyed doll with thick
black lashes that curled their way up into your heart.

All those years ago.

All those years ago . . .

V

I'd got in with the Maximus household through luck. The Lares
must have liked the perfume of my incense. Even though a slave,
the daughter of a slave-daughter of slaves, I was a child who did
not neglect the gods. The Fates spoke in my favour.

At the time my mother Tita was among those serving Auria
senior, Sassia's aunt, and had just had a baby boy. When Sassia's
mother died at childbirth, Auria gave Tita to her brother Aurius
Sassius Maximus in order to nurse the infant girl. To avoid
complications my baby brother was given away to the local
lanista. Unlike me, my brother was swarthy with green eyes and
big bones, fathered by an African, the type excellent in combat.
If someone could be found to look after him, he would make a
great future gladiator; if not, he would make a great meal for the
beast of a present one training in the Ludus. Although I was
sad at his loss, I soon forgot about him in my joy over Sassia;
I had always wanted a sister rather than a brother. My mother
was not too thrilled, and apart from suckling Sassia – out of fear
rather than love, to ease the pain of her swollen breasts than to
assuage the hunger of the child – left her mainly to the care of
a retinue of slaves alloted to her for the purpose. Being a child
of the preferred slave, I had no difficulty in bullying the others
and taking Sassia away from them into my own arms. Maximus

was hardly ever around to see what was going on; Auria senior too preoccupied with her own affairs, and in looking after her two sons and Cluentia, Sassia's sister, who was four.

Those were the best days of my life. Juno had presented me with the most wonderful gift possible. My own little doll. My dark little doll, with dark eyes, dark hair, and a skin that glowed in the dark. A doll so precious that my very life was as nothing compared to the dark smile that played on her lips when she was angry, and the dark laughter that trickled from her throat when she was happy. How I loved her.

She loved me too, even though I was not fit to be the dust beneath her feet.

So began the life of Sassia, my mistress and my lover; born in death, suckled on resentment, cradled in adoration.

And so begin the stories that I, Lucia, her abject slave, will tell you of her fabulous life, and around her fabulous life, to make light the hour and the day as her fabulous 'funeral' dances its way across the harsh Samnium lands to descend upon Rome itself; the same route she took when attending the trial of Cluentius, this time passing not just by, but through Arpinum itself to mock the birthplace of the arrogant knave Cicero.

PART II: THE PASSION

THE WEDDING

June 650* AUC it was, the month of Sassia's first wedding; the second year, I think, of the consulship of Marius. Or the third, I am not quite sure. Oh, yes I am. The third. I think. Shortly after he had rushed off to Africa leaving a whole lot of trouble behind. But then, what could you expect of a commoner. Mind you, he didn't do badly out of it. He, and later on that Sulla. Like this they were – you should see my fingers intertwine – like a couple of dogs in heat after the same bitch, the bitch called Rome. If only poor Jugurtha had managed to survive just another year or two he'd have sorted them both out. But still, he did teach the stuck-up Romans a lesson or two before they could chain him down. What a

* 104 BC.

man he was! Sassia and I would have given the whole of ourselves
for a part of him, with the greatest of pleasure I have no doubt.

But Jugurtha's end was not the end of the problem. Those
giants from the north were on the rampage again, unstiffening
cavalries of Roman·cocks stiffening with fear. Like me they were
– not the Roman cocks, but the giants from the north – Sassia used
to say: blond with eyes of blue marble. Mind you, by that time my
hair was shaved, my head scarred, my legs knocked out of shape,
and one of my marble blue eyes no more than a memory in my
other marble blue eye. All thanks to dear Cluentia, the darling
sister of Sassia who could never do any wrong. She complained
to Maximus that I was much too beautiful, and that was that.
Couldn't be allowed. If only Maximus could see he would have
seen that anyone was much too beautiful compared to the darling
Cluentia. Ah, but she was so virtuous. Who wouldn't be, looking
like her. Virtuous meaning she wasn't putting it about; in every
other way she was all vice.

Nearly destroyed Sassia when she saw me after the treatment. I had to forget my own pain and shame to try and
comfort her. But enough of me. Does me no good to dwell on
me.

She was just fourteen then, my beloved mistress, at the time of
the wedding. How I rubbed the powder of alum in sea water upon
her plucked parts to make her narrow and tight for her nuptial
night, like a real virgin. With any luck she would bleed, and she
did. Who could have guessed she'd given birth to a seven pound
boy only four months ago.

It was too soon for her to wed, after all she had been through.
But would Maximus listen? You guessed it. He thought it was
a wonderful idea, and that if she had any sense she would
be grateful instead of whingeing and whining about it. Grateful *AND* proud. It wasn't every day that a girl could get a
man as *noble AND wealthy AND courteous* as Aulus Cluentius
Habitus. *Even a decent AND modest AND virtuous girl should feel
honoured, much less a tainted trollop like her . . . the devourer of her
own mother.* What could you say to that? Not to Maximus you
couldn't.

Sassia could. If she chose to. But she did not. In her own way
and for her own reasons she was more pleased about the marriage
than she let on to her father. The advantages of becoming a matron
were manifold, as indeed were the advantages of augmenting

her paternal fortune by the wealth of a wealthy husband. She would get back at her father – and at all the others who had conspired against her and against those she loved – in her own time, when she chose to, and when she was better equipped to deal body blows.

Why pick the story of her wedding as the first story to tell at the time of her funeral? I hear someone ask while another jeers, *what funeral!* and more follow with, *why the first wedding? why not the second? the most corrupt; or the third? the most evil; or the fifth? the most disastrous; or the seventh? the most comic.*

It is the dancing fires that remind me of the weddings. They set the world alight now, as they they set the world alight then. Only more voraciously.

Sassia had vowed that the torches of her funeral 'will outnumber and outshine the torches of all my marriages put together . . .' And they did. As to why I choose the first of seven. Because that was the turning point. The unmaking of Sassia as she was, and the making of Sassia as she is.

In order that the inflamed brilliance of the carnival that was her living funeral impacted to the fullest, she resorted to ancient custom by setting out of the house on her alleged final journey during the third watch of the night, at the start of the darkest and the quietest hour.

'But at that time no one will be around to see the theatre of your mourners and revellers breast-beating and merry-making their way through the streets of your beloved Larinum,' Cluentius had objected with thinly disguised irony, knowing that her hatred for Larinum came only after her hatred for Cicero and himself. Not that he had the success of her performance in mind, but he dreaded having to get up at that time of the night and walk the streets in his broken sandals: Sassia had demanded broken sandals as a mark of true sorrow at her '*unexpected and early departure*' from the abode of the living. She had also insisted he not get into his sedan chair until they were out of the city gates.

'Oh yes they will be there to see me go. I can assure you, they will be there. Just remember the town crier makes the appropriate announcement often enough and loudly enough, and have the news written up prominently in the Forum. They will be there.'

And indeed they were there.

As indeed they were there at her wedding.

I remember it like yesterday.

But it wasn't yesterday.

Not the yesterday of men. Not the yesterday of gods either.

I was young then.

I am old now, much too old. Old and tired.

Sassia has provided a litter for me worthy of the noblest of Romans. It is carried by the youngest and strongest of slaves, but even they cannot carry the years away. An agitated inability to relax battles with the compelling urge to rest and gnaws at dissipated nerves; an alliance of sleep and lack of sleep befuddles the mind. February can be a cold and cruel month for emaciated bones and withering flesh. The wild light of the wild torches dancing wildly in the wild and windy night of the wild and windy end of the year plays tricks on my wavering eyes and confuses the senses. The first lady of the funeral becomes the third bride of Aulus Cluentius Habitus, and past and present fuse and diffuse until one becomes the other and both dissolve into the everlasting. And the everlasting, as we all know, is no more than a tantalising mirage. No more, but no less, thank the Fates; for if it weren't for mirages, who would take the next step forward!

Bring me death, merciful Mars; life chills in me the warmth of life, and my blood demands my blood as the price of watering the sod that is my body that was.

Sassia's bier travels next to my litter wherever the streets of Larinum allow: once we are out on the paths left by the Samnium droves there will be no problem of space. I like to keep a watchful eye on her as we move along. She, however, cannot always see my face because of the angle of my litter and the flutter of the curtains, open though they are on both sides and despite the burning glow of the torches. And much glad I am that she cannot always see my face. For when she sees my face she hears my thoughts. And that is not always a wise thing to let happen.

Especially if my thoughts are of death, or despair, or defeat: not three of her favourite words.

Life, and love, and laughter: these were, *are*, her favourites.

And the months preceding the fateful wedding provided the most wonderful opportunities for all of these.

THE LOVE

I

It was the year before the wedding, the month was Quintilis, then the fifth month, before Julius changed it to the seventh and *July*, egomaniac that he was. But no matter, it is still as beautiful a time of the year now as then. Even he couldn't alter the seasons.

I tell a lie.

It was more beautiful then.

I remember it like yesterday.

I lie again.

I remember it better than yesterday.

Wars and rumours of wars had driven us south from north, from east to west, from the Adriatic to the Mediterranean. The savage onslaught of barbarians from way above was bad enough, the threat of another Samnite uprising right under our feet was worse. How much of it was fact and how much the product of puny minds and punier hearts, it is difficult to say, even in hindsight; except that nothing really happened, at least not then and not in or around Larinum. The barbarians turned their steps towards Gaul, and the Samnites lay quiet to rise another day.

Of course Maximus did not admit that he was effectively retreating without a fight; we were just on an extended holiday to the enchanted Campanian city of Pompeii, to stay with one of Sassia's uncles, Aurius, who owned a most magnificent villa within his celebrated vineyards worthy of a Caesar.

To me it was like being in the garden of gods.

I had come to accept my disfigurement: I had seen worse happen to slaves for a crime less audacious than the unwarranted possession of beauty. I was lucky to be alive and have both my arms and both my breasts and the use of my tongue; even my legs were still there, and working; my hair too had grown back, at least in parts where the scalp was not cut too deep. In the Villa of the Grapes I did more than accept all this, I nearly forgot about it. Sassia never accepted, nor forgot. And she certainly did not forgive. I guess she had to face my distorted face and actually look upon the ugliness of it, whereas I hardly noticed even the painful deformity of my legs any more and cheerfully hopped about all over the place, like a child again at the mature age of twenty. It was Sassia's turn to mother me and I revelled in it like a true innocent abroad.

The evil in me started to appear later, when it was Sassia who became the object of Cluentia's hate with the willing compliance of Maximus in all her malicious scheming.

Sassia was already three months pregnant then, and no one knew about it; not Boy, not Sassia, not even me! What a naïve bunch we were. I can hardly credit it now. I, at the very least *I*, should have known, and known better. But no. We were so lost in the newness, in the joy of it all, that nothing else really mattered; certainly not an ugly and irritating concept like *actions have consequences*.

When I said 'newness' a moment ago, I meant the newness of the entire situation: of location, of a sense of freedom; and of love – for Sassia, that is. I didn't mean sex. Sex was not new, not for me it wasn't. Maximus was the first to have me – I was about ten – and many more since. But I knew nothing about being pregnant for I had never conceived. Perhaps my womb was damaged because Maximus took me too strongly when I wasn't quite ready, or so my mother said. She liked blaming Maximus for everything ever since he threw my brother over to the Lanista. After my treatment no one wanted to come near me and I had really forgotten what it was like being with anyone but my beloved mistress. Nor did I crave for anyone else. I had learnt of more ways than one to satisfy myself if the need arose, and that was enough.

II

He had no name.

They called him Boy, those that felt the necessity to call him.

And he was a boy, a mere boy; could have hardly been older than thirteen, the same age as Sassia I would have said; but she looked a grown woman and he a mere boy, as I have said. He was tall as a man though, taller: as tall as six prints of a Roman soldier's foot are long; while his hands and fingers, feet and ankles, neck and shoulders were long and gawky and awkward as that of a half-man-half-boy. He had as yet no signs of hair on his face, or under his arms; just a soft growth on his private parts. Rather, what would have been private parts on a citizen. A slave has no private parts.

It was his private parts that we first saw. Genitals, I should say, he being a slave.

We were in one of the *alae* having a chat about what the kitchen would be preparing for us that day – after my treatment Sassia had kicked up such a fuss that I was officially allowed to be with her almost all the time, even eating with her on occasions – and looking out at the trees and flowers in the garden when through the lattice work in the room to our left we saw what we saw. Boy standing naked in front of Aurius and his wife Julia. His lower parts, being at our eye level as we sat the other side of the wall, were the first to hit our vision. Sassia sneered, as she always did at the mention or sight of male equipment, whereas I showed interest and looked at the specimen to which they were attached. His body glowed darkly in the sunlight streaming into the room, and his eyes appeared to change colour from green to hazel to a translucent amber. His mouth was full and his chin strong, the hair on his head thick and covered in loose curls. It was difficult to say where he came from. Part Greek, part African, part Teuton, part god. I took to him instantly, and at my pleading Sassia gave him another look, this time ignoring the obvious, and this time she too liked what she saw. At least she felt a rush of sympathy for the poor sod. The topic under discussion was the removal of those hanging parts that so simply confronted us. No wonder they looked so downcast and he so downhearted, despite the glint of arrogant defiance in those ever-changing eyes.

From what we could hear it seemed Julia had seen him in the fields as she was out one morning to consume some fresh air with a few of her slave-women. He was in chains and being scourged, and would have been done to death had she not intervened: he had tried to escape, for the third time. He was new in the fields and had been sent from up north where too he had been trouble, and where too he would have been killed had the master not taken pity and sold him to a trader who sold him to someone working down here in Campania. Julia was a careful woman and hated waste of money or goods, and thought the creature might do well as a houseboy where there would be less opportunity to escape with many older and stronger slaves around, some of them ex-gladiators, and quite capable of taking care of a mere stripling.

Aurius was not too sure. Once a runner, always a runner, that was his motto: and the sooner you got rid of one the more you saved in time, effort and food in the long run. However, he was willing to humour Julia provided the lad was castrated. That would save any unpleasant situation from developing through having a growing man as a houseboy around her, and the girls; also it would take the sharpness out of him and tame him accordingly. Julia didn't agree. She said castration was barbaric and that she was no Egyptian. Also, if that was to be his punishment, no use doing it then as he may not realise the true proportion of his loss to the best advantage; it should be done when 'the down down under turned coarse'. Aurius conceded the logic of that and Boy and his parts were spared. I believed Julia had her own reasons for not seeing him carved up, but Sassia hushed me silent and proclaimed yet again that I had a dirty mind.

That would have been the end of that had not the mistress woken me up in the middle of the following night as I lay stretched out asleep on the floor beside her bed, claiming that she had heard unnatural sounds coming from the portico beneath the window which sent her breasts a trembling with unnatural fear.

I am not an easy waker, and by the time I fully came to myself the sounds had apparently stopped. We tried to go back to sleep, but to no avail. We were much too tensed up to relax without some sort of a diversion and decided to go outside for a bit of air and a meander amid the trees and shrubs of the spacious but safely enclosed gardens. Also, though she did not say it in so many words, Sassia was still intrigued by what she had heard, or thought she had heard, and wanted an excuse to be outside and maybe discover the source or cause of the noise.

And she was not to be disappointed.

Hardly had we gone two hundred steps or less when there rose up in the air what could only be described as strangulated guttural moans. I could understand what Sassia had meant by unnatural sounds. I could feel my own breasts trembling with unnatural fear, and no doubt about it. We forgot the heady scent of the lilacs and ignored the unusual paling of the red roses in the light of the summer moon and leant our ears towards the appropriate direction to the exclusion of all other senses. After a moment's petrifaction Sassia pulled me violently against the wind and started dragging me along the reverse path of the groany emanations. Even in those days she could be quite reckless, as long as she had me by her side.

And I could be quite daring, as long as I had her by my side.

So off we went into the throbbing heart of the night.

Not many beats away throbbed another heart. The heart of Boy, in a body that was beaten to a bloodied pulp and chained beneath the statue of a rampantly grinning satyr, links of rusty metal forcing their way into gashed chunks of lean flesh. It was his muted cries that had driven us out into the arms of treacherous fate.

Only the morning before Sassia had seen all that there was to see of Boy, and thought little of it, or him. When she saw him dying in darkness she nearly died in the dark.

Whatever course her life took since then, that night was at the heart of it. And through the long and varied years that followed she sought only Boy through the multitude of bodies that she used and abused; or loved. And there were those she loved, however much they who hate and fear her may deny her the capacity to love.

Swallowing a hushed scream, she pulled at the sleeve of my *subcula* so hard I feared it would come off at the seams – it had seen the days of its strength gradually ebb away over the last few months.

'Do something! Do something, Lucia, my love. Do something. Do anything,' begged my mistress in a voice I did not recognise, with an intensity I did not know she possessed.

I did something.

Ran to fetch Davus, the old freedman with a brain and a heart, and still enough strength in his ancient bones to carry a young body in his arms. Not to mention the fact that he had a small room to himself in which the same young body, if yet alive, could be stowed away in relative safety. The old codger had the face of a dead crocodile, the walk of a dying elephant and the temper of a charging rhino: attributes which kept most people well out of his way, be they slaves, freedmen, or even citizens; excellent as far as we were concerned, and he too was happy to be left alone. His love for mankind did not always stretch out to its individual members in any noticeable way. After taking one look at Boy he mammothed away without saying a word. We thought his nerve had given way: torture and a painful death would surely follow were he to be discovered harbouring the lad. But he had only gone to get a strong file to cut away at the chains.

'The MUSE'

by Mel Calman

Help me, O Muse.
Come & visit me...
    don't desert me in my hour
        of need. PLEASE !!

(SILENCE)... TIME PASSES...

The Next Day...

Please, MUSE —
    you must hear my PLEAS..
    Come.. just for an hour..
    a few minutes... anything but this
        TERRIBLE SILENCE...

A FAINT RUSTLE IS HEARD.. AND.. THEN...

What is all this
NOISE?

I can't be
everywhere at once,
    you know..
    only got one pair
        of hands...

It's just that I'm DESPERATE..
I passed the deadline weeks ago..
and I can't THINK of anything
NOTHING.
It's all BLANK!!
Let's see..
what would you like?
I could suggest a tender love story..
or something SEXY.. always popular.. a spell-binding story of courage and self-discovery.. or a tapestry of family LIFE.. or a Lesbian's struggle to know herself in the foothills of New Zealand..
or FACTION with the spirit of CHARLES DICKENS trying to kill Peter Ackroyd..
or a FAT one with brand names.. a vivid and HAUNTING debut by this influential writer..
A woman's fight against her DESTINY... oh what BLISS!
Just CHOOSE...
choices..
choices..

Choose! I haven't got all DAY..
Hundreds of writers crying out to be visited, you know..
Don't RUSH me!
You MUST decide! I like beginnings, middles and ENDS!
I like a good strong STORY..
and I like a writer who knows what he wants..
FOR HEAVEN'S SAKE..
We don't WANT
wishy-washy... internal brooding..
If this is supposed to be HELPFUL - I was better off on my own..

Can I say something? I don't just need IDEAS..
I need the STAMINA.. the COURAGE.. the sheer BLOODY-MINDEDNESS
to carry on .. To write every day .. to cover the BLANK pieces
of paper with words and then...
the FAITH to go out and see all those BOOKSHOPS
bursting with OTHER PEOPLE'S BOOKS .. and my
POOR LITTLE BABY sitting UNLOVED in the
          far distant corner..
               Completely
                IGNORED!

               I can't stand it..
                    I tell
                    you
                    (SOB)

               IT's HELL .. it's more
          than I can stand..
                    Why should I ?
          WHY? WHY?

Of course - if you can't stand it.. Be something else..
               BE a PLUMBER..
                    OR
               an accountant
               OR a BUS
               DRIVER or .....
               LIFT ATTENDANT
               Be BORED
               day after
                    DAY!

                              see if I care...
                              self-pity..
                              its PATHETIC..

I'm giving you the chance to lead
a HUNDRED different lives.. be other MEN, WOMEN..
CHILDREN.. LOVE.. hate.. KILL.. DIE.. and
only on paper.. never in REALITY.. no price to pay...
it's a chance to be GOD, isn't it?
..

Go on.. pour yourself a stiff drink.. put
a fresh piece of paper in the typewriter..
and BEGIN.. ahh..
BEGINNINGS are such FUN...

We can go anywhere..

BE ANYONE...

Come with me and
TRUST me... .

.. ' Once upon
a time..,'

calman

Essays

The Europe of the Mind

It is odd that so few British consider themselves Europeans. When I first stepped onto Victoria Station platform, a Canadian boy of seven, I knew I was in Europe. It smelled like Europe: the coal smoke from the engine, the Woodbine between the porter's lips, the brown sugary tea in the station restaurant, and the chill London fog that made the pavements glisten and the taxi headlights dim yellow in the gloom. Now that I make my home here, the appeal of Britain remains that it is a European society where I can be at home in my native tongue; for me Britain is just one patch in Europe's quilt of cultures.

But the British keep on insisting they're no part of the European blanket. They keep insisting on their exceptionalism, and of course they have a point. Britain was the first society in Europe where a property-owning class of peasant individualists emerged; the first society to create a common law; the first to make the transition from absolutism to parliamentary democracy; and now the last society to struggle its way into the post-industrial future. Britain can never be European, I am told, because its history is exceptional.

All European nationalisms appeal to a sense of the exceptional character of their history, and all nationalisms are blinkered by provincial self-regard, but the British sense of exceptionalism takes some beating. Instead of exploring the possibility that what is worthy of pride is that Britain stands for values which are essentially European rather than peculiarly British – liberty, tolerance, reason, respect for rights and for human equality – the British pride themselves on collective worship of curious local customs like the monarchy, and on a habit of mind Sigmund Freud called 'the narcissism of minor difference' – the loving exaggeration of every vestigial British difference from the European pattern.

These differences, particularly of political culture, are less and less plausible as grounds for keeping aloof from Europe. During the 1940s and 1950s, when Franco and Salazar were in their palaces and the French Fourth Republic tottered to its end, the British could be forgiven for wishing to give the Continentals lessons in democracy. But since the establishment of French political stability in the Fifth Republic and the passage of Greece, Portugal and Spain into the camp of the democracies, it is less plausible for the British to see their island as a paragon of political moderation on the edge of Continental despotism and political hysteria. A society without a modern Bill of Rights or Freedom of Information Act has more to learn from Europe than its habits of self-congratulation allow.

Between 1918 and 1960 it might have been plausible for the British to distinguish the civility and tolerance of its social life from the often fratricidal character of European social quarrels. But thirty years of economic crisis have limited the welfare state's capacity to conciliate social conflict; Britain is a less civil society than it was a generation ago. In many ways this is a good thing – since civility depended too much on deference – but in any event, the new public culture of the Thatcher era, which made private gain the all but exclusive means to public good, brought British life appreciably closer to the German or American cultural pattern.

Despite these signs of convergence, most British people still distinguish their culture sharply from the European. But now the vocabulary of distanciation is stood on its head. Instead of complacently enumerating all the things they do better than the Continentals, the British now focus neurotically on the uniqueness of their economic and social failure. In the language of invidious comparison which dominates so much public discourse, Britain *has* become more European, but in the worst possible way: in the often incorrect assumption that anything made by Bosch, Braun or Fiat must be better than anything by Rover, Hoover or GEC. These invidious comparisons are not just confined to the contrast between the economic performance of the British and their European partners. The gloomy comparisons now extend to the quality of public culture and state services. Thus the wealth of public provision – museums, subways, monuments – in Paris and Barcelona, for example, becomes a stick to beat poor old London with.

Envy is probably an inevitable phase in leaving behind an excess of imperial self-regard. Invidious comparison is a painful therapy of self-improvement. Societies that do not look enviously, even unhappily, at the success of their neighbours are not struggling with their own limitations. Yet invidious comparison with the Continent has aggravated rather than alleviated the neurosis of provincial self-absorption. Many generations of relative economic decline have produced an inwardly turned national debate marred by all the hallmarks of the depressive, especially the depressive's narcissism. The new British sense of being exceptional (that is, exceptionally incompetent) is surely no improvement on its reverse image: that the Brits do everything better. The one is as parochial and inward-turned as the other.

Just as a depressive breaks the downward spiral by recognising that depression is not a unique personal failing, so British society could do itself some good by recognising how many of its problems it shares with its European partners. Certainly the Germans, the Italians and the French outperform the British, yet beneath the differences there are some long-term similarities in the economic challenge facing all European societies. These economic problems are symptoms of a deeper cultural anxiety. Since the war Europe has been recurrently haunted by the fear that history is passing it by. Behind Europe's resistance to decolonisation in the Fifties lay the fear that Europe might lose its place as the centre of world culture. In the 1980s, the spectre haunting European thought was the fear that the axis of world civilisation was shifting from the North Atlantic to the Pacific rim. When economies shift, cultures follow. When Venice lost its empire, it became a museum. In one of his last interviews, Fernand Braudel, the great French historian of the shift of the axis of the European economy from the Mediterranean to Amsterdam, London and Hamburg, worried aloud that Europe would be turned into a museum culture by the emergence of Los Angeles, Taipei, Singapore, Hong Kong and Tokyo as the economic heart of the global economic order. Europe faces the fate it once visited on its own colonies: becoming an importer of culture and the hired hand of other people's technology. The economic competition with the Americans and with the Far East is ultimately a cultural competition and the worries that it awakens are essentially ones about national identity: do we work hard enough, do we still have the capacity to dare and to innovate, do we still have the national cohesion necessary for collective exercises of the cultural and economic imagination? It is in this European context that the British struggle to remain a viable economy assumes its real historical and cultural significance. This is why it is worth fighting for the economic life of this island: not so that Britain can remain the cosy 'old country' of American tourist brochures, but so that it can join with Europe in defending the best that Europe stands for.

There is no reason to suppose that European societies cannot adapt to a world culture whose economic centre is beyond their borders. Europe's encounter with the cultural and economic penetration of America suggests how resilient and inventive the European response can be. Instead of being the source of European cultures' dilution, American influence has been a key site of its renewal. The British working class's love of blues, country and western and Elvis Presley has produced the international cultural industry which is modern rock and roll. The French passion for American film not only produced *la nouvelle vague* in France but taught a generation of Americans from Scorsese to Coppola to see the achievement of the neglected masters – Ford, Hitchcock, Ray, Walsh – of their own cinema. The Italian affection for the western produced the spaghetti western, and the new German cinema – especially Wim Wender's *American Friend* and *Paris, Texas* – combines a message of poignant envy of American energy and openness with a use of the medium which is unmistakably European.

The question of what Britain does about its identity is thus a question about how Europe refuses the fate of a museum culture, by taking on the forms of a mass global culture and giving them that imprint which makes British television serials, Benetton jumpers, BMW cars, Armani suits and Burberry raincoats a password for design and quality.

If Europe is known to the world for its best products, it can also make itself known again for the quality of its political culture. As the heartland of religious war and political fanaticism, Europe has learned all there is to know about the high moral cost of dogmatism. A pragmatic, sceptical and secular civic character or public temperament has emerged out of Europe's tragic encounter with its own fanaticism, religiosity and nationalist fervour. Having nearly destroyed itself with strong beliefs, the Western European temper now is the most non-ideological, the most sceptical, the least dogmatic on earth. There is no European society where the secular religion of success and the religion of fundamentalist Christianity enjoys the same centrality as in American culture. There is no European society that still believes in the creed of Communist salvation. That is perhaps why European societies have the potential to be less merciless about failure, more tolerant of difference, more open to a world of ambiguity and uncertainty than either of the struggling empires which hem it in on either side.

Figures like Havel in Eastern Europe passionately want their countries to join this Europe of the future and not the religious and nationalist Europe of the past. Whether they get the chance to do so, or whether Eastern Europe goes the way of Serbia, Croatia and Romania, whether it tears itself apart, depends very largely on whether Western Europe believes that what happens in the old Communist empire is part of its own fate. This is more than a question of whether Western bankers and industrialists will detect business opportunities there; it is a question of whether Western Europe will begin to feel, once again, that Diocletian's Split, Kafka's Prague, Grass's Gdansk belong intimately with a common cultural home.

There is a lot of empty talk about a common European culture, empty because it speaks of culture as a commodity, as an artistic experience, to be produced and promoted by market and state. Yet when culture is reduced to the arts, when artistic creation is appreciated in isolation from the values of the political culture in which that creation takes place, devotion to culture becomes an empty form of self-cultivation. Art degenerates into fashion and style. What a culture is, essentially, is a set of attachments to institutions and practices which guarantee, in the European case, political pluralism and personal freedom. Thus culture is too important to be left to artists or artistic administrators. Culture is political or it is nothing but cultivation. To be committed to a European culture is to be committed to a certain kind of freedom: the separation of church and state, the guarantee of minority linguistic and cultural rights, the common provision of social services and cultural goods for all, above all the autonomy of civil society from the state.

Western Europe has taken these values so much for granted, has become so bored with them, that it has taken the revolt of

Eastern Europe to teach us again how precious they are. Havel and Walesa sent us all back to school to learn what we care about, to learn what we cannot live without.

These are values of which Europe has every reason to be proud: not in order to visit European condescension on those who *do* have passionate religious or political belief, but in order to lend support to those in the Third World who know that their own painful experience of Europe's worst – racism, imperialism – need not oblige them to turn away from Europe's best: its traditions of tolerance, respect and equality.

None of this would need saying were it not that Europe is, in the words of Richard Hoggart and Douglas Johnson, a guilty continent, guilty about the contradiction between its 'civilising' airs and the carnage at the heart of its history, guilty that its cultural pretensions bear less and less relation to its economic and political influence.

The most immediate source of this guilt was colonialism. It was inevitable in the struggle for decolonisation that a generation of European intellectuals should have looked on these European values with a certain scorn. Hymns of praise to European liberty rather died on the lips in an era when French troops were torturing Algerian prisoners of war, when British troops were struggling with armed resistance in Kenya, Malaysia and Cyprus. Not surprisingly the best European intellectuals of the post-war period saw it as their task to give comfort to movements of colonial resistance. There resulted in the Fifties and Sixties what the French have labelled 'Tiers-Mondism', a fervent ideological embrace of the values and perspectives of colonial resistance movements and the new post-colonial states. When these new states failed to become democracies, failed to defend European standards of civil and political rights and degenerated either into corrupt bourgeois oligarchies or left-wing tyrannies, Europeans either hesitated to condemn them or justified their failings as evidence of the lingering scars of colonialism. The relativising bias of cultural anthropology encouraged the tendency towards tolerant condescension on the part of European intellectuals. It was held to be unfair to judge tribal and ex-colonial states by the standards of political liberty applicable in Europe. It was forgotten that if colonial rule became indefensible, it became so because it contradicted the European values of freedom and self-determination. What Asian imperium ever taught its subject peoples the values with which to overthrow itself? European colonialism handed its subject peoples the intellectual arms which eventually were turned against itself. Yet if this was so, if the dream of colonial freedom was a dream won in colonial class-rooms, then those who took control of post-colonial states can be fairly criticised for failing to live up to the lessons they were supposed to have learned. By the early 1980s it became apparent, as it should have been all along, that Europeans could both renounce the errors of their imperialist past and uphold the universality of European values, especially the idea of human rights. The post-war period of European self-hatred is properly over. We have entered a period in which it has become possible, once again, to speak up on behalf of that European watchword 'liberty'. There are some French intellectuals of the Left who exploit the traditions of European liberty in a blindly dogmatic denunciation of the Soviet empire; others on the Right who want to defend Europe as a preserve of white culture against the Third World cultures at Europe's gate. But the watchword of liberty – by liberty's very nature – cannot be turned into a slogan or a battle-cry: it is a word to live by, a word to judge one's own failings by.

This Europe of the mind, this Europe of liberty, owes more for its re-discovery to the writers of the Eastern bloc, to men like Milan Kundera and Georgy Konrad, than anyone in Western Europe. They are the ones who have reminded us, if we had forgotten, that Dickens and Joyce and Shakespeare belong as much to Eastern Europe as they do to us; it is they who have made us aware of the mental shutters which prevent us from understanding that there is still one European culture from London to Warsaw, from Paris to Prague. This instinct lay behind the Helsinki process; behind the support in the West for the Charter 77 dissidents in Czechoslovakia; behind Western support for Solidarnosc in Poland. While the Soviet and American empires made the venial pact of detente – which legitimised the Soviet glacis in Eastern Europe – ordinary writers and intellectuals on both side of the Iron Curtain patiently strove to re-knit a common cultural fabric that the superpowers had colluded in ripping apart at Yalta. The pan-European defence of human rights and freedom of expression was never just a defence of courageous individuals: it was a defence of the unity of European culture itself.

Now the walls have come down. The Iron Curtain is no more, and there exists a cultural Europe which runs from Dublin to Budapest. But it does not yet embrace Moscow or Leningrad. We would have to return to the decades before the First World War to recapture a Europe which included the Russian empire. In that last fevered decade of the Czarist regime, Moscow sugar barons collected Matisses and the painters, musicians and poets of Europe's most backward society ushered in European modernism. The Russian élite that was able to consider Baden Baden, Nice, Paris and Dresden as home was admittedly a tiny segment of the population, but nonetheless they were the first generation to successfully resolve the ancient question of whether Russia was an Asian or European nation. The élite which produced Scriabin, Stravinsky, Diaghilev, Kandinsky and Blok was both indubitably Russian and effortlessly European, and they were the last Russian generation to be so. The seventy years of the Soviet experiment re-dug a chasm between European and Russian culture, and it is this chasm that the artists and writers of the Gorbachev era are now beginning to cross. What is ultimately at stake in the Gorbachev reforms, from a cultural point of view, is the possibility that Russia will once again return to the European cultural heartland: not merely that its artists and writers will be able to work freely in the West, but that Soviet society will itself begin to subscribe again to the core values of European tolerance and liberty.

Again, cultural exchanges, even free travel between the Soviet Union and Western Europe do not make for a common cultural home. Party monopolies of power are incompatible with European liberty. Russia cannot rejoin Europe, until the Soviet Union becomes a democratic federation of autonomous republics.

In Germany, in France, this emerging idea of a Europe from Vladivostock to Dublin is a fact of contemporary cultural perception. Not in Britain. She may have joined the EEC in 1974 but she has yet to enter this Europe of the mind. Part of the blame for this must fall on the EEC itself. The Community process has confiscated the energy and commitment behind the cultural idea of Europe and turned the word Europe into a thought-stopping bore, evoking only the grey round of ministerial meetings in concrete bunkers in Strasbourg and Brussels. The grinding quarrels over British budget contributions have allowed us to forget that the institutions of the Community exist, not just

as a cartel of economic advantage, but as the sinews and supports
of a common European culture. The debate about Britain's role
in Europe is not fundamentally about what turn of the ratchet
of national advantage can be applied to the negotiating process
at the next ministerial meeting. It is a debate about what kind
of identity Britain can make for itself in the re-discovery that it
has been a European society all along. That debate has barely
started.

Anglo–English Attitudes

To say that we live in the age of the diaspora is to express a resounding commonplace. Salman Rushdie, John Berger and Edward Said are amongst those who have argued, in a variety of contexts, that ours has been the century of exile, displacement and migration. In search of work or a new way of life, in pursuance of (or escape from) their countries' wars, hitherto unimagined numbers of people have voluntarily emigrated or been forcibly uprooted from their place of birth. Much of the character of modernity and modernism is an expression and product of precisely this experience. So extensive has the phenomenon been that it is difficult to be immune from its consequences. Yet, as far as such a thing *is* possible, I was born into a way of life almost untouched by this quintessential symptom of modernity. My father now lives about two miles from where his father was born. None of his four brothers and sisters live more than three miles away from each other. My mother has moved a little further afield, from a village near Shrewsbury to Cheltenham in Gloucestershire, but migration on this scale could easily be found in early Hardy.

While Hardy's Durbeyfields are astonished to find that they are distantly related to an aristocratic French family, Americans tend to be disappointed if they do not have the blood of at least four or five nations coursing through their veins. 'I'm one part Italian, two parts Irish, one part Jewish and one part Native American' they explain, certain that they are becoming more interesting – more *American* – with every race mentioned. By that reckoning, as Hardy's Edwardian contemporaries used to put it, I'm a dull dog indeed. I am English, so are my parents and so were my grandparents. In contrast to the narrator of Hanif Kureishi's *The Buddha of Suburbia* – 'a funny kind of Englishman, a new breed' – I am a very ordinary sort of Englishman.

I've not bothered to go any further back but it seems unlikely that my great-grandparents and great-great-grandparents were anything other than English. My mother's father went to France in the Great War but as soon as it was over he simply resumed the life he had left. More recently my cousin Ian went to Canada to work for a while prior to full-scale emigration but felt so homesick that he got the next flight home. When asked if he'd ever been abroad, my uncle Harry replied that he'd been there once, years ago, and didn't like it. Apart from drifting over the Welsh border for an hour or two my parents, from the time I was born, did not leave England until 1978 when they were persuaded to go to the Isle of Wight for a week. This was the first time my mother had ever been on a boat; neither she nor my father have ever owned a passport or flown in a plane.

Gloucestershire, where the Dyer anchor has been so firmly planted, is the English mid-West. Cheltenham, in spite of its reputation as a snooty town full of retired colonels, is pretty much like all the other towns in England, with a few Regency buildings thrown in. The signs welcoming you to Cheltenham proclaim it to be 'the centre of the Cotswolds' – and the Cotswolds, well, what could be more English than the not-too-high-not-too-wild-but-very-pleasing-on-the-eye Cotswolds?

Mine, then, are not only poor credentials, from an American point of view, when it comes to being interesting; they are also – the experience of the diaspora being inextricably entwined with the project of modernism – pretty poor credentials for a modern writer. Or at least they are not the kind of credentials shared by many male writers who, in recent years, have made some of the best-known contributions to what seems to be a new wave of English letters. I'm thinking of writers like Salman Rushdie (Anglo-Indian), Kazuo Ishiguro (Anglo-Japanese), Timothy Mo (Anglo-Chinese), Hanif Kureishi (Anglo-Pakistani). UK-born Martin Amis, meanwhile, becomes steadily more Anglo-American by the paragraph.

And me? Anglo-English, mate. But while the distinctive character of the work of the writers mentioned above is felt, quite rightly, to be a product of their tangential relation to England – 'the odd mixture of continents and blood, of here and there, of belonging and not', as Kureishi puts it – my own sense of being out of kilter with English notions of literariness is a product, precisely, of my rootedness in England. There is something ludicrous about this attitude: I can speak and read no other language except menu French – half of the writers I profess to love I have not even read in their original language. This kind of cosmopolitan parochialism also reveals itself in another way: like many people I like to see myself as a citizen of the world, unfettered by nationalist pride. Following the example of Raymond Williams who used to describe himself as a Welsh European, then, maybe I should call myself an English European – except I have never had any sense of being European. In fact I've never had any sense of being British. The truth is I often catch myself on the brink of making that unhip slip (once, almost suicidally, while interviewing James Kelman at the ICA) of saying English when I mean British.

This feeling of being rooted in a culture with which I am at odds informs and fuels my sense of what it is to be a writer in England now. The origins and effects of this feeling – at once ludicrous and contradictory, laughable and illuminating – are worth exploring a little further.

Just before going up to Oxford to read English I got into some trouble, and halfway through my first term had to appear at the magistrate's court in Cheltenham. I hitched back the day before – just forty miles along the A40 – and, as a surprise, turned up at my old junior school canteen where my mother still worked (note again the closed geography and history we are working with). When she came out we both started crying. We were crying because it was the first time I had returned since leaving home but at some level, since this was implicit in the idea of leaving, it was a class thing we were crying about.

Two years later, in my final year, I came home again, this time for a little twenty-first birthday party. My mother had made a cake and she and my father had paid to have it decoratively iced, in the shape of an open book with a bookmark down the middle. Printed across the cake, like print on the open pages, was the name of my college: Corpus Christi. It had the look of a shrine or totem, which in some sense it was, an expression of the vast symbolic power of books. This symbolic power was enhanced by the fact that my father had not actually read one in all of those twenty-one years. Since then he's read three (struggling through the last with the aid of a magnifying glass), all of them by me. While the symbolic book was very much on show (my uncle Peter photographed it), these books are kept hidden safely away in the packaging they arrived in: the family china, to be treasured, not used.

'Books, books, books', as Tony Harrison writes in one of 'The School of Eloquence' poems. Books and class – for in this country, as Harrison poignantly reminds us, you cannot talk about one without the other.

Unlike Tony Harrison and Raymond Williams I grew up in a world where ideas of culture and community – those key Williams words – revolved around the telly. Apart from occasional visits to relatives or Sunday drives we simply stayed at home, the three of us, very happily and cosily. With the testosterone surge of puberty I started doing a bit of reading: *Skinhead, Suedehead* and *Chopper* followed by the complete works of Alistair Maclean, and subsequently, via the pop group Hawkwind, the sword and sorcery novels of Michael Moorcock.

Then suddenly, it happened, the literature thing. Under the spell of my English teacher's enthusiasm I started in on the real stuff: *The Catcher in the Rye, Catch 22, On the Road.* This leisure reading ran parallel with O and A levels and a gradually emerging sense of the Great Tradition of English writing – but the first writers I read for fun were Americans. When it came to applying for university my preference was for UEA where you could read American literature – not because of any great interest in Hawthorne and Melville but because American was synonymous with new (Heller, Salinger, Kerouac) and English with old (Chaucer, Austen, Fielding). It is also worth remembering that your tastes as a reader and ambitions as a writer are formed as much by writers you haven't read as those you have. I was never tempted by the stuff traditionally offered to teenagers as a way of luring them into the pleasures of the text: Kingsley Amis (still haven't read him, never will), Graham Greene (who I now realise was a master) or Evelyn Waugh. I picked up *Brideshead Revisited* but had a visceral aversion to the accent of Waugh's prose which I have never felt the urge to shake off. My love of D.H. Lawrence, meanwhile, expressed itself in terms of a simplistic class solidarity (I was for him and therefore against Bloomsbury) and I baulked at Virginia Woolf and the preoccupation with the exquisite. This was almost instinctive, an involuntary raising of hackles, a bigoted version of Raymond Williams wincing when he read of Henry James referring to 'little Thomas Hardy'.

Literature led to university and a community of sorts, the community of literature-lovers. Later, under the sway of critics like Terry Eagleton, I realised the extent to which not only the values of this community but also the whole notion of the humanities functioned to perpetuate what, until recently, I was content to call bourgeois ideology. Before I was able to see it in these theoretical terms, however, I had already responded in the time-honoured tradition of the scholarship boy – by developing a sizeable chip on my shoulder: certain accents made me want to pull on my Doc Martens (I've never actually owned a pair if we're being perfectly frank). That there is something both comical and revealing about this is made clear by an incident that took place a good few years after leaving university. I emerged from an early evening literary bash with the seething arrogance, the wounded resentment of someone to whom even polite and well-meaning conversation seems provocation enough to merit some class-based retribution. I headed back to Brixton, looking forward to the pub, the boozer, the pisser – my real home. I met up with a friend, stood at the bar and talked books. A drunk started in on us (OK, I'll admit it, I was wearing a corduroy jacket, brogues: like I say, I'd just come from a literary bash), calling us a stuck-up pair of cunts. Two hours earlier my head was full of thoughts of fighting; now, cowed and frightened that this lumpen prick was actually going to hit me, I felt like a mirror, looking out at myself. (Some sort of synthesis in this internalised dialectic of class struggle was subsequently achieved: back home I day-dreamed of dragging him outside and kicking fuck out of him.)

That's how it is in the land of yobs and snobs, there's no getting away from it.

Oxford, much to my parents' disappointment, led not to the financial security of a middle-class career but to the dole-and-squat culture of garret radicals. In an interview with an American magazine, Roland Gift, singer with the Fine Young Cannibals, pointed out that the dole supported a whole generation of musicians, artists and dancers. This is absolutely right and in the early and mid-1980s in certain areas of South London – in Brixton and the area around Bonnington Square in Vauxhall – there was a thriving community of unenfranchised (I mean 'un', not 'dis') people with vaguely creative leanings and no interest in the straight world of careers and jobs. This world still seems to me to represent one of the most important strata of London life. Before moving to Brixton I lived in a house full of apprentice lawyers: every morning there was a stampede of activity in the bathroom and then I'd be left at home lamenting my lot, wishing I too was leading a normal life instead of tampering with a secondhand Olivetti. Once I was installed in a house full of unemployed wasters and was no longer distracted by this perverse urge to get on the tube and go to work, writing was an almost inevitable consequence of having nothing to do all day. Of course we were lucky in that we left university in the days of mass unemployment; by the late 1980s people leaving university were finding the hegemony of success generated by Thatcherism difficult to resist. Lacking the sustaining community of people doing nothing all day, anyone leaving university in recent years is likely to have felt as isolated as I did in Balham and will have been under pressure either to get a job or succumb to the competitive world and short-term gratification of journalism.

Resilient though it is, the kind of world personified by the squats of Bonnington Square is under threat. This is a terrible shame, for that world seems as close as we are ever likely to get in this grim country to any kind of bohemia. As well as campaigning against cuts in education and Arts Council funding we should be lamenting the way that changes in social security legislation and the lure of mortgage and magazine culture have eroded the fertile soil of creative idleness. Now, I don't care about the historical origin of bohemia. What I am talking about is bohemia as traditionally conceived: would-be artists and writers sitting in cafés (which hardly exist here, but never mind), getting up late, living on little money, constantly about to settle down to some major project – a film script, typically – but unable to find the application to see it through because everyone else is also sitting around getting stoned rather than getting on with *their* scripts. The fact that so few of these projects get completed doesn't matter in the slightest: that general culture is a sustaining part of the few that do.

English at Oxford offered a constantly diminishing version of the excitement I'd experienced at school when I read Wordsworth for the first time. In Brixton I discovered a new kind of writing in the work of Adorno, Walter Benjamin, Calvino, Williams, Berger, Foucault and Barthes. Many of these writers were driven or formed by a fierce political commitment and for myself and my friends perhaps the real excitement of Williams and Berger was discovering the point at which literature linked up with broader political issues. For a few years we were on the cusp between the era of political involvement and the political disenchantment of the late 1980s. In 1984 Salman Rushdie published an impressive essay, 'Outside the Whale', arguing for the integration of political and literary endeavour. Since then, as I tried to show in *The Colour of Memory*, politics has receded from the lives of people of my generation. This is not surprising: our only experience has been of defeat – each of the General Elections I have voted in have resulted in Mrs Thatcher becoming prime minister. Lacking a real party of opposition, we gradually fell back on lifestyle as an alternative form of opposition. Martin Amis got onto the anti-nuclear thing in 1987; from then on, though, it seemed the most important political contribution English writers could make was to join Charter 88 and insist on their books being printed on recycled paper.

Notwithstanding this, the lasting effect of encountering writers like Benjamin and Berger is to make you feel frustrated with the English idea that literariness is a quality only of certain narrowly defined forms of writing, that imaginative writing is found solely on the fiction shelves of Waterstone's, in novels and stories. The traditional attraction of the novel from the writer's point of view is that you can do anything with it. All too often, however, the process of novelisation goes hand in hand with a cramping or strait-jacketing of the material's expressive potential. Quintessentially novelistic, books like *Stars and Bars* or *An Ice-Cream War* by William Boyd are anything but novel in the literal sense of the word. (Only a matter of time, surely, before the software – 'Novel Perfect' – becomes available to arrange and structure material automatically along such well-established lines.)

In focusing on novels like Boyd's, I am not making a plea for the experimental writing of someone like Gabriel Josipovici. Most so-called experimental writing seems more hackneyed, more enslaved to worn-out convention than the kind of Booker Prize naturalism it sets itself in defiant opposition to. Freedom from the prerogatives of novelisation, in Bruce Chatwin's *The Song Lines* for example, permits an expansion of imaginative possibilities. In a book like Josipovici's *In the Fertile Land* we see these possibilities being reduced to academic and sub-Beckettian, self-erasing futility.

Ryzard Kapuściński's books *Shah of Shahs* and *The Emperor*, on the other hand, offer a wholly new form of writing, combining reportage and political analysis with all the imaginative daring and linguistic energy of Dickens. *The Soccer War*, a collection of articles that is also a fragmentary autobiography, was reviewed alongside the latest books by Anthony Burgess and John Updike. This was heartening not simply on the level of reputation but for what it revealed of how the kind (not quality) of books that fall within and *determine* the consensual taste of the review pages (which reflect and determine the nation's taste) might be changing. What Terry Eagleton said with regard to the 'classical' canon of English literature applies equally to the processing of contemporary writing: it is not that writing has to be 'fine' to be literary, it has to be of the kind that is judged 'fine'.

Kapuściński not withstanding, English literary life is still characterised by a pervasive parochialism. We are all affectionately familiar with Larkin's insular aversion to all matters foreign but what is most striking about *Haydn and the Valve Trumpet*, a collection of essays by a very different poet, Craig Raine, is how impoverished is his frame of reference. As poet and essayist Raine has enviable fluency, but the way he tackles his subjects and the relish with which he quotes from the Preface to *Lyrical Ballads* ('emotion recollected in tranquility') and T. S. Eliot (the 'dissociation of sensibility') make you wonder if he is still mugging up for his English Finals in Oxford. As with Boyd in relation to the novel so the case of Craig Raine (who, until recently, was poetry editor at Faber) is paradigmatic of a more general debility of outlook within English poetry, which means for example that one of the world's greatest living poets, the Syrian-born Adonis, is almost wholly unknown in this country. Translations of his work reveal a visionary intensity that rivals Neruda's, an imaginative intelligence as sharp as Brodsky's and yet, in spite of his international reputation, his poems are available only in a couple of anthologies in England.

England's cultural insularity is closely allied to the deep-seated and self-congratulatory hostility to that other foreign figure, the intellectual. Foreign not so much by birth as to the idea of what it means to be a man of letters (as opposed to an academic philosopher) in England. Kingsley Amis, of course, is notorious for this particular aversion – which in a fiction writer may be fair enough. But it is depressing when the likes of John Carey and Richard Cobb whose positions, as critics, academics and cultural commentators, embody the status and influence of professional intellectuals, are constantly and spuriously decrying the 'whimsies of the over-educated' and the notion that writers ought to be concerned with ideas. Throughout English cultural life a version of this attitude surfaces harmlessly and often amusingly (in the non-fiction of Raine and Julian Barnes, for example) as a kind of blokeishness. Often this is just a matter of tone which, as Martin Amis's criticism illustrates, can heighten the acuity of your perceptions; but all too often it seeps back, as it were, from the pen to the brain, coarsening your responses to what you are writing about as well as the way you write about it. In other words, the very people who are, by definition, intellectuals are always trying to pass themselves off as a bunch of lads who'd rather watch snooker with their mates than have a bit of a ding-dong with George Steiner (this style is catching).

The effect of writers' aversion to the world of ideas is to leave it vacant for academics and experts to occupy with an idiom hermetically sealed within the conference 'paper' or the Mandarin discourse of *New Left Review*. A tiny circle of people, in other words, facing each other, with their backs to the world, speaking an arcane tongue. The shrinking of the idea of the intellectual to academic or specialist is to replace common ground (where some of the most fruitful creative and intellectual work could be done) with a barren dualism. I am generalising, of course – Michael Ignatieff's *The Needs of Strangers* or Marina Warner's *Monuments and Maidens* or John Barrell's *The Dark Side of the Landscape* are excellent repudiations of this claim – but the insularity of English letters, the robust aversion to matters cerebral, breeds its opposite: a narrowly academic, élitist intolerance for everything that is felt to be inadequately 'theoretical'. (Let me confess immediately, I'm as prone as anyone to enjoy sitting in the Bar Italia, a review copy of Habermas's *The Philosophical Discourse of Modernity* lodged prominently next to my cappuccino.) Unfortunately, once an area of work has been fenced off in this way anything within it is subjected to a very different kind of reading, one immune to the pleasures of imaginative writing and jealousy hostile of any non-specialists having the temerity to stray into their terrain. John Berger, for example, is regarded with distrust by professional art historians because his highly original work lacks the gruelling theoretical grounding and painstaking research of the increasingly unreadable T.J. Clark.

The challenging promise of structuralism and deconstruction, meanwhile, has disintegrated into an alternative orthodoxy – when I see the word 'discourse' these days I reach for my Leavis – which any polytechnic lecturer worth his weight in corduroy has learnt by heart. Confronted with shelves of synoptic books by second-rate Eagletons you are struck by a depressing sense of how utterly alien is this kind of work to the spirit of reading and writing, let alone *living*, literature. It is hardly surprising, then, that an article in the *New Statesman* reassessing the importance of Roland Barthes ten years after his death dwelt almost exclusively on his contribution to semiotics, on works like *Image, Music, Text* and *Mythologies*, while dismissing the late works as 'marginal, lacking the satisfying stamp of authority'. In fact *Barthes by Barthes* (a book to be read 'as if spoken by a character in a novel'), *Camera Lucida* and *A Lover's Discourse* reveal him to be one of the great prose stylists of the century. No one held his pen as lightly or wrote with so fine a nib; no notebook can have loved the touch of ink more than Barthes's (though maybe Nabokov's index cards felt the same way). He mastered all the most difficult forms of writing – the colon, ellipses, the semicolon, italics, parentheses – to evolve a style of punctuation so uniquely his own (and there is nothing more difficult than that) that even while holding the printed book in our hands we feel we are reading his handwriting. Barthes wrote no novel but there is more imaginative daring, more originality in a page of one of his books than in any number of naturalist novels. There is also a good deal of human sympathy. Berger has said somewhere that what he responds to is the pain in Barthes, and this gets us closer to what distinguishes him than any number of semiotics seminars at the ICA. *Camera Lucida* is probably the most original and illuminating book on photography that has ever been written – but it is also a book that makes you cry.

More recently Jean Baudrillard's *America* was subjected to a similar kind of screening as reviewers sought to disentangle a social theory of America from Baudrillard's hyper-oneiric prose. Far from being reliable social theory, these hilarious postcards from Death Valley and the motel outback were better read as a form of wild, meta-fiction. (There are, incidentally, striking similarities between *America* and many of the digressive passages in Don DeLillo's *Americana*.)

I will come back to Barthes and Delillo in a moment, but first let us step sideways and consider the English predilection for irony as a narrative strategy. One of the reasons for the universal success of Kazuo Ishiguro's *The Remains of the Day* was that its ironic scheme fitted exactly with a way of reading which has simmered through two centuries of English literature, indeed was a gentle culmination of it. *The Remains of the Day* was a puzzle whose originality depended precisely on the familiarity of the kind of reading required to solve (that is, enjoy) it. This is all to Ishiguro's credit, but the way that we are so comfortable with his ironic scheme should make us wonder how *un*comfortable, how perplexed we are with the less familiar relations demanded by other forms of writing. Moreover, the opportunity cost of the symbiotic relation of literariness and narrative irony is the virtual impossibility of there being an English equivalent of Richard Ford, Tobias Woolf or Raymond Carver who together represent a similar culmination of a dominant strand of American writing. In England irony as a narrative strategy is, even in the pyrotechnics of *London Fields*, almost inevitably class-derived. Any irony in Carver and Ford, on the other hand, is so open-ended that it amounts to a kind of secular or narrative agnosticism. This is what gives Ford's prose, for example, its blue-collar existentialism, its floorboard-creaking tension. To put it in a nutshell: America enabled Ford to become an excellent writer; in England, someone of similar talents and propensities would *tend* not towards excellence but towards ever more accomplished depictions of the ironies of manners and class.

Either we temper our penchant for irony, then, or ironically we realise that we are not ironic enough. The characteristic irony of English fiction never curls back on itself, is always exempt from its own effects. The irony in DeLillo (the author of *Americana, Ratner's Star, Running Dog, White Noise, Mao II* etc.), on the other hand, is self-devouring, so steeped in the implications of its own unfolding that – as is fitting for the master of the American absurd – his prose approaches, even at its least ingenuous, a condition of utter frankness. This is exactly the pleasure to be had from the late texts of Barthes, whose example is helpful in another way. Rather than importing the works of writers like Barthes, Gaston Bachelard and Baudrillard and processing them as theory as discourse, perhaps we shall see more writers – like Gilbert Adair – internalising their daring and freedom of approach, their ironic delight in the poetry of theory. I am no fan of Derrida but I love the idea of constructing a massive philosophical work around postcards sent by a travelling salesman; I love Barthes building his great book on photography around a few pictures of his mum. If we can Anglicise this spirit of textual ingenuity then criticism will have the inventive vitality of fiction and be read with the same pleasure. As a consequence we will see the publication of more manuscripts which make readers and critics alike shake their heads, not in consternation but delight, and say: what kind of book is this? In this respect the publication a few years back of Barthes's *A Lover's Discourse* as a mass-market paperback was a cause for real jubilation.

As is the fact that we have an English writer to serve as a model: John Berger. Indeed, for me at least, the health of English letters revolves around what we make of his achievement. Because Berger has written in so many kinds of forms people tend only to glimpse his achievement in one or two incarnations. While the careers of most writers reveal a steady mastering of one form, Berger's has been marked by abrupt changes, from art criticism to the European modernism of *G*, to the documentary studies like *A Seventh Man*, to work on photography and, in the last fifteen years, to the trilogy of books on peasant life, *Into their Labours*. He has written only a few good novels – but, as with Barthes, there is more imaginative intensity in a few pages of his study of a country doctor, *A Fortunate Man*, than in most novels. Taken together his is the most varied and exciting body of work of any living English writer, a body of work that forces us to enlarge our idea of what constitutes literariness. When I wrote my book about Berger I argued that he was a great writer. I made that claim not so that his name could be writ larger in the existing map of literary reputations but because his example demands that such a map be fundamentally redrawn. His example suggests too that the contours of the map will be determined less by the kind of critical wrangling I have indulged in here than by new forms of imaginative invention. Not to attempt this topographical reshaping is to accept that in this narrow, class-bound country the most original and challenging work is to be found on the edges, the margins of English literariness.

By contrast, the task of drawing a new map for the future, of using a *new imaginative projection*, recognises that Englishness (like literariness) is not a given set of characteristics which are passively observed but a construct which, although historically rooted, is also actively perpetuated, constantly being renewed (Jonathan Raban's *Coasting* is a succinct example of how this process operates). We are free to forge our cultural identity but, to adapt Marx's famous formula, we are not free to do so under conditions of our own choosing. The conditions exist for the emergence of a *native* voice that, in an attempt to free itself from the defining characteristics of its nativity, is also animated by them.

The Film Set

Like, or so I would imagine, a lot of my fellow cinéphiles, I
confess to being sentimentally, almost tenderly, disposed to those
(rare) films which, in spite of formal and stylistic imperfections as
evident on the umpteenth as on the very first viewing, move me
more than by rights they ought to do. One such is *E la nave va*, or
And the Ship Sails On. Superficially at least, Fellini's film represents
much of what I, though in general a tenacious champion of any
director with nerve enough to repudiate the racy and populist
narrative models by which even the *cinéma d'auteur* (whatever
that now means) has been contaminated of late, still find most
queasily dislikeable about the 'art movie': a big, preprogrammed
theme (here that of the 'ship of fools') which arrives forearmed
with its own smug, narcissistic brand of humanism and which,
like the sort of person who manages to invest himself with an
aura of saintly if entirely unearned generosity by the simple
expedient of making offers of assistance so extravagant that he
need never be concerned about their being taken up by their
potential beneficiaries, tends to leave one with the sour aftertaste
of a self-serving bluff. So why, I ask myself as I watch Fellini's
pleasure liner, the *Gloria N*, an unashamedly artificial film set
immobilised between a hydraulically controlled moiré ocean and
a flagrant scene-painter's sky, its list of passengers comprising
the *crème de la crème* of pre-World War I European society, its
stowaways a boatload of Serbian refugees cast adrift on those
same bogus high seas – why am I moved practically to tears?
And I realise that it's because *the film shoot shows through*.

On the vast draught-haunted sound stages of Cinécitta, with
actors, extras, freaks, sycophants and hangers-on, the by now
familiar fauna and flora of Felliniana, seeming to enjoy absolutely
equal status with one another; with the relaxed and negligent,
on occasion infelicitous but always festive and carnivalesque *mise
en scène* of the completed work tendering the spectator what one
cannot help suspecting is a fairly transparent mirror image of
the noisy, fractious, exuberant caravanserai that was the shoot
that both preceded and engendered it; with, above all, the cast's

and crew's unanimistic faith (in the film's future, in the virtues of communal achievement, in the Maestro's own genially tyrannical presence) exuding from every pore of the screen, that Serbian invasion comes to symbolise for me the contamination of a film's textures by the very means and conditions of its production.

Every film, of course, also constitutes a documentary of its shoot, but Fellini's actually function through a sometimes latent, sometimes overt acknowledgment of filmmaking as a communal undertaking, in so far as they contrive to dissolve the immemorial distinction between those in front of the camera (the cast) and those behind it (the crew), as equally between those up there on the screen and those down here, so to speak, in the auditorium.

Possibly too much has been said and written about the cinema as a solitary, subterranean and voyeuristic medium (one not unworthy of appropriating unto itself André Breton's Surrealist definition of the sexual act as 'a sumptuous ceremony performed underground'), about the screen as a bathysphere immersing each of us, individually, in what is cavalierly referred to as our 'collective unconscious' (less a womb with a view than a whole sad wombing-house), and possibly not enough about that sense of a shared experience, that good-natured unanimism, that infuses *E la nave va*. I happen to have been involved with film, personally, as spectator and fan, as critic and (on a single occasion) scenarist, for longer than I can recall. Or, more precisely, since one Saturday afternoon in my early adolescence when, having arranged with a group of schoolchums to go and see Disney's *Robin Hood*, I slunk off instead, quite alone, as furtively as though to some pornographic movie, and for no more urgent reason than that the mnemonically alliterative name of Marilyn Monroe rang a faint but alluring bell in my head, to a cinema that was screening a garish musical in which she starred, *There's No Business Like Show Business*. (Upon such fragile stems do vocations flower.) It was in the discreet and cloistered obscurity of that auditorium that I encountered for the very first time in my life an authentic specimen of the *genus cinephilum* (an adolescent like myself who was to become, for some years thereafter, my best friend) and dimly began to understand the life-engulfing power of the magic medium.

Modern metropolitan culture is saturated with what one might call the metacinematic. These days I, for one, almost never 'go to the cinema'. Yet, even if I wished to, I seriously doubt whether I could ever really elude its tentacular influence – for the cinema now comes to me.

I regularly view films on TV, for instance: for most of us, indeed, and for good or ill, the dissemination of film history is contingent on television in exactly the way that the dissemination of the history of music has long been contingent on the record industry (and with films seen on television, as once in the cinema itself, aeons ago, when it was still a genuinely populist medium, the pleasure is that one is under no obligation to form, let alone express, an opinion). I videotape films or rent prerecorded tapes, and may divert myself by playing the same sequence again and again as though I were watching successive 'takes' on the set. I read *Cahiers du Cinéma* and *Sight and Sound* and even, for some unfathomable reason, *Variety*, that preposterous 'bible' of American showbusiness which journalists tend to cite as reverently as though it were the Bible itself. I have learned, albeit on an almost subliminal level, to decipher 'cinéliterate' TV commercials full of bogus Bogeys and James Cagney lookalikes. And, most potently of all, I have visited America – America, a metacinematic experience in itself, a veritable Homerica, an entire continent in Cinerama (of which word 'America' is a near-anagram), a living road movie, a circuitous cyberspatial tracking-shot by Wenders.

All of which, in a sense, relates to a critical commonplace, that of the cinema's intertextual and extracurricular 'discourse'. Everyone is a film buff (of sorts) nowadays; in a period of endemic imagorrhea there truly does exist a literacy and illiteracy of the image. Cinéphilia (a crude facsimile of cinéphilia) is currently an essential item in every thinking person's intellectual baggage. Columnists knowing nothing of the history, theory and sociology of the cinema, tending lazily to see the same films everyone else sees (whether *Pretty Woman* or *Cyrano de Bergerac*), toss what were once specialised terms of the initiate like 'auteur' and 'cinémathèque' into their articles with characteristic hack nonchalance. Adolescents for whom Marlon Brando is a fat old slob, and *Rebel Without a Cause* a movie made before they were born, have posters of Brando and James Dean pinned up over their beds and heads. Advertising men who have never heard of Fritz Lang get their greedy hands on *Metropolis*, which they doubtless suppose to be some daft, obscure and long since discarded piece of pulp science-fiction from the 1920s, they graft a pounding rock score on to it, colorise it, chop it up, pop it into the video microwave and, hey presto, a 'postmodern' commercial for alcohol-free lager.* The cinema, a medium to which not a few of the century's supreme artists devoted their lives, as in my rather more modest and partial way have I, has been turned into a branch of 'communications', has been hijacked, snatched from under our noses while we were looking the other way.

But if such a situation represents merely one more *fait accompli* of the rampant eclecticism, the febrile diversification, that are peculiar to contemporary culture, surely, then, there isn't too much to be done about it? And, in fact, from the cinéphile's point of view, a conspiracy of silence having been replaced by a conspiracy of noise, nothing very fundamental has changed.

Consider my own case. As it happens, I feel out of sympathy with a whole lot of modern cinema. I like fewer films than I dislike, and fewer still than those to which I am utterly indifferent. In consequence, I no longer write about film, and hardly miss doing so. Yet there is, after all, something that I do miss. I miss that Fellinian sense of a collective experience, of an autonomous community and its camaraderie. I miss the secret society, the international Masonry, that cinéphilia used to be before it was co-opted by philistines.

At the most ingenuous, infantile level I miss the *frisson* of feeling totally at ease with a lexicon to which I never needed to have recourse in a context of professional responsibility – the thrill, in other words, of airily alluding in conversation with my fellows to 'rough cuts' and 'reaction shots' and 'mike shadows' (I used to fantasise about some B-movie private eye whose name, appropriately enough, would be Mike Shadow). I miss the sensation, not of bristling outrage, but rather of complicitous

---

* In another recent commercial a young woman, promised a new job in Paris, purringly confides to the viewer her chagrin on discovering that Paris, Texas was what was meant. An amusing enough joke, you might suppose, on Wenders' movie, whose two-hour-plus narrative is in true postmodern fashion reduced to a sixty-second atmospheric vignette. But the real if unwitting joke is that, considering all the feverish fantasising that goes on in Europe about the vast and tumbleweedy perspectives of the American hinterland, with no more than a picturesquely lonely filling station or neon-lit diner *à la* Edward Hopper to break the delightful monotony, the prospect of living and working in Paris, Texas would probably strike a number of youthful, movie-mad viewers as far the more appealing of the two.

superiority, that I would enjoy when hearing a journalist mention the 'fact', as he would put it, that the medium 'has only ever had a handful of true artists' who, it would transpire, were always the same few: in the past, say, Chaplin, Eisenstein, Buñuel and Truffaut; in the present, Bergman, Kubrick, Woody Allen and Kurosawa (yes, just about everyone has seen *Kagemusha* and *Ran*, but who, other than the genuine cinéphile, has heard of Mizoguchi or Ozu, not to mention Kinoshita or Naruse?). And why did I feel superior? Because I also knew the work of Dreyer and Dovzhenko, Murnau and Paradjanov, Joseph L. Mankiewicz and Joseph H. Lewis, Fuller and Sirk, Straub and Rossellini, Hawks and Renoir, Ruiz and Terence Davies. Because I knew equally (I did not just believe, I *knew*) that *Lola Montès*, for instance, and *L'Atalante* and *Playtime* and *M* and *To Be or Not to Be* were not simply 'great films' but, by definition thereof, belonged among the greatest works of art of the century. And because I knew finally that, impoverished as is the cinema of the Nineties, notably in relation to its past, it continues to boast a more prestigious pantheon of talents than any comparable art form.

I think it would be fair to say that everyone (that is, the unavoidably élitist, middle-class 'everyone one knows' that I've already employed in this text) is moderately conversant with the history of literature, the theatre, painting and music. In this country, by contrast, those of us who love or have loved the cinema have always been sociocultural outsiders and mavericks; film has always been an art apart, the victim of a form of ostracism which has at least had the virtue of preventing the medium's continuously revised history from ever setting, as it were, from ever congealing into the sterile orthodoxy of the museum. In the recent past it was, with very, very rare exceptions, an object of contemptuously unconcealed suspicion to the British intelligentsia; today, like so many intellectual hovercrafts, sociologists, mythologists and stylologists go skimming over its glittering surface without ever submerging themselves in its depths. But because, as a result, the cinema has always been obliged to demand from its now doubtless dwindling band of devotees a real adventurism in discernment and choice, because, film by film, scene by scene, shot by shot if need be, its authentic values and traditions have been subjected to permanent interrogation and debate, it survived the conspiracy of silence with which it was surrounded in the past and it will survive the current conspiracy of noise.

I myself have naturally had less direct hands-on experience of film-making than anyone for whom it has been a vocation or profession, but rather more, certainly, than that potential reader, 'the next man'. Yet, whether filmmakers or film critics, actors or spectators, best boys or grips, we are all, each according to our lights, the defenders of the faith and the guardians of a flickering flame; whatever our differences, we all know something that those who have not loved the cinema do not know; we all belong, and should feel proud to belong, to what I like to call the film set.

BEN OKRI

Of Poets and their Antagonists

The poet is he who inspires far more
than he who is inspired. — PAUL ELUARD

ONE

The world in which the poet has to live does not necessarily
yield up the poetic. In the hands of the poet, the world is
resistant. It is only with the moulding and the searching that
the unyielding world becomes transformed in a new medium of
song and metaphor.

It is not surprising therefore that poets seem to be set against
the world. The poet needs to be up at night, when the world sleeps;
needs to dwell in odd corners, where Tao is said to reside; needs
to exist in places where spiders forge their webs in silence; near
the gutters, where the underside of our dreams fester. Poets need
to live where others don't care to look, and they need to do this
because if they don't they can't sing to us of all the secret and
public domains of our lives. They need to be multiple figures
round the central masquerades of reality in order to register to
us fully the unimaginable dimensions of the deity's terrible and
enchanting dance.

The great tidal crowds of everyday events pour in one direction, the poet has to move in the other – sometimes moving
directly against them, at other times cutting tangentially across
the morning waves of humanity. The poet seems to be set against
the world because we need him to always show us the falseness
of our limitations, the true extent of our kingdom.

The poet turns the earth into mother, the sky becomes a
shelter, the sun an inscrutable god, and the pragmatists get
irritated: they want the world to come with only one name, one
form. The antagonists of poets and transformants are those who
refuse to see the fluid nature of reality, who cannot perceive that
each individual reality is a different one. Laws do not bind our
perceptions. There are as many worlds as there are lives. It is not
those who have no imagination who are the problem: for that is a
fallacy; we all possess imagination, few of us use it. The problem
is with those who are frightened of the rather unlimited validity
of the imagination, frightened of those who continually extend

the boundaries of the possible, those who ceaselessly re-dream the world and re-invent existence; frontiersmen of the abyss and the uncharted. The enemies of poets are those who have no genuine religious thinking – and by that I do not mean institutionalised religion. To be truly religious requires a sense of terror, compassion, imagination, and a belief in more than three dimensions. Religion touches us at the place where imagination blends into the divine. Poetry touches us where religion is inseparable from the wholly human. In heaven there could be no poetry. The same is true of hell. It is only on a sphere where heaven and hell are mixed into the fabric of mortal frame that poetry is possible.

The poet is set against the world because he cannot accept that what there seems to be is all that there is. Elias Canetti wrote somewhere that: 'The inklings of poets are the forgotten adventures of God.' Poets are not really the unacknowledged legislators of the world. They come with no tablets of stone, and they do not speak to God. They speak to us. Creation speaks to them. They listen. They remake the world in words, from dreams. Intuitions which could only come from the secret mouths of gods whisper to them through all of life, of nature, of visible and invisible agencies. Storms speak to them. Thunder breathes on them. Human suffering forever drives them. Flowers move their pens. Words themselves speak to them and bring forth more words. The poet is the widener of the consciousness. The poet suffers our agonies and combines them with all the forgotten waves of childhood. Out of the mouths of poets speak the yearnings of our lives.

The legislators of the world take the world as given. They dislike mysteries, for mysteries cannot be coded, or legislated, and wonder cannot be made into laws. And so these legislators police the accepted frontiers of things. Politicians, Heads of States, soldiers, the rich, the powerful, kings, religious ministers – they all fancy themselves the monarchs of this earthly kingdom. They speak to us of facts, policies, statistics, programmes, abstract and severe moralities. But the dreams of the people are beyond them, and would frighten them. In the world of the real they would be lost and terrified. It is they who have to curb the poet's vision of reality. It is they who invoke the infamous 'poetic licence' whenever they do not want to face the inescapable tragedy contained in, for example, Okigbo's words: 'I have lived the oracle dry on the cradle of a new generation'. It is they who demand that poetry be partisan, that it takes sides, usually their side; that it rides on the back of causes and issues, their causes, their issues, whoever they may be.

Our lives have become narrow enough as they are. Our dreams strain to widen them, to bring to our waking consciousness the sense of greater discoveries that lie just beyond the limits of our sights. We must not force our poets to limit the world any further. That is a crime against life itself. If the poet begins to speak only of narrow things, of things that we can effortlessly digest and recognise, of things that do not disturb, frighten, stir, or annoy us, or make us restless for more, make us cry for greater justice, make us want to set sail and explore inklings murdered in our youths, if the poet sings only of our restricted angles and in restricted terms and exclusively with restricted language, then what hope is there for any of us on this or any other planet?

Those of us who want this are cowards, in flesh and in spirit. We fear heroic heights. We dread the recombining of the world, dread a greater harvest of being. We sit lazily and demand that our poets draw the horizon closer. Water bursting suddenly into multicoloured spray represents for us something vaguely frightening. We no longer recognise who we are, and have forgotten what we used to be, what states we sometimes inhabited during phases of an extended moment of awareness. It is those who are scared of reality, of their own truths, of their own histories, those who are secretly sickened by what they have become, who are alarmed by the strange mask-like faces that peer back at them from the mirrors of time, it is they who resist the poetic. They resist the poetic with all their hidden might because if they don't, the power of words speaking in their own heads would burst open their inner doors, and all the monsters breeding within would come bounding out and crashing on the floors of their consciousness. What would hold their inner frames together then? They have to suppress the poetic, or accept it only on blurred terms, or promote its cruder imitations, for the simple reason that they have long ago begun suppressing eruptive life and all its irreconcilable shadings, its natural paradoxes.

The antagonists of poetry cannot win. The world seems resistant, but it carries within it forever the desire to be transformed into something higher. The world may seem unyielding but, like certain forces in the air, it merely awaits imagination and will to unloosen the magic within itself. The poet is not a creator, but an alchemist. Poets are helplessly on the side of greater forces, the greatest causes, the highest and the most just future.

And because they are helplessly on the side of the future it may be valid to say that they need their antagonists. The American Indians have a saying: 'May your enemy be strong.' The hardening arteries of our lives are our greatest enemies: that is perhaps why prophets speak out with such incandescent, irrepressible concern at what we are doing to ourselves. In that sense all prophets have something of the poet; not all poets are prophets. The poet as quantum physicist, as healer, as angel and demonologist of the word cannot afford to disdain the world, cannot feel superior to it any more than the scientist can feel superior to thunder, to mountains, or to the constellations. There are no superiorities of functions, only ascendencies. The poet's love shows in the quality of his dreams and his works. The deeper he feels, the deeper is his exploration. The more we want to reconnect, the more we would follow poets in their quest for impossible transformations. They measure the heroism of the consciousness of any age. It is true when they say that poets are never ahead of their times. It is only we who are far behind ours.

TWO

Hunger is an antagonist. Different kinds of hunger. Society can be described as the sphere in which all our hungers meet, as in a great chaotic marketplace. The poet's hunger is our hunger, which is for more life. We all feel that terrible pull sometimes. We are all being herded down, deceived along illusory highways which seem to lead nowhere except, only, to the grave. Did we choose our roads? Did our roads choose us? Did we arrive on them by proxy?

We all feel that pull sometimes, that pull that connects us to Dante's 'love that moves the sun and stars'. And sometimes it comes when we are least prepared, when we are most naked, asleep. It comes in silence. It comes in the dead of night. It comes like Rilke's armies of reality, the armies that besiege 'undisturbed cities', the ones that lie 'outside the walls like a countryside,' and who 'send no one into the city to threaten/or promise, and no one to negotiate.' Yes, sometimes it comes at night. And we awake, sweating. We do not know why, or what, has awoken us. Why have we awoken? What has caused this disturbance of our sleep?

We get out of bed. We wander round the house, to see if everything is all right. Nothing stirs. Everything sleeps. The world snores gently. We try to return to sleep, but the question nags us: why have we woken up? When was the last time we woke suddenly like this for no visible reason? And then gradually, if we are lucky, we realise that something seemingly silent in our lives is trying to speak to us. We realise that we have been woken for the strange and simple reason of having our sleep disturbed. A great fear, or a great yearning, has been forming in us. We cannot tell when it began. We do not know how to deal with the undeciphered terror or fill the sudden emptiness, the foreboding. We may have become aware over the last few days that the sky has been slowly eclipsed by the accumulation of our daily worries, or our deadening habits. Human faces might have been increasingly taking on the polarised forms of those who are for us or those who are against us. They seem more against us. We no longer see the world. We've stopped looking. We no longer marvel at something beautiful. We've stopped noticing. We can't really remember the last time we experienced the quickening of the unknown. The realisations drive away sleep. Something vaguely disconcerting is growing in us, occupying more space, like a sense of guilt freed suddenly from the shackles of our wilful forgetting. Then we might begin to suspect that somewhere, somehow, we took the wrong turning, went up the wrong road. We might have done that a long time ago, in the midst of our confusions. And now we might have travelled far into an undesired destination. Now, in the night, surrounded by the magnifying energies of silence, we look around and we don't recognise either the road or the destination. When did we take the wrong turning? What road were we travelling down in the first place? After some reflection we suspect that it was a branching off from the unsignposted road of youth, that road lined with anxieties and promises, vague notions of a splendid future without too much work, in which the world could have shone with a thousand pleasant colours, in which songs burned the heart with desire, in which our sensations flared brightly.

You turn on the bed: it feels rough. You wonder how you could ever sleep on the same bed, night after night. It feels a little like a limiter of your estate. You get up. You tread the house. The floor doesn't yield. The walls are solid – they don't look as if the armies of reality that Rilke wrote about could break them down in silence. But you look around your room with strange eyes. When did you settle into this? When did your abode become your shell? The house seems unfamiliar, as if it belonged to a stranger who had settled in hastily and never taken the trouble to live in it properly and utilise all its dimensions. Your property, at this moment, looks as if it's all on loan. The house fairly rebukes you. It is one of the turnings. The house, the room, has become your road. You wander deeper into its hidden disintegrations. Everywhere all your dreams are fading, have faded. Photographs of you mock you with their fixity.

You make yourself a drink. Something turns in you. Something seeps into your heart. And then, in an instant, without warning, you remember faces that have disappeared in the turnings you took to avoid being like them. You remember your early dreams, your youthful boasts. You remember those you no longer see. Where are they now? What has the world done to them?

You move in your chair. It creaks. Your life creaks under your weight, slowly giving up the ghost. You try to remember yourself in your best moments. The pictures are dim. The vanities of your triumphs fairly unsettle you with their relative insignificance. Viewing yourself now with the severity you reserve only for others, you suddenly conceive a vague dislike towards yourself. You wonder how you wound up the person you are. Attempting to rally some dignity, you repeat your achievements to yourself in a slightly pompous *sotto voce*. This doesn't improve the unease, the sitting sideways in yourself. What you think you've achieved diminishes as you name them. You ask yourself: what have I done that could outlive me, that could become more beautiful with the merciless clarification of time, that sits quietly in my soul, further aids to greater discoveries? You can't think of any. You sigh. Something sinks in you. Something sad. You are overcome with the absurd notion that your life could be different. You're not sure how or in what way.

Your drink is now definitely lukewarm. You begin to think of trivialities. Your mind, unwilling to face the full implications of your truths, takes the first by-road you can deceive yourself into. You wander down one of the by-roads. You think of finance. You think of something someone said yesterday, something small, but which stung your vanity a little. What did they mean by that remark anyway? You move again in your chair. You realise that your unease is slipping away from you. Your incomprehension is giving way to a petty state of recriminations. There you are, woken by a nameless yearning, a feeling which if followed to its naked conclusion could change your life: and now you begin to find being awake a little boring. I could think these thoughts in the morning, you say to yourself. And this nakedness, this feeling, which lurks at the roots of poetry, conversion, intuition, change – this deceptive gift of the spirit which does its best to warn you, to throw signs at you, is suppressed, eclipsed, by vanity. Saul Bellow was right when he wrote: 'It's too bad, but suffering is about the only reliable burster of the spirit's sleep.'

Your drink, meanwhile, has turned cold. You reach for your slippers. They slide from your toes' grasp. You look at them and somewhat forcefully shove your feet into them. You take the cup to the kitchen, satisfying a lower sense of order. You put the lights off in each room. Nothing feels so strange anymore. It all looks familiar. You recognise it all. You built it thus. You set it up thus. This is your life. It's better, you think, than what millions of people have. As you cross the sitting room you take in the symmetries of the place. Maybe I'll change the curtains, you say out loud. Or get some new carpets. Your eyes fall on the bookshelf. Another time, you think. You put out the light, feeling a little more settled in yourself, a little more at home, a little diminished, but you can't understand why.

It may be that what you *could be* haunts you. It is real. It is a weight you have to carry around. Each failure to become, to be, is a weight. Each state you could inhabit is a burden as heavy as any physical weight, but more so, because it weighs on your soul. It is the ghost of your possibilities hanging round your neck, an invisible albatross, potentials unknowingly murdered. If you could inhabit a higher state, the higher being you could *be* also sits on you, increasing the tensions of your spirit, your moods, your irritations.

And so feeling diminished, and having paradoxically gained a greater burden, you go to bed. But you don't sleep immediately. Repressed faces, forgotten words, replies you failed to deliver in a split second to someone's comment, dance round across your mind. In fact that night you don't sleep soundly at all. That is how in secret moments we repress and deny the poetic. That is how we murder our dreams. Then we carry the suppression of the poetic into our waking lives and wreak our vengeance on the world.

Having avoided a self-confrontation, and being more pompous
in our waking hours for the self-diminishment of our secret ones,
that is how we become the antagonists of poets – enemies of the
widening of the world towards a vaster, more wondrous reality.
That is how we narrow the world's sense of wonder. Antagonists
of poets are among the life-haters, for whom Dante has a special
place in a circle of the Inferno.

THREE

Poets sing for all the world in one breast. They sing for all those
who need its unique nourishment. They may choose to align
themselves with the wretched and the voiceless of this planet.
They may not. But they must draw to themselves cosmic aid, for
their mandate is a relentless and demanding one, as rigorous as
conscience and as elusive as freedom. They could, if they choose
(and their choice is dictated by the quality of their love) – they
could choose to breathe unease on complacency, stir life forces
against injustice, help the blind to see, and, to appropriate what
Pascal said about the parables of Christ, to blind those who can
see. Where there is misery they might be moved to soothe, to stir,
to sing of revolt, to spread hope and deeper dreams of liberation.
The Bible says it clearly: 'For want of vision my people perish.'
A people die not only from hunger and famine, they die also
from spiritual undernourishment, spiritual kwashiorkor, spiritual
AIDS. For at any given time and place there are many inner
selves to feed and we do not have enough good poets to feed us.
Socrates was deeply aware of this when he said: 'There are many
wand-bearers, but few inspired.' The poets who could be better
than good, who breathe their words gusts of an incandescent and
higher oxygen over the lands, wage an unending battle with the
antagonists within and without. Few of these poets come through a
lifetime's struggle, their visions of hell, and can say in their works,
like Homer's Odysseus, and with that fearful Delphic clarity: 'I
have heard the songs of sirens.'

Poets, be cunning. Learn some of the miracles. Survive. Weave
your transformations in your life as well as in your work. Live!
Stay alive! Don't go under, don't go mad, don't let them define
you, or confine you, or buy your silence. If they do confine you,
burst out from their prisons with wilder fatidical songs. Be a
counter-antagonist, break their anti-myths. Where the enemies

breed destructions, sow seeds of startling lights. Keep sowing. Time will reap. Weave your songs by whatever means you can. 'What doesn't kill us makes us stronger,' wrote Nietszche. There is no reason why the poet, who is naturally possessed of a strange and frightening intelligence, cannot survive as well as the politician, or the banker. Don't become a dying breed. Dare to stick around for the hard and beautiful harvest. We need you even as we antagonise you. Remember: it is from the strength of your antagonists that you derive your greater authority. They make it absolutely necessary for you to be more than yourself. Follow Melville's precept, which he had nailed to his writing desk: 'Be true to the dreams of thy youth.' In reality the whole of life is on your side – we would say so after your untimely and much lamented death. Only then would we crow about how much we miss the uniqueness of your voice, your duende, your temperament, your demanding presence.

Poets, be like the tortoise: bear the shell of the world and still manage to sing your transforming dithyrambs woven from our blood, our pain, our loves, our history, our blindness. The lonely and inescapable truth simply is that this is the only kingdom you will ever have. This is the home of your song.

Logical Conclusions

In a crowd awaiting deportation to a concentration camp, a man witnessed the following scene. A Nazi soldier approached a woman who was wearing a large shawl. He pulled the shawl open to find a baby hidden beneath it. He yanked the baby from her arms, threw it on the ground, and shot it.

This is what war is. The murder of women's children. Funnily enough, men treat it as a game. American reporters, holed up in a Baghdad hotel, marvelled at the REAL NOISE of missile explosions, as if it were a NATURAL phenomenon, as if it were the Aurora Borealis! British newsmen held forth on the radio and on TV, on and on, in endless hours of endless speculation, swivelling in their swivel seats as they watched the world crumbling beneath them and let it happen. They questioned and examined the progress of the war in infinite detail, infantile detail, only breaking off for football results. In some confused men's brains, the football results were almost equivalent to the results of the Iraq war.[1] For it was all about male conflict, and in the end it doesn't matter what you're fighting for, be it a football, an oil field or the Rights of MAN. What interests them is the sense of a male struggle. They watch with baited breath to see which rutting stag will win.

They want women off the scene at such times, for women add a cynical note.[2] After all, it doesn't much matter to women which rutting stag wins – biological necessity necessitates that we carry on our biological necessaries with whichever victor turns up.[3] Who catches the ball therefore, or the country, is not of particular concern to women. They are busy tending their children. They are busy tending the children that wanton men kill for their sport.

How can someone pull a baby from its mother's arms, throw a baby to the ground? How can someone SHOOT a baby?

While men on their swivel seats, in their cockpits, speculate about the next duel, women silently speculate on this.

For women, during wartime, are deprived of a voice.[4] No one wants to hear their half-hearted patriotism at such a time, their attachment to life, their appallingly apolitical willingness to be

RED rather than DEAD. Women send their sons to war and receive them home in body bags: such people are unlikely to have a cool, calm and collected approach to the strategic intricacies, the sadistic delicacies of war.

'I've forgotten what it's like to get up in the morning without a dead weight inside me,' said one soldier's mother at the end of the Gulf conflict. But men enjoyed the war. They needed to enjoy it and convince others to enjoy it. This is the only way to whip up enough fuzzy-headed fervour to keep a bloody war afloat.[5] They couldn't bear to let the war die out without a satisfying climax, after all that boring foreplay. Men were turned on by each other's gusto. Blood on their hands makes politicians feel important. And throughout it all they claimed, yes, they claimed that it was for a good cause.

What, you mean Saddam Hussein will be removed from power? Of course. You mean a wholesome leader, democratically elected and all that, will be installed in Kuwait? Natch. And the Palestinian question will finally be answered? Well. You mean you're going to begin a global emancipation programme, saving people from belligerent tyrants? Selectively perhaps. You mean America is not a hypocrisy, run by cynical imperialists, voted for by mentally deficient cinema-goers? Of course not. You mean war is in this particular case necessary and legit and useful and healthy and humanitarian and sensible and that you won't kill any more people than you ABSOLUTELY HAVE TO? Yes, they said, as they bombed Baghdad to smithereens.

Where are they all cowering now, these idealists? Back in front of the telly, watching sports.[6]

Have you BEEN to America lately? It's like the fall of the Roman Empire. Everyone is so FAT. Life is just a matter of cramming enough whopper dinners into yourself to achieve a blissful insensibility. This is the typical state of the people assessing President Bush's performance.[7] The country is doomed anyway, being a huge amoeba unaware of what's going on from one part of itself to the other. Full of people digesting the entire contents of the *Salem News* or the *Klondike Falls Review*. People in Massachusetts never hear about what Teddy Kennedy gets up to outside the state! The most attuned do a few good deeds for the poor; these mainly consist of bundling up FOOD. Thus, eventually perhaps the poor too will become bloated and lethargic, and then the crime rate might go down.

It is the only place in the world where fat people can feel comfortable. Why, in America, fat people even get married! Fat people do all the things thin people usually do (except maybe a little slower). They have jobs. They relax HALF NAKED on beaches.

In England people treat fat people as if they're perpetually on a diet. It is patently obvious by your size that you have thoroughly failed to keep your weight under control, yet they are convinced it must be your utmost concern not to eat too much! They APOLOGISE for feeding you.[8] But in America, and this is perhaps all that can be said for the place, you can be fat and actually overeat in public without anyone displaying surprise, embarrassment, or revulsion. Hollywood be damned! THIS is the only truly seductive thing about America. (It's in fact a *post*-diet society: they talk only of cholesterol and plastic surgery.)[9]

In England, people are still theoretically CAPABLE of thought, but they don't bother. They tend towards complacency. They know they have nothing to be complacent about anymore (unlike Americans, who are told daily how great their country is[10]). So they have to keep creating complacency out of nothing. They search tirelessly for status quo. They leap fearlessly backwards, towards tradition. If there have been boys' schools in which all sorts of sexual shenanigans go on, let there continue to be boys' schools in which, etc. Class differences must be inevitable, since they have existed for some time. If men have been raping their wives for centuries, they must have had good reason. If we've spent so much money on defence, let's kill some people and make it worthwhile. And Englishmen have recently started gloating magnanimously on the supposed progress made by feminists as if, there there, you've had your fun, made your mark, and now you can desist!

It all comes back to women. Because it all comes back to that Nazi who threw the baby on the ground and shot it. Because men have power and no sense. Because women have no voice. Because women are more frequently obese. Because men think war is sport. Because men like war. Because men like sport. Because a man can do something a woman would never do: throw a baby down and shoot it. Because I know this. Because I have my own swivel seat and can secretly speculate, and now and then find my voice.[11]

NOTES ON THE TEXT

1. The early morning news on BBC Radio 4, on the day the Gulf war seemed to have ended, stuck exclusively to the subject of the war – lives lost, atrocities committed, fears raised – until a few minutes before 7:30. This priority slot might well have been reserved for domestic affairs or some such. But no. The second most important topic of the world turned out to be football. Thus, unconsciously, or through mere indifference, the programme revealed the age-old connection between sports and war, presenting them as interchangeable and equally entertaining.

Men are dangerous amoral people. And the end result of all their news reporting is numbness, foolishness and indifference.

2. Men don't want to share the stage with women when anything dramatic is happening. Take my daughter's first History of Britain book (*Please* take it). Women don't seem to have existed, according to this, until the Celts started building proper homes for them. Women apparently had nothing to do with the first million years of human life.

When the going gets tough, only men have a voice, a say in what the next step for humanity will be. Women are allowed to surface when there are fewer questions in the air. They express their peculiar views in high unauthoritative voices, perhaps accompanied by a song or a dance, and then disappear again under the weight of history.

3. Why else are women attracted to so many different types of men? (Speak for yourself, ducky.) We're much more accepting of their imperfections and idiosyncrasies than they are of ours – we make no decisions about whether we like them old or young, big or petite.*

---

* This easy-going nature doesn't stretch to the matter of shorts. No woman can be expected to endure the sight of a man in an unfortunate pair of shorts, especially of the Bermuda variety. In Britain, it is possible to get thoroughly involved with someone before ever seeing what he looks like in shorts. Then one fine day, after some rummaging around in carrier bags, out he'll come, shameless and unabashed, without a by-your-leave sporting legs which suddenly seem overly hairy or hairless, shrimpy, pimply, skimpy, craggy or straggly. There is often an unpleasant pallor about them.

Is it not odd that, between solid months or years spent shrouding these unlikeable limbs in fault-obscuring trousers, men have such unforeseen spasms of assuming that their legs are somehow acceptable and indeed *deserve* to be displayed?

For instance, there was a guy who liked to fuck me every eighteen months or so (this ensured the necessary coolness on my part). The experience was so infrequent it took years for me to distinguish a pattern, and no future.

Then there's the nice young man who wrecked my bicycle. I do not know whether or not, or how, or *why*, to seek compensation. He is too nice and too young and too handsome for me. People find their equals in attractiveness – it's some sort of rough-justice narcissism. People assess potential mates according to their estimation of their own charms. All they want is someone similarly upmarket or downmarket, upbeat, downbeat.

It's a pact: if you don't criticise my buck-teeth, I'll marry you despite your jowls.

4.   Many women were fired from national newspapers during the Gulf war, and few were allowed to mouth on about anything much on TV. I certainly wasn't. But I admit I wasn't fired either. But since I didn't have a job on a national newspaper, that doesn't count for much.

5.   In this rhetorical extravagance, the author seems to have created some sort of apocalyptic hovercraft!?

6.   My ex-husband, a sports-lover, bestirs himself once in a while (except during the cricket season) to come on a train to see his daughter. I pick him up at the station and drop them off at a museum or cinema, a three-minute journey during which he gets so comfortable in my car that it takes him five minutes to remove himself. Add to that the automatic three minutes required to extract the kid from the back seat. I keep the engine running throughout this operation. The extra pollution is regrettable, but otherwise it might take them fifteen minutes to get out of the car.

He leaves his briefcase with me for safe keeping and usually doesn't even bother to feed her during their outing.

7.   The top guys in the government are kept trim, to give the more alert citizens the impression that it is *not* the fall of the Roman Empire.

8.   They suggest ways in which you can work it off! Eyebrows go up when you ask for more, though you're only trying to be polite. Thus they feed your eternal resentment. You soon want to eat *them*.

9.   Of course I shouldn't have gone. I returned to find my house had been occupied in my absence by numerous people I had not

agreed to when originally trying to procure cat-sitters. One guy decided to invite his daughter down from Yorkshire for a week. I do not even know his daughter. Someone else kept turning the temperature gauge on the Aga up and down, as if it were some form of central heating. When the thing eventually stopped heating at all, they complained to my landlord that it was too cold to live here, and proceeded to call a repairman from a company we no longer deal with. Not bothering to be in when he called, they left a key outside under a stone and a blank cheque on the kitchen table, which the repairman duly filled out for an ungodly sum.

A good time was apparently had by all. I found a pubic hair on my TEA-COSY!? The spoons, flung willy-nilly into the cutlery drawer, seemed to have been LICKED clean. And the cat was a nervous wreck.

10. The American flag is treated as a sacred object. There are very complicated ways of folding it into ever-decreasing triangles without letting it touch the ground. If it does touch the ground whilst you are folding it or unfolding it, you go to jail and the flag has to be burnt! That's one crazy country.

11. The author's evident emotion here dissipates her customary objectivity. In her saner moments she is aware that womanhood is no fountain of virtue, nor the answer to all ills. But neither is objectivity. The deadpan, factual approach of men to world events has led to a dullness in our response to such events. Breaking into sorrowful news to give the football results breeds contempt for suffering by miniaturising or at least containing it. The time has come. The time has come for the personalisation of world events – since there is nothing of bigger importance to the individual than a personal event.

Interviews

interviewed by Christopher Bigsby

Martin Amis has a moralist's fascination with the corruption of values, taste, style, form. His early books, *The Rachel Papers* (1973), *Dead Babies* (1975) and *Success* (1979), took a special relish in exploring adolescent and post-adolescent sexuality in a society itself sliding into an aimless materialism. *Money* (1984) extended the setting to America and showed the author at his most stylistically confident. Martin Amis writes a vivid prose, self-consciously distinctive. The apocalyptic mood, evident in the early books and not wholly unconnected with a neurasthenic style, intensified with a volume of short stories, *Einstein's Monsters* (1987) and more particularly with *London Fields* (1989), an allegorical response to the pathology of a nuclear age. His latest book, *Time's Arrow*, shifts that apocalyse back in time to the concentration camps of World War Two, though still searching for a humour born out of disproportion and irony.

CWEB   You bounced around a good deal in terms of education early on. What sort of effect do you think that had on you?

MA   I think it makes you good at ingratiation, basically. It became quite a regular ordeal, the first day at school. Your first challenge is to avoid getting beaten up, then to pick out the more powerful figures, bribe and then win their friendship with cigarettes, jokes or cash payments, whatever is necessary, really. I think it makes you alert socially: you are aware of where the power resides and it makes you: quite expert at self-preservation.

CWEB   Did it alienate you from the whole business of study?

MA   Perhaps it did, at first. I was very, very far behind and in my teens, in my quite late teens, I was still getting an O level a year. Then once I was in the right kind of place I did it all very quickly. So, yes, excitement and distraction and fear are not very conducive to study.

CWEB   Children tend to react against their parents when they are plotting their future. Did you go through a phase like that?

MA No, I think I was rather distastefully emulative. Certainly in my teens for a while I took on some of my father's politics, found myself championing the Vietnam war, for instance; and I thought a writer would be a good thing to be. All I can say is that I conceived the notion of being a writer before I really knew what kind of writer my father was. He could have been writing westerns or supermarket romances or sex and shopping novels for all I knew. Then when I read him I thought, yes, this is very much the kind of thing I would be interested in. So there was no real rebellion period, although our politics are now very different. A reviewer of my first novel said that one way of exorcising the influence would be through imitation, and that, probably, is the way I did it.

CWEB How old were you when you first read his books?

MA Eighteen or nineteen.

CWEB If you go into a library or a bookstore you are going to find your books right alongside your father's books. On the face of it they seem very different from one another. Do they share anything?

MA I think they share a very great deal. If our birth dates had been transposed I would probably have written something like his novels and he might well have written something like mine. The difference is just one of time.

CWEB You mean that you are both tuning in to a cultural tone and mode.

MA Yes, very much, and with the same kind of manner of perception: humorous, slightly mock epic, describing low things in a high voice, and a bit the other way round. But I am writing about a different world and that's it; the big difference between us is the kind of world we are writing about. I think after a certain point a writer disengages from what is really happening in the world and the real world actually looks not only strange but inimical. V.S.Pritchett can't really write about 1991; he writes about a sort of frozen world that existed 20 or 30 years ago. My father put it well the other day when he said that young writers are always saying to older writers, 'It's not like that any more, it's like this,' and it is not a smooth transition. The quote on the back of *Lucky Jim* from Somerset Maugham goes something like this: 'There is a whole new generation of people coming up to the universities from provincial England. Mr Amis's ear is so acute and his eye so sharp that he has captured them exactly.' That is where the quote ends but in the original piece by Maugham the next sentence is: 'They are scum.' I don't know if Maugham had a hand in giving *Lucky Jim* the Somerset Maugham Award, but he saw that my father was talented. On the other hand he hated Jim Dixon and his world. So the figures produced by the next generation are going to seem threatening and repulsive to the established generation and that is why I get on with my father's novels much more easily than he gets on with mine.

CWEB So he is reacting not so much to the novels as to the world the novels are portraying.

MA Yes, and the way that it is portrayed. He can't bear any kind of post-modernist trickiness, for instance; he just completely closes off at that, and I don't blame him in a way. I think post-modernism – this drawing attention to the fact that you are writing a novel – can be and is very annoying to many readers. I do it, but I hope I do it pointfully and amusingly. Otherwise I am wasting my time. But I can understand a certain sense that indecorum has taken place and my father definitely feels that very strongly.

CWEB You are both comic novelists, but is your comedy the same?

MA Pretty close, I think. I think his positive value against which the comedy is played is different from mine. If we could sum it up in a word I would say his positive value is decency and my positive value is innocence. And there is quite a distance between those two notions. Also, I have a sense, which I don't think he has, of a much greater precariousness: I have lived all my life in a kind of modern world and he at least has a prelapsarian period, pre-Second World War, when the planet was very much younger and more innocent, and he is rooted in that and I am rooted in the precariousness of the modern world.

CWEB I am interested that you use the word 'innocent' because it always seems to me that there is a kind of romanticism about you. You are drawn to excess, you are fascinated by degradation, but underneath all this is a nostalgia for innocence.

MA Absolutely. The satire or the comedy wouldn't take unless something of value lay behind it. It strikes me as a self-evident truth, and extra self-evident in the modern age, that the world gets less innocent every day. That is a fact about life: experiences accumulate and attack innocence. History attacks innocence.

CWEB Could you ever see yourself writing a novel in which sexuality was accommodated to simple affection and love was not debased or corrupted: a lyrical, celebratory novel?

MA I don't think so, partly because comedy has no business in that area. It's remarkably hard to make happiness work on the page. Happiness writes white. Perhaps only Tolstoy has made happiness thrilling to read about, an incredible achievement, but not one easily repeated and certainly not easily repeated by a comic writer.

CWEB Jane Austen managed both, didn't she? Irony co-existing with a kind of innocence.

MA Except that it's all wrapped up very quickly, isn't it? Complication is what she is mostly writing about. And then you get those rather contented little afterwords – 'Elizabeth is still shrewish, on occasion,' 'Jane is as forgetful as ever' – or something like that, which Nabokov in *Despair* parodies very amusingly and affectionately. It is all done in the coda and really what she thrives on, and what the reader twists and squirms for, are the misunderstandings, the complications. George Eliot, I think, comes closer to celebrating the happy life. But it sometimes strikes me that the reason comedy, or at least my comedy, is so odd is that comedy is really having to do it *all* these days. The tragic voice has lost its slot on the register; the heroic, the epic, are not really very plausible voices for modern fiction. And the comedy is full of things that shouldn't really be there, like rape and murder and child-abuse, real sin and evil. The comic novelist, of course, doesn't work things out with the strictness of the tragic writer, he doesn't reward and punish and convert; all he can do with these evils is laugh them off the stage. But some things come in that can't be laughed off the stage. I say this having just finished a short novel that is about the paradigmatic unlaughable-off-the-stage matter, which is the Jewish Holocaust of the Second World War. And yet I find that although I am not looking for the funny side of the Holocaust, there isn't a funny side of the Holocaust, I am still writing what is basically a comedy of some kind, a sort of anti-comedy, perhaps. Irony and indirection and humour are still the only things you have to work with. I would maintain that whatever else it was the Nazi project was thoroughly ridiculous.

CWEB Do you feel nervous about approaching a subject like the Holocaust and accommodating it to literary purposes? I am thinking about someone like William Styron and *Sophie's Choice* which still gives me a considerable sense of unease.

MA I hated that book. Primo Levi talks about the dangers of literary lechery when writing fiction about the Holocaust and I think that *Sophie's Choice* commits that sin and many others and it is just not well written. When you start a book like this you are terrified by what George Steiner is going to think of you. I was astonished that this was my subject. If you had asked me two years ago whether I could write about the Holocaust, something I had long been interested in, I would have said that I was perhaps the least qualified living writer to do it. But once you have got over that you have to say to yourself, very early on, that I bring what I bring to this subject. I can't become another kind of writer because of the subject.

CWEB The accusation, I suppose, is that you get a free emotional ride by attaching yourself to such a subject. It is almost as though you wanted to be a Jewish novelist, that there is a subject out there to which you would like access.

MA Well, it is interesting that the only comic novel written about the Holocaust was written not by a Jew but by a German-American, Kurt Vonnegut, a man whose parents and grandparents were German-speakers, and who fought against the Nazis in World War II. I didn't really worry about that at all. I very, very much didn't want to give offence to anyone. I suppose when I was re-writing it for the second time I included, as you do, various cheap shots, but I am definitely going to reserve the right to take them out. I suppose I will be sanitising myself a little bit when in due course I do take them out. But they would be like second-rate metaphors that you would expunge anyway. Three of the first half a dozen people who read it were Jewish and I was more anxious about their response than about any immediate Gentile response. It inhibited me perhaps one or two per cent when I was writing it.

CWEB Are there any doors through which the writer of fiction cannot pass?

MA I might well have said this one until I did it. The 'Do Not Enter' sign is certainly up on this subject but there aren't any 'Do Not Enter' signs. There can't be any more. My father would say there is a 'Do Not Enter' sign on the bedroom door. Other writers might say there is one on the bathroom door. I think they are all notional and to be ignored. You have to have good reason. You don't swagger in there just for the hell of it. You have to have something to say, but that is up to you to decide.

CWEB If I can take you back, you began as a literary journalist. Is that profession wholly different from the writing of fiction?

MA Well, I began writing with right and left hand simultaneously. In fact I started writing a novel before I did a book review, but it does feel like left hand, right hand. It is very different with fiction, it is your own world you create. It doesn't have to be a certain length, written at a certain time, for a certain editor, for a certain paper, for a certain audience. On the other hand, a profile is a kind of short story in a way because as you are entering someone's force field, so to speak, you inevitably foreground yourself. You hire out your senses to take a reading of this person or event and so that is rather like fiction – you are using your nerve ends more than you might otherwise be. But emotionally it is very, very different and when I get out of bed in the morning and all I have got to do that day is write fiction then I get out of bed very happy. When I have got a piece to write it is like working on a railroad by comparison. It is onerous.

CWEB Your first novel, *The Rachel Papers*, centres on a struggle for sexual conquest. In a way that has never been far away in all of your subsequent novels, has it? It is territory that you have marked out for yourself.

MA Yes. I suppose I'd better pack it in soon. I would justify it, excuse it, this way. We reveal so little of ourselves to others, even to those closest to us, and I want more than that fifteen per cent or whatever it is. So almost the first thing I ask myself about a character is, what are they like in the sack? You do find out another biggish chunk about someone that way. You don't have to see them yourself, but if you could, as it were, peep on them, you would find out a great deal.

CWEB But you don't subscribe to the notion that there is a truth to be found there do you? Presumably what you find is just another layer of performance.

MA Increasingly that may be true, but even the type of performance may be important. We are all having to get very good at interpreting performances. But it is nearer the knuckle than most cultural performances. When people are drunk it is not necesssarily *in vino veritas*, but it is definitely something closer to the core. That's also true when people dream. The defences are down. You are not in anything like the same amount of control, and that's true of sexual performance. That is why I wouldn't respect any 'Do Not Enter' sign because I need to know all that. I think it does add up and take you deeper.

CWEB But then in your work that, too, is subverted by comedy.

MA I am certainly not going to be the celebrant of any earth-moving kind of love affair. I don't think there is any act of sex in all my books that goes off without some humiliating hitch or joke, and because I am a comic writer I am always going to be looking for the comedy and humiliation. Not the 'darling, you were marvellous' or 'towards morning he took her again' approach.

CWEB I had a feeling that in one or two of your early books you were almost trying to find the limits in order to transcend them.

MA Transcend is a kind word. I think there was probably a bit of that. Also my craft was at a much more ham-fisted level. All the decisions you make, and writing consists of thousands of decisions, should be to do with the book you are writing. They should be true to that book. Now I would steer away from things not because of any outer decorum, but because of inner decorum to do with the book. There are things I censored in *London Fields*, things that I had Keith doing that I couldn't cope with.

CWEB You surprise me.

MA I surprised myself. I thought, I can't have him doing that. It is too appalling. What kinds of things? Well, low thoughts, really, one sexual transgression, but just low thoughts – of which he has a great many as it is. I just thought this demonises him too much, although he is an incredibly popular character, easily the most popular character I have created, despite his remorseless turpitude. So one never knows with these things.

CWEB Is there, by this stage in your career, a risk of being trapped in your own myth, trapped with a particular kind of character? I can see how the Holocaust book might snap that, but there are now expectations of a Martin Amis novel and a Martin Amis character, and that must be present in your mind when you sit down to write.

MA Yes, except I think you are sunk if you start to worry about that or play up to that. I am sure that the Holocaust book will be seen as a divagation of mine and people will either say it's a good divagation or let's get back to the stuff we expect. I have to admit that on the whole, though, they do tend to say let's get back to the stuff we expect. They do like gratified expectation. Graham Greene wrote the same kind of novel for longer than I have been doing. I think you haven't got many ways of saying what you have to say, and that what you are really doing is running through them again with the advantage of being a little older every time. The novel I put aside to write the Holocaust novel is pretty much what people would expect, maybe a bit lighter, but the same kind of thing, to do with rivalry, lying, deception, slightly unstable identities, that kind of thing.

CWEB It sounds like low-rent Tom Stoppard.

MA Well I think that is what I do seem to write about. That is the rough frame.

CWEB You yourself once confessed that you would have reviewed your own book *Dead Babies* unfavourably. What would you have gone for?

MA Well, after a while it's the flaws which stand out, not whatever is left. Just as when you are thinking about yourself the thoughts that won't go away are the ones where you behaved embarrassingly or badly. Those are the ones that make you shout to drown out the memory, Not much time is spent in contented review of one's supposed achievements. As you move on you have got less to criticise, perhaps, with each book, depending on how recent it is. There is not much I would change in the books I have written since 1980, because you hit your stride, basically, after making these appalling errors of judgement.

CWEB You do have a fascination, almost a Gothic fascination, with excess and decadence. What is the root of that?

MA I think early, in the second and third novels, perhaps . . .

CWEB There was a kind of decadence, surely in *Money*.

MA I think it is more decline than decadence. The society one is writing about in England is to do with decline rather than decadence.

CWEB Does that imply that you are a realist?

MA Like a fly in a bottle of milk, you can't help but soak up some of that. I heighten it and exaggerate it and cartoonify it, grotesquify it, but one is certainly alive to all that. But bad behaviour, sleaze, well, I certainly must be very interested in it. Leavis said famously that the first question of morality a writer faces is the choice of his material. Now I know for a fact that it is not a choice; it is a recognition. As a writer you may even say with a weary shrug, this is my subject, you may not like your subject that much, you may disapprove of it in all kinds of ways but when you sit down to write, this is your subject. Bad behaviour, sleaze, decadence, decline certainly go on appearing. They must be my subject. But I didn't choose them.

CWEB If you are a satirist, does that mean that you are a moralist?

MA I fear so, yes. But I don't think I am a satirist. If you define satire as militant irony you are nailing your colours halfway up the mast. You are making it acidly clear what you disapprove of without actually having to say what you approve of. But I would say I am not terribly interested in disapproval.

CWEB But a moralist in the sense that there is a kind of still point from which you operate.

MA Yes, I am fantastically clear in my own mind about the degrees to which my characters transgress. I think I am a sort of helpless Freudian about that. I just think they are like that because of things that have happened to them, because of where they live, what chances they have had. I even have sympathy for my Nazi doctor, or something approaching sympathy. I can't imagine creating a character I hated. I don't think the perpetrators, even of the most spectacularly dreadful and bestial crimes, escape. I think a huge price is exacted from them.

CWEB Is writing a way of flirting with danger? Is it a kind of controlled envisaging of alternative paths?

MA Yes, as Philip Roth said – and Philip Roth I think has perhaps on occasion gone too close to life – you write not about what happened but about what didn't happen. You may have a situation with real people in it but that's never going to be interesting enough for a novel; it is never going to be shapely enough, it is never going to mean anything, it is never going to have literary form. So you think 'what would have happened if *she* married *him*?' And that is where you start from.

CWEB But it is also a way of licensing your own libido, perhaps, sending it off on a journey that you would hesitate to take.

MA Libido, yes, also frustration and aggression. Take the opening scene of *Money*. The vile taxi driver says you ought to kill all the blacks. That happened. It was a fact. But I didn't challenge it in the way that my hero does. For me that was more wish-fulfilment in a way than any sexual episode. You have more courage. In actuality you think, 'Oh Christ, life's too short to get into a row with this monster behind the wheel,' but in your novels you can imagine you did, and how it would have gone. Perhaps it's more a kind of projection than wish-fulfilment.

CWEB Do you feel that in writing novels in England you don't have quite the role that, say, a writer in South America has or a writer in Eastern Europe, that you become marginal, a licensed entertainer?

MA Yes, but I am quite happy to do without that. I think some writers yearn for the centrality of the writer's role in other societies but that offers an extra burnish I am happy to do without. That's the tradition I'm in.

CWEB Your father once complained that you had a terrible compulsive vividness to your style. Do you think there is any truth in that?

MA On occasion, probably, but it is a question of taste. He said that there should be more sentences in my books which go, 'He finished his drink and left'. Well, I think there should be *fewer* sentences like that in his books. I think you don't waste anything; every bit of a novel should be pulling its weight. There should be no dead areas. Of course I believe in modulation but if it's quiet it should be quiet for a very good reason. Style is not an icing but an ingredient, perhaps the main ingredient of your way of perceiving things. When you are writing you are trying to make that perception as clear as possible: that's really all you're doing. If it's a complicated perception it will need a complicated sentence. I don't like this clear-as-a-mountain-creek kind of writing, this vow-of-poverty prose. It doesn't suit my character. I would rather be in the counting house than wandering the lanes in a loin cloth.

CWEB Indeed you've said that, for you, writing is what it is about, not story.

MA Much more writing than story, yes. What I want from a plot or a structure is something that will let comic invention flow, and interesting situations. I'm looking for chances to describe the things I am interested in.

CWEB So how would a book like *Other People* fit into that? I can see that in a way it is born out of a desire to see things afresh, to add a kind of edge to reality, but, on the other hand, the narrative drive of that book is just as important, isn't it?

MA It is more plotty than most of my stuff, yes, but the plot got going quite a way in. The premise was what drew me to it. The Holocaust book is one of those, too, in that it's written backwards in time, in a backwards physical universe. So once again you are having to re-examine the tiniest gestures with few preconceptions. Similarly, having *Money* narrated by a drunk, who kept forgetting what he had done, is another way of saying, let's start again. Because I think that every writer is trying to do this in every book. Every writer is saying, 'Let's take another look at it'. I do it perhaps more literal-mindedly than most, but that's what writing is, isn't it? Let's look at this again and notice something that hasn't been noticed.

CWEB A lot of novelists edge their way towards the novel through short stories. Paradoxically you seem to find novels easier to write than you do short stories.

MA Yes, again borne out in the Holocaust book. I thought very early on this would be an eight-page short story. Then I thought, for an intoxicated period, this is a novella. But it actually became a short novel. I am definitely a putter-in rather than a leaver-out. There are writers who get praised for what they leave out, but I never see the virtue of that. I sort of know what is meant, but either you are an exclusive or inclusive kind of writer. I think I got less interested in formal considerations, in a neat, well-made book. It doesn't interest me so much partly because it's easy – anyone can do it. What makes you an individual as a writer is something else, a kind of flow which is to do with the voice. Once you get that going it's your job to cultivate that, not suppress it, and say, 'wait a minute, this paragraph should not necessarily be in this book.' Never mind about that. There are always going to be plenty of people who can write those formal books with nice decor and everything. Anyone who has done it knows it's not the most difficult thing. The most difficult thing is that kind of flow.

CWEB When you did produce a book of short stories, *Einstein's Monster*, it was prefaced by an essay about nuclear war that was full of a sense of shock and outrage. But it also implied that you had found an explanation for something in your own work.

MA Yes, I think I probably erred in the direction of supposing I'd found the explanation for *everything*. But it was certainly written with that sort of indignation: I'd always felt that there was something peculiar to my time, and outrageous, and that this was very much to do with me. So I did feel indignation on behalf of my childhood, I think, all the terrors I'd felt and had suppressed; and when I had children of my own I felt a double indignation, about the disgraceful state of affairs, the humiliating state of affairs, and it did account for certain things in my books. It accounted for this tremendous interest in self-destruction which takes several forms in my work. Yes, that produced the anger or sense of indignity that

I have suffered from all my life. Those who were born post 1945 have never known a time when it wasn't there, so it was harder to recognise as intolerable. You can't go around minding about it the whole of the time, so you become numb to it and that is not a healthy response either. There is no safety anywhere because of this reality which we have inherited and tolerated. Everyone is in uniform. How did this get going?

CWEB Something of the pressure of that has gone now.

MA Well, four tons of TNT per human being has been whittled down to 3.8 tons. No, it's certainly a new world and a different world, but in a way the world has been made safe for nuclear weapons as it's no longer a stand-off. How quick we were to think in terms of nuclear weapons when the Gulf War began and how we all thought, I thought, if Saddam attacks Israel with chemical weapons there will probably be a nuclear response but that will be survivable, it will be bloody awful, but it will be survivable because the trip wire has gone, certainly for now. It's not the old NATO policy: fight like mad for three days then blow up the world. That kind of absurdity has receded.

CWEB Is there any sense in which that pressure having gone has led you to another enormity, hence the Holocaust.

MA No, I don't think so, although it was begun in 1989 when the Berlin Wall was coming down. But I don't think it happened like that. It happened much more accidentally. I had an idea to write a life backward in time. I did not have much opinion about what kind of life it was going to be. Then, I was playing tennis with a friend at Cape Cod, and he gave me his latest book, *The Nazi Doctors*, a great, a monumental book. I read that and I thought with horror and recognition that there would be a real point to writing life backwards if the life was of a Nazi doctor, and that was how it got going, idle coincidence.

CWEB You write with a fair deal of irony, one thing that is sometimes difficult to export to other countries. Did you have a problem with that at first in America?

MA I have had my ups and downs in America. Although it didn't sell very well, the book that made a difference was *Money*, which surprised me very much. America has to have a limited sense of irony because it has so many different kinds of people in it. As I say in *Money*, if you have a fully active sense of humour in America you would be sobbing with laughter all the hours there are – it would incapacitate you entirely. But that book went down much more easily there than it did here, as did *London Fields*.

CWEB Why do you think that was?

MA It baffles me, but I think they are not annoyed by large books that splutter and sound off and are full of energy. These are the words I use that make my father's head drop. Whenever he hears a novel is full of energy, he despairs. I think he stands for a certain British taste there, but the Americans, as we know, are gluttons for energy.

CWEB You've suggested that Americans never cease to write *USA*, to try to capture the mood, the myths, the reality of America. I wonder, though, if with *Money* in particular you don't try to write *USA* yourself. You certainly have a fascination with America. In *Money* you take a character to America. In *London Fields* you bring a character from America.

MA And in the Holocaust book, the first half of which is set in America. Well, I feel very North Atlantic. I am like Thatcher, I feel much more strongly linked to America than to France, Spain or Italy. And the link is very simple; it is language. Also, I spent time in America when I was a child, my wife is American, and I loved living there for many years. It was my beat as a journalist. I think one is always attracted towards the centre of the earth, which is really, culturally, America. It's never going to be Japan, culturally. There aren't any Sushi bars in Hendon. That kind of culture doesn't travel. There is never going to be a Japanese Clint Eastwood. It is too alien. Nineteenth century England is the time of our big novels, our centre-of-the-world novels. That imperial confidence has now shifted to America and you think quite coldbloodedly, quite selfishly, I want some of that. I want that amplitude that is no longer appropriate to England.

CWEB It is interesting that you mentioned the 19th century because in the 1980s so many British writers turned back to the 19th century. They wrote pastiche or at the very least turned back to the Empire and the Second World War. They evacuated the 80s, whereas you actually made the 80s very much your subject.

MA Yes, there is something in that, although I have now done it and gone back, literally backwards in time, to the Second World War. But not out of a David Hare kind of interest in the political implications of the Second World War. I think what is going on in England is incredibly interesting and we will go on writing about it: although we are not at the forefront of anything else, we are at the forefront of decline and what happens to a developed nation after its manly noon has passed is uniquely interesting.

CWEB You mean that paradoxically Britain has suddenly become the future because it is going through a process of decline just marginally ahead of the United States and the Soviet Union.

MA It's going through its own state of decline. In America it's a different spectacle because the society is so much younger. We got our revolution out of the way in the 17th century. We were way ahead and we still are but, then, even being at the forefront of something always drives you back into the past, simply because things don't travel in a straight line. When I was writing about a future London in *London Fields*, Dickens was the writer I thought of most. There will be regression and illusion and it will be to do with the past because the future is so much emptier, at least for the English.

CWEB Is Dickens a point of reference in other senses, too?

MA Yes, he likes to write about the whole of society. He likes to see what links Lady Dedlock and Joe the Sweep, and that's very much what I am interested in, too. He likes to see society as one thing, mysteriously interdependent.

CWEB *London Fields* is a millennial novel, not merely in the sense that it's set in 1999. Almost everything is in decline. It's a dying century, a dying millennium, a dying almost everything.

MA Yes, the end of history. That is the millenial theme. But there is a longing for renewal, for redemption, for a new start.

CWEB You once said that Saul Bellow was lucky to have Chicago. Are you equally lucky to have London?

MA It suits me fine. I don't think I am distorting when I write about London. If people complain, I just say you are not looking where I am looking. I am not saying that my truth is the only truth, but it's very definitely part of the truth. If you are interested in ugliness and sleaze, the comedy of all that, then London is absolutely the place to be.

CWEB You've said that you get terrific comfort thinking that when you die your sons will know a lot about you from reading your books. What will they discover?

MA That I noticed things and was amusing, mainly. They'll discover the kind of things I noticed and the kind of things I found funny. When I first read my father's books I thought it was like talking to him only better, more concentrated, and I assume that that will be what they would get from me, from reading my books. It's the voice, you recognise the voice. When I read my father's books I can hear him speaking. I hope they'll hear me.

interviewed by Lorna Sage

Angela Carter's new novel *Wise Children* is a Shakespearean soap opera about a British stage dynasty in which the men belong to the legitimate theatre and the women to vaudeville. It's an acrobatic romp through the branches of the family tree, posing questions about gender and generation, and about the genres of the novel – the latest instalment in an *oeuvre* that unravels the romance of exclusion.

'I've always covered a lot of ground,' she says. This time, she wanted lightness: '*Nights at the Circus* hasn't got enough air in it, it's a big thick heavy nineteenth-century novel. There should be more holes in the text, it should be airy, with spaces on the page. One of the most difficult things about writing this book was that I wanted to have a transparent prose that just ran, and I wanted it to be very funny, and at the same time I wanted the complex of ideas about paternity, and the idea of Shakespeare as a cultural ideology.'

She has come a long way since she first cruelly, and wittily, held up the mirror to 1960s narcissism. Of those early books *The Magic Toyshop* (1967) and *Love* (1971, revised and reissued 1987) in particular have become classics of a kind. *The Magic Toyshop* indeed has turned into a set text: a once Gothic and alien object that is now an indispensible part of the contemporary canon, taught in schools and theorised in theses. Her work has proved, again and again, uncannily timely (though it used to take a while before people could see it). The new novel's Shakespearean rag coincides with a renewed public debate about the national bard's centrality or otherwise, sparked off by Prince Charles – 'his roots are ours, his language is ours, his culture is ours' – an assertion that immediately raises awkward questions about who 'we' are. For Carter, the short answer is that Shakespeare is anybody's and everybody's: 'When I was writer in residence in Sheffield [in the mid 1970s] there were some Chilean refugee kids staying in the same house, finishing off school. One of them, Cecilia, was shown the Olivier *Hamlet*, and when she came home we said – because we very much wanted her to enjoy her first Shakespeare

– "Well, did you enjoy it?" and she said, "What do you mean enjoy it, I *hated* it, I hated every minute of it!" and we were crestfallen. She said, "That Ophelia, he shouldn't have done it to her, that Hamlet, I cried my eyes out, and now you ask me did I *enjoy* it!" I'm sure that Shakespeare would have been very pleased after four hundred years. She was having exactly the same reaction to it that Dr Johnson had to the end of *Lear*. What was really interesting was that Cecilia homed in immediately on the bit that was made for her, for teenage girls. I do think there's something about Shakespeare that converts the most sophisticated person into the naive observer: *this time*, you know, Othello will see sense about the handkerchief. They played *Lear* with a happy ending for two hundred years, and it's perfectly possible that *Lear* with a happy ending would have sent you from the theatre with a great surge of joy, it would turn into a late comedy, a successful *Cymbeline* . . .'

Criticism – or praise – of Shakespeare as the homogenising factor in the national heritage doesn't, consequently, move her. She says, with some irony, 'It's a real shame that we've got Shakespeare as opposed to, say, Goethe, who was a great poet and a great dramatist and a great intellectual, and a rather good diplomat besides being a snappy little natural philosopher. Shakespeare just isn't an intellectual, and I think this is one of the reasons why intellectuals get so pissed-off with him. They are still reluctant to treat him as popular culture. It's altogether too carnivalesque, there's still the shadow of Leavis, we still feel we have to take it seriously. The extraordinary thing about English literature is that actually our greatest writer is the intellectual equivalent of bubble-gum, but can make twelve-year-old girls cry, can foment revolutions in Africa, can be translated into Japanese and leave not a dry eye in the house. You mention folk culture and people immediately assume you're going to talk about porridge and clog-dancing, there's this William Morris and Arnold Wesker prospect – truly the bourne from which no traveller returns. Shakespeare, like Picasso, is one of the great hinge-figures that sum up the past – one of the great Janus-figures that sum up the past as well as opening all the doors towards the future. I tend to agree that his politics were diabolical. I think I know the sort of person he was, the sort of wet war-hating liberal who was all gung-ho for the Falklands, who in taking sides would have said, you know, it's a sorry business, but once we have embarked on it

... signed William Shakespeare, Highgate Village. That sort of intellectual dishonesty seems to me to *reek* from all the political aspects of the plays, but the plays themselves add up to something else. You can play them any way you want. It must be obvious that I *really like* Shakespeare.'

It's equally obvious that popular culture is for her neither innocent not crudely representational. Her Shakespeare is in the tradition of Chaucer and Boccaccio, ribald, magical and a bricoleur. The play that's at the centre of the new novel is *A Midsummer Night's Dream*, restaged with loving irreverence as a 1930s Hollywood spectacular.

'I like *A Midsummer Night's Dream* almost beyond reason, because it's beautiful and funny and camp – and glamorous, and cynical. It's not sophisticated like *Love's Labour's Lost*, which I think is Shakespeare's only attempt at a sort of campus novel. English popular culture is very odd, it's got some very odd and unreconstructed elements in it. There's no other country in the world where you have pantomime with men dressed as women and women dressed as men, and everybody thinks this is perfectly suitable entertainment for children. It's part of the great tradition of British art, is all that 'smut' and transvestism and so on.'

Her *Virago Book of Fairy Tales*, 1990, made the same point in a different way (some are definitely adult fairy tales). The stories she chose play disconcerting games with pieties about gender old and new. Now she says darkly, 'That sorted out the men from the boys. Can you see Martin Amis allowing himself to be observed leafing through something called *The Virago Book of Fairy Tales*? He'd rather be seen reading *Guns and Ammunition*.' (This in jokey allusion to Amis having come out, in *Einstein's Monsters*, as a concerned father in the nuclear age.)

Fairy tales and folk tales provide a clue, for her, to the alternatives to social (not to say socialist) realism. Calvino's career – he started off in the post-war neo-realist mould – is in this sense exemplary: 'His fairy tale book had a transformational effect on his entire career. I think it made him write and think in a completely different way. If he hadn't at some point read Vladimir Propp he wouldn't have written *Invisible Cities*. What happened with Calvino was that he thought he'd better check out what 'the people' really liked. You discover that they are capable of the most extraordinary and fantastic reinterpretations of their situation, and you also find out that they are ideologically impure to a degree. After that, there are a number of things you can do. One is to systematically re-write your source material, another is simply to retreat into it where no one can get you, another is to give it all up and go and work in a factory, though I've noticed that intellectuals are loath to do this. But social realism isn't an option any more. In any case, a book like *Germinal* is not at all a naturalist novel. It's the most terrifying and hallucinatory and strange novel, the final scene of which is necrophilia. In that community love can only be consummated posthumously, you're too hungry or too tired or too dirty when you are alive.'

Propp and structuralist theory in general were certainly part of her own early reading. After *Nights at the Circus* people assumed that Bakhtin on the carnivalesque was too, but not so: she eventually read him because he was invoked so often by readers. 'It's wonderful, exactly what criticism ought to be. When I was doing the reading for this latest book, I reread *Measure for Measure*, thinking about the Falstaffian character in my novel, and very much post-Bakhtin, and the play just gave a shake and turned into something completely different. Lucio became the only sane person in Vienna, he became the central figure, and it was a play about the unconquerability and resilience of the libido. The law is a complete ass in that play. It's always supposed to be one of the crabbed, difficult problem plays, but my feeling is that it's a pure groundlings' play. It's people like Arsenal supporters who'd recognise its lawlessness. And that dreadful ending – there was a recent production where they explain the fact that Isabella never says anything after the Duke tells her they're going to be married by having her faint. I like that.'

Nonetheless, and notwithstanding her pleasure in Bakhtin and her feeling that he's right to claim Dostoevsky as a polyphonous writer ('he's very sound on women, some male writers invite me to read them, it's nothing to do with how they think they organise their world'), she is characteristically sceptical about the vogue for the carnivalesque: 'It's interesting that Bakhtin became very fashionable in the 1980s, during the demise of the particular kind of theory that would have put all kinds of question marks around the whole idea of the carnivalesque. I'm thinking about Marcuse and repressive desublimation, which tells you exactly what carnivals are for. The carnival has to stop. The whole point about the feast of fools is that things went on as they did before, after it stopped.'

Wise Children has a lot of singing and dancing, but it's professional 'show business' – 'That's what Fevvers [in *Nights at the Circus*] was about as well. Dora and her twin Nora are tough old girls, they can hold onto the fact that their roles aren't all they are, although they're constantly reinterpreted by everyone who meets them.' She has given her narrator Dora 'elements of a parodic South London voice. Though the snag is that people do talk like that, generic South London "common"'. (The female line is not only illegitimate, they live south of the river, in Brixton.) 'Though she's very fluent, very articulate, she doesn't use standard English.' (Dora gets her education in Hollywood, at the hands of an Irish writer who's sold his soul for drink, and casts her in the role of Muse.) 'That's a reflection of my story "Black Venus". Dora finds herself reformulated, you're being presented with two versions of Dora. Her own version of herself isn't anyway particularly sympathetic, she's perfectly straightforward about the fact that she's been two-timing. She's behaving, as they say, like a man. And she gets nothing out of the experience of being a Muse – except a course in world literature from Austen to Wedekind, and of course the ability to formulate a grammatical sentence.

'Every time you read a male writer's female characters you're reading reinventions. Being a woman you register it unconsciously. Dora registers it consciously.'

There's a passage in Levi-Strauss about exogamy where he points out that the women act as messages passed between men, which is very much what this novel takes apart. 'Dora and Nora know they are messages. There's a quotation from one of Wedekind's Lulu plays – I guess a lot of Lulu's personality, which I find very attractive, has gone into my twins – where at one point Lulu says, "Everybody who looks at me sees something different, but I know who I am and I hang onto it." She says to her men, "I can't help how you see me, what you see" – I paraphrase – "is what you want, what you see is your own invention." Very few men are in fact bothered to find out what is going on, whereas women have to because of sheer self-preservation. It's one of the great differences between the sexes. I think it's one of the differences between gay men and heterosexual men. The minute that you realise you're not simply natural you really need to know what's going on. I'm very fond of the passage where Dora and Nora do themselves up to go to the party, and Nora says, "It's

every woman's tragedy that, after a certain age, she looks like a
female impersonator." And Dora says, "Mind you, we've known
some lovely female impersonators, in our time."'

The climactic party (itself the climax to a whole set of parties)
is one of the novel's soap opera ploys – 'You *could* say it's one of the
most basic forms of realism, the row at the birthday party, people
slamming doors . . .' Her grand theatrical family have come down
in the world. The (legitimate) Hazards are doing television (not
to say commercials), the (illegitimate) Chances find themselves,
in their old age, on a level with their much-mythologised father
at last, and contemplate the dizzying thought that he too was
a bit of an invention – 'I sometimes wonder,' says Nora, 'if we
haven't been making him up all along. . . . If he isn't just a
collection of our hopes and dreams and wishful thinking in the
afternoons . . .' This is vintage Carter magic-in-reverse (with an
appropriate hint of the bard, and 'our revels now are ended') –
the kind of metafictional gesture that infuriates readers, when
it doesn't delight them, tongue-in-cheek and resolutely sceptical
about the prospect of a wise child really knowing her own father.
Or mother for that matter (this is a book full of surprises).

She has often been asked, she says, why there are so few mothers
in her books, and has realised that all along the houses have stood
in for mother. 'In *Heroes and Villains*, it's the crumbling mansion of
the Gothic novel, open to the sky. Twenty or twenty-five years ago
I was on holiday in Ireland, and came up to a cliff where there
was an abandoned house. And you could see right through the
house, it scared me stiff, you could see the sky on the other side.
I was convinced, in a temporary access of irrationality, that there
would be nowhere for the ghosts to hide. It was like something out
of Magritte, very striking. Like a good Freudian, I was thinking of
houses as being mothers, so there was this empty mother, with the
sky on the other side. Bare ruined choirs . . . ? When mother is
dead, all the life has gone out of the house. The shop in *The Magic
Toyshop* gets burnt down, the old dark house, and adult life begins.
In this novel, though either way mother is dead, her spirit lives on
and the house survives. I don't think it's anything to do with *my*
mother, but the kind of power mothers have is enormous. Take
the skyline of Istambul – enormous breasts, pathetic little willies,
a final revenge on Islam. I was so scared I had to crouch in the
bottom of the boat when I saw it. This is about real power, the kind
of thing Hitler and Stalin wanted – to be *mothers* of their country,

and suffering from bad pre-menstrual tension too, I would say. In this book, in mother's house, mother's ghost attacks them when they're just about to have a crippling attack of nostalgia, it saves them ... Father's house, on the other hand, is very grand and unliveable in.'

A recent, uncollected short story, 'The Curious Room', her contribution to a Swiss conference on 'Strangeness' at the University of Basel (where, as she reminds the reader, Paracelsus graduated), provides a series of surreal footnotes for this version of fictional space. In this tale Lewis Carroll's Alice has gone through the looking glass and found herself in Rudolph II's Prague, in the den of 'English expatriate alchemist' John Dee, along with the mandrakes and automata. Carter refers to it as a 'piece of speculation in the form of a short story', with all the mirror-puns on 'speculation', and it features a paragraph of exquisite and lawless authorial intrusion:

> There's a theory, one I find persuasive, that the quest for knowledge is, at bottom, the search for the answer to the question: 'Where was I before I was born.'
>
> In the beginning, was ... what?
>
> Perhaps, in the beginning, there was a curious room, a room like this one, crammed with wonders; and now the room and all it contains are forbidden you, although it was made just for you, had been prepared for you since time began, and you will spend all your life trying to remember it.

'The Curious Room' is a reminder that her fictional territory is so distinctive precisely because she has always refused to draw the boundaries that would allow her to be comfortably classified as *either* 'fantastic' or 'mainstream'.

She says now, in some frustration, 'I can only write a story *about* Dada, I can't *do* it. Dada is the authentic festival of the dispossessed. The older I grow the more convinced I am that Dada is the real twentieth-century thing – utopian anti-art. In a hundred years, perhaps this will look like the century of Dada. A lot else will have fallen away. Dada will seem to have created the flavour of the entire century, art which self-destructs. 1968 was the last great explosion of it, but it tends to recur every twenty to thirty years.'

The question of who your forefathers and -mothers are, what

'line' you belong to, the new novel's question, is for her capable of being asked and answered in many different ways. The form she's chosen is deliberately hybrid, impure, a family saga; and at the same time spiked with abstraction (not just twins, but twins in every generation, as well as 'holes in the text'). In a sense, she's parodying the stuff of Leavis's great tradition (George Eliot, Lawrence) in a postmodern perspective. Though she has never read those novels quite as he did. 'In *Middlemarch* you can see Ladislaw as representing Europe, a refugee from a world with a different kind of history, history running at a different pace. When you think of later nineteenth century London, it was a seething mass of people who seldom show up in the novels, people whose 'realism' got left out. Whose realism are we talking about? In *The Rainbow* there's the Polish woman who brings echoes from a different world.' And in *Wise Children*, true to this formula, there's Brecht in the Hollywood episode. 'He makes a cameo guest appearance.' Brecht was another who knew when the carnival had to stop – 'there's this poem of his against laughter, that people who laugh haven't heard the news.' History has been bent, in the sense that Brecht didn't get there until the 1940s, but the point is that in history, as against the narratives that seem most obviously to ape history, such collocations (Brecht, say, and Busby Berkeley) are not rare.

Nor can the novel entirely levitate out of history. Modernism, she thinks, never exactly happens in writing: 'My idea of modernism is very much to do with Picasso, and certain styles of architecture, the skyline of New York, the unprecedented things of the twentieth century. It's not to do (despite Bakhtin) with the messiness of life, that is why it's sometimes fascistic, obsessed with heroic systems of control. Think of Wallace Stevens on the 'rage for order'. It's the American century, too. . . .' Her friend, painter Gillian Ayres, 'says it's an unfortunate fact, but the greatest painting of the twentieth century has been abstract. It's not something you can do in language, language is something else. My relation with folk literature is not accidental, it's something one comes back to, because the problem with literature is that it's impure, it's not a pure system. There's a striving for a transcendental quality, Wallace Stevens's jar in Tennessee, Mallarmé and the perfume never inhaled. . . . Maybe you can do it in French, God knows. It's possible that you can do it in some languages and not others, that you can do it if you're

Japanese – a perfect abstraction from language. I spent a lot of time in the early 1970s [when she was in Japan] thinking about abstraction. That's why Gertrude Stein is important, she tried to evolve some way of using language that would do the trick ... Then she ended up influencing Hemingway.'

The novel, Carter concedes, is a messy genre – 'part of social practice in a way the fine arts are not.' But then, it occurs to me again, that fact – or rather, her bold and ingenious use of it – is the reason why her fiction can't be consigned to some timeless realm of otherness. We return to forests, *A Midsummer Night's Dream*, and Hollywood – 'It is the wood I like in *A Midsummer Night's Dream*, the forest where you go mad and become sane, I'm very fond of forests. Medieval literature is one great forest where you go to be alone, it's an allegorical forest, although England at that time *was* forested to a degree we can't conceive of any more. The play on Hollywood was a happy accident, I didn't really think of it until I had finished that section – 'wood' and the Old English word for mad, the relations between woods and madness, that was pure serendipity that they go to the wood that makes you mad. But the more I thought of it, I thought that it's actually a rather good description of Hollywood in its heyday, this kind of magic forest.'

In fact, she says, there was a 1935 film of *A Midsummer Night's Dream*, done by the German director, Max Reinhardt, from which she borrowed some details from the set. For instance, 'he had made the wood so thick that they had to spray it with silver paint.' Hollywood is the dream-*factory*, and so fits her purposes by demonstrating with complete literalness that the 'stuff ... dreams are made on' is material, paint and pasteboard and dry ice. Shakespeare's wood, Hollywood, the narrative forests that branch out on Carter's pages, are of the nature of artifice, they come to us out of history. It's that mysterious provenance ('Father Time has many children' someone pointed out in *Nights at the Circus*) that *Wise Children* tracks down to its lair across the generations.

Spring Gardens
by Paul Cox

Spring Gardens ...

Carlton House Terrace ...

THE BRITISH COUNCIL

Spring Gardens—

Mick's stall, Trafalgar Square ...

Henry Moore
at Admiralty Arch --

Overviews

The Novelist Today: Still at the Crossroads?

One can consider the situation of the contemporary novelist either aesthetically or institutionally. Under the aesthetic I include questions of genre, of formal and stylistic choice or fashion – what French critics call *écriture*. In the category of the institutional I include questions about the material conditions of writing, how writing today is produced, circulated, received and rewarded. The two are, of course, connected.

Both the aesthetic and the institutional state of writing today can be viewed from the perspective of either the critic or of the creative writer. As I function in both capacities, this is for me a splitting of the subject in a double sense. For most of my adult life, from 1960 to 1987, I combined an academic career as a university teacher and scholar with writing novels. I tried to keep a balance between these two activities; and throughout this period I published, more or less by design, a novel and a work of literary criticism in alternation. In 1987 I retired from university teaching, and although I expect to go on writing literary criticism, I doubt whether it will be oriented towards an academic readership. One component of that decision was a feeling that it was becoming harder and harder to make meaningful connections between an academic criticism increasingly dominated by questions of Theory, and the practice of creative writing.

Both the critic and the creative writer can address themselves to the subject of writing either descriptively or prescriptively. My own preference has always been for the descriptive. Nothing, it seems to me, is more futile or arrogant than for critics to tell novelists what they should write about or how they should write about it or what it is no longer possible to write. Writers themselves may be excused for doing this as a way of defending or publicising or creating a receptive climate for their work or the work of their friends. There is a long and honourable tradition of discourse about the state of writing known as the manifesto, but for reasons I shall come to I do not think it is appropriate to the present literary moment, and I certainly do not have one to proclaim.

So these are the coordinates of my observations: aesthetic/institutional, critical/creative, descriptive/prescriptive.

About twenty years ago I published an essay called 'The Novelist at the Crossroads' which was aesthetic, critical and descriptive in orientation: that is, it was intended as a descriptive survey of the aesthetics of the contemporary novel, drawing indirectly on my experience as a novelist but written essentially within the conventions of academic criticism. My starting point or springboard was a short but potent book of prescriptive criticism by the American academic critic Robert Scholes, called *The Fabulators*. (It is, incidentally, difficult to imagine an ambitious young scholar of Scholes's ability choosing today to write a book about contemporary fiction; he or she would almost certainly be working in the field of Theory, or applying Theory to the revisionist reading of classic texts). The realistic novel was obsolete, Scholes argued; writers should leave realism to other media, such as film, which could imitate reality more faithfully, and instead develop the purely fictive potential of narrative. His prime example was John Barth's *Giles Goat-boy*, a huge allegorical romance that presented the modern world as divided into an East Campus and a West Campus, which the hero, conceived by a virgin impregnated by a computer programme and brought up as a goat, has a mission to save. Lawrence Durrell, Iris Murdoch, John Hawkes, Terry Southern and Kurt Vonnegut were the other chief exemplars of a kind of writing that Scholes called 'fabulation'.

To resist, or at least question, this manifesto, I invoked Scholes's own generic theory of the novel, expounded in an earlier book that he had co-authored with Robert Kellogg, *The Nature of Narrative*: that the novel was generically an unstable mixture of the fictional and the empirical, of romance and allegory on the one hand and history and mimesis (realistic imitation of ordinary life) on the other. Granting that the viability of the traditional realistic novel had been called in question on several grounds (for instance, the bizarre, extreme, absurd nature of modern 'reality'), I suggested that the excessive cultivation of the fictional through fabulation was not the only possible response. A writer might equally well decide to develop the *empirical* style of narrative exclusively – as in the so-called non-fiction novels of Capote (*In Cold Blood*) and Mailer (*Armies of the*

Night), and in the experimental autobiographical novels of B.S. Johnson.

The contemporary novelist was therefore in the situation of a man (or woman) at a crossroads. Before him stretched the way of traditional realism, now alleged to be a very boring route, and possibly a dead end. To the left and right were the ways of fabulation and non-fictional narrative. Many writers, I suggested, unable to choose between these three routes, built their hesitation into their fiction, made the problems of writing a novel the subject of the novel. I called this the problematic novel; later it was christened, by Bob Scholes again I seem to remember, metafiction: a name that achieved wider currency. An important example of this kind of novel, it seemed to me, was Doris Lessing's *The Golden Notebook*, in which a blocked novelist writes about various aspects of her life, including her own writing, in various differently coloured notebooks and then unites her fractured imagination in a Golden Notebook. I concluded my essay with a 'modest affirmation of faith in the future of the traditional realistic novel.' It was probably not coincidental that I was about to publish such a novel myself, *Out of the Shelter*. But the essay was essentially a plea for aesthetic pluralism. There was, I argued, no dominant style or *écriture*, such as obtained in the Fifties, or the Thirties. 'We seem to be living through a period of unprecedented cultural pluralism which allows, in all the arts, an astonishing variety of styles to flourish simultaneously.'

Twenty years later, I think that generalisation still holds good; but I am also struck by how sturdily traditional realism has survived the obsequies pronounced over it by Scholes, and by a number of other writers and critics in the Sixties and Seventies, and how clearly it remains a serious option for the literary novelist today. (By realism I mean not only a mimetic representation of experience, but also the organisation of narrative according to a logic of causality and temporal sequence.)

Fabulation in Scholes's sense has certainly flourished in the last twenty years, encouraged by the discovery and dissemination of South American magic realism in Europe and the USA. In British writing, Salman Rushdie, Angela Carter, the later Fay Weldon come to mind in this connection. The blurb's description of Rushdie's *Satanic Verses*, for instance, suggests a family resemblance to *Giles Goat-boy*:

Just before dawn one winter's morning a hijacked jumbo jet blows apart high above the English Channel. Through the debris of limbs, drinks trolleys, memories, blankets and oxygen masks, two figures fall towards the sea without benefit of parachutes: Gibreel Farishta, India's legendary movie star, and Saladin Chamcha, the man of a thousand voices, self-made man and Anglophile supreme. Clinging to each other, singing rival songs, they plunge downward, and are finally washed up, alive, on the snow-covered sands of an English beach. A miracle; but an ambiguous one, because it soon becomes apparent that curious changes are coming over them. Gibreel seems to have acquired a halo, while, to Saladin's dismay, his legs grow hairier, his feet turn into hoofs, and there are bumps burgeoning at his temples.

The combination of the exploding jumbo jet, as real and topical as yesterday's newsreel, and the miraculous survival and mythical metamorphosis of the leading characters, is typical of fabulation. It aims to entertain us with the humorous extravagance and inventiveness of its story while offering this as a kind of metaphor, or objective correlative in T.S. Eliot's now rather outmoded jargon, for the extreme contrasts and conflicts of modern experience. Humour is a very important component of this kind of writing, for without humour it is apt to become portentous, laboured and ultimately boring; and of course a sense of humour is absolutely essential for an appropriate reading of it – a faculty Ayatollahs are notoriously lacking in. The model for this kind of fiction is Rabelais' *Gargantua and Pantagruel*, and its poetics Bakhtin's theory of the carnivalesque.

Fabulation has certainly flourished in the last twenty years, but it has not conquered the fictional scene. It remains a marginal form of fiction, at least in Britain.

The non-fiction novel, which applies fictional techniques, such as free indirect style, scenic construction, present-tense narration, prolepsis, iterative symbolism, etc., to factual narratives, was always more of an American than a British genre. The poetics of this form of writing were formulated by Tom Wolfe in his anthology *The New Journalism*, and in that anthology he included only one specimen by a British writer (Nicholas Tomalin). Tom Wolfe's own *Radical Chic* and *The Right Stuff* are classics of the genre, along with Norman Mailer's *The Executioner's Song*. The nearest approximation to this kind of writing in English outside America is perhaps the Australian Thomas Keneally's *Schindler's Ark*, which demonstrated its generic ambiguity by being published as non-fiction in the USA and winning the Booker Prize for best novel in 1982. There has been in Britain in recent years, however, something of a renaissance of literary travel writing in Britain, much of which perhaps belongs in this category of the non-fiction novel. Names that come to mind in this connection: James Fenton, Jonathan Raban, Bruce Chatwin, Redmond O'Hanlon, and two Americans who have made their homes in Britain, Paul Theroux and Bill Bryson. Such writing combines factual reporting with cultural and philosophic musing and a slightly teasing autobiographical subtext, both components of modern fiction. Probably the most prestigious and influential outlet for new writing in England today is the paperback book-cum-magazine *Granta*, and it may be significant that its travel number, featuring several of the writers I have named, was its best-selling issue; also that Richard Rayner, author of the very funny *Los Angeles Without a Map*, worked for *Granta* when he wrote it. This book describes the bizarre, mainly sexual adventures of a narrator indistinguishable from the real author; it reads like autobiography but was shortlisted for the *Sunday Express* Fiction prize in 1988.

There have certainly been many examples of the problematic or metafictional novel produced since I wrote my essay, and still more examples of novels which have a strain of metafiction in them, without being primarily metafictional in motivation. For example, Margaret Drabble's novels from *The Ice Age* onwards, Malcolm Bradbury's *The History Man*, Martin Amis's *Money*, and my own *How Far Can You Go?* are all novels primarily focused on developments in contemporary society, but all refer to and in some cases actually introduce the author into the text, as a character on the same ontological level as the fictional characters: a device which exposes the fictionality of texts in a peculiarly drastic way, and invariably reveals some anxiety about the ethical and epistemological nature of fictional discourse and its relationship to the world.

Indeed I would say that my model or metaphor of the crossroads now seems to me inadequate chiefly because it doesn't allow for such mixing of genres and styles within a single text. Such mixing, what one might call 'crossover' fiction, seems to me to be a salient feature of writing today. That is to say, relatively few novelists are wholly and exclusively committed to fabulation or the non-fiction novel, or metafiction. Instead they combine one or more of these modes with realism, often in a startling, deliberately disjunctive way. Vonnegut's *Slaughterhouse Five* (1970) was an early and influential American example of crossover fiction. British examples would include some of Doris Lessing's later work (for instance *Briefing for a Descent into Hell*), Julian Barnes's books from *Flaubert's Parrot* onward, and D.M. Thomas's *The White Hotel*. Foregrounded intertextuality, the overt citation or simulation of older texts in a modern text, has frequently been used to achieve the crossover effect in this period, from John Fowles' *The French Lieutenant's Woman* at the beginning of it, through Peter Ackroyd's *Hawksmoor* and *Chatterton*, to Antonia Byatt's recent *Possession*. My own *Small World* might be mentioned in this context. But one has also to say that a great many of the most admired novels of the present time are written wholly in the discourse mode of traditional realism, employing either first-person character-narrators or covert authorial narrators in a way designed to create an illusion of the reality of the story that is not fundamentally challenged or questioned within the text.

In 1989 I was chairman of the judges for the Booker Prize, Britain's premier literary prize. We read, or at least scrutinised, over a hundred new novels. The great majority of them were written within the conventions of fictional realism. The shortlist of six that we selected were all realistic novels. I should say that it was a matter of great regret to me that Martin Amis's *London Fields* was not shortlisted, due to the strong objections of two members of the jury. Had it been, our list would have looked somewhat different, for there are important metafictional and fabulatory elements in this novel. None of the six novels we ended up with could be said to deviate from the conventions of modern realistic narrative.

They were: Kazuo Ishiguro's *The Remains of the Day*, which of course was the eventual winner, John Banville's *The Book of Evidence*, Rose Tremain's *Restoration*, James Kelman's *A Disaffection*, Margaret Atwood's *Cat's Eye*, and Sybille Bedford's *Jigsaw*. Five of them, though we didn't realise it at the time we selected them, are first-person narratives, and the sixth, Kelman's *A Disaffection*, is written from a single point of view, often in interior monologue.

First-person narration appeals to contemporary novelists because it permits the writer to remain within the conventions of realism without claiming the kind of authority which belongs to the authorial narrative method of the classic realistic novel. In the case of the Bedford and the Atwood, the voice of the narrator is hardly distanced from that of the implied author; in the Ishiguro, the Banville and the Tremain, the narrators are very different from their authors, created by rhetorical means. These three are virtuoso feats of writing, but they are not formally innovatory. Indeed Banville's novel is perhaps the most conventional he has written, in form. Of the six, Kelman's was regarded as carrying the flag of the avant-garde, but though I greatly admired this novel, and was indeed its chief advocate on the jury, I did not see it as formally adventurous. It is written in a mixture of interior monologue and free indirect style, rather like the early chapters of *Ulysses*, but quite without Joyce's mythic design or the stylistic experiments of the later chapters of *Ulysses*. Its aesthetic motivation is entirely mimetic. It challenges the reader primarily by its content and use of Glaswegian dialect, not by its narrative form.

In short, the aesthetic pluralism I sought to defend in my 'Novelist at the Crossroads' essay seems to me to be now a generally accepted fact of literary life. It is sometimes described as a post-modern condition, but if so then we can no longer use post-modernism as a term for a new kind of avant-garde experimentalism. The astonishing variety of styles on offer today, as if in an aesthetic supermarket, includes traditional as well as innovative styles, minimalism as well as excess, nostalgia as well as prophecy.

The triumph of pluralism also no doubt has something to do with the absence of any dominating literary critics or school of criticism actively engaged with the interpretation and evaluation of contemporary literature, a function performed in earlier periods by Eliot, Leavis, and the American New Critics. This is partly due to the increasing professionalisation of academic criticism and its preoccupation with Theory. It is criticism which defines literary movements, determines or sets up debates about what is important and what is not important, what is in and what is out. What we have now is a literary situation in which everything is in and nothing is out. One symptom of this state of affairs is the hopeless failure of a critic like D.J. Taylor (*A Vain Conceit* (1989)) to write prescriptive criticism that carries any conviction or is even internally coherent.

This situation has an upside and a downside. The upside is that the literary world is open to anybody with talent. When you have a dominant *écriture* there is a danger that good work that is unfashionable will be neglected, and mediocre work will enjoy an inflated reputation because it is fashionable. The Thirties and Fifties provided plenty of examples. The downside is that, in the absence of any consensus about aesthetic value, some other value system will take over. And given the nature of our society it is not surprising that a somewhat materialistic notion of success, as measured by sales, advances, prizes, media celebrity, etc. has filled the vacuum. To state it summarily: success has supplanted fashionableness as the reference point of the literary world; or, if you like, success has become an index of fashionableness. It was not always so. In the heyday of modernism, you could hardly be considered an important literary writer if you were commercially successful. It is interesting that Martin Amis, whom many consider the representative novelist of his generation, has written two novels called *Success* and *Money*.

I am now of course viewing my subject under its institutional aspect, and I am well aware that what I am talking about may be partly an effect of a change in my own position within the institution, inasmuch as I have in recent years enjoyed some success of the kind I have just referred to; but I don't think it is entirely a subjective impression. It is a commonplace that the literary novel acquired a new commercial significance in the 1980s, and of course it is no coincidence that it was a decade dedicated to Enterprise culture and the deregulation and internationalisation of high finance. In this climate publishing houses became desirable objects for financial mergers and takeovers. Prestigious literary writers became valuable assets, like brand names in the commodity market, worth far more than the income they actually generated – though they could, in certain circumstances, generate a good deal. The literary bestseller was born, a concept that would have seemed a contradiction in terms to Frank and Queenie Leavis. Umberto Eco's *The Name of the Rose* was a paradigm case. Salman Rushdie's *Midnight's Children* was another. In the 1980s the Booker Prize, which had made little or no impact on sales in the previous decade, suddenly developed the power to make any book that won it a bestseller. Publishers began to search and compete for potential literary bestsellers. In consequence, literary novelists have probably been, in the recent past, better rewarded financially than at any earlier time in this century. It never has been, and it never will be, possible for everybody who would like to earn their living as a full-time writer, to do so; but in the 1980s it seemed to be a more attainable ambition than ever before.

The economic recession of the early 1990s has changed this picture considerably. While the market was buoyant, the large advances commanded by bestselling authors led to a general enhancement of novelists' financial rewards. In today's harsh economic climate, however, many of those huge advances have not been earned, while the sales of less commercial fiction have apparently plummeted. Novelists are finding it harder to place their work and to earn a living from it. There has been a painful shakeout of personnel in the publishing industry and a corresponding shakeout in publishers' lists. Whether this is altogether a bad thing depends, of course, on what books are being eliminated by the financial squeeze. There are so many novels published in Britain that a great proportion of them never get properly reviewed, and never thus really enter into the public consciousness at all. It's possible that some novels of real distinction are being published, but not being noticed, because they are swamped by a mass of decently competent, but not really *necessary* novels. In any event, the effects of the structural changes in the publishing of literary fiction that occurred in the 1980s will not quickly disappear.

The novel has from its very beginnings had an equivocal status, somewhere between a work of art and a commodity; but in the twentieth century, under the impact of modernism, it seemed to split into two kinds of fiction – the highbrow novel of aesthetic ambition, which sold in small numbers to a discriminating élite, and the popular or middlebrow novel of entertainment which sold in much large numbers to a mass audience. Now the gap seems to be narrowing again, and this has changed the attitude of the literary writer towards his audience and his peers, and his work.

The successful marketing of literary fiction depends upon a collaboration between the writer, the publisher and the mass media. Publisher and writer have a common interest, and the media have been very eager to collaborate with them for their own reasons. Developments in print and communications technology in the last decade have led to a vast expansion and diversification of media outlets – newspapers, magazines, supplements, TV channels and radio stations. They all have an inexhaustible appetite for raw material; discussion and gossip about books and writers is a cheap source of such material.

So, if you are a novelist with any kind of reputation, publishing a new novel no longer consists of sending off the manuscript to your publisher and waiting for the reviews to appear nine months or so later. It means delicate negotiations, probably via your agent, over terms, possibly an auction. Once the contract is signed it means consultation with the publisher over the timing of the book's publication, the design of the jacket and other details of production. You might be asked to talk to the firm's sales force, or to a convention of booksellers. Around the time of publication you will be asked to give interviews to press and broadcasting media, perhaps do bookshop readings, signings, attend literary festivals. If you are lucky enough to win or even just be shortlisted for a major literary prize, that will lead to more publicity events. And there will be yet more interviews, readings, signings, etc., if and when the book is paperbacked, turned into a film or TV series, and published in foreign countries. You may be invited to tour foreign countries by the British Council, reading from your work or lecturing on the state of the novel. It is an interesting and significant fact that at the very moment when post-structuralist academic criticism has been proclaiming the Death of the Author as a theoretical axiom, an unprecedented degree of public attention has been focused on contemporary authors as living, breathing human beings.

Some authors collaborate in this process more enthusiastically than others; but very few eschew it entirely. Why? For a number of reasons. The present climate encourages the writer to think of himself not only as an artist, but as a professional, in a business partnership with his publisher. If the publisher has invested a large advance in a book the writer may feel a moral obligation to help him sell it, as well as self-interest. He may get some ego-gratification from contact with admiring readers, or from the performance element in public readings. He may be glad to get out of the house, away from the loneliness of his study, and to travel abroad at someone else's expense.

There are obvious dangers in this new literary lifestyle – I speak as one who has knowingly exposed himself to them. There is the danger that all the media exposure will encourage the vanity, jealousy and paranoia to which writers are constitutionally prone in any case. There is a danger that all the interviews, readings, lecture tours, signing sessions, festival attendances, etc., will consume time and energy that should have been dedicated to the production of new work. There is, perhaps most importantly, a danger that the writer's raised consciousness of the market dimension of his work will interfere with the artistic dimension, making the work less innovative, less ambitious, less inclined to explore new territory, than it might otherwise have been. Indeed it is possible to argue that there is a direct connection between the power of the media and the market in today's literary world, and the aesthetic pluralism, in which realism remains a dominating force, of contemporary fiction. J.G. Ballard made a waspish comment to this effect recently in reviewing a biography of William Burroughs in the *Guardian*:

> At a time when the bourgeois novel has triumphed, and career novelists jet around the world on Arts Council tours and pontificate like game-show celebrities at literary festivals, it is heartening to know that Burroughs at least is still working away quietly in Lawrence, Kansas, creating what I feel is the most original and important body of fiction to appear since the Second World War.

'Arts Council' here is presumably a slip for 'British Council'. The Arts Council doesn't send British writers jetting around the world, it sends them pottering round the country on British Rail, or sets them up as Writers in Residence in regional community centres, though I don't suppose Ballard approves of such enterprises either. The really interesting phrase in this passage is 'career novelist'. It seems to be formed on the model of 'career woman': a somewhat sexist phrase, now becoming rare, used to denote a woman who has sacrificed or subordinated the traditional female occupation of homemaking and childrearing to the pursuit of a career of a traditionally masculine kind, involving the acquisition of power and wealth. Implied in Ballard's locution there is a distinction between writing as a vocation and writing as a profession, writing as the pursuit of importance and writing as the pursuit of success. I must confess that I find that tiresome old bore, William Burroughs, a very unconvincing specimen of literary importance, but let us not be distracted by that from what Ballard is saying.

There are, undoubtedly, dangers in the current literary situation of the contamination of literary values by considerations of fame and money. But they differ only in degree, not in kind, from what has always been the case, at least from the eighteenth century onwards, when writers became professionals, and ceased to rely on patronage, and the printing press turned fiction into a mass-market commodity. It has always been necessary for novelists to struggle to reconcile, in their ways of working, pragmatic institutional considerations with aesthetic integrity. It has always been necessary to be an artist while writing your novel, and a man (or woman) of business when publishing it. All one can say is that the conditions of modern cultural production and circulation make this balancing act particularly difficult, and require from the writer a particularly clear head.

What cannot be denied, I think – and it is perhaps what Ballard means by the triumph of the bourgeois novel – is that contemporary writing, whatever particular style or mode it follows, whether realist or nonrealist, whether fabulation or metafiction or non-fiction novel, or a combination of all of these, is likely to be reader-friendly. The contemporary writer is interested in communicating. This was not always the case. Romantic writers saw their art as primarily self-expression; modernist writers as the making of symbols, or verbal objects. Contemporary critical theory tells us that the very idea of communication is an illusion, or fallacy, though it is not clear what it thinks it is doing when it tells us that. Contemporary writers, however, perhaps partly as a result of the explosion of methods and techniques of communication in modern society – satellite telephone links, video, fax machines, photocopiers, word-processors, etc. – and certainly because of their greater professional involvement in the publishing and marketing of their fiction, and its adaptation to other media such as TV and film, cannot but see themselves as engaged in a process of communication with an actual or potential audience. This it seems to me is, for good or ill, an irresistible effect of living in the modern world, and it has undoubtedly had an effect on the form of contemporary fiction.

British Fiction of the 1980s

Probably the most striking feature of British fiction of the 1980s is how much of it is set neither in Britain nor the 1980s. In a decade when the heritage industry boomed, heritage – not usually cosy and not always British – became a central fictional commodity.

One way in which this showed itself was an enthralment with empire. For serious British fiction – Paul Scott, J.G. Farrell – the 1970s had been the decade of depicting imperial disillusion and dissolution. In the 1980s, the picture changes. Though crumbling empires still stretch across the fictional scene, new vistas of post-colonialism open up.

The most eye-catching instance of this is the fiction of Salman Rushdie. With *Midnight's Children* (1981), he takes up where the *Raj Quartet* left off: the departure of the British from India. But his commentary on what ensued is very differently accented from Scott's mainstream British fictional voice. In Rushdie's crowded comic saga about the children born as midnight struck the dawn of India's independence, it's alleged there were 1001 of them: an obeisance towards the presiding genius that hovers over all his work, the spirit of *The 1001 Nights*. Though European influences – *Tristram Shandy*, Günter Grass, Italo Calvino – are perceptible in his pages, he is most eager to advertise his affinities with a more indigenous mode of writing. For his chronicles of post-colonialism, he creates a post-colonial style. Heavily spiced with Eastern fable, it's one that also shows a keen taste for eclecticism: Hindu myth, Islamic lore, Bombay cinema, cartoon strips and Third World magic realism all contribute to the mix.

Behind the fictional miscellaneousness is a political rationale: a desire to parade the animating results of intermingling diverse cultures. Designed to flabbergast bigotry, Rushdie's fiction calls commitment to notions of ethnic or ideological untaintedness 'the absolutism of the Pure'. Against this 'fantasy of purity', his novels pit extravaganzas of variousness. Amid the carnivals of metamorphosis they let loose, racial or religious creeds of unbending rigidity look arthritically outmoded. The hardline is

sinuously satirised as characters mutate, situations turn themselves inside out, fluctuating actualities re-form in fresh guises,
and metaphor ceaselessly transforms the look of things. In
Midnight's Children whose narrator surreally embodies India's
altering aspects after Independence, in *Shame* (1983) with its
scarifying parables about Pakistan, and in *The Satanic Verses*
(1988), Rushdie's sulphurous phantasmagoria about migration
and displacement, fabulous shape-changings, inter-tangled tales,
robust cross-fertilisations and vigorous fusions unrestingly dem-
onstrate the post-colonial virtues of flexibility and assimilation.

Other authors, in the meantime, were still gazetting episodes
of imperial ignominy. J.G. Ballard's semi-autobiographical novel,
Empire of the Sun (1984), recorded – like Farrell's *The Singapore
Grip* (1978) – the routing of European colonists from South-East
Asia by the Japanese during the Second World War. In this case,
the setting was Shanghai, and Ballard's skills as a science fiction
conjurer-up of weird, doomed worlds was brilliantly redirected
to raise from his boyhood memories the spectacle of a bizarre
city in a state of lurid breakdown. Starting as a pampered
colonial child, his young alter ego soon finds himself adrift in
nightmarishly inverted circumstances where destitute Europeans
beg for admission to Japanese POW camps as sanctuary against
the even more implacably antagonistic Chinese.

An earlier affray with the Chinese – the Opium Wars – was
charted in another outstanding imperial-retrospect novel of the
decade, Timothy Mo's *An Insular Possession* (1986). Prior to this,
Mo – his imagination invariably stirred by themes of empire and
combat – had written (in *The Monkey King*, 1978) about family in-
fighting in Hong Kong, and (in *Sour Sweet*, 1982) about gangland
vendettas in London's Chinatown. With *An Insular Possession*, a
massive, masterly extension of his range, he responded to two
strong impulses in 1980s British fiction: to look back at starting-
points, and to write period pastiche. Set on the South China coast
early in the nineteenth century, the novel narrated events leading
to the founding of Hong Kong, and did so in a style that emulated
the rhetorical mannerisms – buttonholings of the reader, ironic
sallies and circumlocutions – likely to be the stock-in-trade of a
novelist contemporary with what was portrayed. Artfully simu-
lated extracts from journals, letters and early nineteenth-century
newspapers with their array of classical tags, ponderous puns,
elegant variations and formally phrased vituperation amplified

this echoing of the sound of an era. Visually, there were set-pieces – the Storming of the Heights of Canton, the war-junks and fire-rafts of the Celestial Empire kept at bay by British cannonades – that a nineteenth-century Royal Academician would have been proud to put his brush to. But always, with the mercantile rapacity of empire kept well in the foreground, Mo's perspective gave a strongly post-colonial slant to things. Bringing his interest in imperialism back to the present day, *The Redundancy of Courage* (1991) inspected what happened when the Portuguese withdrew from East Timor and the Indonesians moved in.

Another Far Eastern empire, Japan, found its annalist – and analyst – in Kazuo Ishiguro. From devastated Nagasaki (his birth-place), *A Pale View of Hills* (1982) contemplated the grim aftermath to Japanese expansionism. *An Artist of the Floating World* (1986), as spare and refined as the Japanese prints at the centre of its story, stepped further back to observe how a painter's work and life became insidiously coarsened during the 1930s by allegiance to the Emperor and a growingly authoritarian ethos. With *The Remains of the Day* (1989), another quietly resonant novel, Ishiguro lit upon an analogy in 1930s England to his Japanese artist's plight. This time, the figure delineated with a sensitive mix of empathy and regret is an impeccable butler whose life has been blighted by unquestioning subservience to his master, an aristocrat of Fascist sympathies.

Harking back to the end of Africa's colonial era was how William Boyd began his fictional career. Leafy Morgan, the seedy, perspiring diplomat of *A Good Man in Africa* (1981), seems the last in a long line of such personnel, often memorably put in satiric post in books by Graham Greene or Evelyn Waugh. Starting in a well-trodden rut of expatriate farce, the novel gradually ventured out on to the trickier terrain of contemporary African politics, tribalism and dictators. From that point on, Boyd – almost as engrossed as Mo by colonialism and conflict – has filed fictional stories on a range of overseas struggles. *An Ice-Cream War* (1982) watched the British and German empires clash in East Africa during the First World War. *The New Confessions* (1987), whose hero works as a photographer on the Western Front, reels out searing battle sequences as well as later touring the shattered Berlin of 1946. Returning to Boyd's favourite fictional locale, the Africa where he was born, *Brazzaville Beach* (1990) juxtaposes a post-colonial civil war with an internecine war that scientists have been perturbed to find raging among chimpanzees.

Writers such as Ben Okri and Buchi Emecheta used fiction to

give a native African's eye-view of calamities like the Nigerian civil war. The latter novelist also excels in communicating, with sturdy, matter-of-fact immediacy, oppressions hampering the progress of bright, energetic Nigerian girls who (like her) make their educationally emancipated way from bush village to Lagos city life to immigrant existence in London. Pluckily trekking from tribal huts and polygamy to council flats and single-parenthood, her heroines – time-travellers as much as emigrants – don't merely journey hundreds of miles but appear to leap centuries.

Where former imperial bonds chafed closest to home, of course, was Northern Ireland. An instance of the way concern with this became exacerbated during the 1980s was the fictional change of ground effected by William Trevor. When the decade began, he had apparently settled into a rather formulaic kind of comedy that delighted in bringing the sedate and the sleazy into discomfiting collision. With pursed amusement, his novels and stories tweaked into view nastinesses tucked away in the privacies of ostensibly nice people inhabiting genteel suburbs, decorous villages or staid seaside towns. *Beyond the Pale* in 1981 signalled a moving out towards wider concerns. Though the title story in this collection still harboured its quota of Trevor's former preoccupations – prim-lipped lubricity, a couple of furtive adulterers – it was essentially devoted to exposing the ugly coupling of terrorism and despair in Ireland. Subsequently, several of his novels enlarged on this, most hauntingly *The Silence in the Garden* (1988). Telling of an Anglo-Irish family stunned into sterility by guilt and violence, it takes as its central symbol for a society mildewed by history a once-fine old house eaten into by lichen.

Dilapidated mansions occupied by the vestigial remnants of a colonial caste are stock properties in the fictional landscapes of Molly Keane, for over sixty years an unflagging recorder of the hypocrisies and voracities of the Protestant gentry. During the 1980s, with a trio of cuttingly funny novels (*Good Behaviour (1981)*, *Time After Time (1983)*, *Loving and Giving* (1988)) she pushed even deeper her sardonic incursions into the horsey, philistine and covertly disreputable milieu of the Ascendancy in the later stages of its decline.

Across the border, Ulster was grimly fertile in novels documenting a seemingly inextricable post-colonial tangle. Bernard MacLaverty, the most gifted new writer to emerge from the province, produced with *Cal* (1983), a bleak Ulster *Romeo and Juliet*.

Brian Moore, born in Belfast but long an émigré from it to North America, imaginatively returned to the riven city with *Lies of Silence* (1990), whose fast thriller-ish narrative twists through scenes that disclose different suppressions and repressions contributing to Ulster's crisis.

In keeping with the prevailing atmosphere, Scotland had post-colonial things to say too, and the novelists who said them tended to be clustered around Glasgow. From there, in styles ranging from the quirky fables of Alasdair Gray to the dour minimalist monologues of James Kelman, came books portraying the region as a still-exploited fiefdom of England.

The most far-reaching attempt to map the historical dimensions of colonialism hailed from Wales in the unfinished form of Raymond Williams's novel-sequence, *People of the Black Mountains* (1989, 1990). Making *The Forsyte Saga* seem a mere news-flash, this 250-century Cymric cavalcade chronicled life in the region from 23,000 BC to the present-day. What its multiplicitous flashbacks were all tilted to illuminate was the process by which the local folk – after aeons of blameless tribal co-operation, respect for the environment and hospitality to strangers – were inexorably oppressed by in-comers. A more humanly convincing depiction of lives stunted by social circumstances in the same area was *On the Black Hill* (1982) by Bruce Chatwin, whose other books (*In Patagonia* (1978), The Viceroy of Ouidah (1980), The Songlines (1987), *Utz* (1988)) explored more exotic or deadly colonial encroachments.

In the 1980s, empires were to be found everywhere in fiction. Doris Lessing located three in outer space: Canopus, Sirius and Puttiora. Representing different imperial ideologies, these stellar dominions allowed her to project ideas shaped by her early experiences in Rhodesia out into the sphere of galactic-didactic science fiction. At the other extreme, Philip Glazebrook, in books like *Captain Vinegar's Commission* (1987) and *The Gate at the End of the World*, (1989) re-entered the realm of imperial romance, sending two young Victorians adventuring out into the wilder reaches of the Ottoman and Russian empires but unearthing evidence of commercial greed and cynical realpolitik amid the gaudy dazzle and stir.

The most indefatigable tourer of empires in 1980s fiction was Barry Unsworth. At the start of the decade he seemed, like Glazebrook, particularly fascinated by the Turkish suzerainty, inspecting its fraying outer fringes in *Pascali's Island* (1980) and peering into its decaying core, Constantinople, with *The Rage of the Vulture* (1982). Venice, seen in *Stone Virgin* (1985) at different phases of its history, was the next stopping-point. Then, with *Sugar and Rum* in 1988 came Liverpool, a city once aggrandised by imperial trade, now pauperised by its loss, which Unsworth used as a vantage post from which to survey past vistas of empire and present social prospects in Britain. Contrasts ran through the novel: between elegant merchant mansions and the fetid slave-hulks that helped to finance them; between the affluent enclaves of Thatcherite Tories and the derelict quarters of the unemployed.

Social crevasses of the latter kind are the most prominent feature in fictional panoramas of 1980s Britain. A novel starkly displaying this is David Caute's *Veronica or The Two Nations* (1989), whose narrative viewpoint is polarised between that of a Conservative cabinet minister and that of a left-wing journalist from the East End slums. At one point, the MP encounters Margaret Thatcher (a frequent strider into novels of the decade from Jeffery Archer's *First Among Equals* (1984) to Pete Davies's *The Last Election* (1986)). She is got up in 'a terracotta outfit . . . with a busy pattern of what looked all too like snakes and ladders'. This pattern, with its motif of escalated rise and helpless descent, is also woven into the novel's fabric. As Caute's title indicates, behind his vision of a bifurcated Britain stands an earlier portrayal of the country as deplorably split between rich and poor: Disraeli's *Sybil or The Two Nations*.

Nineteenth-century Condition of England novels became regular phantom presences in fiction of the 1980s, invoked by authors who felt the divides such books had helped to narrow were being prised wide again by Thatcherism. Though Margaret Thatcher's call for a return to 'Victorian values' failed to win any appreciable response from novelists, a desire to document the social results of her policies did send a great many of them back to Victorian fictional prototypes. David Lodge's elegant, ironic *Nice Work* (1988) is a prime instance of this. As a post-structuralist feminist lecturer and an unreconstructed Midlands industrialist learn about each other's very different field of employment, Lodge makes witty play with allusions to, and plot-patterns from, books like *Sybil*, *Shirley*, *North and South* and *Hard Times*. Like them, Lodge's novel looks at a nation cleft by social, economic and regional gulfs. Where there's a difference is in his characters' awareness that the real sphere of power and prestige lies outside both their orbits: in the City.

As the financial hub of monetarism, the City of London generated quite a lot of literature during the decade. With the

Square Mile suddenly appearing glitzily fashionable, a new genre emerged. In the theatre, 'City Comedy', a term once denoting rather obscure seventeenth-century plays mocking the dowdy habits of Cheapside merchants, took on fresh significance as dramatists, in plays like *Serious Money, Fashion* or *Speculators*, trained satiric eyes on the manic acquisitiveness of commodity-brokers, *arbitrageurs* and associated PR or advertising agency types. Novelists were alert to the almost lurid pre-eminence money-markets achieved during the Thatcher era, too. Symptomatically, the two fictional works Malcolm Bradbury published were both labelled with phrases from the financial lexicon. *Rates of Exchange* (1982), though mainly a comedy of cultural misunderstandings in Eastern Europe, sardonically nodded towards the dominant Thatcherite 'sado-monetarist' ethos with its title and pervading imagery. *Cuts* (1987), a subsequent novella, incisively itemised the financial cutbacks and social scissorings-apart the decade was witnessing.

If Caryl Churchill's *Serious Money* ('Sexy greed *is* the late Eighties') was the play that encapsulated the high-adrenalin buzz and thrusty rapacity of the decade's finance frenzy, Martin Amis's *Money* (1984) was the novel that came closest to doing the same. Unlike Churchill, Amis doesn't underpin his scathing, scabrous burlesque with hard knowledge about the means by which characters amass the money they are selling out their humanity for. As in his earlier semi-satires of contemporary decadence, he settles for sending the strobe-lights of his Walpurgisnacht prose raking garishly over monsters and freaks spawned by an outlandish status quo. Another favoured fictional motif of the 1980s – the metropolis as hell – heightens the infernal glare. With both London and New York put on show as Gehennas of voracity and violence, *Money* deplores and revels in a culture expiring from nightmarish glut.

Things are even more drastically terminal in Amis's last novel of the decade, *London Fields* (1989): a book that carries his habitual sense of scary precariousness out into new areas. Vibrating with sinister, destructive energies, this is a ferociously apocalyptic work. In the ecologically ravaged near-future it envisages, 'multi-megaton hurricanes' and 'gigawatt thunderstorms' turbulently shroud the planet. Under this canopy of meteorological menace, the political climate is equally worrying: an international crisis boils up towards nuclear war. Further darkening the atmosphere, the sun, already abnormally low on the horizon, is due to go into total eclipse on November 5th ('bombfire night', as a cockney cabbie has it). Characters silhouetted against all this are a narrator apparently expiring from radiation sickness, a psychotic woman seeking someone to kill her, a devitalised yuppie and an emotionally dead proletarian thug. The only discernible gleam of hope is the presence of a patient, angelic little girl.

That she is eventually revealed to be a victim of child abuse will come as no surprise to regular readers of 1980s fiction. Never before in English literature can so many molested juveniles have been brought into view. Partly, this seems a response to growing contemporary awareness of the problem. Partly, it seems an aspect of the pervading tendency to scrutinise often traumatic starting-points. Partly – in finding present-day equivalents to the jeopardised waifs of Victorian fiction – it connects with the keenness on reactivating nineteenth-century fictional fixtures.

David Cook, an unsurpassed depicter of the disadvantaged and damaged, pointed up the last of these links when he published, in *Sunrising* (1984), a very Dickensian narrative about endangered children straying through nineteenth-century London and a desperately impoverished countryside. With *Crying Aloud* (1986), he focused on more recent child-abuse and its propensity to recur through generations of a family. Numerous other novelists put together fictional case studies too. Deborah Moggach's *Porky* (1983) confronted father-daughter incest with unblinking directness. In Beryl Bainbridge's *An Awfully Big Adventure* (1989), it led to tragedy. Alexander Stuart strove to cause shocks with a variant on it in *The War Zone* (1989). Paternal abuse of a daughter flickered into view in *Veronica* and lurked in the background of the trilogy Alice Thomas Ellis wrote during the decade, *The Clothes in the Wardrobe* (1987), *The Skeleton in the Cupboard* (1988) and *The Fly in the Ointment* (1989). Detective novelists – P. D. James, Ruth Rendell, Simon Brett – unmasked female murderers as victims of the continuing repercussions of sexual abuse by a father. Buchi Emecheta, long an observer of the patriarchal pitfalls hindering her heroines' progress, brought father–daughter incest to the fore with *Gwendolen* (1989). Abuse of children was central to Margaret Drabble's *The Radiant Way* (1987) and its successor, *A Natural Curiosity* (1989).

During the 1970s, under-age protagonists in Ian McEwan's fiction were as likely to be damaging as damaged. In the 1980s this changed. Now his concern became, if not exactly tampered-with children, at least tampered-with childhoods. Ostensibly about the loss of a child through kidnapping, *The Child in Time* (1987) was actually about loss of childhood and the toll this can exact in later life. A sub-plot, in which a Gradgrindish Tory MP reverts to puerility and living on toffee in a tree-house, illustrated this in fantasy-parable fashion. More realistically, McEwan shows the novel's hero, repressed and regimented when young, needing to re-establish contact with the openness and spontaneity this cut him off from. With *The Innocent* (1990), which took as its protagonist another inhibited and emotionally cramped English male, McEwan made even clearer a distinction crucial in his work: that between childishness and childlikeness. For him, men tend to manifest the worst aspects of the former – self-centredness, impatience, violence; women, the best aspects of the latter – trust, candour, attachment. *The Child in Time* and *The Innocent* are both placed in crudely divided communities: a near-future Britain of plutocracy and state registered beggars, the politically partitioned Berlin of the 1950s. Against these backdrops, McEwan subtly examines healing modes of psychological and emotional integration.

The most thorough-going survey of the fissures the decade saw opening up in Britain was Margaret Drabble's *The Radiant Way*. Beginning with a New Year party ushering in the 1980s, the novel rapidly became less festive. Once again, a Two Nations formula was employed as Drabble returned to the North–South contrast that had stood her in such good stead in earlier books. Casting an elaborate narrative network over both regions, the novel showed a desire, reminiscent of Dickens or George Eliot, to encompass the whole of contemporary British society and what were viewed as its alarmingly widening gulfs. Everywhere the story turned, devastation loomed. Talk of mugggings, cuts, ruinous strikes and ruined public services cast a continuing pall. A typical scene had a disillusioned social worker stranded in her broken-down car amid inner-city dereliction during a relentless downpour on the night of the winter solstice. On the prowl in the dark streets around her was a murderous psychopath, known to the press as 'The Horror of Harrow Road'.

In the book's sequel, *A Natural Curiosity*, he is brought under the spotlight (and, like so many mentally disturbed figures in 1980s fiction, is diagnosed as having been deranged by parental abuse). His prominence in this novel accords with Drabble's conviction that the date of its setting, 1987, was 'a psychotic year, the year of abnormality'. As part of her attempt to convey this, the narrative tone – low-keyed and depressed in *The Radiant Way* – becomes more clamorously insistent. Presenting itself as the fictional record of a disturbed phase in British life, the novel deepens its scope by constantly delving into history to come up with earlier instances of cruel aberration. Archaeology books perused in prison by The Horror afford graphic illustrations of ancient atrocities: mass slaughterings and ritual killings.

Digging back into the past is a popular occupation in 1980s fiction, and has obvious affinities with the prevailing desire to probe to imperialism's foundations or to uncover the maltreated child behind the malformed adult. Assisted by the fact that its narrator is a history teacher, *Waterland* (1983), Graham Swift's novel set in the Fens, dredged up data from both the recent and distant past to elucidate the present. Excavation into a prehistoric barrow has its progress charted throughout Peter Ackroyd's *First Light* (1989). Near the tumulus in that novel is a high-tech observatory. Attention paid to its sophisticated monitoring of the heavens aligns the book with another 1980s trait: an eagerness by novelists to incorporate scientific material into their art. Quantum physics and time theory attract McEwan's interest. Amis saturation-bombs *London Fields* with nuclear terminology. Mathematical geniuses figure in Boyd's *The New Confessions* and *Brazzaville Beach*.

Physicians and mathematicians, it has to be said, are on record as less than impressed by some of these portrayals of their proceedings. Where contemporary novelists were on surer ground was in their assimilating of components from earlier novels into their own. Recycling literary prototypes was a boom industry in 1980s fiction. Placed amid the Hardyesque contours of Dorset, for instance, *First Light* reworks his *Two on a Tower*. Similar impulses actuated preceding Ackroyd books. Reminders of *Little Dorrit* flicker through *The Great Fire of London* (1982). *The Last Testament of Oscar Wilde* (1983)was a feat of virtuoso ventriloquism. *Chatterton* (1985) and *Hawksmoor* (1987) are structured round sizeable stretches of finely replicated nineteenth- and seventeenth-century prose.

Other novelists shared this taste for replica and remoulding. Boyd's *The New Confessions* was a homage to Rousseau. Bainbridge's *An Awfully Big Adventure* toyed with plot situations from *Peter Pan*. Anita Brookner's first novel, *A Start in Life* (1981), is modelled on *Eugénie Grandet*; her second, *Providence* (1982), on *Adolphe*. Muriel Spark's *Symposium* (1990) inventively responded to both

Plato's dialogue and Lucian's satire of that name. David Lodge's farce about international conference-circuit academics, *Small World* (1984), mimicked the tropes of verse-romance, sprinkling its pages with cross-reference to Ariosto, Grail myths and the like.

Many writers turned their pens to pastiche. With *A Maggot* (1985), John Fowles offered facsimile eighteenth-century fiction. Philip Glazebrook reproduced nineteenth-century imperial adventure-and-travel tales. Intertextual panache packed A. S. Byatt's *Possession* (1990) with sheaves of high-quality pastiche from Browningesque monologues and Emily Dickinson-like lyrics through William Morris-ish sagas to post-structuralist feminist prose. As two 1980s academics rummaged into the clandestinely linked lives of two nineteenth-century poets, the novel, counterpointing the Victorian age and the present day, zestfully demonstrated how creativity and critical interpretation are shaped by the pressures of personality, gender and the atmosphere of an era.

The most impressive fictional sequence of the 1980s, William Golding's trilogy *Rites of Passage, Close Quarters,* and *Fire Down Below* (1980, 1987, 1989) constituted an especially masterly excursion into the past and pastiche. As its narrator, Edmund Talbot, set sail during the Napoleonic wars to Sydney Cove and a high-ranking government post, Golding's fiction put itself on course to revisit an early phase of British colonialism. Penned for the most part in Augustan prose, the trilogy matched its subject with a stylistic harking-back. And, as Talbot's hidebound mentality, still redolent of the late eighteenth century, encountered manifestations of Romanticism, the novels evoked with dazzling immediacy a crucial watershed in Britain's cultural and political development.

Golding's battered, barnacled old sailing ship creaking its leaky way over the Equator to the Antipodes was the most unforgettable fictional vessel in the 1980s. A more widely employed one was, rather surprisingly, Noah's Ark, which hove into view from many compass points during the decade. The cosiest outing it was given was in Barbara Trapido's *Noah's Ark* (1984), where it afforded a wooden image for the sentimental tale of the family a Noah Glazer had assembled under his roof. More often, it was commandeered by feminists eager to remodel this patriarchal archetype which had only accommodated conventional connubial couples. The results – Jeanette Winterson's *Boating for Beginners* (1985), *Arky Types* (1987) by Sara Maitland and Michelene Wandor – could be over-freighted with whimsical preachiness. But the best of the novels in this line, Michèle Roberts's *The Book of Mrs Noah* (1987), which converted the Ark into a floating conference centre where women from different backgrounds congregated, wrote and discussed, did adroitly combine the buoyant and the substantial.

Roberts steered her Ark to Venice, a city whose associations with androgyny, carnival and moist intricacy made it a favoured feminist port of call. Winterson's *The Passion* (1987) journeyed there too, finding as its heroine a boatsman's daughter with webbed feet. Women possessing unorthodox physical attributes weren't unusual in feminist fiction of this decade. The heroine of Angela Carter's gaudy extravaganza, *Nights at the Circus* (1984), has wings. In *Sexing the Cherry* (1989), Winterson employs as her protagonist a Rabelaisian giantess capable of engulfing men in her vagina. As such features indicate, fantasy was a popular mode in 1980s feminist novels. Just as Rushdie and his growing band of imitators (I. Allan Sealy, Shashi Tharoor) used myth, magic and fable as a kind of stylistic mutiny against the supremacy of Anglo-Saxon realism, so feminist writers revelled in the gothic, fairy-tale and absurd as counter-effects to the 'patriarchal discourse' of rationality, logic and linear narrative. Occupying a zone of its own between this type of writing and the more documentary feminism of Margaret Drabble, Pat Barker and the like was the fiction of Fay Weldon in which comic-strip indictment and nemesis unreeled amid scenes striving for social actuality.

The most notable 1980s Noah's Ark book, Julian Barnes's *A History of the World in 10 1/2 Chapters* (1989), took on board some elements from the feminist flotilla of novels in this genre (one of the participants in *Arky Types* was a chatty worm: Barnes's first chapter gives a woodworm's eye view of life on the Ark; another of his chapters elaborates on something Winterson's novel alludes to, an American expedition to Mount Ararat in search of relics of the Ark). Deftly picked up bits and pieces like this are then worked into a novel collage.

Always an eclectic talent (his previous output included adolescent-memoir fiction, a marital-stress novel, jaunty detective stories, fiction that jumps from past to future, and a creative blend of narrative and literary criticism) Barnes produced with *A History of the World in 10 1/2 Chapters* a work that is itself a marvellous miscellany of facts and fictions, pastiche, autobiography, essays and reportage. Settings shift from the Aegean to Australia, from Biblical times to the present day via medieval France and nineteenth-century Armenia. Different ways of viewing the world – artistic, scientific, religious, 'sophisticated', 'primitive' – are inspected from different angles and in different genres. Parody gives way to documentary. Jokes jostle horrors. Satiric mimicry counterpoints intimately personal talk. In true post-modernist style, the book utilises a mix of styles. Running through the multiplicity are insistent connections, though. Barnes's bobbings into the past repeatedly sight factors, especially bigotry and prejudice, that have bedevilled humanity's history. The ever-returning image of the Ark is a reminder to the planet's variegated inhabitants that, essentially, we are all in the same boat. This affirmation of global unity along with an enjoyment of cultural diverseness gives the book its distinctive quality – and makes it an ingeniously crafted summation of British fictional trends in the decade at whose conclusion it appeared.

Facing the New

The glory is departed from Israel. So, famously, lamented the pregnant wife of Phinehas, when her husband and his brother were slain in battle by the Philistines, the Ark of the Lord in their custody was carried off and their father, old Eli the national Judge, collapsed at the news and broke his neck. All these shocks brought on her labour. She named the child Ichabod, meaning Where Is the Glory?, a name that entered the English language as the apt title of any lost Christian cause, a closing-down chapel, it might be, or a sect on its last legs. Ichabod, Ichabod, the Glory is Departed: that's what nineteenth-century Nonconformists thought should be written up over places the Spirit had departed from. And it's what mournful souls have been writing over the forms of narration known as the Novel, for as long as anyone can recall. In history the middle classes always seem to be rising; in literary history their favourite form, the novel, is always said to be dying. Especially the so-called English novel.

The allegations about the 'crisis' in Our Novel Now are awfully familiar. It's too bourgeois. It's too English. It's certainly no longer new enough. It's stifling to death on old-fashioned technique, allegiance to Jane Austen, or Classic Realism, or Humanism, and the like. On the other hand, it's claimed Our Novel is also being killed off by sordid and ill-advised experimenters. There's been nothing good after – and because of – *Ulysses* or *Finnegans Wake* and their heirs and assigns. So bring back Jane Austen. Or, 'Who's Jorge Luis Borges?' as Philip Larkin, Dick Francis's most literate fan, once memorably put it. 'Nothing makes me feel more thoroughly old than to realise that there is nothing but a bloody great hole where quite an important part of my life once was.' Thus Kingsley Amis in his recent *Memoirs*, talking about the early styles of jazz that he likes and can no longer find in sufficient quantity. He doesn't feel new writing is in quite such bad odour as new jazz – it hasn't caused all the old stuff actually to *disappear* – but it is nearly so: 'I mean, poetry, the novel and much more besides have gone off all right'. He's starting telling interviewers that he can only now bear to read Amis junior, out of all the younger novelists.

But neither the pro- nor the anti-modern wailers and bemoaners are in close touch with what is really happening in 'English' fiction. For good stuff pours incessantly out from the presses. The dross-purveyors – and of course, there is dross; there always has been – have classy rivals in great number. And it's been almost a criterion of good fictional stuff, just as it has been of serious-reader-appealing stuff, that it eschews the opposed extremes of novelty and convention that the lamenters tend, absurdly, to make the burden of their negative cases. It is possible, no doubt, to imagine a readership for utterly unchanging, traditional fiction, even if it's difficult to imagine that readership not signing off pretty sharply if what is repeatedly offered is actually only warmed-up pastiches of past modes. And in practice it is very hard to track down utterly old-fashioned or simply repetitive conventional novels. Catherine Cookson – who usually gets cited hereabouts – is, in her way, quite an up-to-date fictionist. Her sexual explicitness, for instance, was simply not available to a popular Victorian novelist such as Mrs Oliphant, and was certainly not indulged in popular fiction before the Second World War. D.H. Lawrence and James Joyce had novels pulped and banned for far less than is normal in Ms Cookson's pages. Just so, while Jilly Cooper, say, may be conventional as to form, she is manifestly an end-of-the-twentieth-century novelist in relation to subject-matter, vocabulary and tone.

As for the great innovators, even the most notorious ones have innovated only patchily – in terms of subject here, language there or form there – and they've normally done it within recognisably conventional bounds. Fielding shifted the novel's ground dramatically, but it was on post-Homeric and Cervantick lines. Much of our period's most innovative fiction has been consciously revived Shandyesque. We're all of us – to coin a phrase – Joyceans nowadays. And this drag of the conventional upon the new is to a large extent inevitable. A completely new text would be simply illegible. Keeping faith with the incessant promise of newness suggested by every 'new novel' inevitably means also keeping up some kind of pact with the tradition or traditions. Experiment that halts anywhere this side of gobbledegook or glossalalia is unavoidably a compromise with the past. And making the run-in with convention – or conventions, for by this time there are inevitably many, many fictional conventions on offer – more or less self-conscious, signalling the process of allusion and intertextuality, foregrounding it as self-conscious critics say, that is playing games with it, manipulating it, is what marks out much of what's arresting in current 'English' fiction.

A strong case in point is Patrick McGrath, who in only three volumes of fiction – the stories of *Blood and Water* (published in the US in 1988, and in Britain in 1989 in the shortlived Penguin Originals series) and the two novels *The Grotesque* (1989) and *Spider* (1991) – has proved himself a masterful modern updater and exploiter of the traditional devices of Gothic. McGrath is a devoted Gothic revivalist – unsurprisingly enough, one of his published stories, 'The Angel', has a character who's fond of Victorian Gothic Revivalist architecture and the Anglo-Catholic religiosity that went with it – and a resurrection man who is not at all trading in Gothic out of mere antiquarian interest or only with a Literary Comp winning eye to the joys of pastiche. 'I'm trying to achieve an elegant weirdness in my work,' he's declared, but his writing wagers on the significance of gothic blackness as a sign-system as potent as any for registering the terrible things in our unprecedently evil century. McGrath's human monsters, the rotting flesh his narratives expose beneath the corsets of his respectable-looking people, his oddballs and madmen, are all, inter al, post-colonialist, post-Auschwitz ones. The strange man Spider Cleg, the most unreliable narrator of McGrath's *Spider* who turns out so demented and dementing as his narrative unfolds, is a child of East End streets that are full of the traces of a dubious British imperial past, Kitchener Street, Omdurman Close, and that come into a terrifying familiarity with the horrors of Europe and the Hitler struggle that might at first have seemed appropriately far off. German bombs will blitz these cosy streets to pieces, and Spider's own story will finally reveal him as a kind of domestic blitzer on a miniature Hitlerite model. It's not only the Nazis, out there in Eastern Europe, who will use gas as a murder weapon. The murderous apocalyptic tendencies of his, and our, times are in him. The poisonous pong of gas – and right from the start of Spider's story there's an increasingly ominous gasometer at the end of his street – will eventually take over the novel, as it took over Europe and European history, completely. And this is only one of the telling, chilling junctures McGrath arranges between some nightmarish piece of local gothicised narrative matter and the larger awful history of our times. In such ways McGrath uses his chosen convention, updates it, strips away its acquired layers of Dracula-Frankenstein-Hollywoodised farcicality, makes it serve powerfully bleak satiric purposes.

Not all new novelists manage their selected conventions as successfully as they might and McGrath does. The poet and biographer Andrew Motion, for example, has launched himself into what was promised as a grand *roman fleuve* about a public-schoolboy called Francis Mayne with very great energy, but also with a worryingly pronounced kind of genre speed-wobble. Motion's first volume, *The Pale Companion* (1989), tried re-articulating the customary tropes of its Sixties story of adolescent all-boys boarding school pashes as a story of growth into historical consciousness, but the mix would keep slipping back into a mere sequence of rather familiar enemies-of-promise-style sessions of mutual masturbation behind the cricket pavilion. In this novel's successor, *Famous for the Creatures* (1991), Francis Mayne is to be found up at Oxford where, useful for self-reflexion, and marking his author's try at another type of beginning novel, he's joined the novel-writing, diary-keeping classes. But to watch Mayne watching himself seeking to capture his relationship with the lovely fellow-undergraduate Sylvie Shepherd in his diary and in his novel that's entitled – yes! – *Famous for the Creatures*, is to be moving only among pale echoes of Martin Amis's famously sharp debut in his self-reflexive Oxford fiction *The Rachel Papers*. Motion must, in the words of the ushers who so far people his fictional imagination rather thickly, try harder next term.

Motion's initiate fumbling of catches is worth mentioning because it makes an instructive contrast with the generic sureness of touch instantly displayed by Lucy Ellmann and Paul Watkins. Both of these were, of course, like Amis *fils*, born mouth stuffed full of literary silver spoons – she, a daughter of Joyce biographer Richard Ellmann; he, 'educated at the Dragon School, Eton and Yale' – and so knowing a thing or two about how writings go. Like Motion's novels, Lucy Ellmann's first novel *Sweet Desserts* (1988) is manifestly autobiographical. Its author's own experience obviously fires its portrait of Suzy Schwarz, the irked sibling of a rising academic star of a sister and the angry, yearning daughter of a famous Oxford academic daddy who lies dying. But nothing goes awry with this novel's array of opening-life motifs – the wry, adolescent clever-dickery, the awed discovery of sex, the intertwining lives of the body and the mind, the blend of fucking and food-ism – right down to the smart post-modernist trickery of the joke-index (knowing shades of Christine Brooke-Rose). Lucy Ellmann is already clearly on top of her chosen mode. So, too, is Paul Watkins, and several times over, for he's already turned out to be a deft manipulator of several fictional kinds. His first novel, *Night Over Day Over Night* (1988), rightly reminded readers of *All Quiet on the Western Front*. His second, *Calm At Sunset, Calm At Dawn* (1989), an extraordinary story of a youth working with fishermen on the eastern seaboard of the United States, laconic and tough, reads like mightily freshened up Hemingway. In his third novel, *In the Blue Light of African Dreams* (1990), the preferred model is St-Exupéry in a story about one Charlie Halifax, First World War flyer now caught up in a war between the French Foreign Legion and the Arabs. What's compelling about Watkins is not only this astonishingly versatile power to command different fictional kinds – which makes him one of the flashiest of, as it were, post-modernist flaunters of stylistic variety around – but also his reinstatement of the rights of the story of male adventure. It's taken William Boyd and Ian McEwan – and their critics – time, I think, to get around to realising that they are in effect rewriting and recuperating certain kinds of once unfashionable, and certainly anti-feminist, male-action fiction. That Watkins has reached this realisation of what he's about so early in his career is a key part of his power.

Seeking to express kinds of selfhood through fiction set, like Watkins's *In the Blue Light of African Dreams*, in the past – in that case 1926 – is, of course, something that 'English' novels have long been good at. Like realism, though, historicism has come under steady critical fire in our present deconstructionist era, no doubt because the historical is easy to perceive as a threateningly heightened domain of the realistic. How interesting, then, to observe that some of our best new novelists are defying such Higher Critical prejudices, are refusing to allow mere costume dramas (*à la* Catherine Cookson) to hog historical narrative, and are, like Watkins, attractively reinvesting in the realistic via the historical.

Duncan Sprott's *The Clopton Hercules* (1991) – a hugely confident first novel, and the first novel, it's said, to be published by Faber and Faber from the slush-pile since *Lord of the Flies* in 1954 – is set in Shakespeare country in the 1840s. Built on the true story of gigantic Charles Warde of Clopton House, Stratford-upon-Avon, it narrates the rise and fall of a moneyed Victorian rake who flouts the sexual conventions of his time and is dragged down by his sturdily individualistic investment in a very bizarre mix of sexual and social defiance.

An equally promising grotesque realism of character and action, but mapped this time on a far larger historical scale, is what preoccupies Michael Ignatieff's first novel *Asya* (1991), about the career of a fearless Russian woman who traverses our century from the Bolshevik Revolution, through pre-war Paris, blitzed London and post-war Eaton Square, ending up back in Gorbachev's Moscow. Ignatieff undoubtedly has trouble managing the crowdedness of his great canvas, and the crowdedness of his literary memory. Like all the smart pen-pushers of our *fin-de-siècle*, he is inevitably steeped in the vast intertextual debris of our awfully 'literatured' (to borrow a word from Joyce) times. It's no surprise to find his narrative reading like something by Chekhov layered onto a Conradianism that's not only – naturally – familiar with Dickens, but also, less expectably, with John Le Carré. Asya's great love Sergei greatly resembles Le Carré's Carla, the intriguing face of the Cold War Soviet opposition. Her questing life of Dickensian path-crossings and coincidences leads to an extremely Dickensian end, with Asya as Lady Dedlock in a Moscow graveyard. And there are many ghosts of a more personal kind that Ignatieff clearly feels compelled to try and cope with. His own family was, like Asya, once in trans-world flight from Russia and Bolshevik terror. The pull of the literary and historical past is immense and understandably aweing; but Ignatieff's past-animating reach and political scope are never swamped by the massiveness of these various memories.

Much more stay-at-home in its affections, and more inclined to embrace its particular past of an English childhood in a larkily farcical way – a keynote of English fictional approaches to youthful selfhood since the 18th century: our *Bildungsromane* run heavily to farce and send-up – is Ivor Gould's charmingly pretend-memoir of one Jeffrey Cork, *A Smoking Dot in the*

Distance (1991). What makes this large saga of growing up
in a balmily nostalgic amalgam of wartime Spitfire-spotting,
cinematic news-dramas, Richmal Crompton's Just William
stories, trips to Whipsnade Zoo and BBC wireless dance-bands
so particularly fetching is Gould's magic materialism – the
capacity to animate the contents of kitchen cupboards, medicine
chests and the window displays of once important high street
purveyors of essential domestic gear, such as J. Dunne the
Hatter and Timothy White's and Taylor, the pharmacists.
Here things like Zebo, Scott's Emulsion, Germoline, Vironita,
Carnation Milk, Gee's Linctus, Victory Vee Lozenges, Tizer
the Appetizer, Palm Toffee and Zubes live, and live again, in
the most user-friendly commodity fetishism possible, held on
the page, as in the memory, by their names, titles lovingly
released from the Pandora's Box of the immediate past, along
with whole lists of contextualising, history-animating tags,
slogans, phrases: Britain Can Take It, Phone Whitehall 1212,
Friday Night is Amami Night. Gould's home-brewed version
of magic realism does that mode's business of simultaneous
familiarising and defamiliarisation with great aplomb. The
distancing announced in Gould's title and practised in his
choice of a setting in the past has often proved a necessary
device for imaginative focussing. Some form of self-sought
alienation from the fictional subject is anyway quite normal.
In particular, when novelists of any period have approached
the perennially interesting subject of the present, taking up the
traditional fictional concern with the Condition of England,
life in the contemporary City, selfhood and sexuality under
whatever conditions and constraints happen to be current,
they've often done so from some distanced standpoint.

Satiric vexation anyway estranges, but it's often been enforced by the alienations of class, region, nationality. Not
for nothing are our greatest novelists marked by the class
estrangements of a Dickens or a Lawrence, the foreignness of
a Joyce, a Conrad or Beckett. And so it is now with many of
our best new novelists. Not only are numbers of them aroused to
satiric anger over the contemporary social and political climate
– which has been a subject to over-heating and over-heatedness,
in what novelists widely perceive to have been the wrongs of
'Thatcher's Britain', no less than the over-heating meteorology
of the globe – but the fulcrum of the new satiric fictions is

commonly some overt and pronounced point of recognisable social disadvantage. To put this bluntly: a very large number of our most promising new novelists are in some degree outside the Arnoldian 'tone of the centre' and writing from within some form of enforced internal exile – femaleness, homosexuality, Irishness, blackness of skin. It is, I think, no accident that Patrick McGrath should have spent so much of his early life at the gates of Broadmoor mental hospital, where his father was medical superintendent, and should live in the USA; nor that Lucy Ellmann should have been born in the USA and been brought up by US citizens living in Britain, and that Michael Ignatieff is by birth Russian Canadian or that Paul Watkins was educated in the USA.

You don't necessarily, of course, have to be 'foreign' to be able to produce biting political satires and radical social comedy, or undertake bad-mouthing forays into the desperate worlds of the urban homeless, the social-security dependent, the down-and-out, the floating, alienated, cynical youth-masses of the metropolis. That's clear from the strong first novels along these lines by writers of, so far as one can judge, straightforward British pedigree: *The Way You Tell Them* (1990) by Alan Brownjohn, the poet; or *Rebuilding Coventry* (1988) by Sue Townsend, the playwright and renowned inventor of the pimpled diarist Adrian Mole; or *The Colour of Memory* (1989) by streetwise journalist Geoff Dyer; or the comic geriatric-hospital exposé *Asleep at the Wheel* (1989) by Moy McCrory, former waitress, sandwich delivery girl and nurse on the psychiatric and geriatric wards. Alienated cursing of modern Gradgrindery and Circumlocution Office lunacies and prevarications comes rather naturally in hard times and crumbling post-imperialist cultures even to otherwise settled native souls. But some extra estranging thrust clearly does help energise your fiction no end. And some specialised, particular, skewing angle on the reality of modern Britain is what unites and empowers important beginning fictionists as various as Alan Hollinghurst, poet, literary editor, homosexual and Robert Mapplethorpe apologist; Hanif Kureishi, film-maker and Man of Kent, but one with Indian parents and so a brown skin; Hugo Hamilton, born in Dublin, with an Irish mother and a German father, who lives and writes in Germany and Austria; and Adam Zameenzad, yet another modern Man of Kent to be born outside the kingdom, this time in Pakistan, and brought up elsewhere, in

East Africa. Such are our modern 'English' novelists; from such matrices our most interesting current fiction is arising.

Kureishi's first novel, *The Buddha of Suburbia* (1990), is a wonderfully comic English *Bildungsroman* with the pronounced edgy difference that its wry presentation of adolescent English life in the grey South London suburbs – the very world of Prime Minister John Major's allegedly ordinary English citizen – features the ambitious, fantasizing Karim Amir, 'an Englishman born and bred – almost'. And the benefits, painful, angering, but wonderfully strengthening, packed into that 'almost' are visible all over the writings of those of our new novelists who are, *mutatis mutandis*, in a similar case.

Alan Hollinghurst's extraordinary first novel *The Swimming Pool Library* (1989) is an anglicised version of what is relatively more common in the USA, the homophiliac bath-house fiction. This plunge into the narcissistic, manichean world of London clubland's male body-cultists is all at once that well-known creature, the literate Oxbridge novel gone slightly punk, all toughed-over E.M. Forster, bristling with the abutting frissons of yobbery and thuggishness (bad boy, Martin Amis kind of stuff), and that relative novelty in above-ground bookshops, a fictionalised history of twentieth-century poshocratic gays. Here serious fiction gains access to a whole world formerly closed off to it by internalised repressions as well as by law-enforced embargoes, and does so in a single stride as dramatic for fiction as, on another occasion and in connexion with the working-classes, *Sons and Lovers* was.

In a still more obvious acknowledgement of the power of the marginal, tangential vision, Hugo Hamilton comes to contemporary urban life in his *Surrogate City* (1990) in terms of a quite foreign *urbs*, the Berlin of now. Here is all of Geoff Dyers's fictional world, the youthful, spry, anxious, put-upon, wise-guy underbelly of the city (*The Colour of Memory*) seen through the eyes of an Irish girl, pregnant in the estranging metropolis, questing for her lost man. Not, as is more normal in these circumstances, on her own in London, but alone in Berlin where the grimly-treated underclass of drifters, musicians and other semi-criminalised outsiders is a predominantly Turkish element. In *Surrogate City* the Isherwood-like promise of Hugo Hamilton's stories that appeared in Faber's *First Fictions: Introductions 10* (1989), especially 'The Compound

Assembly of E. Richter', about an impecunious Irish musician in Berlin, is wonderfully fulfilled. As Isherwood read his times, including his London times, through reading Thirties Berlin, so Hamilton reads his native Dublin and its neighbour London, and the modernity they house and represent, through the lens of Berlin in the Eighties and Nineties. If this novelist is a camera, the camera is emphatically Made Elsewhere. Which couldn't be more dramatically true of the potent fictions of Adam Zameenzad.

Zameenzad started off in *The Thirteenth House* (1987) in a wryly comic R.K. Narayan sort of vein, investing in the nicely self-protective ironies that clever anglophone Indian and Pakistani writers are well schooled at wrapping their social criticisms in. But he's gradually turned himself into a moral and political allegorist of the most fearlessly open kind, wielding scathing apocalyptic parables about evil and oppression in our time as, almost, no other 'English' writer does. His third novel, *Love, Bones and Water* (1989), is a classic dystopia that savagely presents the wicked schemings of the politically powerful against the shanty-town poor in the so-called democratic, sub-South American republic of New Heaven. In this novel the critical scalpel is still partly sheathed by the pseudonymity of the target. But in his majestic, huge, fourth fiction, *Cyrus, Cyrus* (1990), Zameenzad has shed the traditional maskings of the dystopian mode and named the names with a courage reminiscent of Salman Rushdie – who is clearly, in some senses, a model for Zameenzad. This novel has real places in its sights: India, where the fabulous globe-trotter Cyrus Cyrus is born; California of the gurus, to which Cyrus is inevitably drawn; London, where Cyrus is just one more abused Paki, alone in a city of racists. The nearest comparison for this novel is, of course, with Zameenzad's fellow-countryman – in every sense – Salman Rushdie. There are, though, significant differences from Rushdie. Strikingly, Zameenzad's account of the suffering under-class alien in his various modern Babylons looks for salvation to Christ-resembling male saviours. This is true in *Love, Bones and Water*, a text dominated by an enigmatic, physically desperate (and incidentally very Goldingesque) charismatic figure apparently risen from he dead, as it is in *Cyrus, Cyrus* where it's only the Man on the Donkey who can take on the money-changers in the London where these cashiers have taken over. In this City, classically inspired Hades stories blur into the tropes of the

Biblical mysteries of the End Times, making a striking combined apocalyptic of extraodinary multivalent hellishness.

Some sort of transcendence or investment in religiose reflections, magics, spiritual sources of salvation and respite is often a part of the parabolic mystagoguery of the fabulous realism that Zameenzad has, like many another 'European' novelist, learned, and is importing, from South America. His 'South Americanism' yet one more sign of the directions that the best of new 'English' novels are taking, emphatically away from mere Englishness, into the decidedly mixed enthnicity of a culture now unignorably a compound of former insiders and newer 'outsiders'– with Pakistanis like Zameenzad crowding in to join Irishmen like Hamilton and all the other traditionally native foreigners – in a New Britishness that looks to the world not just for its clientele, the personnel of those who will be its writers, a group that now manifestly comes from all over the globe, but that also looks outwards for what are, and I take it will increasingly be, its global modes and means and its globalised subjects. Now, more than ever, it is clear, Daniel Defoe's 'True-Born Englishman' is, like his and her fiction, genetically, as generically, no longer able to be thought of as something single, whole, white, male, centralised, predictable, pure. At the end of the century 'English' fiction is assuming, as 'England' has taken in, the world.

Poems

History

(*To Peter Vansittart*)

The last war-horse slaughtered and eaten
long ago. Not a rat, not a crow-crumb
left; the polluted water scarce;
the vile flies settling on the famous
enlarged eyes of skeleton children.

Tonight the moon's open-mouthed. I must
surrender in the morning. But those
cipher tribes out there, those Golden Hordes,
those shit! They'll loot and maim and rape.
What textbook atrocities in the morning?

Now, solitary, my hip-joint aching,
half-lame, I climb the high battlements
carrying a musical instrument.
Why not? What's better? The bedlam of sleep
or the clarities of insomnia?

Look! Below, most fearful perspective:
cloud-fleeing shadows of unending
flatlands; enemy tent after tent
pegged to the unstable moonlight.
You'd think the moon, exposed, would howl.

Besieged city, in some future
history book (aseptic page or footnote)
they'll fable your finale: how
your huck-shouldered, arthritic General,
silhouette on the dark battlements,

played on his pipe a Mongolian song,
an enemy song, played so purely
the Past disrobed, memory made audible,
(sharp as a blade, lonely, most consequent,
that soul-naked melody of the steppes);

how, below, the Mongol soldiers awoke,
listened, leaned on their elbows tamed,

became so utterly homesick, wretched,
so inflamed, that by the cold sweats
of dawnlight, they decamped, departed.

Ha! Such a pleasing, shameless story,
to be told over and over by these
and by those: by propagandists of music;
by descendants of the Mongols.
But, alas, only a scribe's invention.

The truth? I play pianissimo
and not very well. The sleepers
in their tents sleep on, the sentries
hardly stir. I loiter on the battlements.
Stars! Stars! I put away my pipe and weep.

FRED D'AGUIAR

Dread

I saw what I took for waves
roping off into strands
that combine to make a fat rope
breaking on mud banks and turning pebbles.

But the strands formed ropes of their own
and before I could name what they were
the ingenious head to which they were plaited
reared up from the tide, widening rings
that marked new heights on the South Bank.

Marley's unmistakable smile
shone through the wash released over his face
by the matted locks. He shook them free
and it was like the Crystal Palace Bowl all over again:
Bob under the lights, when, between chanting down
Babylon
he shook his dread, and in shaking them a tremor
ran through the city knocking points off

the stocks and shares at the Exchange
and noughts off some dealers' profits.

He spoke through that smile at me.
'I an' I don't need no man to speak for I.
Though you see dust where there was a tongue
I man still loud an' clear on platinum.
Check your history and you will see
all through it some other man speaking for we;
and when they talk they sounding wise and pure
but when you check it all they spouting is pure lie.
Lies about Africa, home of the first upright man.
Lies about how many of us didn't get to the
Caribbean.
Lies about black people's true contribution
To building and civilising their Great Britain.
Look in the river it's a crystal ball;
Shout about the pain but don't shut out the bachanal.'

Right then Marley start to skank
his big steps threatened to make the water
breach its banks, Barrier or no Barrier,
this was the dance of the warrior;
the more he stamped the lower in the water he sank
until his dreadlocks returned to the waves I mistook
for plaits doing and undoing themselves.

▄▄▄ **WENDY COPE** ▄▄▄▄▄▄▄▄▄▄▄▄▄▄▄▄▄

Poem composed in Santa Barbara

The poets talk. They talk a lot.
They talk of T.S. Eliot.
One is anti. One is pro.
How hard they think! How much they know!
They're happy. A cicada sings.
We women talk of other things.

Letter

Alone too much this week,
I'm in my poet mode –
Awake at half past five and writing,
Dozing on the sofa-bed by ten.

You're there, of course, my absent angel,
But for once we don't make love
Or even talk. You have been working
In another room and then

You come in, carrying a blanket,
And cover me while I'm asleep.
It's cold today. I need the blanket.
You do it over and over again.

Reflections on a Royalty Statement

They've given me a number
So they will know it's me
And not some other Wendy Cope
(They publish two or three).
When I go to see them
I wear a number-plate
Or sometimes I salute and say,
'032838'.

What a lot of authors!
The digits make it clear
That publishers are busy –
You can phone them once a year
But it isn't done to grumble
If the cheque's a little late:
'Look, we've other things to think about,
032838.'

Sometimes they give a party
And all the numbers go.
'It's 027564!'
'036040!'
'Hey, have you seen 014's book?
You're right. He's second-rate.
But even so he's better than
032838.'

We're one big happy family
(My eyes are getting runny)
And, what is more, if we do well
They give us pocket-money!
Some publishers are terrible
But mine are really great.
OK? Can this go in my book? –
032838.

CAROL ANN DUFFY

Before You Were Mine

I'm ten years away from the corner you laugh on
with your pals, Maggie McGeeney and Jean Duff.
The three of you bend from the waist, holding
each other, or your knees, and shriek at the pavement.
Your polka dot dress blows round your legs. Marilyn.

I'm not here yet. The thought of me doesn't occur
in the ballroom with the thousand eyes, the fizzy, movie
tomorrows
the right walk home could bring. I knew you would
dance
like that. Before you were mine, your Ma stands at the
close
with leather for the late one. You reckon it's worth it.

The decade ahead of my loud, possessive yell was the best
one, eh?

I remember my hands in the high heeled red shoes, relics,
and now your ghost clatters toward me over George Square
till I see you, clear as braille, under the tree,
with its lights, and whose small bites on your neck, sweetheart?

Cha cha cha! You'd teach me the steps on the way home
from Mass,
stamping stars from the wrong pavement. Even then
I wanted the bold girl winking in Portobello, somewhere
in Scotland, before I was born. That glamorous love
lasts,
where you sparkle and waltz and laugh before you were
mine.

Away and See

Away and see an ocean suck at a boiled sun
and say to someone things I'd blush even to dream.
Slip off your dress in a high room over the harbour.
Write to me soon.

New fruits sing on the flipside of night in a market
of language, light, a tune from the chapel nearby
stopping you dead, the peach in your palm respiring.
Taste it for me.

Away and see the things that words give a name to,
the flight
of syllables, wingspan stretching a noun. Test words
wherever they live; listen and touch, smell, believe.
Spell them with love.

Skedaddle. Somebody chaps at the door at a year's end,
hopeful.
Away and see who it is. Let in the new, the vivid,
horror and pity, passion, the stranger holding the future.
Ask him his name.

Nothing's the same as anything else. Away and see
for yourself. Walk. Fly. Take a boat till land reappears,
altered forever, ringing its bells, alive. Go on. G'on. Gon.
Away and see.

■■■ **GLYN MAXWELL** ■■■■■■■■■■■■■■

Tale of Robbing Wood

When what the hell was written on the sky
'Oh look at this' said Hobden looking down
At the page spread of print: 'this Robbing Wood
   He's at it again, he found
Our finest quartering a doe and said
Or – so it says down here – *demanded* why!'

'Why' monotoned his woman, knitting a woman:
'Why' 'Why indeed!' spluttered her rising lord:
'Presumably he believes he's in his rights
   To strut about the wood –
It's in his name! Wood! yes? – picking fights
With noble – noblemen. Outrageous! Someone

Should put a stop to this!' 'Yes,' said his wife,
'Why were they quartering a doe, I mean.'
'Wh – ? Wh – ? Wh – ?' And a slamming door,
   And then, on the village green
That afternoon a kind of council of war
With the mercer, the fletcher, the chandler and chief

Crier: 'Master Hobden, it don't stop there!
I heard he knobbled the County Hunt last week!
Just him and this clergyman he stuck the fox
   Right up his tussock! The cheek!'
'It can't go on,' said the manufacturer of clocks,
Walking towards them carrying a chair.

The fletcher whispered 'they say he is actually green.
Comes from a green tribe, sort of, they wants
To do us all in but first them in the north.

I heard this at the wantz.'
They looked at him. 'But what about us down south,
When are we?' one called from his demesne.

Later they had some other names: Skillet,
Jonson, Tuck, and soon some news to swallow
Somehow: Wood had disturbed an entire chapter
   Of noblemen in a hollow
Having their way with the digenous pop. 'He stopped a
Sheriff – would you please – and a whole billet

Of lads like mine were holed up in a tree
For days!' bubbled Hobden: 'when in the name
Of God and King will we put an end to this?'
   But then the cooper came
With more: 'We just got this: Three hundred horse
Surprised in a forest glade. Apparently

Some thousand thousand sovereign taken. No
Deaths.' 'A th – a th – a th –' the men
Contributed: 'T-t-t-taken where?'
   'No one knows. But a green
Leaf was found nearby the place.' 'There,
I warned you,' hissed the fletcher, 'I did so!'

They stood in growing silence, growing what
Silence grows. 'What will the man do next?'
'Who knows, he has shown himself entirely without
   Scruple, he clearly attacks
Even the worthiest, noblest men and will flout
Every law of the land. Manifestly not

An Englishman.' They muttered and dispersed
Towards their tensing women. The sun came out.
Way up in Nottinghamshire the sun went in
   And a staggered, spreading shout
Rose from the tiniest places, where every bin
Yielded an amber sovereign, and the worst

Befalling on that day was a light shower.
The worst that week a couple of colds. The kids
Compared dates on their coins and showed the women.
   The elders looked to the clouds

Every day, but the dimmest blinked at the bowmen
They were sure they saw in the tops of trees. An hour

Later Hobden and several hundred men
Found what they were looking for: a wood.
They neighed and dismounted, flattened a useless chart
   They thought they understood
And rubbed their hands and made an early start,
Watching the ground, heading towards the glen.

Poem in Blank Rhyme

This isn't very difficult to do.
The sky's pink, the morning pretty new.

Last night I met a mate from the old crew.
We walked too far too late and turned a U

Out of the woods as it got dark. He knew
I'd spend the evening talking about you

But didn't mind, and, when we had to queue,
He made the time fly quickly with his two

Hundred unfunny jokes, plus a big clue
About his own big heart. Well the sky's blue

Now over there, I'm standing in the dew
Remembering and hoping. But it's true:

Days are very many. Days are few.
I want to be with someone and you're who.

CRAIG RAINE

Scrap

Starved
on turnip tops
on onion skins potato peelings

the second River War
had stopped

(and the third
had not begun)

Past the only petrol pump
in Jam Jar City

pushing a KFA
with a broken belt

this dealer in scrap
was heading for home
heading for home

The pump held
a gun to its head
an empty
theatrical gesture

a seagull
blew on a blade of grass

He
was making a song

for his wife
happy loving foolish
heading for home

He had only finished
one verse
when he came to the orchard

(beyond it the house)

and propped the KFA
beside a bicycle asleep
in its cobwebs
in its oxygen tent

and other dim machinery
machinery

the baby
would have been a boy
he saw

he saw at once

when he saw
she was dead

the foetus unearthed
slateblue face carved
carved hands
between her legs

tiny waistcoat of ribs

on the bloody
divan

He straightened
the rug

and turned his
head from
side to side to side to
side like a baby

grazed
by a nipple

hungry
he had finished
one verse

turbot move like magic carpets
undulating at a lick
caterpillars move by peristalsis
jellyfish

   by being sick

heading for home

PETER READING

From Evagatory

Newspapers there (the sumps of society,
draining off, holding up for inspection a
   corporate concentrated slurry)
retail, with relish, mayhem and much of a
     clapped-out, subliterate, scrap-stuffed fake state:
   23.3 million vehicles,
   29.8 million drivers,
300 000 maimed on their ludicrous
   tarmac p.a., 5000 flenched dead –
    fortunate, then, that it doesn't matter
(for they are far too philoprogenitive).

*

upon an island where the natives venerated a deity. It was
soon apprehended that the object of their adoration was a
species of duck, *Anas platyrhynchos* (the mallard). Anyone
unenlightened enough to revere, say, the pochard (*Aythya
ferina*), the wigeon (*Anas penelope*) or the smew (*Mergus
albellus*) was subjected to corrective interrogation by a
most venerable committee and, invariably, sentenced to
suffer personal destruction.

    There was one in that place, cowering in the police-
protected exile of a concrete bunker, who had advocated,
ill-advisedly, the omniscient immutability of the velvet
scoter (*Melanitta fusca*), and

*

Doyle's on the harbour, dusk, pulse of warning light,
octopus, crayfish, chill gold dry semillon's
   bouquet of ripe grapes/pollen; plum-mauve
    Rothko of afterglow on which silent
slow-flapping fruit-bats' transient silhouettes . . .

a.m., a carcinogenic sunrise
(**15% of population . . .**),
shrieking, an iridescence of lorikeets
raucous from palms and blossoming eucalypts;
Sydney, *The Age* screwed up in a trash-bucket.

*

sea-level newly pole-augmented,
 mutated arthropods, algae, UV,
force 12s dispersing disbound **Collected Works**

*

heliopause, inertia of solar winds,
 energy particles streamed from Sun cease,
Voyager, 40 years since lift-off,
 power from plutonium generator
greatly reduced, continues trajectory,

hurtling, 40 000 years afterwards,
 trillions of miles near Ross 248,

drifting, 290 000
years beyond launch-pad, in towards Sirius

Above Ryotsu

Come here in the rain, under the dark pines,
Late afternoon in mid-November.
The steady rain drips from your umbrella.
No one visits the shrine above the little port.
It is not a famous place, this temple,
Unmentioned in the guidebooks. The stone lions
Grimace with ordinary rage, stare down
The avenue towards the new hotel.
Below, the ferry's foghorn blares twice, stops.

What strange needs made them build it here, and when,
Seems beyond explanation. Standing here
Under the rain, with nowhere to go
Except back to the hotel, is a banality
Equally inexplicable. This holiday
Comes at the wrong end of the year, away
From all the urgencies you've vanished from,
But satisfies another need, somehow:
To be foreign, tied to nothing, and yet happy.

No one will watch you, alone here in the rain:
Even the straggling schoolboys, going home,
Won't notice you, another dark dim shape
Beyond the torii, hidden in the mist.
Tomorrow you will take the ferry back,
Leaving the little port, the new hotel,
The temple with its lions, the wet pines;
And no one will have noticed anything,
Even your absence unremarked, at peace.

The Rug

Among the red and yellow tangles
Grubs squirm, wings brush the rotten weavings,
The fabrications of a Basra market.

The old couple have not noticed. They sit
Among their trophies of Iraq and India,
Accumulations of five decades' journeys.

He was an envoy. Now he tells us how
He will write a book that proves the Maori
Voyaged from Libya, left inscriptions there.

She was a pianist, studied under Schnabel.
She thinks she remembers Schoenberg. Her legs swell,
Her tight white bandage stained with orange pus.

In the corner of their room, along a shelf,
Six Buddhas squat and praise longevity.
The rug from Basra crawls with bright decay.

HUGO WILLIAMS

Self-Portrait in Old Age

I have put on a grotesque mask
to write these lines. I sit
staring at myself
in a mirror propped on my desk.

I hold up my head
like one of those Chinese lanterns
hollowed out of a pumpkin,
swinging from a broom.

I peer through the eye-holes
into that little lighted room
where a candle burns,
making me feel drowsy.

I must try not to spill the flame
wobbling in its pool of wax.
It sheds no light on the scene,
only shadows flickering up the walls.

In the narrow slit of my mouth
my tongue appears,
darting back and forth
between the bars of my lips.

I have put on a grotesque mask
to write these lines. I sit
staring at myself
in a mirror propped on my desk.

Standstill

A last visit to the long-abandoned 'Gosses' on Harold Macmillan's Birch Grove estate, soon to be levelled as part of the Birch Grove Golf Course.

I apologise to the driver
for the branches closing in,
almost bringing us to a standstill.
He doesn't seem to mind.
'I'm like you,' he tells me, as we move aside
a tree blown across the drive by the storm.

'I had to come back home
to see my own particular corner of the UK
before I died. Our daughter wanted to stay out there
in New Zealand and get married.
Don't ask me why.
She's a karate champion.'

We have turned a corner in the drive, past the swing,
past the gibbet, past the tree
where we buried the screaming idol's head
of Elsie Byers, the American agent.
Flowering creepers and bushes
crowd round the old house,

as if some great party were being given there
long ago, the party of the season.
Look, the same door! The same knocker!
The same doorhandle I held
when I came back from going round the world!
The same footscraper!

The driver seems to share my astonishment
that everything is the same yet different
when you look through a window
into your old room
and see your head lying there on the pillow,
innocent of your life, but dreaming your dreams.

'Where is it you say old Supermac used to live?
I want to see the field
where President Kennedy landed in his helicopter.
I was cheering and waving the American flag.
Our daughter had just been born. We were on our way
to start a new life in New Zealand.'

Fiction

Art Work

In 1947 Matisse painted *Le silence habite des maisons*. It is reproduced in Sir Lawrence Gowing's *Matisse*, only very small and in black and white. Two people sit at the corner of a table. The mother, it may be, has a reflective chin propped on a hand propped on the table. The child, it may be, turns the page of a huge white book, whose arch of paper makes an integral curve with his/her lower arm. In front, a vase of flowers. Behind, six huge panes of window, behind them, a mass of trees and perhaps sunlight. The people's faces are perfect blank ovals, featureless. Up above them, in the top left-hand corner of the canvas, level with the top of the window, is a chalked outline, done as it might be by a child, of a round on a stalk, above bricks. It is a pity there are no colours but it is possible, tempting, to imagine them, sumptuous as they were in what Gowing says was 'the reconciliation which is only within the reach of great painters in old age.' The pictures, Gowing says, have extraordinary virility. 'At last Matisse is wholly at ease with the fierce impulse.' It is a dark little image on the page, charcoal grey, slate grey, soft pale pencil-grey, subdued, demure. We may imagine it flaming, in carmine or vermilion, or swaying in indigo darkness, or perhaps – outdoors – gold and green. We may imagine it. The darkness of the child may be black on black or black on blue or blue on some sort of red. The book is white. Who is the watching totem under the ceiling?

There is an inhabited silence in 49 Alma Road, in the sense that there are no voices, though there are various sounds, some of them even pervasive and raucous sounds, which an unconcerned ear might construe as the background din of a sort of silence. There is the churning hum of the washing-machine, a kind of splashy mechanical giggle, with a grinding note in it, tossing its wet mass one way, resting and simmering, tossing it the other. A real *habitué* of this noise will tense him or herself against the coming banshee-scream of the spin-cycle, accompanied by a drumming tattoo of machine feet scrabbling on the tiles.

The drier is chuntering too. It is not a new drier, its carbon brushes are worn, it thumps and creaks and screeches in its slow circling. The mass of cloth inside it flails, flops with a crash, rises, flails, flops with a crash. An attentive ear could hear the difference in the texture and mass of the flop as the sleeves and stockings are bound into sausages and balls by the fine straps of petticoats and bras.

In the front room, chanting to itself, for no one is watching it, the television is full on in mid-morning. Not loudly, there are rules about noise. The noise it is making is the wilfully upbeat cheery squitter of female presenters of children's TV, accented with regular, repetitive amazement, mixed in with the grunts and cackles and high-pitched squeaks of a flock of furry puppets, a cross-eyed magenta haystack with a snout, a kingfisher blue gerbil with a whirling tail, a torpid emerald green coiled serpent, with a pillar-box red dangling tongue and movable fringed eyelids. At regular intervals, between the bouts of presenter-squitter and puppet snorts and squawks, come, analogous to the spin-cycle, the musical outbursts, a drumroll, a squeal on a woodwind, a percussion battery, a ta-ta-ta-TA, for punctuation, for a roseate full-frame with a lime-coloured logo T–NE–TV.

On the first floor, behind a closed door, the circular rush and swish of Jamie's electric trains can be heard. Nothing can be heard of Natasha's record-player, and Natasha cannot hear the outside world, for her whole head is stuffed with beating vibrations and exploding howls and ululations. She lies on her bed and twitches in rhythm. Anyone coming in could well hear, from the other side of the corridor, the twangling tinny bumps made by the baffled sound trying to break out of its boxer-glove packaging. Natasha's face has the empty beatific intelligence of some of Matisse's supine women. Her face is white and oval and luminous with youth. Her hair is inky blue-black, and fanned across her not-too-clean pillows. Her bedspread is jazzy black forms of ferns or seaweeds, on a scarlet ground, forms the textile designer would never have seen, without Matisse. Her arms and legs dangle beyond the confines of the ruffled rectangle of this spread, too gawky to be an odalisque, but just as delicious in their curves. White, limp, relaxed, twitching. Twitches can't be painted.

From Debbie's room comes the sound of the typewriter. It is an old mechanical typewriter, its noises are metallic and clicking. It chitters on to the end of a line, then there is the clash of the return, and the musical, or almost musical 'cling' of the little bell.

Tap tap tap tap tappety tappety tappety clash cling tappety tap tap. A silence. Debbie sits over her typewriter with her oval chin in her long hands, and her black hair coiled gracefully in her neck. It is easy to see where Natasha's ink-and-ivory beauty comes from. Debbie frowns. She taps a tooth (ivory lacquer, a shade darker than the skin) with an oval nail, rose madder. Debbie's office, or study, is very cramped. There is a drawing-board, but if it is not in use, it is blocked up against the window, obscuring much of the light, and all of the vision of pillar-box red geraniums and cobalt blue lobelias in a window box on the sill. Debbie can work at her desk or work at her drawing-board, but not both at once, though she would like to be able to; she is the design editor of *A Woman's Place*, of which the, perhaps obscure, premise, is that a woman's place is not only, perhaps not even primarily, in the Home. Debbie is working at home at the moment because Jamie has chicken pox and the doctor is coming, and the doctor cannot say at what time he will or won't call, there is too much pressure. Jamie has the same inky hair as his mother and sister, and has even longer blacker lashes over black eyes. He has the same skin too, but at the moment it is a wonderfully humped and varied terrain of rosy peaks and hummocks, mostly the pink of those boring little begonias with fleshy leaves, but some raging into salmon-deeps and some extinct volcanoes, with umber and ochre crusts. It was Jamie who was watching the TV but he cannot stick at anything, he itches too wildly, he tears at his flesh with his bitten-down nails, he rubs himself against chairs. Debbie stood him on a coffee table and swabbed and painted him with calamine lotion, creating a kind of streaked sugar or plaster of Paris mannikin, with powdery pinky-beige crude surfaces, rough make-up, failed paint, a dull bland colour, under which the bumpy buds of the pox heated themselves into re-emergence. 'War-paint,' Debbie said to her son, squeezing and stippling the liquid on his round little belly, between his poor hot legs. 'You could put stripes of cocoa on,' said Jamie. 'And icing sugar. That would make three colours of stripes.' Debbie would have liked to paint him all over, with fern-green cake dye and cochineal, if that would have distracted or assuaged him, but she had to get the piece done she was writing, which was about the new wave of kitchen plastic design, wacky colours, staggering new streamlined shapes.

On Debbie's walls, which are lemon-coloured, are photographs of Natasha and Jamie as naked babies, and later, gap-toothed, grinning school heads and shoulders, a series of very small woodcuts, illustrating fairy tales, a mermaid, an old witch with a spindle, a bear and two roses, and in a quite different style a small painting of a table, a hyper-realist wooden table with a blue vase and a small Rubik's cube on it. Also, in white frames, two paintings done by a younger Natasha, a vase of anemones, watery crimsons and purples, a dress flung over a chair, blue dress, grey chair, promising folds, in a probably unintentional void.

Debbie types, and cocks her head for the sound of the doorbell. She types 'a peculiarly luscious new purple, like bilberry juice with a little cream swirled in it.' She jumps at the sound not of the doorbell but of her telephone, one of the new fluttering burrs, disconcertingly high-pitched. It is her editor, asking when she will be able to make a layout conference. She speaks, placating, explaining, just sketching in an appeal for sympathy. The editor of *A Woman's Place* is a man, who reads and slightly despises the pieces about the guilt of the working mother which his periodical periodically puts out. Debbie changes tack, and makes him laugh with a description of where poor Jamie's spots have managed to sprout. 'Poor little bugger,' quacks the editor into Debbie's ear, inaudible to the rest of the house.

Up and down the stairs, joining all three floors, surges a roaring and wheezing noise, a rhythmic and complex and swelling crescendo, snorting, sucking, with a high-pitched drone planing over a kind of grinding sound, interrupted every now and then by a frenetic rattle, accompanied by a new, menacing whine. Behind the Hoover, upwards and downwards, comes Mrs Brown, without whom, it must immediately be said, Debbie's world would not hold together.

Mrs Brown came ten years ago, in answer to an advertisement in the local paper. Natasha was four, and Jamie was on the way. Debbie was unwell and at her wits' end, with fear of losing her job. She put 'artistic family' in the advertisement, expecting perhaps to evoke some tolerance, if not positive affection, for the tattered wallpaper and burgeoning mess. She didn't have much response – a couple of art students, one an unmarried mum who wanted to share babysitting, painting-time, and chores; a very old, purblind tortoise-paced ex-parlourmaid; and Mrs Brown. Mrs Brown had a skin which was neither black nor brown but a kind of amber yellow, the sort of yellow bruises go, before they vanish, but all over. She had a lot of wiry soot-coloured hair, which rose, like the crown of a playing-card king, out of a bandeau of flowery material, tied tightly about her brow, like the towelling of a tennis star, or the lace cap of an old-fashioned maid. Mrs Brown's clothes were, and are, flowery and surprising, jumble sale remnants, rejects and ends of lines, rainbow-coloured jumpers made from the ping-pong-ball-sized unwanted residues of other people's knitting. She came for her interview in a not too clean (but not too dirty) film star's trench coat, which she didn't take off until Debbie had said, dry-mouthed with anxiety, 'I think you and I might manage to get on, don't you?' And Mrs Brown had nodded decisively, accepted a cup of coffee, and divested herself of the trench coat, revealing pantaloons made of some kind of thick cream-coloured upholstery linen, wonderfully traversed by crimson open-mouthed Indian flowers and birds of paradise and tendrils of unearthly creepers, and a royal blue jumper embroidered all over with woollen daisies, white marguerites, orange black-eyed Susans.

Mrs Brown does not smile very much. Her face has some resemblance to a primitive mask, cheeks in triangular planes, long, straight, salient nose, a mouth usually tightly closed. Her expression can be read as prim, or grim, or watchful or perhaps – though this is not the first idea that comes to mind – resigned. She likes to go barefoot in the house, it turns out – she is not used to this level of heating, she explains, implying (or does Debbie misread her?) that the heating is an unhealthy extravagance. She comes up behind you with no warning, and at first this used to irritate Debbie most frightfully, but now she is used to it, she is used to Mrs Brown, her most powerful emotion in relation to Mrs Brown is terror that she will leave. If Mrs Brown is not Debbie's friend, she is the closest person to Debbie on earth, excluding perhaps the immediate family. Debbie and Mrs Brown do not share the usual intimacies, they have no common chatter about other people, but they have a kind of rock-bottom knowledge of each other's fears and pains, or so Debbie thinks, knowing, nevertheless, that Mrs Brown knows more about her than she will ever know about Mrs Brown, since it is in Debbie's house that the relationship is carried out. Mrs Brown washes Debbie's underwear and tidies Debbie's desk, putting Debbie's letters, private and official, threatening and secret, in tidy heaps. Mrs Brown counts the bottles and sweeps up the broken glass after parties, though she does not partake of the festive food. Mrs Brown changes Debbie's sheets.

Debbie did not ask Mrs Brown at that decisive interview whether Mrs Brown had children, though she was dying to, because she, Debbie, so resents being asked, by those interviewing her for jobs, whether she has children, what she would do with them. She did ask if Mrs Brown had a telephone, and Mrs Brown said yes, she did, she found it essential, she used the word 'essential' tidily and drily, just like that, without elaboration. 'So you will tell me in advance, if at all possible,' says Debbie, trying to sound sweet and commonly courteous, 'if you can't come ever, if you aren't going to be able to come ever, because I have to make such complicated arrangements if people are going to let me down, that is, can't make it for any reason.' 'I think you'll find I'm reliable,' says Mrs Brown. 'But it's no good me saying so, you'll have to see. You needn't worry though, bar the unforeseen.' 'Acts of God,' says Debbie. 'Well, and acts of Hooker too,' says Mrs Brown, without saying who Hooker might be.

Debbie did find that Mrs Brown was, as she had said, reliable. She also discovered, not immediately, that Mrs Brown had two sons, Lawrence and Gareth, shortened to Gary by his friends but not by Mrs Brown. These boys were already ten and eight when Mrs Brown came to Debbie. Lawrence is now at Newcastle University — 'the lodgings are cheaper up there' says Mrs Brown. Gareth has left home without many qualifications and works, Mrs Brown says 'in distribution.' He has made the wrong sort of friends, Mrs Brown says, but does not elaborate. Hooker is the father of Lawrence and Gareth. Debbie does not know, and does not ask, whether Hooker is or is not Mr Brown. During the early childhood of Natasha and Jamie, Hooker would make sudden forays into Mrs Brown's life and council flat, from which he had departed before she took to going out to clean up after people like Debbie. One of Mrs Brown's rare days off was her court appearance to get an injunction to stop Hooker coming round. Hooker was the cause of Mrs Brown's bruises, the chocolate and violet stains on the gold skin, the bloody cushions in the hair and the wine-coloured efflorescence on her lips. Once, and once only, at this time, Debbie found Mrs Brown sitting on the bathroom stool, howling, and brought her cups of coffee, and held her hands, and sent her home in a taxi. It was Mrs Brown who saw Debbie through the depression after the birth of Jamie, with a mixture of carefully timed indulgences and requirements. 'I've brought you a bowl of soup, you'll do no good in the world if you don't

eat.' 'I've brought Baby up to you, Mrs Dennison, he's crying
his heart out with hunger, he needs his mother, that's what it is.'
They call each other Mrs Dennison and Mrs Brown. They rely
on the kind of distance and breathing space this courtesy gives
them. Mrs Brown was scathing about the days in hospital, when
she was concussed, after one of Hooker's visits. 'They call you
love, and dearie, and pet. I say, I need a bit of respect, my name
is Mrs Brown.'

Debbie types 'new moulding techniques give new streamlined
shapes to the most banal objects. Sink trays and storage jars . . .'
Banal is the wrong word, she thinks. Everyday? Wrong too. The
Hoover snorts on the turning of the stair. The doorbell rings. A
voice of pure male rage rings out from the top floor.

'Debbie. Debbie, are you there? Just come here a moment.'
Debbie is torn. Mrs Brown abandons the Hoover and all its
slack, defunct-seeming tubes, along the bannisters.

'You attend to *him*, and I'll just let the doctor in and say you'll
be down directly.'

Debbie negotiates the Hoover and goes up the attic stairs.

'Look,' says Debbie's husband, Robin. 'Look what she has done.
If you can't get it into her head that she mustn't muck about with
my work things she'll have to go.'

Robin has the whole third floor, once three bedrooms, a tiny
room with a sink and a lavatory, as his studio. He has had large
pivoting windows set into the roof, with linen blinds, a natural
cream, a terracotta. He can have almost whatever light he likes
from whatever angle. Debbie feels her usual knot of emotions, fear
that Robin will shout at Mrs Brown, fear that Mrs Brown will
take offence, rage and grim gratitude mixed that it is always to
her that he addresses his complaints.

'The doctor has come for Jamie, darling,' Debbie says. 'I must
go, he won't have long.'

'This bowl,' says Robin Dennison, 'this bowl, as anyone can see,
is a work of art. Look at that glaze. Look at those huge satisfactory
blue and orange fruits in it, look at the green leaves and the bits of
yellow, just *look*, Debbie. Now I ask you, would anyone suppose
this bowl was a kind of *dustbin* for things they were too lazy to put
away or carry off, would they, do you suppose, anyone *with their
wits about them*, would they?'

'What's the matter?' says Debbie neutrally, her ear turned to
the stairs.

'*Look,*' cries Robin. The bowl, both sumptuously decorated and dusty, contains a few random elastic bands, a chain of paperclips, an obscure plastic cog from some tiny clock, a battered but unused stamp, two oil pastels, blue and orange, a piece of dried bread, a very short length of electric wire, a dead chrysanthemum, three coloured thumbtacks (red, blue, green) a single lapis cufflink, an electric bulb with a burnt patch on its curve, a box of matches, a china keyhole cover, two indiarubbers, a dead bluebottle and two live ants, running in circles, possibly busy, possibly frantically lost.

'Her habits are filthy,' says Robin.

Debbie looks around the studio, which is not the habitation of a tidy man. Apart from the inevitable mess, splashed palettes, drying canvases, jars of water, there are other heaps and dumps. Magazines, opened and closed, wineglasses, beer glasses, bottles, constellations of crayons and pencils, unopened messages from the Income Tax, saucers of clips and pins.

'It is hard for anyone to tell what to leave alone, up here, and what to clear up.'

'No, it isn't. Dirt is dirt, and personal *things*, things in use, are things in use. All it requires is intelligence.'

'She seems to have found that cufflink you were going on about.'

'I expect I found it myself, and put it down somewhere safe, and she interfered with it.'

All this is part of a ritual dialogue which Debbie can hardly bear to hear again, let alone to utter her own banal parts of it, and yet she senses it is somehow necessary to their survival. She does not wholly know whether it is necessary because Robin needs to assert himself and win, or because if she does not stand between Robin and Mrs Brown Mrs Brown will leave. She does not need to think about it any more; she turns and hearkens to it, like Donne's other compass half, like a heliotrope.

'She could see I was painting *exactly* that dish.'

Indeed, there are sketches in charcoal, in coloured chalks, of exactly that dish, on an expanse of grained wood, propped up around the studio.

It crosses Debbie's mind that Mrs Brown used exactly that dish as a picking-up receptacle for exactly that reason. Mrs Brown has her own modes of silent aggression. She does not raise this idea. Robin is neither moved by nor interested in Mrs Brown's feelings.

'Shall I take them all and throw them away in the bin in my study, darling. And dust your bowl for you?'

'Wait a minute. Those are quite all right rubber bands. I was using that bread for rubbing out. The matches are OK, nothing wrong with them. Some of us can't afford to throw good tools away, you know.'

'Where shall I put them?'

'Just stick them on the table over there. I'll see to them myself. Dust the bowl please.'

Debbie does as he asks, abstracting the cufflink, which she will return to his dressing-table. She looks at her husband, who glares back at her, and then gives a smile, like a rueful boy. He is a long, thin, unsubstantial man in jeans and a fisherman's smock, with big joints, knuckles and wrists and ankles, like an adolescent, which he is not. He has a very English face, long and fine and pink and white, like a worried colt. His soft hair is pushed up all round his head like a hedgehog and is more or less the same colour as one. His eyes are an intense blue, like speedwells. A photographer could choose between making him look like a gentle mystic and making him look like a dedicated cricketer. A painter could choose between a haziness at the edges, always light, never heavy, and very clear sketched in features, bones, a brow, a chin, a clearcut nose, in a kind of pale space.

'You *have* managed to make her understand about the fetishes.'

'It took long enough,' he grumbles. 'I even gave her lectures on tones and complementary colours, I just *stood* there with the things and showed her.'

'I should think that was interesting for her.'

'She should know her job, without all that fuss. Anyway, it worked, I grant you that it worked.'

'I must go, darling, the doctor's here. Do you want coffee when he's gone, shall I bring you a mug?'

'Yes please. That will be nice.'

He is not apologising, but the ritual confrontation is over. Debbie kisses him. His cheek is soft. She says,

'Have you heard from that girl from the Callisto gallery, yet?'

'I don't think she'll come. I don't think she ever meant to come.'

'Yes, she did,' said Debbie. 'I talked to her, too. She really liked that blue and yellow plate picture Toby has got in his loo. She said she didn't think much of Toby's taste in general, but that was exquisite, she said, she said she just sat there staring at it and caused an awful queue.'

'She was probably drunk.'

'Don't be *silly*, Robin. She'll turn up, I know. I don't say things I don't mean, do I?'

Debbie doesn't know whether the girl, Shona McRury, will turn up or not, but she says she will, with force, because it is better for her, as well as for Robin, if he is in a hopeful mood. Deborah loves Robin. She has loved him since they met at Art School, where she studied Graphic design and he studied Fine Art. She wanted to be a wood engraver and illustrate children's books. What she loved about Robin was the quality of his total dedication to his work, which had a certain austere separateness from everyone else's work. Those were the days of the Sixties, in fact the early Seventies, when much painting was abstract, washes of colour and no colour, geometric patterns, games with the nature of canvas and pigment and the colours of light and their effect on the eye. Robin was a neo-realist before neo-realism. He painted what he saw, metal surfaces, wooden surfaces, plaster surfaces, with hallucinatory skill and accuracy. He painted expanses of neutral colours – wooden planks, glass table-tops, beige linen, crumbling plaster, and somewhere, somewhere unexpected, not quite in a corner, not quite in the centre, not where the folds were pulling from or the planks ran, he painted something very small and very brilliant, a glass ball, a lustre vase, a bouquet of bone china flowers (never anything alive) a heap of feathers. It was just this side of kitsch, then and now. It could have been turned into sweet prints and sold in folders in gift shops, then for its wit, now for its nostalgic emptiness containing verisimilitude. But Debbie saw that it was a serious attempt at a serious and terrible problem, an attempt to answer the question every artist must ask him or herself, at some time, why bother, why make representations of anything at all?

She said to him, seeing her first two of the series, a hexagonal Chinese yellow box on a grey blanket, a paperweight on a kitchen table, 'They are miraculous, they are like those times when time seems to stop, and you just *look* at something, and *see* it, out of time, and you feel surprised that you can see at all, you are *so surprised*, and the seeing goes on and on, and gets better and better . . .'

'Is that what you see in them?' he said.

'Oh yes. Isn't that what you meant?'

'It is exactly what I meant. But nobody's ever seen it. Or nobody's ever said it, anyway.'

'I expect they do, really.'

'Sometimes I think, it just looks ... ordinary ... to other people. *Unprivileged* things, you know.'

'How could it?' said Debbie.

Sex makes everything shine, even if it is not privileged, and Debbie made Robin happy and their happiness made his pictures seem stranger and brighter, perhaps even made them, absolutely, stranger and brighter. When they got married, Robin had a few hours part-time teaching in a college, and Debbie, whose degree gave her more marketable skills, got a job doing layout on a corset-trade magazine, and then a subordinate job in *A Woman's Place*, and then promotion. She was good, she was well-paid, she was the breadwinner. It seemed silly for Robin to go on teaching at all, his contribution was so meagre. Debbie's head was full of snazzy swimsuits and orange vats of carrot soup with emerald parsley sprinkled in it, with lipsticks from grape and plum to poppy and rose, with eyegloss and blusher and the ghosts of unmade woodcuts. Her fingers remembered the slow, careful work in the wood, with a quiet grief, that didn't diminish, but was manageable. She hated Robin because he never once mentioned the unmade wood-engravings. It is possible to feel love and hate quite quietly, side by side, if one is a self-contained person. Debbie continued to love Robin, whilst hating him because of the woodcuts, because of the extent of his absence of interest in how she managed the house, the children, the money, her profession, his needs and wants, and because of his resolute attempts to unsettle, humiliate, or drive away Mrs Brown, without whom all Debbie's balancing acts would clatter and fall in wounding disarray.

Left to himself, Robin Dennison walks agitated up and down his studio. He is over forty. He thinks, I am over forty. He prevents himself, all the time now, from seeing his enterprise, his work, his life, as absurd. He is not suited to the artistic life, in most ways. By upbringing and temperament, he should have been a solicitor or an accountant, he should have worn a suit and fished for trout and played cricket. He has no great self-confidence, no braggadocio, no real or absolute disposition to the sort of self-centred isolation he practises. He does it out of a stubborn faithfulness to a vision he had, a long time ago now, a vision which has never expanded or diminished or taken its teeth out of him. He was given a set of gouache paints by an aunt when he was a boy, and painted a geranium, and then a fish-tank. He can still remember the illicit, it seemed to him, burst of sensuous delight with which he saw the wet carmine trail of his first flick of the brush, the slow circling of the wet hairs in a cobalt pool, the dashes of yellow ochre and orange, as he conjured up, on matt white, wet and sinuous fishtails and fins. He was not much good at anything else, which muted any familial conflict over his choice of future. With his brushes in his hand he could *see,* he told himself, through art school. Without them, he was grey fog in a world of grey fog. He painted small bright things in large expanses of grey and buff and beige. Everyone said, 'He's *got* something,' or more dubiously, 'He's got *something.*' Probably not enough, they qualified this, silently to themselves, but Robin heard them well enough, for all that.

He could talk to Debbie. Debbie knew about his vision of colour, he had told her, and she had listened. He talked to her agitatedly at night about Matisse, about the paradoxical way in which the pure sensuousness of *Luxe, Calme, et Volupté* could be a religious experience of the nature of things. Not softness, he said to Debbie, *power*, calm power.

Debbie said yes, she understood, and they went to the South of France for a holiday, to be in the strong light là-bas. This was a disaster. He tried putting great washes of strong colour on the canvas, à la Matisse, à la Van Gogh, and it came out watery and feeble and absurd, there was nothing he could do. His only successful picture of that time was a kind of red beetle or bug and a large shining green-black scarab and a sulphurous butterfly on a sea of pebbles, grey and pinkish and sandy and buff and white and terracotta, you can imagine the kind of thing, it is everywhere in all countries, a variegated expanse of muted pebbles. Extending to all the four corners of the world of the canvas, a stony desert, with a dead leaf or two, and some random straws, and the baleful insects. He sold that one to a gallery and had hopes, but heard no more, his career did not take off, and they never went back to the strong light, they take their holidays in the Cotswolds.

Robin has ritualised his life dangerously, but this is not, as he thinks it is, entirely because of his precarious vocation. His father, a Borough Surveyor, behaved in much the same way, particularly with regard to his distinction between his own untouchable 'things' and other people's, especially the cleaning-lady's 'filth'. Mr Dennison, Mr Rodney Dennison, used to shout at and about the 'charwoman' if pipe-dottle was thrown away, or soap-fragments amalgamated, or scattered bills tidily gathered. He, like Robin with Mrs Brown, used to feel a kind of panic of constriction, like the pain of sinus fluid thickening in the skull pockets, when threatened by tidy touches. He, like Robin, used to see Mrs Briggs's progress like a snail-trail across his private spaces. Robin puts it all down to Art. He does not ask himself if his hatred of Mrs Brown is a deflected resentment of his helplessness in the capable hands of his wife, breadwinner and life-manager. He knows it is not so: Debbie is beautiful and clean and represents order. Mrs Brown is chaotic and wild to look at and a secret smoker and represents – even while dispersing or redistributing it – 'filth'.

Mrs Brown has always had an awkward habit of presuming to give the family gifts. She possesses a knitting-machine, which Hooker got off the back of a lorry, and she is also good with knitting-needles, crochet-hooks, embroidery silks and tapestry (not often, these two last, they are too expensive.) She makes all her own clothes, out of whatever comes to hand, old plush curtains, Arab blankets, parachute silk, his own discarded trousers. She makes them flamboyantly, with patches and fringes and braid and bizarre buttons. The epitome of tat, Robin considers, and he has to consider, for she always strikes the eye, in a magenta and vermilion overall over salmon pink crepe pantaloons, in a lime-green shift with black lacy inserts. This would not be so bad, if she didn't make, hadn't made for years, awful jumpers for Natasha and Jamie, awful rainbow jumpers in screaming hues, candy-striped jumpers, jumpers with bobble-cherries bouncing on them, long peculiar rainbow scarves in fluffy angora, all sickly ice-cream colours. Robin tells Debbie these things must be sent back *at once,* his children can't be seen *dead* in them. The children are ambivalent, depending on age and circumstances. Jamie wore out one jumper with red engines and blue cows when he was six and would not be parted from it. Natasha in her early teens had an unexpected success at a disco in a kind of dayglo fringed bolero (acid yellow, salmon pink, swimming-pool blue) but has rejected other offerings with her father's fastidious distaste. The real sufferer is Debbie, whose imagination is torn all ways. She knows from her own childhood exactly how it feels to wear clothes one doesn't like, isn't comfortable and invisible in, is embarrassed by. She also believes very strongly that there is more true kindness and courtesy in accepting gifts gratefully and enthusiastically than in making them. And, more selfishly, she simply cannot do without Mrs Brown, she needs Mrs Brown, her breakfast table is ornamented with patchwork tea cosies contributed by Mrs Brown, her study chairs have circular cushions knitted in sugar-pink and orange by Mrs Brown. Mrs Brown stands in Debbie's study door sometimes and expounds her colour theory.

'They always told us, didn't they, the teachers and grans, orange and pink, they make you blink, blue and green should not be seen, mauve and red cannot be wed, but I say, they're all there, the colours, God made 'em all and mixes 'em all in His creatures, what exists goes together somehow or other, don't you think, Mrs Dennison?'

'Well, yes, but there are rules too, you know, Mrs Brown, how to get certain effects, there are *rules*, complementary colours and things . . .'

'I'm learning all that. *He* tells me, when I move his things by accident, or whatever. Fascinating.'

'Mrs Brown's yellow face is long, unsmiling and judicious. She adds, 'If Jamie's got no use for that nice sky-blue tank-top I did for him I'll have it back if you don't mind, I've got a use for a bit of sky-blue.'

'Oh, he *loves it*, Mrs Brown, it's just a wee bit tight under the arm-pits, you understand . . .'

'As I said, I've got a use for a bit of sky-blue.' Implacably. Debbie feels terrible. Mrs Brown goes through Jamie's drawers and points out that there are holes in his red sweatshirt, that those rugger socks are shockingly shrunk, look at those tiddly feet. She puts them in a plastic dustbin bag. Debbie adds a cocktail dress she made a mistake about, mulberry shot silk, and two of Robin's ties, presents from his auntie Nem, which he will never wear, because they are a horrid mustard colour with plummy flowers.

'*Interesting*,' says Mrs Brown, holding them up like captured eels, and adding them to her spoils. She is mollified, Debbie thinks, the mulberry dress has mollified her. She balks at knowing what Mrs Brown will do with the mulberry dress.

Robin Dennison's 'fetishes' have a table of their own, a white-painted wooden table, very simple. Once they were mantelpiece 'things', but as they took on their status of 'fetishes' they were given this stolidly unassuming English altar. What they have in common is a certain kind of glossy, very brightly coloured solidity. They are the small icons of a cult of colour. They began with the soldier, who cost 5s 6d when Robin was little, and is made of painted wood, with red trousers and a blue jacket and a tall, bulbous black wooden bearskin. His red is a fading cherry-crimson, his blue is a fading colour between royal and ultramarine. He has a gold strap under his wooden chin and a pair of hectic pink circular spots on his wooden cheeks. Robin does not often paint him now – he cannot clear him of his double connotations of militarism and infantilism, and he loves him for neither of these, but because he was his first model for slivers of shine on rounded surfaces. Sometimes Robin paints his *shadow* into little crowds of the other things.

Some of the other things are pure representations of single colours. Of these, two are glass – a cobalt blue candlestick from the glassworks at Biot, and a round heavy grass-green, golden-green apple made by Wedgwood, greener and greener in its depths. The yellow thing was much the most expensive. It is not pure yellow as the candlestick is blue, and the apple is green, it is sunny-yellow, butter-yellow, buttercup-yellow with a blue rim, a reproduction sauceboat from Monet's self-designed breakfast service for his house at Giverny. It cost £50 which Robin did not have, but spent, he wanted *that* yellow so much. He did not really want the sauceboat, but anything else he wanted cost money which even in his madness he saw he didn't have. Robin in his fit of educating Mrs Brown observes to her that the blue rim makes the yellow colour sing out because the colours are almost complementary. He would, however, still like to find a yellow thing without the blue. There is no orange thing either. Robin often stands an orange and a lemon amongst the things, to make the colours complete, and Mrs Brown's habit of moving these, or even throwing them away when they begin to soften and darken and grow patches of sage-green, blue-specked mould, is one of the things that makes Robin see red and roar.

Purple is represented by a rather sweet handmade china sculpture of a round bowl of violets. These are both pale mauve and deep purple; they have a few, not many, green leaves in a wishy-washy apple colour, and their container is a softly-glazed black. Sometimes Robin leaves the leaves out, when he doesn't want that colour. He knows the fetishes so well, he can allow for the effect of the leaves on the violets. Sometimes he wishes the leaves weren't there and sometimes he *makes* them fit into his colour-scheme with delicate shifts of tones and accommodations in other places. There was a problem with red for years and years. There was a banal red German plate, modern and utilitarian, a good strong red, that stood in, but could not make itself sing out or be loved. When Robin found the present red thing he felt very uneasy because he knew immediately it was the, or a, *right thing*, and at the same time he didn't like it. He still doesn't. Like the poor soldier, but in more sinister ways, it has too much meaning. He found it in a Chinese bric-à-brac shop, in a dump-bin with hundreds of others. It is a large red, heart-shaped pincushion, plumply and gleamingly covered in a poppy-red silk which is *exactly* what he wants, at once soft and shining, delicate and glossy. It had a vulgar white lace frill, like a choirboy's collar, which Robin took off. Sometimes he puts into it some of his grandmother's old hatpins, imitation jewels, or lumps of jet. But he doesn't quite like this, it borders on the surrealist, and though he senses that *might* be interesting, it also worries him. He did buy a box of multi-coloured glass-headed pins which he occasionally displays in a random scattering shape, or once, a tight half-moon.

Besides the single-coloured things, there are a few, a very few, multi-coloured things. A 1950s Venetian glass tree, picked up in a second-hand shop, bearing little round fruits of many colours – emerald-green, ruby and dark-sapphire, amethyst and topaz. A pottery jug from Deruta with a huge triangular beak-like spout, covered with bright round-petalled childish flowers in all the colours, and a pair of chirpy primitive singing-birds, in brown. A pot, also from Deruta, with a tawny-gold and blue-crested grotesque merman, or human-headed dragon, bearded and breathing a comma-shaped cloud of russet fire. There is a kite on the wall, a Korean kite in puce and yellow and blue and green and scarlet, and there are two large Chinese silk pipe-cleaner birds, crested and flaunting long tails, one predominantly crimson, with a yellow and acquamarine crest, one blue and green. The birds, too, the most fragile things, are a point of contention between Robin and Mrs Brown. She says they collect dust. He says she bends their legs and squashes their down and interferes with the way they turn their necks to preen. She says, they don't balance, the way he fixes them. Once she balanced one on the bough of the glass tree. There was a sulk that lasted weeks, and Mrs Brown talked of leaving.

It was after Debbie patched up this difference that Robin explained to Mrs Brown about red and green. He moved the apple back next to the pincushion, and redeployed the violets in front of the Monet sauceboat, beside the cobalt-blue candlestick, which was shaped a little like a gentian, a tall cup on a stem. Mrs Brown's preference was for standing the fetishes in a rainbow line, from infra-red to ultraviolet, so to speak. Robin said,

'Certain combinations have certain effects. For instance the opposition of yellow and violet, blue and orange, that can appear *natural* in a way, because natural shadows are blue or violet. Light and shade, you see? Whereas red and green, if you put them next to each other – sometimes you can see a kind of dancing yellow line where they meet – and this isn't to do with light and shade, it's to do, possibly, with the fact that if you *add* certain reds to certain greens you can *make* yellow, which you would never have guessed.'

'Geraniums are natural,' said Mrs Brown.

Robin stared at her abstractedly.

'Natural red and green. They don't make yellow.'

'*Look*,' said Robin, pushing together the soft heart and the hard apple. He could see the dance of unreal yellow. He was entranced.

'Hmn,' said Mrs Brown.

'Can you see yellow?'

'Well, a sort of, how shall I say, a sort of wriggling, a sort of shimmering. I see what you mean.'

'I try to make that happen, in the paintings.'

'So I see. It's interesting, once I know what you're up to.'

The sentence was a concession, unsmiling, not wholly gracious. She accepted that he had given her what he could, the battle was, she obviously considered, won, and by her. Robin was relieved, really. He was not so far out of touch with real life that he could not sense Debbie's fear of losing Mrs Brown. So he had given Mrs Brown his secret vision of the yellow line. Mrs Brown went out, head high. She was wearing a kind of orange and green camouflage Afro-wrapper, and a pink headband.

Shona McRury telephones. She asks to speak to Debbie, who has in fact answered the phone, and spends a long time congratulating Debbie on an article on Feminist art in *A Woman's Place*, an article about the amorphous things that women make that do not claim the 'authority' of 'art-works', the undignified things women 'frame' that male artists have never noticed, tampons and nappies but not only those, and the painted interior cavities of women, not the soft fleshy desirable superficies explored/exploited by men. Debbie has made a lovely centre-spread of the crayon drawings of an artist called Brenda Murphy, who works in the kitchen with her children, using *their* materials, crayons and felt-tips on paper, creating works that are a savage and loving commentary on their lives together. Shona asks Debbie if she knows if Ms Murphy has an agent or a gallery, and Debbie answers abstractedly, praises the interesting variety, the eclectic brilliance of Callisto's shows, and is rewarded by Shona McRury's request to see Debbie's husband's work, which is so *witty*, she thinks, she just loves that mysteriously funny little painting in Toby's loo, a jewel in a desert. Debbie thinks a jewel in a desert is a good phrase, but is not sure the idea of *wit* bodes well, Robin is, she recognises, somewhat humourless in his driven state. But she fixes something exact, for this coming Wednesday, without consulting Robin.

Robin is perturbed and threatened by the closeness of Wednesday, as Debbie has foreseen. She becomes ever so slightly minatory, and at the same time plaintive. 'It isn't so easy to get a chance of getting the work seen by a gallery, you can't just pick and choose your moments or you end up with *none*, as you ought to know by now, and I've done my best for you, I pinned her down, you have to, she's so busy, even with the best will in the world . . .'

Robin condescends, in terror, to have his work viewed.

Shona McRury has topaz eyes and long, silky brown hair, like a huge ribbon, caught up at the back with a tortoiseshell comb. She wears topaz earrings, little spheres on gold chains, that exactly match her eyes, and an olive silk suit, with a loose jacket and a pleated skirt, over a lemon yellow silk shirt, all of which tone in impeccably with her eyes. (Debbie who is now a professional in these matters sees immediately how the whole delicate and powerful effect is constructed around the eyes, reinforced by a subtle powdering of olive and gold shadow shot with a sharper green, almost malachite.) She climbs up to Robin's attic on dark green lizard-skin shoes. Between the lizard skin and the olive silk are slightly golden metallic stockings on legs not quite beautiful, too thin, too straight. Robin goes first, then Shona McRury, then Debbie, then Mrs Brown, with a bottle of chilled Sauvignon and three glasses on a Japanese lacquer tray. Mrs Brown is wearing her bird-of-paradise-upholstery trousers and a patchwork shirt in rainbow colours, stitched together with red feather-stitching. Although she has not brought herself a glass, she positions herself inside the studio door for the showing, and makes no attempt to go away, staring with sombre interest at Shona McRury's elegance and Robin's canvases.

Debbie has not decided whether to leave Robin alone with Shona McRury, or to stay and put in a word here and there. Mrs Brown's odd behaviour decides her, and is perhaps altogether decisive. It is not in Debbie's power to say anything like 'You may go now, Mrs Brown', but she can say to her, 'Come on, let's leave them to it', so she does, and she and Mrs Brown go downstairs together.

Shona McRury prowls in Robin's studio in her topaz earrings and lizard shoes. She rearranges the fetishes absentmindedly, rattling the Monet dish in its saucer. Robin puts up a series of paintings of the fetishes on different backgrounds, in different numbers, in different lights. White silk like a glacier, crumpled newspaper, dark boards, pale boards. Her mouth is large and soft and brown. She lights a cigarette. She says 'I *like* that', and 'I *like* that', and nothing else for a bit, and then begins to read the paintings as allegories. 'They're modern *vanitases*, I see,' says Shona McRury, 'they're about the *littleness* of our life.' Robin tries to keep quiet. He cannot overbear her as if she were Mrs Brown, he cannot tell her that they are not about littleness but about the infinite terror of the brilliance of colour, of which he could almost die, he doesn't think those things in words anyway. He does at first say things like 'Hmn, well, this one is solving a different kind of problem, d'you see?' and then he doesn't say anything because he can see she doesn't see, she isn't the slightest bit interested in the fact that the pictures, of which there are a very large number, never repeat, though they are all in a sense the same, they never set themselves exactly the same problem. She doesn't see that. She says, 'It's a bit frightening, a bit depressing, all that empty space, isn't it, it reminds you of coffins and bare kitchen tables with no food, no sustenance, all those bare boards, don't they?'

'I don't think of it that way,' says Robin.

'How do you think of it?'

'Well, as a series of problems, really, inexhaustible problems, of light and colour, you know.'

He does not say, because he does not articulate, the sense he has that he is *allowed* his patch of brilliance *because* he has dutifully and accurately and even beautifully painted all these null and neutral tones, the doves, the dusts, the dead leaves.

'Do you have any inkling of a change of direction, a next phase coming up, you know, a new focus of interest, anything like that?'

'I think if I had a big show – if it were all *on show together*, all the different – hm – aspects – hm – solutions, so to speak, temporary solutions – I might want to – move on to something else. It's hard to imagine, really.'

'Is it?'

He does not see how crucial this little question is.

'Oh yes. One thing at a time. I seem to have my work cut out, cut out, you know, for me, as it were, yes.'

Shona McRury says, 'All those prints of lonely deckchairs in little winds, in gardens and on beaches. When you see the first, you think, how moving, how interesting. And when you see the tenth, or the twentieth, you think, oh, *another* solitary deckchair with a bit of wind in it, what else is there? You know?'

'I think so.'

'I can *see* your work isn't like that.'

'Oh no. Not at all like that.'

'But it might look like that. To the uneducated eye.'

'Might it?'

'It might.'

Debbie watches Shona McRury walk away down Alma Road. How beautifully her olive skirt sits on her thin haunches, how perfectly, how expensively, those pleats are coerced to caress. Robin says his talk with her went well, but Debbie thinks nothing of Robin's judgement, and he does not seem seized with hope or vigour. Shona McRury's long straight band of hair flaps and sidles. Mrs Brown, in her trenchcoat, catches up with Shona McRury. Mrs Brown's hair stands up like a wiry plant in

a pot, inside a coil of plaited scarves, orange and lime. Mrs Brown
says something to Shona McRury who varies her pace, turns her
head, strokes her head, answers. Mrs Brown says something else.
What can Mrs Brown have to say to Shona McRury? Debbie's
mind fantastically meditates treason, subversion, sabotage. But
Mrs Brown has always been so good, so patient, despite her
disdainful *look*, to which she has a right. Mrs Brown could not
want to *hurt* Robin? Mrs Brown is in no position to hurt Robin,
surely, if she did. Why should Shona McRury listen, more than
out of politeness, to anything Mrs Brown has to say? They turn
the corner. Debbie feels tears bursting, somewhere inside the flesh
of her cheeks, in the ducts round her nose and eyes. She hears
Robin's voice on the stairs, saying it is *just like that woman* to go
home without removing the wineglasses or wiping up the rings
on his desk and drawing-table.

Shona McRury sends a gallery postcard to Robin and Debbie
jointly, saying that she really *loved* seeing the pictures, which have
real integrity, and that things are very crowded and confused in the
life of her gallery just now. Debbie knows that this means no, and
suspects that the kindnesses are for her, Debbie's, possible future
usefulness, that is, *A Woman's Place*'s possible future usefulness,
to the Callisto Gallery. She does not say that to Robin, whom
she is beginning to treat like a backward and stupid child, which
worries her, since that is not what he is. And when *A Woman's Place*
sends her off a month or two later to the Callisto Gallery with
a photographer, a nice enough on-the-make Liverpudlian called
Tom Sprot, to illustrate an article on a new feminist installation,
she goes in a friendly enough mood. She is a reasonable woman,
she could not have expected more from Shona McRury, and
knows it.

Tom Sprot has brilliantined blond hair and baggy tartan
trousers. He is very laid-back, very calm. When he gets inside
the gallery, which is normally creamy and airy, he says 'Wow!'
and starts rushing about, peering through his lens with alacrity.
The whole space has been transformed into a kind of soft, even
squashy, brilliantly coloured Aladdin's cave. The walls are hung
with what seem like huge tapestries, partly knitted, partly made
like rag rugs, with shifting streams and islands of colour, which
when looked at closely reveal little peering mad embroidered
faces, green with blue eyes, black with red eyes, pink with

silver eyes. Swaying crocheted cobwebs hang from the ceiling, inhabited by dusky spiders and swarms of sequinned blue flies with gauzy wings. These things are brilliantly pretty, but not like a stage set, they are elegant and sinister, there is something horrid about the netted pockets with the heaped blue bodies. The spiders themselves are menaced by phalanxes of feather dusters, all kinds of feathers, a peacock fan, a fluffy nylon cyan blue and shocking pink tube, a lime green and orange palm tree on a golden staff, wound with lamé. The cavern has a crazy kind of resemblance to a lived-in room. Chests of drawers, made of orange boxes covered with patchworks of wallpaper, from vulgar silver roses to William Morris birds, from Regency plum stripes to Laura Ashley pink sprigs, reveal half-open treasure chests with mazy compartments containing crazy collections of things. White bone buttons. Glass stoppers. Chicken bones. Cufflinks, all single. Medicine bottles with lacquered labels, full of iridescent beads and codliver oil capsules. Pearlised plastic poppet beads and sunflower seeds, dolls' teaspoons and drifts of variegated tealeaves and dead rose-petals. Sugar mice, some half chewed. String, bright green, waxed red, hairy brown, running from compartment to compartment.

There are pieces of furniture, or creatures, standing about in all this. A large tump, or possibly a giant pouffe, layered in skirts of scarlet and orange, grass green and emerald, dazzlingly juxtaposed, reveals, if the wools are parted, a circle of twenty or thirty little knitted pink breasts, and above that another of little chocolate coloured satin ones, a kind of squat Diana of Ephesus without face or hands. A long bolster-like creature might be a thin woman or a kind of lizard or even a piece of the seashore. It is mostly knitted, in rich browns and greens, with scalloped fronds and trailing, weedy 'limbs' or maybe tentacles – there are more, when it has been walked round, than four. From a distance it has a pleasing look of rock-pools crusted with limpets and anemones. Closer, it can be seen to be plated with a kind of armour of crocheted bosses, violet and saffron, some tufted with crimson, or trailing threads of blood-coloured embroidery silks.

The centrepiece is a kind of dragon and chained lady, St George and the Princess Saba. Perseus and Andromeda. The dragon has a cubic blue body and a long concertina neck. It has a crest of mulberry taffeta plates, blanket-stitched, something like the horrent scallops of the Stegosaurus. It is an odd dragon, recumbent amongst its own coils, a dragon related to a millipede, with hundreds of black shining wiry tentacular legs, which expose their scarlet linings and metal filaments. It is knitted yet solid, it raises a square jaw with a woollen beard and some teeth dripping with matted hair and broken hairpins, multicoloured fluffy foam and cotton spittle. Its eyes are bland blue rounds with soft chenille lashes. It is a Hoover and a dragon, inert and suffocating.

And the lady is flesh-coloured and twisted, her body is broken and concertina'd, she is draped flat on a large stone, her long limbs are pink nylon, her chains are twisted brassieres and demented petticoats, pyjama cords and sinister strained tights. She has a cubist aspect, crossed with Diana of Ephesus again, her breasts are a string of detached and battered shoulder-pads, three above two, her pubic hair is a shrunk angora bonnet. Her face is embroidered on petit-point canvas on a round embroidery-frame, it is half-done, a Botticelli Venus with a chalk outline, a few blonde tresses, cut-out eyeholes, stitched round with spiky black lashes. At first you think that the male figure is totally absent, and then you see him, them, minuscule in the crannies of the rock, a plastic knight on a horse, once silver, now mud-green, a toy soldier with a broken sword and a battered helmet, who have both obviously been through the wheel of the washing-machine, more than once.

There is someone in the window hanging a series of letters, gold on rich chocolate, on a kind of high-tech washing-line with tiny crimson pegs. It says

SHEBA BROWN WORK IN VARIOUS MATERIALS   1975–1990

Underneath the line of letters a photograph goes up. Debbie goes out into the street to look at it, a photograph of Mrs Brown under a kind of wild crown of woven scarves, with her old carved look and an added look of sly amusement, in the corners of mouth and eyes. Her skin has come out duskier than it 'really' is, her bones are sculpted, she resembles a cross between the Mona Lisa and a Benin bronze.

As far as Debbie knows, Mrs Brown is at this moment Hoovering her stairs. She cannot think. She thinks several things at once. She thinks with pure delight of the unexpectedness and splendour of Sheba, for Mrs Brown. She thinks inconsequentially of a ball she once went to, a Chelsea Arts Ball, in the mulberry-coloured dress which is now the dragon-scales. She thinks, with a terrible flutter of unreadiness to think about this, that Mrs Brown will now for certain leave. She wonders why Mrs Brown said nothing – was it a desire to shock, or a simpler desire to startle, or the courtesy of the old Mrs Brown, aware that Debbie could not do without her, thinking how to break the news, or was she – she certainly is in part – *simply* secretive and cautious? She thinks with terrible protectiveness of Robin in his attic, explaining his fetishes to Mrs Brown, and roaring as he will roar no more, about her forays into his workplace. She does not feel for a moment that Mrs Brown has 'stolen' Robin's exhibition, but she has a miserable fear that Robin may think that.

And she feels something else, looking at Sheba Brown's apparently inexhaustible and profligate energy of colourful invention. She feels a kind of subdued envy which carries with it an invigorating sting. She thinks of the feel of the wooden blocks she used to cut.

Tom Sprot comes up, full of excitement. He has discovered a chest of drawers full of tangled thread and smaller chests of drawers all full of tangled thread and smaller still chests of drawers. He has got the text of an interview done by Richard Cork for *A Woman's Place,* the text of which has just been delivered hot to the gallery by a messenger on a motor-bike. Debbie skims through it.

Sheba Brown lives in a council flat, surrounded by her own work, wall-hangings and cushions. She is in her forties, of part-Guyanese, part-Irish ancestry, and has had a hard life. Her work is full of feminist comments on the trivia of our daily life, on the boredom of the quotidian, but she has no sour reflections, no chip on her shoulder, she simply makes everything absurd and surprisingly beautiful with an excess of inventive wit. Some of her hangings resemble the work of Richard Dadd, with their intricate woven backgrounds, though they obviously owe something also to the luxurious innovations of Kaffe Fassett. But Sheba Brown, unlike Richard Dadd, is not mad or obsessed; she is richly sane and her conversation is good-humoured and funny.

She has brought up two sons, and gathered the materials for her work on a mixture of Social Security and her meagre

earnings as a cleaner. She gets her materials from everywhere
– skips, jumble sales, cast-offs, going through other people's
rubbish, clearing up after school fetes. She says she began on
her 'soft sculpture' by accident really – she had an 'urge to
construct' but had to make things that could be packed away
into small spaces at night. Her two most prized possessions
are a knitting-machine and a lockup room in the basement
of her block of flats which she has by arrangement with the
caretaker. 'Once I had the room, I could make box-like things
as well as squashy ones,' she says, smiling with satisfaction.

She says she owes a great deal to one family for whom she
has worked, an 'artistic family' who taught her about colours
(not that she needed 'teaching' – her instinct for new shocking
effects and juxtapositions is staggering) and broadened her
ideas of what a work of art might be . . .

Debbie goes home thoughtful. Mrs Brown has done her day's work
and left. Robin is fretful. He does not want spaghetti for supper, he
is sick of pasta, he thinks they must have had pasta every night for
a fortnight. Debbie considers him, as he sits twisting his fettucine
with a fork and thinks that on the whole it is probably safe to tell
him *nothing* about Mrs Brown and her Aladdin's cave, since he
never takes an interest in *A Woman's Place*, she can hide that from
him, and she can probably keep other criticism from him too, he
doesn't read much, it depresses him.

No sooner has she worked all this out than it is all ruined by
Jamie, who rushes into the kitchen crying, come and see, come
and see, Mrs Brown is on the telly. When neither of his parents
moves he cries louder,

'She's got an exhibition of things like Muppets with that gallery-
lady who came here, do come and look, Daddy, they're *bizarre*.'

So Robin goes and looks. Sheba Brown looks down her long
nose at him out of the screen and says,

'Well, it all just comes to me in a kind of coloured rush, I just
like putting things together, there's so much in the world isn't
there, and making things is a natural enough way of showing
your excitement . . .'

The screen briefly displays the Hoover-dragon and the washing-
bound lady.

'No, no, I don't do it out of *resentment*,' says Sheba Brown, enthusiastically in voice-over, as the camera pursues the strangling

twisted tights. 'No, I find it all *interesting*, I told you. Working
as a cleaning-lady, OK, you learn a lot, it's honest, you can see
things *anywhere at all* to make things up from, that's one thing I
know. People are funny really, you can't be a cleaning-lady for
long without learning *that* . . .'

Debbie looks at Robin. Robin looks at Sheba Brown. Sheba
Brown vanishes and is replaced by a jolly avuncular tar surrounded by simpering infants, brandishing a plate full of steaming
rectangular Fishy Morsels. Robin says,

'That, round that woman-sort-of-thing's neck, that was that
school tie I lost.'

'You didn't lose it. You threw it out.'

'No, I didn't. How would I have done that? I might go back
to some school reunion, might I not, you never know, and it isn't
likely I shall go and waste any money on *another* hideous purple
tie, is it?'

'It was in the waste-paper basket. I said she could have
it.'

'Mummy,' says Jamie, 'can we go and *see* Mrs Brown's squashy
sculptures?'

'We will all go,' says Robin. 'Courtesy requires that we all go.
And see what else she has filched.'

Mrs Brown comes in the next day accompanied by a grey-haired
sylph in ballet tights and trainers.

'Mrs Brown, Mrs Brown,' says Jamie (it is the school holidays),
'Mrs Brown, we saw you on the telly. And your name is beautiful,
and I think the muffet sort of things and the little faces are
stupiferous.'

Mrs Brown says,

'It looks as though I can't come for a bit, Mrs Dennison. I
hadn't quite taken what a change in my life it was going to
make, showing anyone my things. I just suddenly got it into
my head that it was time they were seen by someone, you
know how it is, and things got taken on from there, out of
my control rather, though I'm not complaining. I kept meaning
to say something, but it didn't seem to be the moment, and
I was concerned for you, how you would take it, for you do
need someone to rely on, as we both know. Now this here is
Mrs Stimpson, who will do exactly what I did, I'll show her
all the ropes, and how not to interfere with Mr Dennison, and

I really do think you'll hardly notice, Mrs Dennison. It'll be just the same.'

Debbie stares silently at Mrs Brown. Mrs Brown drops her eyes and then looks up slightly flushed.

'You do see how it was?' she asks, steadily enough. Debbie thinks, the worst thing is, if we had been friends, she would have shown *me* her things. But we weren't. I only thought we were.

Sheba Brown says, 'We understood each other, Mrs Dennison. But no one's unique. Mrs Stimpson is quite reliable and resourceful. I wouldn't let you down by bringing anyone who wasn't. She'll be just like me.'

Debbie says, 'And does Mrs Stimpson make secret works of art?'

'Now *that*,' says Sheba Brown, 'you will have to find out for yourself.'

Mrs Stimpson's young-old face has a firm, knowing little smile on it. She says,

'We can but try, Mrs Dennison. Without prejudice.'

'I suppose so,' says Debbie. Before she can open her mouth again Mrs Brown and Mrs Stimpson have gone into the kitchen. Debbie hears the coffee-grinder. They will bring her a cup of coffee. It will all be more or less the same.

Or not quite the same. For one thing, Debbie goes back to making wood engravings. *A Book of Bad Fairies* and *A Book of Good Fairies*, which have a certain success in the world of book illustration. Some of the more exotic fairies have the carved, haughty face of Sheba Brown, and the sweet, timeless face of Mrs Stimpson. And Robin? He roars at Mrs Stimpson, who humours him by appearing to be very flurried and rushing energetically to and fro at his behest. He also develops an interest in Oriental mythology, and buys several books of tantric mandalas and prayer-wheels. One day Debbie goes up to his room and finds a new kind of painting on the easel, geometric, brightly coloured, highly organised, a kind of woven pattern of flames and limbs with a recurring motif of a dark, glaring face with red eyes and a protruding red tongue. 'Kali the Destroyer,' says Mrs Stimpson, knowledgeably at Debbie's elbow. 'It's a picture of Kali the Destroyer.' It is not right, thinks Debbie, that the black goddess should be a simplified travesty of Sheba Brown, that prolific weaver of bright webs.

But at the same time she recognises a new kind of loosed, slightly savage energy in Robin's use of colour and movement. 'It's *got* something,' says Mrs Stimpson pleasantly. 'I do really think it's *got* something.' Debbie has to agree. It has indeed got something.

Over

Waking is the hardest thing they ask of him.

The nurse always wakes him with the word 'morning', and the word 'morning' brings a hurting into his head which he cannot control or ameliorate or do anything about. Very often, the word 'morning' interrupts his dreams. In these dreams there was a stoat somewhere. This is all he can say about them.

The nurse opens his mouth, which tastes of seed and fills it with teeth. 'These teeth have got too big for me,' he sometimes remarks, but neither the nurse nor his wife replies to this just as neither the nurse nor his wife laughs when from some part of his ancient self he brings out a joke he did not know he could still remember. He isn't even certain they smile at his jokes because he can't see faces any longer unless they are no more and no less than two feet from his eyes. 'Aren't you even smiling?' he sometimes shouts.

'I'm smiling, Sir,' says the nurse.

'Naturally, I'm smiling,' says his wife.

His curtains are drawn back and light floods into the room. To him, light is time. Until nightfall, it lies on his skin, seeping just a little into the pores yet never penetrating inside him, neither into his brain nor into his heart nor into any crevice or crease of him. Light and time, time and light lie on him as weightless as the sheet. He is somewhere else. He is in the place where the jokes come from, where the dreams of stoats lie. He refuses ever to leave it except upon one condition.

That condition is so seldom satisfied, yet every morning, after his teeth are in, he asks the nurse: 'Is my son coming today?'

'Not that I know of, Sir,' she replies.

So then he takes no notice of the things he does. He eats his boiled egg. He pisses into a jar. He puts a kiss as thin as air on his wife's cheek. He tells the nurse the joke about the Talking Dog. He folds his arms across his chest. He dreams of being asleep.

But once in a while – once a fortnight perhaps, or once a month? – the nurse will say as she lifts him up onto his pillows: 'Your son's arrived, Sir.'

Then he'll reach up and try to neaten the silk scarf he wears at his throat. He will ask for his window to be opened wider. He will sniff the room and wonder whether it doesn't smell peculiarly of water-weed.

The son is a big man, balding, with kind eyes. Always and without fail he arrives in the room with a bottle of champagne and two glasses held upside down between his first and second finger.

'How are you?' he asks.

'That's a stupid question,' says the father.

The son sits by the bed and the father looks and looks for him with his faded eyes and they sip the drink. Neither the nurse nor the wife disturbs them.

'Stay a bit,' says the father, 'won't you?'

'I can't stay long,' says the son.

Sometimes the father weeps without knowing it. All he knows is that with his son here, time is no longer a thing that covers him, but an element in which he floats and which fills his head and his heart until he is both brimming with it and buoyant on the current of it.

When the champagne has all been drunk, the son and the nurse carry the father downstairs and put him into the son's Jaguar and cover his knees with a rug. The father and the son drive off down the Hampshire lanes. Light falls in dapples on the old man's temples and on his folded hands.

There was a period of years that arrived as the father was beginning to get old when the son went to work in the Middle East and came home only once or twice a year, bringing presents made in Japan which the father did not trust.

It was then that the old man began his hatred of time. He couldn't bear to see anything endure. What he longed for was for things to be over. He did the *Times* crossword only to fill up the waiting spaces. He read the newspaper only to finish it and fold it and place it in the waste-paper basket. He snipped off from the rose bushes not only the dead heads but the blooms that were still living. At mealtimes, he cleared the cutlery from the table before the meal was finished. He drove out with his wife to visit friends to find that he longed, upon arrival, for the moment of departure. When he made his bed in the morning, he would put on the bedcover then turn it down again, ready for the night.

His wife watched and suffered. She felt he was robbing her of life. She was his second wife, less beautiful and less loved than the first (the mother of his son) who had been a dancer and who had liked to spring into his arms from a sequence of three cartwheels. He sometimes dismayed the second wife by telling her about the day when the first wife did a cartwheel in the revolving doors of the Ritz. 'I've heard that story, darling,' she'd say politely, ashamed for him that he could tell it so proudly. And to her bridge friends she'd confide: 'It's as if he believes that by rushing through the *now* he'll get back to the *then*.'

He began a practice of adding things up. He would try to put a finite number on the oysters he had eaten since the war. He counted the cigarettes his wife smoked in a day and the number of times she mislaid her lighter. He tried to make a sum of the remembered cartwheels. Then when he had done these additions, he would draw a neat line through them, like the line a captive draws through each recorded clutch of days, and fold the paper in half and then in quarters and so on until it could not be folded any smaller and then place it carefully in the waste-paper basket next to the finished *Times*.

'Now we know,' his wife once heard him mutter. 'Now we know all about it.'

When the war ended he was still married to the dancer. His son was five years old. They lived in a manor house with an ancient tennis court and an east-facing croquet lawn. Though his head was still full of the war, he had a touching faith in the future and he usually knew, as each night descended, that he was looking forward to the day.

Very often, in the summer of 1946, he would wake when the sun came up and, leaving the dancer sleeping, would go out onto the croquet lawn wearing his dressing gown and his slippers from Simpson's of Piccadilly and stare at the dew on the grass, at the shine on the croquet hoops and at the sky, turning. He had the feeling that he and the world made a handsome pair.

One morning, he saw a stoat on the lawn. The stoat was running round the croquet hoops and then in and out of them in a strange repeated pattern, as if it were taking part in a stoat gymkhana. The man did not move, but stood and watched. Then he backed off into the house and ran up the stairs to the room where his son was sleeping.

'Wake up!' he said to the little boy. 'I've got something to show you!'

He took his son's hand and led him barefoot down the stairs and out into the garden. The stoat was still running round and through the croquet hoops and now, as the man and the boy stood watching, it decided to leap over the hoops, jumping twice its height into the air and rolling over in a somersault as it landed, then flicking its tail as it turned and ran in for another leap.

The boy, still dizzy with sleep, opened his mouth and opened wide his blue eyes. He knew he must not move so he did not even look round when his father left his side and went back into the house. He shivered a little in the dewy air. He wanted to creep forward so that he could be in the sun. He tiptoed out across the gravel that hurt his feet onto the soft wet lawn. The stoat saw him and whipped its body to a halt, head up, tail flat, regarding the boy. The boy could see its eyes. He thought how sleek and slippery it looked and how he would like to stroke its head with his finger.

The father returned. 'Don't move!' he whispered to his son, so the boy did not turn.

The father took aim with his shotgun and fired. He hit the stoat right in the head and its body flew up into the air before it fell without a sound. The man laughed with joy at the cleanness and beauty of the shot. He laughed a loud, happy laugh and then he looked down at his son to get his approval. But the boy was not there. The boy had walked back inside the house, leaving his father alone in the bright morning.

Serrusalmus

One wall of Marjorie's living room swims with brightness. Each tank is a separate glowing world, where fish flicker through swaying weed. There is no sound but the hum of the electric pumps, aerating the water. The fish mouth silently to Marjorie through the glass.

The opposite wall of her room is also glass, window glass. If she cares to look through it, the flickerings she sees are the tiny busy cars, the movements of the miniature people down below. The people are featureless so far away – Marjorie lives on the nineteenth floor. The people scurry like ants. Once, as a girl, she had been taken to the zoo for a birthday treat. The thing she liked best, better than the elephants or the tigers, was the formicary. In the large glass-topped box was the ants' nest, a pyramid of earth, laced with holes. There were leaves for them to gather, and at the end of a ramp, a bottle full of sugar solution for them to collect. The ants lived out their busy lives in the box, oblivious to the people pressing their faces against the roof of their world, misting it with their breath. They toiled up and down the ramp, stopping to exchange a few words with their fellows now and then; one ant would drag a leaf a hundred times its own size to the nest; another would carry the dead or dying body of another upon its back. Marjorie could have watched all day. Her mother had eventually pulled her away. 'It's like a real little world all on its own,' Marjorie had said on the way home. 'The ants are just like people.'

It is more than forty years since that trip to the zoo and during that time there has been a reversal in Marjorie's mind. Now it is the people that are like the ants.

It is seldom that Marjorie meets a person face to face. She suffers from a condition that does not show. It is all in her head. 'Pull yourself together,' her mother would have said. Her glass-fronted room is balanced up in the sky where the clouds wrap around it in the winter so that looking out is like nothing so much as staring into grey water, where occasionally, a sparrow-fish swims by. Marjorie rarely ventures out of her room. 'Agoraphobia,' the doctor said when she tried to explain, and gave her some pills. 'Don't give in to it,' he advised. 'It can take you over if you let it. Don't.'

Marjorie's mother would have scoffed. All in the mind, she'd have said. Marjorie's mother had a fear of the mind. Marjorie swallows the pills and tries to fight, but the agoraphobia has her in its clutches.

Marjorie presses her face against the aquarium glass where her darlings swim coldly night and day. After her trip to the zoo, she'd vowed to have a formicary when she grew up. She wanted a little world all of her own, just to watch. But the ants were too much like people, she decided as she grew older, too busy, too social. Marjorie has developed a dread of people, most people – not Ron from Fish'n Feathers, the supplier of all her stock and equipment – but of most others. Particularly Mick.

It is bright in the tanks, brighter and realler behind that glass than the greyness behind the window. It soothes her to watch the fish. They aren't busy like the ants and the people. They are peaceful behind their wall of glass, in the warm tanks and the cold. It soothes her to watch the bubbles streaming from the pumps, and to listen to the electric hum that keeps conditions perfect for all the many species. There are angel fish, big and flat as her outstretched palms; neon tetras, bright firework sparks; cat-fish, with tabby bodies, their mouths glued to the glass like snails. There are carp that glisten like silver-foil, and blind cave fish, with piquant, eyeless faces. There are eels winding their bodies through the gravel. Her new boy, of the genus Serrusalmus, glides patiently from one end of his tank to the other. He is a beautiful boy, and although she does not have favourites, if the truth be told he is her pride and joy. She calls him Russ for short.

It is the way they are so contained that soothes Marjorie. Each species in its own glass-walled world, entirely safe, pampered one might almost say, entirely safe from predators. If Marjorie could be so contained she would be happy. In her dreams, on good nights, sleeping nights, she is silver slick and silent, gliding from one glass wall to the other, enclosed and yet entirely free.

Now watching Russ, she almost wishes Mick would come.

It has been months. But he will be back, eventually, and Marjorie will be there. Mick is a predator, and Marjorie his prey. She supposes he has others in his thrall, but she knows nothing of them. All she knows is the fear he brought her, and the fear he left behind, dripping from the glass like condensation.

Marjorie blames the school. They obtained her name from a list given them by the Social Services, and included her in their Community Scheme. This means that every Friday afternoon they turn loose all their yobs and troublemakers. They send them into the community to offer unsupervised solace to the old and the sick and the lonely.

He has never actually harmed her, not physically. He has simply terrorised her. He's borrowed money from her time and again, with never a please or a thank-you. He must owe Marjorie about fifty pounds, not that she's ever kept a tally. She's never been naive enough to expect it back. Mick only came twice, officially. Marjorie telephoned the school to complain of his behaviour, and of the intrusion. She telephoned the Social Services and tore them off a strip for giving out her name and address. That made her feel better, briefly. The school told Mick not to call on her again, but he knew when he was onto a good thing. Even after he left school he'd turn up out of the blue, after weeks, just as Marjorie began to relax, to hope he'd given her up. He helped himself to food from the refrigerator, and in the most uncouth way, swigging milk straight from the bottle, taking a bite from a lump of cheese, spitting fruit pips onto the floor. He swore at her, and he threatened her. If she phoned the police she would be dead, he said. However, none of these were the worst thing he had done.

He pretended once to take an interest in the fish – and she had been taken in. He'd called on her at a most distressing time; a nightmare of a time, when her fish had a fungal infection. It was the angel fish that suffered most, and Marjorie watched helplessly as their beautiful chiffon fins and tails rotted, and their eyes skinned over with a soggy membrane. She rang Ron at Fish'n Feathers every day, but all he could offer was sympathy. She'd done the necessary: isolated the sufferers in a healing solution of Phenoxetol, sterilised the tanks, the pumps, the gravel.

Mick turned up just as she was about to transfer an angel fish from his tank to a bucket of treated water. He had been a magnificent fish before the disease had reduced him to tatters. She was all ready with the net and the bucket when Mick arrived. She should never have let him in. There was no need. She had a little spyhole in her door, a tiny glass bubble. When she'd peered through, she'd seen quite clearly that it was Mick. The curved glass distorted his face, drew out his nose, pushed back his forehead and chin, slid his eyes round to the side of his head so that he looked curiously fishy. Like a tooth carp, perhaps, of the vicious Belonesox type. Perhaps it was this fishiness that made her open the door, that made her believe, stupidly, that he was really interested. He'd listened without the usual sneer as she explained the problem, pointed out the suffering fish.

'Perhaps you'd like to help?' she'd suggested.

'OK,' he'd said, and taken the net. He'd scooped the fish up without any trouble.

'Now the bucket, quickly,' Marjorie had said.

'What's it worth?' he'd said, holding the net aloft so that the poor fish gaped and burned in the parching air.

'Please,' Marjorie said.

'What's it worth?' he'd repeated.

Marjorie's mouth was dry, she was weak with anxiety, with empathy for the suffering creature, with rage. 'Anything,' she whispered. 'Just put him in the bucket.'

'A hundred quid, then,' Mick said.

'I haven't got . . .'

'A hundred . . .'

'But . . .'

'Better put the poor bleeder out of its misery then,' he said, almost amiably.

Marjorie's arms reached out and her mouth opened and closed helplessly as he opened the window and flipped the fish out. Impossibly, it seemed to hang in the air for a few long seconds, doomed angel, before it plummeted out of sight to join the scattered rubbish on the ground below.

Mick had laughed at her face. Her mouth gaped open as if *she* was drowning in air. He had laughed uneasily as she sank to her knees beside the bucket. There had been a pause as Marjorie stared first at the empty water, then at the open window, and finally at Mick's face. He could have killed her then. She wouldn't have made a murmur. But over his face passed a new expression. Marjorie glimpsed weakness and fear, just for a second, before the cockiness was back. The sharkish triumph. He shouted something at her before he went, some obscenity. By the time Marjorie had regained enough strength to go to the window, he was down below, kicking and grinding his boots amongst the rubbish.

When Mick finally turns up again, he is different. Even through the spyhole she can detect a change. He has been in a fight by the look of it: black eye, swollen lips, bloodied nose. He limps inside without a word and flops down on the sofa. He is in a bad way altogether, Marjorie can see. His swagger has gone. He looks smaller, his shoulders narrow under the scuffed leather of his jacket.

'Well,' says Marjorie.

'Don't fuckin' open the door to no one else,' Mick says. 'Need a drink. Fetch me a fuckin' drink.'

'What right . . .' begins Marjorie, and then stops. There is no need to go getting on her high horse now. She has him now. 'I'll see what I can do,' she says.

She pours him a glass of whisky and drops into it several of her tablets, the ones the doctor prescribed for her agoraphobia. She crushes them against the side of the glass with a spoon, and mixes them in.

'Here,' she says. She watches him swig the drink down in one gulp. She turns to put the kettle on the gas stove. He rolls a thin cigarette, lights it and puts it between his lips. But he is already too far gone to smoke. The pills *are* strong. The correct dose is only one per night, and they are not to be mixed with alcohol. There is a warning on the bottle. Mick passes out right there on her sofa, slumping down, his head upon the arm, his eyes glazed and only half closed.

Marjorie removes the cigarette from between his fingers. He doesn't stir. She studies him, grimy and greasy and half-starved. Sometimes Marjorie regrets not having had a child, but when she looks at the likes of him she thanks her lucky stars.

Marjorie turns to the fish. They swim slickly backwards and forwards in the bright heaven of their tanks: white gravel, silver bubbles, green weed and the iridescence of their scales. They cheer her. How much more beautiful fish are than people, she thinks for the thousandth time. No ungainliness, no filth, no stupidity. The tanks hum. There is the guttering sound of Mick's breath. The kettle whistles and Marjorie goes to turn it off. Plenty of time for tea later. Since Mick's asleep she'll get on as usual. It is time to feed the fish. She pinches into each tank the correct share of daphnia and tubifex worms, enjoying their eagerness, their hunger and its satisfaction. She saves Russ until last. She feeds him slivers of ham from last night's tea. He attacks them madly as if they are alive. She savours his excitement, his frenzy. He is her favourite boy. In their natural habitat these creatures can strip the flesh from an animal or another fish is seconds. Piranha is their common name. Marjorie looks at Russ, hungry boy, growing boy.

Mick is fast asleep. She shakes his shoulder, gives him a chance, but he never stirs. His mouth hangs open and a dark pool of saliva stains the arm of the sofa. His filthy hand trails on the floor, like a careless hand trailed from a boat. She considers what this hand has done, remembers her helpless Angel plummeting through the air.

She fills her bucket. She scoops Russ from his tank, enjoying just for a moment the muscular weight of his thrashing body before she releases him into the bucket. He swims round, curiously, and she pauses to watch him before stooping to pick up the limp hand and drop it in the water. Mick never even stirs. Russ swims against the hand for a moment, butts it with his nose. And then suddenly the water boils red and rises in the bucket. Mick makes a strange noise, jerks himself away, but Marjorie is ready. She presses her weight against his puniness, forcing his arm to remain still, and his resistance is only temporary. Marjorie holds him where he is until Russ has finished, until the churning in the bucket ceases.

She lifts his arm clear and returns the sated fish to his tank; she tips the rosy water into the bath; she mops the splashes on the floor beside the sofa. And then she makes the tea. She lays a tray nicely, with two cups, in case Mick comes round. She arranges custard creams upon a plate. She bears no grudge now. No need. The boot is on the other foot.

Marjorie sits down beside him. He doesn't look at all well, poor boy. His hand trails on the floor out of the dampened ragged cuff of his jacket. It is clean now, bluish shining bone clean. Marjorie takes a sip of tea and sits back to look at Russ. Through the glass she could swear that he's blowing her kisses.

The Coat

It was a light summer coat of yellow velvet with a silk lining. The velvet was soft and smooth. It might have been cut from the petals of an enormous primrose.

It had been given to Muriel by a dear friend (this was the term she had settled on), a veterinary surgeon, who had treated Muffy, Muriel's dog, for the numerous ailments she was suffering from when Muriel had first taken her in.

The pockets with their deep silk interiors were very cool to the touch. There were three buttons; ivory coloured, with sunflowers moulded in relief on each. The shoulders were styled a little outward, a little upward, not padded, but giving just a hint of regal breadth. The skirting tapered inward – a note of playful severity – stopping just high enough to disclose its owner's ankles, which, as the dear friend constantly averred, and as Muriel did not mind admitting herself, were something a seventeen-year-old girl could have been proud of.

In fact the whole garment flattered her. The colour revived a lustre in the remaining honey colour of her hair; the cut did credit to her figure which if nothing else was still erect. Wearing it Muriel felt a little more radiant, a little lighter-hearted than usual. It was, she sometimes felt, like being sheathed in an emanation from her own youth.

For this reason she wore it sparingly. She was in good health, not yet sixty, still worked in the college where she had been registrar since her husband's death. But after all, one's youth was not something to be called up indefinitely: its residue was volatile, like an ancient chrism that too much exposure might vaporise.

Then too, by an instinct for the higher subtleties of sympathetic magic, she made a point of never putting on the coat with a view to *inducing* livelier spirits; never wearing it to 'cheer herself up', as some of her more simple-minded acquaintances imagined they could by dressing up in some gaudy retrieval from the depths of their closets. No. She wore it only when the rare mood, the distant intimation of gaiety, was already stirring inside her. Then and only then would she wear it: not to coax but to facilitate, to enhance.

After checking the sky and the hall barometer (the dear friend had cautioned that water might spot the material), she would lift the coat from its padded hanger, swim her hands into the stream-cool sleeves, button up the three sunflower buttons, and step out from her small brick house (she preferred not to think of it as a bungalow), onto the lane that led to the village, pausing to smell a neighbour's honeysuckle, or buy stamps, or pick up groceries at the village store. Invariably someone would admire the coat, remark how well it suited her, how elegant she looked in it, how young, and she would answer graciously, feeling a sensation of calm delight arising in her, as if a cool flame were waving through her body.

The dear friend was a gentle, quiet soul called Donald Costane. Their attachment was more consolatory than passionate – they had come late into one another's lives – though once or twice a remote craving had passed through Muriel as she watched Donald's long, white, well-manicured hands pick their way through the mangy tufts of Muffy's ochre hair in search of sores and parasites, then lave themselves in disinfectant soap, and rub each other dry with a crisply starched hand-towel. However, his regard for her appeared to be restricted to the scope of formal veneration. He admired her spirit, which he considered both proud and refined. He cherished a notion that the two of them were each other's reward for maintaining dignity in the face of unspecified suffering. It was understood that if they were not 'above' other people, they were at least 'apart' from them, in possessing virtues too subtle and discreet for the world to recognise; that they must bear their obscurity with fortitude, but that now at least they had each other to help them. Such, at any rate, was how she interpreted his attentions.

And in a very little time she came to see that the limits he tacitly set were not only sensible, but were also conducive to unexpectedly rich and gratifying feelings; feelings that had more to do with possibility than actuality; suggestion than statement; with consummations subtly deferred that at another time might have been eagerly sought. So that their friendship had acquired the air of an eternal courtship; two parallel lines moving together over horizon after horizon toward some infinitely distant but perpetually beckoning point of convergence.

'I must admit I always believed I would come into my own at sixty,' Donald said once during a mild post-prandial haze; 'Even, would you believe, it when I was quite a young child.'

Muriel had laughed. 'It is a shame we didn't meet when we were younger,' she had ventured, then realising from his abstracted look that she had missed the point, added, 'but perhaps we would not have recognised each other.'

He was handsome in his own way; shiny grey hair always neatly brushed and set; dignified profile; grave, pouchy eyes that seemed to indicate a bottomless fund of sympathy. He collected Victorian pewter, dressed in well-cut suits or sports jackets, drove a plushly upholstered car, and was dependably punctilious in the matter of flowers and notes and little gifts at appropriate moments – all of them well-chosen, though none as bold, as presumptuous, as the coat, which he had presented to Muriel after their first outing to London, when she had complained of looking and feeling like all the other dowdy provincial ladies at the theatre.

It had astonished her, arriving by delivery van one afternoon, in a shallow box the length of a body, wrapped in several layers of tissue; lying there buttoned up, primrose yellow, with a fresh rose in its lapel, and a little mauve envelope with a note saying simply 'For the Metropolis'.

He spoke little about his past, and seldom asked Muriel about hers. The agreement seemed to be to banish all ghosts for the duration of their meetings; to create passages of perfect happiness while they were in each other's company.

Their outings were elaborate, and no doubt costly, though Muriel herself never saw a bill. They occurred perhaps once every six weeks, more in summer, a little less in winter. They had quickly established themselves as the high point in Muriel's routine, becoming downright necessary after her son Billy joined the navy and was out of the country for most of the year, so that aside from the trivial solace of gossiping with the neighbours, there was effectively nothing but Donald between herself and whatever it was that pressed upon one during the quiet afternoons when there were no letters to write, no cardigan about to go at the sleeves, nothing to weed or prune in the garden, and one could see as if through glass straight into the empty ocean of the day.

But the coat.

There had been the occasion of the Losing of the Button.

It had happened during one of the outings to London. Donald

had picked Muriel up as usual at eleven o'clock in the morning. They had driven to the city, eaten lunch at an Italian restaurant in Charlotte Street, strolled to the Embankment and taken a boat ride along the river. Gulls, bridges, boat crews flat in the water like pond-skimmers, the Parliament buildings rising from the thumbed bronze Thames like needles of caramel combed up out of molten sugar ... Donald had inquired in his solicitous way after Billy; Muriel began a lament about her son's deficiencies as a correspondent, then, hearing the unpermitted note of complaint in her voice, stopped herself and changed the subject, which Donald graciously pretended not to notice. After a drink at a newly restored Victorian pub in Shoreditch that Donald had wanted to investigate, they had gone to a musical in the West End, finishing off their evening with a light supper at a crowded brasserie in St Martin's Lane.

It had been an entirely satisfactory outing. Donald had told amusing stories about some of his animal patients, for whom he bore a tender and unashamedly personal affection. The musical had been cheerful and tasteful. The weather had been sunny but cool, and she had worn the coat all day except when they were indoors.

On the drive home, as she was drawing it a little tighter against the evening chill, her fingers had registered a bobble of thread where the middle of the three sunflower buttons should have been.

She waited until Donald stopped for petrol o.. the motorway, when she took the opportunity to make a search of the car; to no avail. Suspecting Donald would feel obliged to turn back in search of the button if he thought she was upset, and equally that he would be offended if she affected not to care, she refrained from saying anything when he returned to the car.

But all the small contentments of the day, stored up in her mind to be fondly relived later, had seemed to pour out of her in a single rush of annoyance.

The following morning she phoned the coat's makers and found that neither the coat nor the buttons were being manufactured any more. Without pausing – she did not want to give herself time to question what she was doing – she drove herself to the station (driving in the city made her nervous), and took a train to London. Thinking she had probably lost the button towards the end of the outing – else she would surely have noticed it – she began retracing her itinerary of the previous day in reverse.

Nothing had been found at the car park or the brasserie. The cloakroom attendant at the theatre in Piccadilly had a box with odds and ends in it that people had left behind in the theatre; keys, gloves, fountain pens, a pocket-sized television, but no buttons of any description. Staving off her disappointment, Muriel took a bus to Shoreditch and walked to the Victorian pub. With its gilded cherubs and mirrors, its scrimshawed narwhal horns and enormous buttoned-leather sofas, the pub might have been expressly designed as a haystack for the concealment of her particular needle. A group of young men, catching on to her predicament, made a raucous display of searching every nook and cranny of the lounge and saloon and public bar, much to the irritation of the other patrons. The exercise was as fruitless as it was embarrassing. And what with the commotion, the heat, and the smell of beer and spirits, it left her feeling distinctly weak on her knees.

She took a taxi to the little shack on the Embankment that served as the offices of the pleasure boat company. The lady who sold tickets remembered her; remembered the coat at any rate, as soon as Muriel described it, and seemed as concerned as Muriel herself at the loss of the button, entering Muriel's by now unconcealable anxiety with a fullness of sympathy that made her feel at least that she was not being wholly ridiculous. It did not, however, produce the button.

At the Italian restaurant in Charlotte Street, the bow-tied manager who had attended to her with studied gallantry the day before, helping her both into and out of the coat, today not only failed to remember her, but treated her with thinly veiled suspicion, only grudgingly allowing her to inspect the cloakroom at the back of the restaurant, eyeing her all the while as if she had come here to steal the silver. Glimpsing herself in a mirror on the way out she had had an inkling why. She looked frayed, haggard, dishevelled and a little crazed.

So she had emerged into the afternoon heat of the city.

There was an hour before her train left, and she wandered slowly towards Charing Cross. A muffled sensation came into her. She felt dimmed somehow, and cut off from the buildings and people passing on either side of her. Confronted with the failure of her mission, she began to wonder why she had embarked on it in the first place. What had possessed her to waste a day in such a senseless fashion? If she couldn't replace the button, she could find three others that would look just as nice as the sunflowers. Really, she told herself, it had been altogether rather a shameful exercise. And futile.

But even as she admitted these things, something in her rose obstinately to her own defence. There *was* something worth clinging to in the idea of perfection. A thing once blemished was never the same, however much you forgave it. At any rate she herself was so constituted as to be sensitive to the small things that made the difference. If that was a fault in her then so be it. She was not responsible for the aspirations of her own soul.

She marched on, squinting into a glare that seemed to radiate equally from the street, the sky, and her own exhaustion. Turning a corner she came to a crossroads where the flow of people and cars was held up by what appeared to be the demolition of an underground public convenience. Giant excavating machines were grouped around a crater in which were exposed – among clay, rubble, creeper-like armatures of plumbing, and some patches of broken mosaic – several doorless toilet cubicles with the white porcelain bowls still nakedly in place. Verdigris-streaked pipes led up from them like stalks from enormous onion bulbs. A horrible odour hung in the heat. She tried to hurry by but the cordoned walkway past the site had narrowed pedestrian traffic to single file. For several unpleasant seconds she was caught in a slow-moving human crush. By the end of it a sweat had broken out on her lip, and she was feeling dizzy. Just as she emerged, a pigeon flew down slantwise right across her face, so close she felt a buffeting of hot air on her eyelids. She gave a soft cry and put her hand to her heart, which had at once begun knocking in her chest. The pigeon landed in one of those arid patches of earth left unpaved at the base of city trees. It scrabbled there with its wormy toes; a filthy bird, looking as if some passing god of the metropolis had seen fit to breathe life into a broken lump of pavement with a smear of oil on it. Muriel caught its bulbous eye as she paused for breath. Cigarette butts, sweet wrappers, bleached excrement, lay around it on the sandy earth. It hopped between two gnarled claws of root, jabbed at the ground, and then took off with a wheezy flapping.

And there between the roots, pristine and gleaming, as if the pigeon had just that moment laid it, was the sunflower button.

A sensation of hot triumph had come into Muriel as she stooped for it. She felt both elated and defiant, as if in retrieving the button she had confounded some opposing law of existence.

It was warm from the summer heat, and mysteriously communicative as only an inanimate object can be.

She had been even more sparing in her use of the coat after that, restricting herself for the most part to admiring it in passing as she picked something less hazardous from her bedroom closet. She hung it on its padded hanger, with a net bag full of cedar chips to keep away the moths. It was hanging there, of course, the weekend her son Billy came to visit with Vanessa.

Billy had met Vanessa three weeks earlier, on his first weekend of shoreleave. It was unlike him to bring home a girl, particularly one he had known for so short a time. Sensing something momentous, Muriel had gone out of her way to extend a welcome. But it had soon become apparent that the weekend was going to be a trial.

By Saturday night the young lady had distinguished herself by lounging around the house with next to nothing on, feeding Muffy chocolates till the poor thing was sick, sitting on Billy's lap at mealtimes, spoonfeeding him, cooing babytalk at him, signalling at him while Muriel attempted to make conversation with him about his tour of duty in the Arctic, until with a sheepish grin he had sidled off after the girl and followed her upstairs. Muriel had not been born yesterday, but there are certain sounds that she considered a mother's ears better off not hearing, and she had had to go outside and prune the roses in the twilight rather than endure them, though even there she had heard her son's name called out in a startlingly piercing cry; *Billy, Billy* . . . My God.

It was as she had suspected. On Sunday morning Billy took her aside to ask what she thought of Vanessa. She had begun to make a reply, choosing her words carefully, with an equal view to truth and tact, when Billy burst out that he had proposed to the girl and that they were going to get married on his next leave.

So that Muriel had felt it her uncomfortable duty to take them to the Sandbourne Hotel at lunchtime, for a celebratory glass of champagne . . . The girl's idea of dressing up had been to exchange her negligee for a lederhosen outfit with a loose, sleeveless top that seemed designed to draw every male eye deep into the ripe shadows of its shoulder halters. It had certainly caused a stir in the lounge of the Sandbourne, and the girl had clearly revelled in the attention, letting her eye stray about the room, babbling her silly nonsense in a loud voice that got louder the more she drank.

Under the circumstances it was difficult not to contemplate the crude perils awaiting Billy in his long absences at sea. But with luck perhaps the young lady would find herself unable to manage even the few months of solitude that lay ahead of her, and Billy might learn his lesson without the added humiliation of being actually married to his teacher.

Shortly before they left the hotel, something behind Muriel caught the girl's attention. Her eyes kept moving slyly to a point just over Muriel's shoulder, then sliding back to Billy's with a look of suppressed mirth. A few times Billy looked covertly over at the bar, then met Vanessa's glance with expressions that changed gradually from perplexity to the same reined-in hilarity as if he were slowly cottoning on to some private game. Muriel did her best to ignore it, but at last turned round to see what they were looking at. There was an elderly man in a brass-buttoned blazer sitting at the bar; red-faced, white-haired, and with long, stiff, white moustaches twirled and waxed at the ends and sticking out absolutely horizontally above his lip. He was drinking gin and tonic and sitting with a very straight back. He looked with a stony or perhaps merely blank expression at Muriel's party.

Muriel turned reproachfully back to Billy, but before she could speak, Vanessa broke out with a peal of giggles, and after a feeble attempt at self-restraint, gave in to a fit of wild and rather terrifying laughter which seemed to Muriel, however mysterious its precise cause, to be formed unmistakably of an inseparable cruelty and dirty-mindedness, and which twisted and crumpled the girl until, with tears streaming down her face, she had run off to the Ladies' Room.

That afternoon Muriel had decided it would be in everyone's interest if she absented herself from the house for a few hours. Apart from anything else it might earn her a little of Billy's attention in the evening.

On the pretext of errands to run she drove off with Muffy to the nearby reservoir where a footpath led around the shore.

People were out sailing in dinghies – snub-nosed Mirrors, and the flotilla of pretty, leaf-shaped Larks owned by the Sailing Club.

It had been warm for days, and dry for most of the summer. The water level had sunk quite low, leaving a wide band of dried froth and ribbon weed on the pebbly shore.

Muriel clipped the lead to Muffy's collar and set off along the dusty footpath, bordered by the reservoir on one side, and on the other by a flat wilderness of broom, gorse and bilberry bushes. There was a smell of warm creosote from the Water Authority huts dotted along the shore, and an occasional dank algal breath from the lapping water carried upward on the breeze.

The place had always had a calming effect on Muriel, and it was not long before she began to feel a little less agitated.

She thought about Billy and Vanessa, and reflected that a father might have been useful to Billy at this moment in his life; even his own father, who had maintained high standards in his judgments of others, if not of himself. It was a pity, too, that Donald and Billy didn't get on – not that anything had been said, but it would be hard to imagine Donald offering to take the boy aside for a chat, let alone Billy submitting to such an offer.

Anyway, much as she loved her son, she knew that he was in some respects a fool, and that even if he were saved from this particular folly he would sooner or later find another one to commit in its place.

And then too, she thought with sudden gentleness, there was always the chance that Vanessa herself would improve. She was very young after all. The shrillness and flimsiness of her outward manner might disappear over time, and reveal a decent sort of soul. Her faults might not be deep; at any rate might not be irredeemable. You never knew what might happen to a person; it was a mistake to trust only in the worst.

A couple with a Labrador approached along the footpath. Muffy stood still to be sniffed, then sniffed the Labrador in return. She trotted towards the owners with her tail wagging, and Muriel let her stay a moment to be patted, though she kept the leash tight and watched her closely: Donald had said Muffy had probably been beaten as a puppy, and would never be a hundred per cent dependable.

She had appeared at Muriel's door one winter morning, her skin covered with bald patches and sores, and her skeleton visible beneath it. One ear had been badly chewed up, and one hind leg was in the air; apparently too tender to put on the ground.

Muriel had thrown her some bacon rinds, which the dog came

warily forward to snatch up, limping off with them through the wet grass into the woods at the end of Muriel's back lawn. That evening she had returned, soaked and shivering. Muriel had thrown her some more scraps. The dog gobbled them, this time staying where she was, and staring up at Muriel with her head cocked to one side when she had finished. Muriel had been touched by the sight, and had called her inside, giving her more food and putting down a blanket for her on the floor of the mud-room.

An acquaintance had recently suggested she get a dog for the companionship now that Billy was gone. She had taken no notice of the idea, never having considered herself a dog lover, but she found it difficult to turn the animal out of the house the next morning, and she soon realised she was becoming attached to the creature.

It had sharp, almost dainty features, like a very small Alsatian. Its cindery ochre coat had a reddish tinge on top that suggested red-setter. After a few days Muriel had decided to adopt her, and inquired about a vet to have her examined. It was in this way that she had met Donald.

Under his care, the dog recovered from her sores and grew back the fur on her bald patches. After a few weeks in a splint, the fractured bone in her hind leg mended perfectly. She lost her slightly unpleasant derelict odour, and began to smell of ginger biscuits, if rather stale ones. She grew healthy and sleek and alert; turning in fact into a very pretty animal, with bright girlish eyes, and a way of tilting her head to form a certain pathetic expression that never failed to arouse a pang of protective affection in Muriel.

Her nervousness had been slower to cure. She barked furiously at anyone who came to the house, and had once chased the child of a neighbour out onto the road, after which Muriel kept her tied up whenever she was outside. But in time the sedate rhythms of Muriel's life seemed to soothe the animal, and she had grown less noisy and excitable, becoming even a little bit slothful in recent months.

Muriel passed the Sailing Club, which marked the halfway point of her circuit. The sun was low in the sky, and a lance of light had begun to probe across the reservoir. From the far shore ripples shot across the water like footprints of a swift, invisible herald.

A breeze blew up. Sails filled out and surged forward, tilting over as they were hauled in for speed.

Muriel remembered bringing Billy to the Sailing Club once when he was a small boy, and watching anxiously as the little Lark he was put in with an instructor raced off across the water at what had seemed a dangerously unstable angle. He hadn't enjoyed the experience any more than she had, and never showed any desire to repeat it; a fact she had not failed to remind him of when he arrived home from his job at the local estate agents one day a few months after the Falklands War, and announced that he was going to join the Royal Navy.

The breeze died, then came back, stiffer than before. By the time Muriel completed her circuit, the reservoir had blossomed with brightly striped spinnaker sails billowing out in front of their craft and towing them along so fast that even the smallest cut a wake of orange light on the water. For a moment she stood and watched. They were lovely to look at, and she felt gladdened and lightened by the sight.

She drove home in good spirits, exercised and refreshed, sanguine about the chances of a civilised final evening with her son.

There was a note on the kitchen table when she got in: 'Gone to the pub. See you later.'

Assuming this meant they would be back in time for supper, Muriel put the casserole she had prepared into the oven and set the table. For a while she sat in the living room reading the papers. But she was unable to concentrate, and fearing that her good mood might not survive if she sat there with just her thoughts, she went back outside to finish pruning the roses.

It was almost dark by the time she finished. Billy and Vanessa had not returned. She raked up the pruned stalks and carried them in bundles to the steel basket incinerator at the bottom of the back lawn. Putting in as many as she could, she poured petrol over them and set them alight. Flames shot up into the dusk. A few pearl-sized drops of water glinted in the firelight, falling to earth. She hadn't realised it had started raining.

Back inside, she ate her supper and cleared it away. Thinking it would be a triumph of sorts if she were to wait up for Billy and Vanessa and receive them without a trace of reproach, she went back into the living room, and had another go at the papers.

But the silence of the room, so familiar to her, and usually not oppressive, made her suddenly desolate. It really was a little inconsiderate of them to disappear like this, she couldn't help thinking, though she immediately chided herself; probably Billy had wanted to celebrate with some of his old friends from the village. Well, that was understandable. She resisted the temptation to feel hurt by him; there was no limit to how far you could slide in that direction once you started.

She stood up and went upstairs, thinking her best bet would be to go to sleep.

To her surprise she could smell Vanessa's scent as she went into her bedroom. She turned on the light. The slide door to the closet was open. She went over to inspect it. A pair of high heels on the floor had been tipped over. A tweed jacket had been taken out and put back with its collar twisted. There was a padded hanger with a net bag of cedar chips at a gap where the row of clothes had been divided. The yellow coat was gone.

Muriel sat back on the foot of her bed, a little stunned. For a while she neither moved nor formed a thought, but merely sat, coiled into herself like a person who has just been hit. Then gradually she began to make an assessment of the situation.

Obviously the girl had not taken the coat in order to spite her. She knew nothing of its preciousness to Muriel. She had taken it because the evening had turned out to be cool and she needed something to wear. No doubt she had asked Billy's permission, and Billy had told her to help herself.

It was unfortunate that the weather had broken, but Vanessa could hardly be blamed for that. Anyway, Donald's warning that rain would ruin the velvet might well have been alarmist – he did tend to be a little over-cautious. But even if he was right, so what? It was only a coat after all, and one shouldn't make a fetish of such things. She had perhaps set too much store by it in the first place; certainly her day in London in search of the button filled her with a half-shameful feeling whenever she remembered it.

These last reflections were formed more in a spirit of wishfulness than conviction, but they helped Muriel stave off the feelings of annoyance that had begun to rise in her.

She felt it necessary to do this; in recent months she had noticed herself becoming prone to fits of irritation, often for quite trivial reasons. Something would vex her, and before she knew it she would have passed into a dreamlike state of silent fury, where the most violent punishments would be meted out in an atmosphere of obscure malediction. She would emerge from these states feeling shaken and vaguely guilty, as if after an over-indulgence. She had no wish to end her days in a permanent twilight of bitterness and anger. Why such a fate should threaten her, she had no idea; these things were apparently not in one's hands. But it was becoming a matter of conscious vigilance to maintain a pleasant disposition, and keep the more disagreeable tendencies of her imagination in check.

She no longer had any desire to go to sleep, and went back downstairs.

Passing the open door of the mud-room she saw a short red suede coat on a hook and remembered that Vanessa had brought this with her. Because of the fine weather, she had not worn it all weekend, and Muriel had forgotten about it. Seeing it now was like being struck again. For this argued, did it not, an indifference verging on contempt?

A feeling that had in it both dismay and bewilderment came into Muriel. She pictured the girl putting on her own coat then discarding it and running upstairs to Muriel's bedroom and riffling through her closet, trying on one thing after another, posing in the mirror, calling out to Billy for approval. The idea was peculiarly distressing; it unfolded in Muriel like an extremely unpleasant physical sensation.

So that it was again necessary to get a grip on herself.

She went into the living room and sat in an armchair without turning on the light. She thought of ringing Donald – it might have helped to talk to someone – but dismissed the thought. Idle telephone chats were not a part of their arrangement. Donald would assume a calamity had occurred and start flapping, then wonder why she had rung. Worse, he might attempt to rise to the occasion and encourage her for once to pour out her heart, and she dreaded to think what that might bring forth. Either way, she was certain to regret disturbing him.

And at this she found herself struggling against a sudden impulse to denigrate, even to revile, her friendship with Donald. What sort of friendship was it after all? What did it mean? An infinitely deferred promise of love; an offer of intimacy that would never survive being taken up ... She thought of him with his sombre, considerate manner that seemed to invite confidences, yet somehow always contrived to deflect them; his elaborate attempts to procure a frail feeling of enchantment that was really nothing but a kind of sweetened anaesthesis . . . Was that all she could hope for any longer? A feeling of disgust rose in her: for his tepid notion of happiness, for her own collaboration in it, for his fussy habits, his clean hands, his cabinets with their carefully labelled curios, his cautious driving, his conscientious gifts and notes . . . God, he was like the ghost that didn't know it was a ghost. He was like the void of a person not there . . . And if their time together was an improvement on their respective solitude, it was only as an exchange of the despair that knows it is despair for the despair that imagines it is not, and is therefore even further from hope . . .

She felt as if the darkness of the room were seeping into her soul. Morbid and bitter thoughts began to take hold of her. She saw herself quarrelling with Billy and Donald – even heard herself spit out the withering remarks that would bring about these quarrels – then sitting alone here in the living room like someone in a ship drifting towards some vast and empty darkness.

She stood up and went outside.

Cool, light rain was falling steadily now, pattering on the grass, swishing through the woods at the end of the garden.

She walked to the garden gate and stood looking along the lane that led to the village. In her mind's eye she saw Vanessa putting on the coat as she and Billy left the pub, and going out into the rain. She followed the girl's carefree steps, imagining the first drops of rain falling onto the material of the coat. A sharp spasm of anger went through her, but it was followed by a feeling of helplessness.

Smells of wet soil and wet vegetation filled the air, sweet and fresh under the acrid driftings from the incinerator. In a few days the first brown marks would be appearing on the roses. Trees that had fallen in the big spring winds would start succumbing to mosses, fungus, lichen; the wood growing soft, pulpy, then powdery, eaten up by insects and mould, blackening, disintegrating, disappearing into the soil . . . She had heard woods described as being like an hourglass; the life sifting from the trees into the earth, then the hourglass turned around and the life sifting back into the trees. The new grew off the old, the living off the dying. But it was never the same thing that grew back. Life poured into you, then the hourglass was turned and it began to pour out of you.

The moon was high in the sky above her, muffled in cloud,

its light falling in showers through the upper air, glittering in dimness on the wet hydrangeas and feathery yew shrubs of the house opposite, pooled in the giant leaves of the gunnera plants in the border along the fence, dripping from branches, pouring in plaited trickles from the gutter on the garden shed.

After a while she heard the girl's voice from far off. The two figures appeared, Vanessa hanging on Billy's arm, both of them walking a little unsteadily. The girl's hair was plastered to her skull, giving her face a rudimentary look; a knot of sense organs. The coat looked more silver than yellow in its sheen of rain and moonlight.

DHSS

The young woman on the pavement's edge was facing in, not out to the street, and she moved about there indecisively, but with a stubborn look. Several times she seemed about to approach somebody who had just come out of the Underground to walk up the street, but then she stopped and retreated. At last she moved in to block the advance of a smartly dressed matron with a toy dog on a leash that came to sniff around her legs as she said hurriedly, 'Please give me some money. I've got to have it. The Social Security's on strike and I've got to feed my kids.' Resentment made her stumble over her words. The woman examined her, nodded, took a five pound note from her handbag, then put it back and chose a ten pound note. She handed it over. The young woman stood with it in her hand, looking at it disbelievingly. She muttered a reluctant 'Thanks', and at once turned and crossed the street in a blind, determined way, holding up one hand to halt the traffic. She was going to the supermarket opposite the Underground station, but at the entrance stopped to glance back at the woman who had given her the money. She was standing there watching her, the little dog yapping and bouncing at the end of its leash. 'Fucking cheek. Checking to see if I was lying,' muttered the young woman. But she was a girl, really. 'I'll kill her. I'll kill them . . .' And she went in, took a basket, and began selecting bread, margarine, peanut butter, cans of soup.

This incident had been observed by a man sitting in a shabby blue Datsun at the kerb. He had got out of the car and crossed the street just behind her, holding up his hand against the traffic to support her. He followed her in to the supermarket. He was a few paces behind her during her progress through the shop. At the check-out desk, when she took out the ten pound note, her face tense with the anxiety of wondering if it would be enough, he interposed his own ten pound note, forcing it into the check-out girl's hand. By the time the girl he had been following understood what he was doing it was too late. 'OK,' he said, 'let's fight it out outside.' She looked angrily at him, and at the check-out girl, who was already busy with the next customer. Then she went out on to the pavement, following him. She was not looking at him to find out what he was like, but how to quarrel with him. In fact he was a man of perhaps forty, with nothing particular about him, and dressed as casually as she was. But he had all the carelessness of confidence. Her clothes were ordinary, that is to say jeans and a sweater, but she had a drab appearance, not so much dirty as stale. Her hands were nicotine stained. She was probably not much more than twenty-two or twenty-three.

'Look,' he said, taking all this in, 'I know what you want to say, but why don't we have a cup of coffee?'

She just stood there. She was frozen . . . it was with suspicion. She looked trapped. A few yards away a couple of tables with chairs around them stood outside a café.

'Come on,' said he, with a jerk of his head towards the tables. He sat down at one, and she did too, in a helpless, lethargic way, but as if she was about to leap up again. At once she started peering into the carrier bags for the just-bought cigarettes. She lit a cigarette and sat with her eyes closed, and smoked as if trying to drown in smoke, drawing deep breaths of it into her lungs. He said, 'I'm going to order. Coffee?' No movement from her. 'I'll get coffee, then. And I know you are hungry. What do you want to eat?' No response. She went on drawing in smoke from the cigarette held to her lips in a childish grubby hand.

He went into the café. His quick glance back showed he was afraid she would be off. But when he came back with two cups of coffee she had not moved. He sat down, putting the two cups on the table, and she at once pulled a cup towards her, piled in sugar and drank it in big gulps, though it was too hot. Before she had finished it, he went back in and returned with another cup which he put down before her.

'Don't think you're going to get something out of this because you won't,' she said angrily.

'I know that,' he said, in a voice kept reasonable. He was sorry for her and could not keep this out of his face and eyes. But she had not looked at him properly, not once.

There arrived before them a large plate of sandwiches.

'Go on, eat,' he said.

She took up a sandwich without enthusiasm, sat with it in her hand, and at last did look at him. This was a rapid once-over, expecting the worst: her face seemed forever set in sarcastic rage.

'Well, then, what's all this for?' she asked, cold.

'I used to work in a DHSS office,' he said, as if this were an explanation. Her face – if this was possible – got even harder and angrier. Her eyes narrowed and shot out beams of hate. 'Yes, yes,' he said, 'I know what you want to say.'

'No you don't. You don't know anything about me.'

'I'm making a fair old guess,' he said, with deliberate humour, but she wasn't going to have that.

'You don't know a bloody thing about me and you're not going to.'

'I know you haven't got the money to feed your kids.'

'How do you know I've got kids?'

He smiled, mildly impatient. 'I wouldn't have to be Sherlock Holmes. And I'm sure you wouldn't be begging if you didn't need it for your kids.'

This froze her up. She had not known, it seemed, that she had been observed begging. Then she decided not to care. She crammed in a big bite of the sandwich, holding her cigarette at the ready in the other hand. 'I suppose you're full of remorse about being on strike,' she jeered, as soon as her mouth was empty.

'I told you, I *used* to work there. I don't now. I left a year ago. I left because I couldn't stand it.'

It was evident he needed to go on telling her, but she shook her head to say she wasn't interested.

'I'd like to kill them,' she said, meaning it. 'I would if I could. What do they think . . . they *don't* think. I haven't been able to collect any money for three weeks and it was their mistake in the first place, not mine. And now they're on strike. They owe me a full month. I haven't paid my rent. I borrowed money from someone who doesn't have any either. Then they go on strike for a rise . . . they don't care about us, they never think about what is happening to us. I could kill them.'

He said uncomfortably, his eyes bright with sympathy for her, 'Look at it from their point of view . . .'

'What point of view?' she cut in. 'I'm only interested in my point of view. I had a friend downstairs, she killed herself last time they decided to treat themselves going on strike. She had two kids. They're in care now. I got myself a job a couple of months ago. It wasn't much of a job but it was a job. But hanging around Social Security day after day to try and get my money out of them, I lost it. Now I haven't even got that. I'm not going to try for another job, what's the point? If I did get one, the shitting DHSS would decide to go on strike again.' She delivered all this in a cold level tone, her eyes – the vulnerable eyes of a girl – staring off at nothing. She was probably seeing visions of herself killing enemies.

He said, sounding discouraged, 'Not everyone in the Social Security agrees with the strike, I'm sure of that.'

'I don't care. Well, I've come to begging. I did it last time they went on strike. I shoplifted too. If I hadn't, the kids'd've starved.'

'How many have you got?'

'What's it to you? I'm not telling you anything.'

He leaned forward, peering into the cloud of smoke she sat in, and said, speaking slowly and deliberately, to make her listen to him, 'When I started working there it was all different. Fifteen years ago . . . I really liked it then, I liked . . .' Here he censored 'helping people', but she heard it and gave him a sour and derisive smile.

'But then everything slowly went to pot. In those days there was a good atmosphere, not like it is now. We were understaffed suddenly. Then the cuts . . . suddenly they put up partitions and glass panels and bars in the windows. We were shut off from the customers, so to speak. It was like being in a cage. Not that I wasn't sometimes glad of the protection.' He laughed: it sounded like grudging admiration. He held out his arm and pulled back the sleeve of his jacket, showing a reddened lump just above his wrist. 'See that? That's where a girl bit me. She went berserk . . .'

'Probably me,' she said, not looking at him. Her pose said she didn't want to listen to all this. His attitude said that he had to say it: he was full of the need to tell her.

'No, it wasn't you. I'll never forget that girl.'

'Could have been, though.'

'Then you'd have been in the wrong of it. That time it wasn't our fault. She got herself in a muddle and blamed us.'

'If you say so. If you say something then it has to be true. No appeal. Going berserk, is that what you call it?' She was stubbing out a cigarette and wondering whether to light another. She looked at her watch: yes, she had a bit more time.

He said, 'Ten quid's worth of food isn't going to get you very far.'

'I've got the ten that rich cow gave me.'

He took out his wallet, extracted a ten pound note, then a five

pound note, and handed them to her. 'Go into the shop again.
Stock up a bit.'

She looked at the money in her hand, her mouth ugly, bitter.
She got up, then remembered the carrier bags on the chair beside
her, and was about to take them into the shop with her.

'Do you think I'm going to steal them?' He sounded hurt, but
she only shrugged, and went into the supermarket. While she was
gone he allowed his face to show what he was feeling: anger, but it
was different from hers, and he did not seem able to believe what
he was remembering, what he was thinking. Pity, but it was a
reminiscent pity, and he was full of frustration.

When she came back laden he was smiling. She could hardly
walk as she returned to the table so as to heave up the bags she
had left there. He said, 'Sit down, finish your sandwiches.'

She considered this on its merits. She sat. And ate up the
sandwiches slowly, methodically, without appetite.

He watched her. He said, 'I've been driving a minicab for a
year now. I don't earn what I did, but we manage.'

No response. She had lit another cigarette.

'I've got a wife and two kids,' he said.

'Good for them.'

'If you want to put that stuff in my car I'll run you home.'

'What sort of a fool do you take me for? For twenty-five quid
and some coffee and sandwiches you'd know where I live.'

Now he sat silenced.

She glanced up because he had not replied, saw his face, and
said, 'No, I *don't* trust anyone. And I never will again.'

'You're going to stagger home with all that stuff rather than
trust me?'

'That's right.' She stood, and hoisted up the bags. One held
twenty pounds of potatoes.

He got up too. 'If you put that stuff in my car I'll run you
somewhere near where you live. You can tell me where to stop.
It'll cut down the distance a bit.'

'I don't know why you're doing this. And I don't care. I don't
give a fuck.'

'All right,' he said patiently, though he sounded fed up. 'I
didn't ask you to care. I made you an offer. Anyway, don't
be so bloody stupid. If I wanted to find out where you live
all I'd have to do is hang around the schools in the area. It's
probably Fortescue, isn't it?' He was going on, but stopped,

because of her face. She looked helpless, dragged down by the heavy carriers.

'All right,' she said, not looking at him.

He took a couple of the carriers from her, and went across the road in front of her, holding up his hand to slow a car. She followed. She got into the back seat. He put the carriers in beside her. He got into the front seat and said, 'Where to?'

'Just drive down this street.'

After about a mile, near Kentish Town, she said, 'This'll do.'

He stopped the car. She got out. He was gazing in front of him, not at her.

She said, and it killed her to say it, 'Thanks.'

'Don't mention it,' he said.

He sat on there, watching her go slowly along the pavement, her shoulders pulled down with the weight of the bags. She turned into a street he knew she did not live in. He was waiting to see if she would turn and wave or smile or even just look at him, but she did not.

L'Hotel des Grands Hommes

L'Hotel des Grands Hommes is an ordinary looking little French hotel on the far side of the Place du Panthéon. Three well-scrubbed steps lead up to it. Flanking the steps are two identical fir trees in white wooden boxes, so green and so identical you might doubt they were real except for the moist squares of well-turned earth in which each is planted, a rich dark red, particularly in the evenings when the sun slews down over L'Église de la Sorbonne and the whole square is filled with subdued ruby.

The hotel gets its name from the domed and decaying grandeur of the Panthéon itself, in which are housed the remains of famous men, of Hugo, Zola and the inimitable Voltaire. But one cannot say, though the hotel brochure claims it, that the best rooms overlook the Panthéon. All you can see from your window is a flat expanse of dressed stone, pale ochre in the early mornings, orange at midday, and the gangs of local children rollerskating on the pavement, with patches on the backsides of their trousers and an abundance of unkempt hair.

Marsha and Tony were staying in the Hotel des Grands Hommes by accident. Marsha had found it in a guide book she'd picked up at the Bureau de Tourisme, and was attracted by the name, and the fact that it was situated in the *cinquième*. They'd both wanted to get away from the *huitième* which was beginning to seem just a little pretentious now that summer was coming and the real Parisiennes were making way for the tourists and you heard almost entirely American voices as you strolled, occasionally checking your reflection, past the elegant windows of the Rue Faubourg St Honoré.

The move made them slightly uncomfortable at first. The *cinquième* is very different from the *huitième* and they needed time to adjust. It was difficult to know what to wear. But perhaps they would have been uncomfortable anywhere. They had come to Paris for a holiday but also because there were things between them which needed to be seen to. They thought it would be easier to discuss in a foreign city those things it seemed impossible to contemplate at home.

Marsha and Tony were no longer in love. Perhaps they had never been in love. Perhaps love did not exist. Perhaps the only thing that existed was philosophy. You could tell they didn't love each other. He kept away from her and her movements, when she inadvertently got near him, were unnatural and stiff.

They were a prosperous looking couple, in a middle-of-the-road way. They had recently made money and he was very involved in his business. She had that dissatisfied look that comes to some women. When they were in a restaurant he sat with his back to the room and she looked past him and generally they left early and walked through the dusk without talking, taking the long way back to the hotel.

On their third morning, the sun rose very gold over the dome of the Panthéon. They were late getting down to breakfast. Marsha had been slow in the shower and Tony had wanted to finish the final chapter of *Thérèse Raquin*. He rather liked the book. His view was, old Zola could put together a good story. That Thérèse. She was really something. But the parts about passion were well portrayed.

They took the lift all the way down to the vaulted basement where breakfast was served, and tried not to look at each other in the mirrors which covered the inside of the lift. As they got out of the lift Tony thought that Marsha was still a good looking woman. Marsha thought this morning they ought to talk. They sat down to their croissants in silence and felt uncomfortable in the empty room.

They began talking about Zola but it was difficult because Marsha didn't know *Thérèse Raquin*.

'There are some real brutish bits,' said Tony, putting a lot of butter on his croissant. Marsha had read *Germinal* and gave her opinion that Zola had a tendency to go over the top. A wrangle began between them, of no very great significance. Marsha was spirited in her own defence. She wrote a little, and had plans to produce the Great English Novel. She'd thought about taking a villa for a month. She knew that was what you had to do. Writers needed space. Maybe she'd take a villa at the end of this Paris thing. She shushed her husband who was talking too loudly and waving his hands. He held a piece of croissant in one hand and waved it in front of her. She told him they weren't alone and he quietened down. Two men were breakfasting behind one of the pillars.

Marsha thought, 'Well, now we *can't* talk,' and was relieved. Tony began listening to the men's conversation in a quite uninhibited way. He pushed away his plate and lit a cigarette and pushed his chair back from the table. He asked the waitress in very bad French for more coffee. She brought it grudgingly, which annoyed him. The two men were American and one was interviewing the other. He listened for a few minutes, nodded a couple of times, pursed his lips, drank more coffee, and soon stopped listening, or listened only partially because half his mind was back home, and thinking about his business, and wondering how he could make sure his order books stayed full.

Marsha was in seventh heaven. When she thought about it afterwards going up in the lift, she could hardly believe her luck.

'But didn't you recognise him?' she said to her husband, her voice pitching and tossing like a boat on a swollen sea. 'I mean, didn't you *hear*? Weren't you listening, for God's sake?'

She made a strange little noise when Tony said he hadn't been listening particularly. It was a little snorting noise, somewhere between incredulity and contempt.

'It was Carver, for God's sake. *Raymond Carver*! A real, live writer. *Everyone's* read Carver. My God, if only you'd listened! You can really learn something, listening to a man like that.'

Tony pooh-poohed it, saying what could Carver tell him that he didn't already know? But underneath he was annoyed. You couldn't often listen in on what somebody famous was saying. Marsha kept referring to it. They toured the Musée de l'Orangerie because Tony said it was small enough to get around, and right in front of Picasso's *L'Étreinte* Marsha said again,

'That Carver. The things he said about chaos. You'd be surprised.'

That night she told her husband she was going to take a villa straight after Paris. Nothing very much. Not too expensive. Something simple up in the hills. They spent the evening in because Tony had some calls to make. He needed to call America. Lack of progress on some deals there was scaring him. Marsha sat at a table in the corner and got out a pencil and paper and tried to write. It was some months since she'd written anything and the pencil felt odd in her fingers and the empty pages gave her a stretched feeling in her head. She thought she'd write a story, maybe call it 'L'Hotel des Grands Hommes'. It was a good title. If she handled it right, she could make it reverberate. She started it several times but it didn't sound right. She sat gripping the pencil and stared out into the courtyard. They had a bedroom which looked out over a small square courtyard. The courtyard was enclosed on all sides, seven storeys high. Across it, on the same level she was, someone was playing Brahms. The piano tinkled as if it were slightly out of tune. Marsha heard traffic revving in the distance and felt claustrophobic. She thought about how it would be when she was really writing. She'd sit by an open window on a terrace with the sun coming slowly towards her, eating up the shade. She wasn't sure what she'd write about. But that would come. There were so many things to write about. 'Order trembling at the edge of chaos.' Had Carver said that? She remembered it from somewhere. She felt happier than she had in a long time. There was so *much* to write about. She understood about chaos. She could write about chaos. As long as she was writing about it she could conquer chaos and be strong.

Tony finished on the telephone and asked if she wanted to go for a drink, but she said no. The next morning she got up early and spent an hour on 'L'Hotel des Grands Hommes'. Then Tony woke up and got out of bed and farted on his way to the bathroom and Marsha thought how white his body was, and decided not to write any more for the time being.

At breakfast the waitress was affable and Tony seemed good humoured. Carver was there on his own. He sat very still with his coffee in front of him and his shoulders hunched, staring at the table cloth.

'Why don't you go up and introduce yourself?' Tony said. 'You know – writer to writer.'

He said it just loud enough so that Carver would have heard if he'd been listening. But Carver gave no sign, and Marsha shushed her husband angrily. Later she wondered what it would be like to introduce herself to Carver. Maybe she'd do it. There wasn't any reason why not. And yet, when you got down to it, you couldn't possibly do it, not just like that, not go and introduce yourself out of the blue.

She didn't see Carver again that day. But the idea of introducing herself to him stayed in her head. It stayed with her while she and Tony went around the Panthéon. They could only go around part of it because it had been crumbling since the beginning of the century, and was in a bad state of repair.

'We could go up,' Tony said to her. 'There's supposed to be a great view from the walkway that goes round the outside of the dome. You can see everything. There's a great view of Paris. You can even see the Eiffel Tower. And I hear there's a tremendous perspective of Notre Dame.'

She liked the view of the city with its endlessly overlapping roofs. There was something perversely medieval about the tall eighteenth-century houses and the ramshackle roofs. When the sun hit the roofs you could see it shimmering off again and everything was very white, there was a white behind the colours of things which was stronger than the colours themselves. In the streets where the sun couldn't get to, everything looked black in comparison. The window boxes punctuating this expanse of white and blackness looked like something which had been spilled.

'There's the hotel,' she said to Tony, glad to have spotted it and in doing so to have got her bearings.

'I wonder if we can see our room? I don't suppose so. It's on the other side. I left our curtain not quite pulled back.'

They had to climb some narrow steps to get to the upper walkway. Marsha was afraid of heights, especially when you were exposed, and she held on to her husband's arm. He said,

'Don't look down. You'll make it,' and let go of her as soon as they got onto the walkway. She didn't like the city quite as much this time. The view was too high. Everything took on a miniature look which unsettled her. The wind came from across the city in a shifting way. She moved from pillar to pillar, stopping a little in the protection of each one. They soon went down.

It was a long way down. The crypt was cool and the soft lights made it difficult for her to see after the intense directness of everything outside. That white colour in the roofs. That had been intense. Quite a few people were in the crypt and their footsteps echoed on the stone, making a geometric sound. She stopped and bent down to look at the inscriptions next to each stone compartment. You could look through into the compartments where a piece of glass was set into the wall. Tony wandered off somewhere. In one compartment they'd put Zola and Hugo. She was surprised. She wouldn't have thought Zola and Hugo would have sat all that well together. Zola's stone coffin had nothing on it. Hugo's had a flag and a letter and some dried flowers. It looked rather ornate. She was drawn back to look at that compartment again on the way out. Some of the others didn't interest her as much. There were a lot of dead generals.

From somewhere they were piping through profound music. It sounded like Wagner but she wasn't sufficiently into Wagner to say. On the way out was a benign statue of Voltaire. The wall plaque next to it seemed to be trying to make out that Voltaire was a defender of Catholicism. She said,

'Hey, Tony,' and Tony came round from the back of Voltaire where he'd been intrigued by the effect the fall of his cloak had, it was really amazing how those guys could make things out of stone.

'Hey Tony. You know. This is crazy. Remember *Candide*? Was Voltaire an atheist or *was* he?'

Tony was in a fooling kind of mood, and struck up an attitude. It annoyed Marsha.

'Don't you remember how it ends?' she persisted. '*We should go and work in the garden.*'

Tony shrugged and said,

'Well. Maybe they got it wrong.'

A blue-jacketed official walked by and looked at them queerly. Marsha turned to Tony to tell him they ought to be going but he had wandered off.

The Wagner had stopped and Marsha became aware of how quiet everything was. A few people were still moving about the crypt, like bluish-looking shadows. Voltaire's benignity disturbed her. Surely you couldn't get it wrong about your own hero. Perhaps he had been a defender of Catholicism after all. Perhaps he hadn't been an atheist. She could understand that. You had to believe in something.

She decided, quite suddenly, that she would introduce herself to Carver. There was something about Carver. Tony came up to her again and took her arm and together they left the cool gloom of the hallway and went out into the bright sunshine. As they walked along, Marsha found the thought that she would introduce herself to Carver a consoling one.

Next morning Marsha and Tony woke up on opposite sides of the bed. They'd been out to a bad Italian restaurant and got rather drunk, and on the way back to the hotel they'd quarrelled.

Marsha, making erratic progress from streetlight to streetlight, appealed for support to the darkness which was fixed over the city like a dome.

'I *ask* y', she said, the edges of her voice rather husky.

'*You* ask me? You ask *me*!'. Tony was at the gesturing stage. The quarrel had started over nothing, in the restaurant.

'Oh,' said Marsha. 'Oh.' She didn't know why she said 'Oh'. She said 'Oh' out of a sense, way out on a limb away from every other sense, of something cataclysmic. Her mouth made a little impregnable circle when she said it.

When they got back to the hotel Tony came out of the bathroom with a hard on and Marsha pretended to be asleep. Sometime in the night, probably about three or four, Marsha woke up. The drink had worn off and everything seemed very bleak. She lay with her back to her husband, and thought about Carver. Then she thought about 'L'Hotel des Grands Hommes'. She knew she had to try and finish it before they left the next day. It would be impossible to finish it anywhere else. The atmosphere would be wrong, somehow. She lay awake for a while, feeling panicky, but keeping the panic down by breathing slowly, and opening and closing her hands.

They had a rather silent breakfast in the vaulted chamber. Marsha found the *confiture* too sickly. Carver was nowhere to be seen. Tony told her there wouldn't be time for her to work, they had to leave by 10.30.

'You know we said we'd head off down to Perpignan. Perpignan's a long haul.'

There was an artist down in Perpignan who Marsha had a yen for. She'd bought a little nude of his at the Marché de Poésie last time they were in Paris. She'd hung it in her dressing room back home in Baltimore and she looked at it every morning on her way to the shower. The way she'd hung it, the light really picked it out. The little nude had her arms raised, pinning up her hair. There was a lot of tension in her elbows. Sometimes it surprised Marsha she wasn't actually alive.

Marsha didn't write anything else but applied herself to the packing. By about ten everything was in and Marsha was pinning up the sides of her hair. She asked Tony if he thought it made her look more sophisticated and he said,

'I guess.'

Down in the lobby it took a long time for the clerk to prepare their bill. The Carver party was before them. Marsha nudged Tony and said,

'Look. That must be his wife.'

Carver's wife was about fifty, the same age as Carver, and had long brown hair loose to the waist except where it was held up over her ears with two bright red slides. She was deep in conversation with a young Frenchman. Marsha wondered if he was Carver's publisher. It must be really something to have a foreign publisher. She'd have a foreign publisher one day. The young Frenchman held Carver's wife's hands and they looked at each other and smiled a lot. Carver was sitting in the corner and looking out of the window and smoking. Carver's wife seemed very lively. They went outside and got a stranger to take their photograph. It was Carver's wife's idea. She had to call Carver twice before he'd come. In the end they stood together, the three of them, Carver's wife in the middle with her arms draped over both men's shoulders. It was an instant picture and there was great hilarity when she discovered she'd left her flies undone.

'Oh God!' she squealed. 'Just look at me!'

She planted an excited kiss on the Frenchman's cheek and her lipstick came off and left a red impression there. Carver's wife and the Frenchman went inside and sat in the corner talking and laughing. Marsha thought, there was only one thing that made a man and a woman talk and laugh like that. Carver stayed leaning in the doorway, looking out over the Place du Panthéon. It was a Saturday morning and there wasn't much traffic. It was a dull day and the Place looked smaller somehow, without the sun. Marsha stood watching Carver and Carver stood watching the Panthéon. Tony paid the bill and said,

'Are you coming, Marsha?'

She said, 'Sure', and picked up one of the cases and walked with her husband down the hotel steps and over to the car.

'That Carver sure looks miserable.'

'Doesn't he just.'

As Tony unlocked the car Marsha looked round and saw Carver still standing in the doorway. He'd finished his cigarette and his hands were hanging down by his sides. The light reflecting off the side of the Panthéon made his face, especially his cheekbones, look bronze. Marsha felt very strongly she wanted to go over to him. She waved Tony out of the parking space and got into the car. The flags that decorated the upper walkway of the Panthéon lifted in a cross wind then went limp. As the car circled the Place and approached the hotel entrance for the final time, Marsha hoped Carver would still be standing there. But as the two green trees in their neat white boxes came into view she saw, with a disproportionate sense of sorrow, that Carver had gone.

Conspirators

The first word that came to me when I heard how Benjy had killed himself was 'loud'. Isn't that peculiar? A 'loud' suicide doesn't make sense. I mean, you don't say of someone that 'he did it loudly', do you? Well, Benjy did do it loudly, because he was the quietest man alive, and the last person you'd imagine ending it in such a theatrical, such a *loud*, manner. It's history now, the kind of history that only affects a few people, but it still surprises me, that loud exit of Benjy's. Eighteen years ago, on a hot morning in June, very like today, Benjy was found by his daughter, Vile, hanging from a rope tied to a hook stuck in the kitchen ceiling – the selfsame hook that usually supported Benjy's beloved copper mixing bowl, which he always kept in sparkling condition with the aid of salt and lemon juice. He was fastidious by nature.

Vile had no idea where her mother was that terrible morning, so she phoned me, her father's best friend, instead.

'Daddy's gone and done something strange, Uncle Joe,' she began.

'In what way strange, Vile? I'm all ears.'

'He's hanged himself.'

'No, he hasn't, Vile. Hanged himself? Benjy? No, he hasn't.'

'He has, Uncle Joe.'

I laughed, I remember, in disbelief.

'It's true, Uncle Joe.'

'But Benjy wouldn't, couldn't, be so – so – so loud.'

Why, out of the dozens of words I might have chosen, did I decide that 'loud' was the most appropriate? It just seemed to be spot-on.

'He needs to be taken down,' was what Vile said next. 'Can you come round and do it, Uncle Joe? Seb and I don't want to.'

Vile isn't vile in the least. Vile is as Vile does, which is enchanting. If you called her by her real name, Viola, she probably wouldn't respond. Seb, alias Sebastian, is her twin. Naming them Viola and Sebastian was Claudia's little conceit, not Benjy's. Viola became Vile at school, I can't think why, and Vile she's remained.

On my way to Benjy and Claudia's house, I anticipated I don't
know what – sobbing and howling; the complete waterworks,
perhaps. I advised myself to be calm, since I would have to
be a calming influence. Yet would I? Suppose the twins were
playing a nasty trick on me? Fifteen is the ideal age for bad
taste, and Vile and Seb were at that awful age. But no, not *them*,
I reasoned. They loved their quiet, doting father too much, and
they loved and respected their Uncle Joe, I hoped. They weren't
up to, weren't capable of, mischief like that.

On the doorstep, though, my hand reaching for the knocker, I
suddenly wished they were. Let it be their grim practical joke, I
think I muttered. I'll give them a sharp ticking-off, and the silly
business will be finished with.

Seb let me in. 'Dad's in the kitchen, Uncle Joe,' he said.

'Cooking?' I asked, convinced now as I was by the boy's
calmness that, yes, a game was indeed being played.

'Of course not cooking. Are you trying to be funny?'

'No, Seb. It's just that I can't believe –' That I was about to
see Benjy hanging from the ceiling, I was unable to say.

'What's the expression, Uncle Joe? "Seeing is believing."'

Then I saw, and believed. And then I had to excuse myself and
go to the bathroom, where I was epically sick.

The twins had thought of ringing the police, but on second
thoughts had agreed that I should do the 'dirty work' for them.

'Aren't you going to take Daddy down, Uncle Joe?'

'No, Vile. That's their job. Shall we go and sit in another room
until they come?'

She replied that she'd really rather stay where she was, so that
she and Seb could keep an eye on Daddy. 'The rope might break,'
she explained.

So we stayed in the kitchen, I with my back to my dead friend,
the twins dry-eyed and silent and watchful.

Later that day, after Benjy had been removed to the mortuary and
Vile and Seb had answered unanswerable questions about their
father's state of mind, I suggested to the twins that we should go
somewhere and try to enjoy ourselves.

'Where's somewhere, Uncle Joe?'

'Where do you fancy, Vile?'

'Surprise us.'

I accepted the challenge. I told them to put on their very smartest clothes, the kind you wear for hitting the town. We would make a night of it.

What madness was I planning? I wasn't certain, and that was part of the fun. I'm known – actually, I'm notorious – for my wild moods, my habit of swinging from high to low and back again, but the wild mood I shared with Vile and Seb that June evening was the wildest of my life. I was aware that it had to be, even before it began.

It began, I recall, in my austere flat in Pimlico, where I lived with the absolute necessities – a bed, a table and two chairs, a wardrobe, and a refrigerator permanently stocked with champagne.

'Do you want us to get drunk, Uncle Joe?'

'I think I do, Vile. Gradually.'

'Why?'

'Why not?'

'Is Daddy the reason for the celebration?'

'Yes, Vile, he is.'

(It was then, Vile says, that she fell in love with me. Had I replied 'No, Vile, he isn't', perhaps she would have accounted me totally frivolous. With that honest answer, she told me seven years later, I ceased being her *soi-disant* Uncle Joe and became – she laughed at the cliché – the 'man of her dreams'. Ergo: I owe my present happiness to four unpremeditated words – 'Yes, Vile, he is.')

'That's a good enough reason, isn't it, Seb?'

Seb nodded, and drained his glass, which he held out to be refilled.

'I'm going to take you,' I said, 'to my favourite restaurant.' I did not add that it was Benjy's, too.

La Boîte de Pandore had a garden at the back, which boasted one of London's few thriving gingko trees. It was there we dined on the evening of the day of Benjy's death.

The *sommelier* knew what Monsieur Joseph required, and was pouring it out for him as soon as we sat down.

Vile giggled. 'This is ridiculous. This is completely bloody ridiculous.'

'*D'accord*,' said Seb.

How long would it stay so? I wondered. How long before the

expected, the predictable happened? How long could I keep *that* in abeyance?

'We lied to you this morning, Uncle Joe.'

'Lied, Seb?'

'Yes. When we – when Vile, rather – said we didn't know where our mother was. We knew all right; we knew exactly. We could have phoned her, but we didn't.'

'It seems we're conspirators, then. I know where she is, and I haven't phoned her either. We've been cruel, haven't we?'

'Oh, terribly. Positively wicked. Why did you mention her, Seb? Please let's just be ridiculous.'

'Sorry, Vile. *Mea culpa.*'

'And let's be extravagant as well,' I said. 'I'll order us a feast.'

We feasted. We feasted, extravagantly, on frog's legs, on *foie gras*, on *bouillabaisse*, on quail, on *filets de boeuf*, on Roquefort, on *compote de pêches*, on Sancerre, on Margaux, and then, at the last, on champagne. And all through the long, long meal I talked – of the uselessness of my monied, idle life; of Benjy's quiet goodness; of the moderate nature of his temperament, compared to mine; of his worldwide fame as a musicologist, and he only forty-two; of his skill as a cook, subtle and unassertive; of my romantic – if that was the word – exploits, and how I was for ever falling in and out of love, always bewitched by a girl's bright eyes, or tantalising smile, but never by anything *serious* in her character, since seriousness and I had signed a pact as far back as my childhood never, never to confront each other on equal terms . . . On and on I gabbled, until the day was over and then beyond – and there was wildness in my talk, I have to remember; a wildness inspired by the *loud* manner of Benjy's going, a wildness I could not acknowledge – then – as the prelude to a later calm. I am notorious, as I say, for my wild moods, but my notoriety dates from that wasted time before the evening at *La Boîte de Pandore*, when I entertained the children of my dear, unlikely friend, whose wife had deserted him for a wastrel (what a quaint word that is!) like me. A younger wastrel, I should add, scarcely older than the twins.

Wild though I was, I said nothing of Claudia and her lover, Henry. That subject was taboo.

We sang and danced, after our drunken fashion, along the Thames embankment. We kissed a minutes-before-dawn good-night.

Claudia learned of Benjy's death the following day, when she read his obituary in *The Times*.

'Why didn't the kids tell me, Joe? Why didn't you?'

'You were otherwise occupied,' I answered – I, who had slept with other men's wives.

'What did he die of? *The Times* doesn't say.'

'Heartbreak, Claudia.'

She rang off.

I was still a conspirator, it seemed.

It was a secular funeral, on Benjy's instructions, at a crematorium in west London. I read from Marcus Aurelius and the hymn-less service ended with Elena Gerhardt singing *An die Musik* on a cracked record.

The twins sat together, but apart from their mother. At the very moment the coffin began to slide away, Claudia got up and walked briskly out of the chapel. Nobody commented on her hasty disappearance.

I went abroad, to Italy, where I had the last of my frivolous affairs – with God, no less, to whom I found myself turning for some explanation of Benjy's loud departure. He and I could not reach agreement on that little matter, and so we split up – in the Capella Brancacci in Florence, as it happens.

My return to London was brought about by an unexpected letter from Vile, who wrote that she wanted to see me again, desperately, to make sure that her dreams were not deluding her. Her message made no sense, yet I obeyed her summons.

'I love your white hair,' were the words with which she greeted me.

I learned, on that afternoon of now perpetual sunlight, how she and her brother had fared after Benjy's death – of their joint silence and moroseness, of their unspoken conspiracy to kill Claudia by absenting themselves from her hated presence. 'She's deader than Dad is, Joey.'

Eleven years later, we thought we might just marry, to seal our bliss.

Ours was a quiet wedding, at a registrar's office. Seb flew over from Africa for the occasion. We held the reception at the restaurant that had replaced *La Boîte de Pandore*. It no longer had a gingko tree, and the food was indigestible, but we drank lots of champagne, to compensate. We toasted Benjy, the cause of first, our grief and, latterly, our joy. And then Seb said, 'I feel like a stranger here, with you two. I really hate to see people so contented.' He stood up. He kissed us. 'Dad's legacy to me is different from yours, Vile. I must get back to the starving and dying. I should have sent you a telegram, and stayed where I was. I'm happier there, if you can believe it.'

He left, with his mother's brisk stride.

We hear from him every so often. We let him have all our news, and we try not to sound too smug, too pleased with our lot.

The Squire's Treasure

We came to the tumulus at first light and the Squire rammed the spade all but to the haft, it was that soft. God knows what we expected to find. He had on his pince-nez and Homburg, with a snappy knee-length twill which flapped and muddied itself as he dug. The earth came out on the spade in chunks bristling with tussocks. At lunch it began to rain again in slanting gusts right across the downs and some of us held umbrellas for the spadework. They grunted and hewed all through the afternoon and my legs were sodden at the backs of the knees; nothing was found that day. By the time we stopped the Squire was a sight, splattered in mud up to the neck-button, a wild streak across his forehead where he'd wiped the sweat off.

It was that day (or the day after, I forget now) that Austria declared war on Serbia.

We went deeper the next morning. Still nothing. The summer rain squalls had left a fresh breeze that made the digging easier. Butterflies, as if dazed by the sudden removal of a favourite haunt, dallied above our heads and Ernest, the schoolteacher, his little moustache wet with exertion, managed to net an Admiral that blazed in his chloroform bottle like a blown coal.

In the village it was all talk of the war, or the expectation of it. As a retired lawyer I was circumspect. Men leaned on their bicycles and nodded. The vicar, after the evening service, bestowed himself in my rocking chair and through a glow of sherry made quite plain that 'this Slav business, trivial as it may seem, serves a higher purpose.' The creaking of the runners through this teleological treatise annoyed me somewhat. I vowed to oil them.

I could not sleep at all. To be truthful, I was somewhat unused to all that brisk air and simple exertion; not, of course, that I ever achieved more than an hour of digging at a stretch. My arthritis, hovering at that time around the second joint of the third finger, saw to that. But it was enough to cajole me into sitting for at least ten minutes while I recovered my strength; and in those frequent pauses, before I set to on some less strenuous occupation for a while, I saw nothing but fields and copses stretching away to infinity under the graze of sheep and sun; heard nothing but the murmur of voices, the odd grunt, and the satisfying splice of the spades attacking in a kind of natural rhythm. This was not what I was used to. I think it might have been the first time since I was a boy that the crack of a book's spine had not interrupted the day's pleasures. Knee-deep in downland, scraping at chalk, I shared the calm the farm labourer must feel when the job in hand is immediate and clear and devoid of words.

The soil changed colour the day the Germans violated Belgian neutrality. It was a sign, apparently, that something, perhaps wooden, had rotted there. The Squire, wiping his pince-nez on a bright blue kerchief, cautioned us to proceed carefully. He replaced the glasses, I remember, with a victorious air, looking up at the August sky as if something had been answered from that quarter. And a moment of absolute peace ensued, a sort of pause in which everyone present girded their loins, as it were, leaning on their spades: Ernest, biting his lip; Trevick, the head gardener; Allun, the chauffeur from Cardiff; the young lad Terence, whose mother had just died in labour; Sedgwick, the woodsman; and Dart, the blacksmith's assistant with the flared nostrils and low intelligence. Across the downland came the usual medley of sheep-bells superseded by our distant church. The Cabbage Whites and Common Blues fluttered about our heads so close we could hear, it seemed, their wings. Even Dart, wiping his nose, appeared aware of the moment's portentousness.

We carried on until, just before dusk, with a chorus of rooks scouring the tree-tops on the rise beyond, Trevick shouted and the squire scrambled down from the rim where he had been discussing the need for safeguards at night if anything valuable were to be found, and bent down over the spot Trevick was pointing at. Within minutes he had lifted up a small pot in which, as we quickly discovered, huddled the burnt remains of some Bronze Age inhabitant. We whooped with delight, and my blisters were forgotten. Ernest made elaborate notes while the rest of us uncorked our water-bottles and drank a rather tepid toast. I recall quite distinctly the warmth of the leather round the metal – its sun's heat in my hand like the body of something live, gurgling when I shook it.

Toller was the Manor's under-gardener at the time. He had refused to take part in the dig 'for fear of summat, and 'cos its

wrong.' He confided more when I was out walking round the
back of the estate several Sundays before the excavations were
due to begin. It was early in July, and the ragwort had already
begun to splash its defiant yellow along the path. I switched at
it vaguely with my walking stick, until I noticed, looking hard
at me under a cloth cap, the gardener with a sickle in the field
beyond. He nodded and I stopped.

After the usual pleasantries over the gate I told him that it
was a pity he had decided not to join us in the treasure-hunt. I
meant this in jest – the Squire had always insisted on the academic
nature of his interest, which explained the presence of Ernest and
his notepad – but Toller took it as literal.

'There's the trouble, sir. An't right, disturbin' the dead for
silver.'

I smiled.

'We hope for more than silver. We hope for gold.'

'There. An't right.'

'But my dear man,' I said, a little more seriously, 'we're not in
this for the money. We hope to gain knowledge, and the sight of the
artistic achievements of our forebears. Necklaces, carved artefacts,
or whatever. And what's more the sight of someone who lived and
breathed thousands of years ago on this very soil.'

His features barely altered.

'And died,' he said.

I smiled again. There was no doubting it: the man was as
superstitious as they come, and evinced in me a certain pleasure
that such deeply-rooted instincts still held on in a scientific age.

'Well,' I said, making ready to go, 'if I see the remotest hint of
a haunting, I'll be the first to run blubbering into your cottage. But
as it is I am convinced that nothing remains there but the breeze
and the grass. I am in need of the exercise and the change.'

'Yes,' he nodded, 'the master told me. I am sorry, sir.'

I thanked him for his thoughts – the mention of my wife's death
had cast a pall on the erstwhile subject of our conversation – and
carried on down the perimeter path until the sound of the sickle,
like a man hissing between his teeth, had been obliterated by the
summer afternoon and all its attendant din. Bees hummed over
the dog rose that clung to the wall of the estate, and I paused,
remembering how my wife had looked forward to its gentle scent
each year. I cried a little and felt foolish.

The Squire was understandably furious. Not so much for the

loss of a strong pair of shoulders – Toller was a big man – but
for the implication of moral judgement that his non-participation
implied. A rather bristly, pale man, the Squire was easily offended,
and would rub his pince-nez vigorously when he was annoyed.
He must have cleaned them six or seven times in the space of our
thirty-minute encounter the next week, by the church wall, and
I conjectured that the glass in them was thinner by the end.

We had begun by discussing the nature of the physical work
involved, as I had expressed a doubt the previous week over my
abilities, as a man of past sixty, to contribute to any fruitful
degree. The Squire dismissed this once more as a feeble apology,
and stated that my exact mind and quiet presence would make
up for any muscular defects.

'And what's more,' he added, placing his hands on his hips,
and stretching his waistcoat, 'an enterprise of this magnitude
needs more than muscular dolts. That damn Toller has refused,
you know.'

'I do,' I said.

'Damn annoying. The silly bugger's not only craven but damned
impudent. Good mind to fire him. What d'you think?'

He glared at me in his cream suit like some avenging angel
paused in mid-flight. The church tower behind tolled the quarter
as I considered – or rather, pretended to consider.

'One has to respect,' I said slowly, 'the honesty of his feelings.'

'Yes, there's the trouble. Servants who speak their own mind
always are a damned nuisance. I'm a fair man, Ridley. But a
servant who passes moral judgement on his superiors has to be
treated briskly. Any more mention of our motives and he's out. I
hear, Ridley, the word "greed" passed his lips in the Green Man
the other day. I think I'll tell him.'

'Tell him?'

'To keep his mouth shut. He's behaving out of position. Even
the Reverend approached me after luncheon yesterday.'

He began rubbing his pince-nez like a man possessed.

'Approached you?' I ventured, describing a guarded circle with
my stick in the dust of the road. A carriage passed and he waited
until its clops and creaks had turned the corner.

'Got wind of it, y'see. An ill wind. Know what he called it?'

I shook my head, vaguely.

'Treasure-hunt! Damned impudence. Treasure-hunt! "Is it
wise," he said, "to bear on things material, to disturb the

dead for gain, to meddle with a pagan site . . . ?" and so on and so forth. Now where d'you think he got all that from, eh? You've noticed his breath, have you?'

'Whose?' (tracing a cross in my circle).

'The Reverend's. Light a match with it. A tipple becomes a topple, as my father used to say. Sermons are shorter, thank God.'

On the 4th of August, the day of that first find, war was declared. That evening I folded up my copy of *The Times* as a souvenir issue for my grand-nieces and nephews (assuming I were to have any). A meeting was declared a few days later: children with hoops (I seem to recall them as very much in fashion at the time) stood by as the posters were nailed to the wooden boards.

With hindsight, of course, one can hear that rat-a-tat-tat of the hammer clamouring back from the stone walls of the square as the nailing of the coffin on the bright joys of that summer and all summers since. Then, however, as I passed on my way up to the tumulus, my luncheon bobbing in my pack, the water-bottle gurgling as I crossed the slabbed square, it sent nothing more than a brief shiver of excitement through my belly, a sense that history was gathering to some head whose proportions and appearance were not yet clear, and were certainly not those of horror. Up on the downs, with the wind blowing the heat away and shifting the gnats in clouds, the war was all but forgotten. Trevick, Sedgwick, Allun, Terence, and Dart with his smut-dark skin, simply got on with the job in hand. Now, of course, they were brushing the soil with trowels, the Squire eagle-eyed lest one of their broad hands should move too quickly and threaten whatever he was hoping we would find. Surprisingly, only one urn and a small food vessel were uncovered from the layers we penetrated in those days before the meeting. Ernest sketched the finds, sucking the point of his pencil, holding it up to his eye then attacking the paper vigorously, while all around him the summer slumbered or buzzed in the rich fields, the peewits and larks vying for attention beneath the tufts of cloud.

The meeting was attended by the whole village. These were, after all, the days before the wireless, when any event would be an excuse for breaking the monotony of long evenings in cramped cottages. A small podium had been erected in the middle, with a flag borrowed from the Women's Institute draped across the front. Three chairs and a table occupied most of the raised space, and the Squire, the Vicar, and a uniformed gentleman had difficulty in finding their places without toppling the furniture. The local photographer – a small, bent man with very˙long fingers – was attempting to keep the space in front of him clear of the crowd, which was very difficult. Hoops clattered across the slabs behind us, the children weaving through the women who stood in groups at the edge of the crowd, their broad skirts tugged at by infants, shielding their eyes from the sun and no doubt acknowledging that this was man's business.

Outside the New Inn, to the right side of the podium, some thirty yards away, the old men sat in chairs or leaned on their sticks, nodding and talking all the way through the first speech. It was only when the uniformed gentleman – a major, apparently – had sat down, that I noticed, turning round in my chair which I had positioned close to the podium, Toller among them, his hand around a pint tankard, smiling. I was just close enough to see his eyes. They were watching something above and beyond the speakers, and when I looked in that direction I saw a house martin busy in the eaves of the post office, flashing its white patch as it swooped and scurried. Perhaps affected by that smiling gaze, I found it hard to concentrate on the Vicar as he declaimed in his piping voice of God's crusade and the Sword of Righteousness; the bird focused all my attention, despite its distance (some fifty yards) and the bald head in between grew blurred as it bobbed and glittered in the late sun. It was only, indeed, when the Squire stood up, adjusting his pince-nez, that I folded my arms, leaned forward, and listened.

'We are,' he said, 'profoundly fortunate. We have the chance to partake of history, to follow our forefathers into glorious battle. This sabre,' he announced, drawing a polished blade from its scabbard, and almost impaling the Vicar in the process, 'is – or was – my grandfather's. He carried it at Waterloo.'

An *Oooo* from the crowd appeared to extend the last syllable. Up to that point the villagers had been singularly unstirred. They had little respect for the Reverend, who had stumbled the previous Sunday down the lectern steps and knocked the verger off his stool, and the Major had simply shouted as if the square were his parade ground, most of the speech drowned in the echoing backwash off the church wall. But the visual impact of the blade flashing the last of the evening into their upraised eyes achieved what words could not; they shifted as one. Something had welded. The Squire smiled.

'We are, as I have said, profoundly fortunate. The young men among us again have the chance to join that great march, to wield that same sword, to follow that same flag.' Here he touched the point of the sabre lightly against the flag draped at the front. A small breeze, full of the sweetness of evening grass, billowed it slightly. It was like a sign. I confess that my own chest was swelling with a small excitement. I turned to look at Toller. His eyes were fixed on the bird.

The Squire went on.

'The Major has asked me to tell you that any man here who is willing to defend our country and fight for God may step forward and declare himself. We need men, and the more men we have the quicker victory over the Hun will come and we can all return to our daily tasks in the honourable knowledge that Ulverton has done its part!'

A great roar bathed the Squire in a wave of adulation; his hair, sheened with oil, gleamed in the late sun as it shafted across the square, gilding the cock on the church tower. The bell rang the quarter. The crowd shifted and swelled behind me and like a tide leaving its wrack, receded from the sudden line of young men who stood beneath the podium, wiping their noses and chuckling in an attempt at cockiness. I shifted my chair to the side (I felt uncomfortably exposed so close to them) and scanned their faces. It was then that I noticed an absence. Trevick and the other 'diggers' were missing. And they were nowhere in the crowd behind.

The photographer was positioning his camera just in front of me, darting in and out from under his black cloth. The Squire and the Major posed with the men, frozen for many seconds in a handshake. The flashlight exploded like a little bomb, catching the whites of eyes and the Squire's teeth and the little buttons on the Major's cavalry twill. Beyond, out of focus (I have the photograph still), women shielded their eyes with the older men, and a child was a pale blur as she ran with her hoop between.

It was then, as the Squire relaxed from rigidity, that he noticed Toller. I turned myself and was somewhat amused to see him standing alone by the water-pump that in those days dripped into its trough betwen the inn and the middle of the square. His smile had not changed. He leaned against the pump-handle and continued to watch the martin busy itself in its nest.

The crowd appeared to sense something and turned their

heads towards the solitary man, differentiated from them not by physical distance so much as the mental separation of complete indifference, on his part, to the proceedings in hand. The Squire's lips tightened in the silence (for silence there suddenly was). The flag swelled briefly on the podium.

He knew he had to say something. As a (retired) lawyer, I would certainly have advised the contrary. I had seen too many cases, terrible cases, whose seed had been just such a moment's errant decision. 'The greatest events,' as Fielding puts it, 'are produced by a nice train of little circumstances.' An invisible glove had been thrown between the two men, and the plump hand of the Squire took it up.

'Ah! Toller!' he called. His voice was hoarse, and he cleared his throat. The big face turned. 'Well, man, are you joining us?' The Major, evidently impressed by Toller's build, muttered something to the Vicar, who nodded and rubbed his hands. The Major rocked back and forth on his heels, a one-man welcoming party.

The under-gardener frowned a little, as if he had been asked a curious question.

The Squire glanced at the crowd. They had began to murmur. Small beads of perspiration rolled down his nose. He reached for his pince-nez and thought better of it.

'Well? Are you joining . . . us?'

The words, isolated in the near-silence, sounded faintly ridiculous. My chair creaked. The flag sagged to a stillness. Big whorls of horse-dung buzzed with flies. A lark, somewhere over the churchyard, bubbled irreverently. I remember noticing these things one by one, as if each lay beyond the other, like further rooms with doors.

The man shifted on his boots, pushed himself off from the pump (which squeaked and dribbled a palmful of water) and walked towards myself and the Squire and the Major and the Vicar and the line of men. Each step rang across the square. I recall the ease of his movement, the almost shambling, relaxed gait of those big limbs and his shadow dancing over the slabs and the dung.

He stopped several yards short, just in front of me. The Squire's head was rigid. The Major had extended his hand, which now hung there in its buttoned cuff like a clown's. The vicar was swaying slightly with his head on one side, his palms ready to grant their blessing. The men were watching Toller from the corner of their eyes. The crowd were silent again.

'I'd rather,' said Toller, 'bide at 'ome.'

Even the old men in front of the inn heard it. Toller's simple sentence seemed to strike the church wall and the walls of the square with the ease of a mallet. The old men glanced at one another, then shook their heads.

The Squire swallowed.

'Stay at home, Toller?'

The man nodded slowly.

'What,' said the Squire, in as firm a voice as he could muster, 'you would rather do, and what is your duty, are two quite different things. I would be proud for one of my servants to be involved in such a cause. Kitchener calls you, Toller.'

The Major's hand dropped. The Vicar frowned.

'I'd rather bide at 'ome, sir. That's all.'

The crowd chuckled. The young men in the line shifted from foot to foot.

'I see,' said the Squire. He looked about him. People averted their eyes. He glanced down at me. I smiled encouragingly. I noticed two small spots of red rise in his cheeks. He began to glower.

'Yes. I see. Very well. Very well. He would rather *bide* at home. If that's what a man would rather do, then who is to stop him? Thank you, *Toller*.' He fairly spat the name out. The crowd murmured. Toller turned and walked away, every eye following his long stride. He disappeared around the corner of the church wall.

Activity broke out again in the square: the crowd began to disperse into small knots, the young men gave their names to a dapper clerk who had suddenly appeared from the side of the crowd, the hoops rattled and a green-liveried automobile roared to a stop outside the post office and diverted everyone's attention. It was the Major's. When I looked above it, at the eaves, I saw nothing. The house martin had gone.

Within days the young men had packed their bags and, via a brief licking-into-shape session somewhere nearer, joined the ranks grinning their way down to Flanders. Up on the downland, nose against the English chalk, I worked shoulder to shoulder with those the Squire had requested not to attend the recruitment meeting. But the encounter with Toller had introduced a factor the Squire had never bargained for. It made him the paragon of manly sacrifice – or rather, the persuader of it in others. The rhetorical flourish of the sabre had worked too effectively, and Toller's apparent cowardice, or blunt irresponsibility, had driven the reputation deeper. Ulverton had more volunteers than any other village in the county, and it was, people agreed, the Squire who had 'done 'em proud.' But this left the 'diggers' even more uncomfortable. And the Squire had had a more difficult task explaining their absence than he had expected. All this only made his resentment against Toller rankle deeper.

So it was not unexpected when Trevick stood up at the end of the day's excavation and announced that this was to be his last week. His leggings were white with chalk; his face streaked. He said that he could no longer face Mrs Wayland, a widow whose only son had been the first of Ulverton's casualties, killed at Mauberge on August 21st, and was going out to join the boys forthwith. Jimmy Wayland was a pale lad with a stutter who had done me some service by mending the stone outhouse roof at the bottom of my garden – which, in good weather, served as a buddleia-scented study and gave me some of my happiest moments through those golden evenings. I honestly believe that the whole village was surprised when the telegram came. Not so much at his death, but at the fact that he had fallen in action. It was reliably reported by his fellows, some time later, that very little of his body had been recovered, and that the weight of the coffin was more stones than flesh. It was as if the sabre had proved deadly, after all; that the war was a real one.

'It's your decision,' said the Squire, blanching a little. Ernest, whom he had been consulting, sucked his pencil.

'Duty,' said Trevick, glancing at the others, who were wiping their trowels on the soft tussocks. 'You talked of duty at the meeting, so we understand. We've been told, you see. That's why all the young lads have gone. You and your sword from Waterloo, sir.'

'Yes,' the Squire replied, looking down.

Ernest began to flick through his drawings. Urns, shards, an iron hair-pin, yesterday's broken beaker, impressed with a comb in crude diamond-shaped patterns. Nothing of significance or value.

'Yes,' he said, again, and smiled.

Trevick, Allun the chauffeur, Terence, and the woodsman

Sedgwick, all left at the end of the week. Only Dart, nostrils quivering like a horse, too stupid to comprehend notions of duty and sacrifice, stayed on under the September sun. The Squire was devastated, and cancelled the dig for a week while he took refuge in the shooting of pigeons through Bailey's Wood. A month of disappointing finds had taken its toll, and now war had interrupted his long-held ambition to take possession of an ancient treasure.

Sometime during this week Ernest called round and sipped pallid tea while he explained the various stages through which the barrow had passed before resting content with tussocks and butterflies for four thousand or so years. His enthusiasm was tempered by the possibility that the Squire had lost interest. This was, he claimed, the sign of an amateur.

'Though, of course, I cannot, um, blame him. Of course.'

I nodded. His moustache was wiped free of tea and malt biscuit and he spread out a diagram on the table between us.

'Here,' he said, pointing to a large oblong ringing the welter of circles and crosses, 'here is the latest burial-phase. A ditch dug around the mound in which, um, we have found evidence of burial by cremation. The discolouration of the soil is probably due to the rotting of wooden stakes surrounding the most recent, um, mound phase.'

He paused. I was impressed.

'From previous expeditions which I have been party to I predict that, um, an earlier phase will yield something much more exciting.'

'Why should it?'

He smiled.

'The initial justification for such a sizeable mound,' he said, as if that explained everything. His moustache quivered. 'These recent finds were simply additions. And cremation is, I believe, associated with later centuries. If we continue I confidently predict that, um, we will uncover a rich burial, uncremated, with grave-goods to match. It might take many weeks, but I am sure it will be, um, worth it.'

I sat back and pondered his assertions. In truth, I was hardly bothered one way or another. If anything, with such recent memories of my wife's last illness, I'd rather we didn't find anything at all. To uncover the dead is not to release them.

'I see. But with whom? Dart? He's more a liability than a help.

He still believes the trowel is his hammer and the chalk the anvil, if I'm not mistaken. He would smash the skull before we saw it.'

Ernest laughed – or rather, giggled.

'Yes, there's the problem. Um, I've often wondered why the under-gardener hasn't joined us. He's, um, very strong.'

'Toller?'

'Yes.'

I sighed. 'That man has strong opinions of his own. As you saw, or rather, would have seen, at the meeting.'

'I heard, yes,' he said, frowning a little. 'But what are these opinions? Concerning the excavation, I mean.' He coughed and blew his nose, as if asserting the fact that his asthma made any talk of war redundant. 'He never,' he added, 'says very much.'

'That's because the Squire has forbidden him to do so. Button your lip, he was told, apparently. So that is what Toller has done. I used to have most fruitful discussions with him on notions of life and death, religious matters, even politics. Apart from botany and biology, of course. Now it is exceedingly difficult to extract the shortest of sentences from him, unless you are talking of the weather, or the crops, or such like.'

'Ah,' Ernest nodded, and wiped his moustache with the corner of his handkerchief. 'Then we will have to work slowly. Or recruit others. Older men. A pity, a pity. Um, yourself excused of course. The new chauffeur looks very, um, frail. And the harvest is at its height. Pray for a fine autumn.'

After the Battle of the Marne, which raged from the 5th to the 9th of September, and in which our county regiment was not involved, thank God, the Germans dug in at the Aisne and trench warfare began. It was around that time that my depressions started, a late hangover from my wife's death, clearly. That week of enforced idleness, coupled with a certain absence in the village, played on my nerves. I dreamt of digging up endless skeletons, all of which turned their hideous heads to reveal my wife's face grinning at me. When the excavations resumed in the middle of the month, with Dart, Ernest, the Squire, and the new chauffeur, Lock, I had half a mind to give the whole adventure up. But I persisted, partly for the sake of the Squire, whose pale complexion now bore small vein-marks of anxiety across his cheeks, and partly for the sake of the exercise and fresh air. Ernest had succeeded in persuading the Squire to continue, and as each scrape of the trowel rang on the flints across the pasture, a new sense of excitement hovered over the enterprise, although I missed Trevick's growl and the laughter of the others.

Well after harvest I was walking that same back-path that comes out behind the brick wall of the estate and its effulgent dog rose when I glimpsed Toller pouring feed into a tin trough. The sheep were running towards him and pressed quite happily about his knees as he shook the sack out. The dust hazed him in a kind of aura as the autumn sun levelled itself through the leaves of the wood behind. He saw me, and raised his hand in greeting. I thought how clear and simple that life was, how like the ancient shepherds on the slopes of Attica he must look! I walked to the gate.

He came over and leaned on the iron. Flecks of bran nestled in his hair and in his stubble. His jacket was buttonless. He rested a boot on the lower cross-piece. His repose was one of energy held in check, his big arms the calmer for the exertion they were used to.

'Decent weather,' he said. He sucked on a tooth.

'Very decent,' I replied. I tapped a flint with my stick. I waited.

'Doin' the animals now,' he said.

'Yes. That was Trevick's job, wasn't it?'

He nodded and smiled. I smiled back.

'I miss them. Do you?'

He smiled again, albeit ambiguously. He looked down for a moment. He sucked on his tooth.

We did not notice the horse until it had rounded the corner and, as the gate was well tucked in to the hedgerow, was still half-hidden by the tall bobbing splash-red of mallow and knapweed along the wayside. It was the Squire. He pulled to a stop in a cloud of dust and nodded at us both. For a moment I felt conspiratorial.

'See about the fence at the bottom of Grange Field,' he said. He looked at me with what I can only describe as small eyes and switched at the horse with his crop. We watched him go, clattering into a gallop as the track meandered onto the open downland. Bluebottles clamped themselves without a moment's hesitation on the fresh dung. Toller shrugged at my raised eyebrows.

'Best see about it,' he said.

'Well, he was to the point.'

Toller nodded and walked off, touching his brow. The nuzzling of the sheep in their feed almost drowned all the other sounds that certain evening (the woods alive with birdsong, the rattle of a distant cart) in which two forces came together for a moment, bristled, and departed, as if all that is irreconcilable was not in the far-off thump and whistle and wet of the Aisne but there, in that golden English dusk, that glimpse of Attica!

It was, I think, at the beginning of the next week, when I had shoved a ladder into the branches of my apple tree, and was twirling the russets easily off their stems of an evening, when Lock, assigned to a corner of the (by now) vast digging area, clambered up the stepped side of the excavation and thrust a dagger at Ernest, who almost fell off his canvas stool in fright. The Squire was relieving himself against an elm and hurtled back still buttoning himself into decency when he heard Ernest's excited shriek. Lock's eyes were wide in his small face as he pointed out the exact spot in which the dagger had lain. It was, Ernest said, of bronze or copper, with a simple triangular blade and a pointed tang to which a wooden hilt would have been tied by twine.

We were each assigned a tiny area and given a brush – except for Dart, who continued to wield his trowel elsewhere. It was a tedious business, especially as the soil was wet and gathered into small clods with each stroke. Ernest joined us and it was he, fortunately, who first revealed the hump that stroke by stroke, hour by hour, turned inexorably into the cranium of a buried ancient. The Squire bent down with his mouth open, his eyes wild with excitement, as the brush unveiled the sockets, the nose cavity, and finally the grin of those broken teeth, like the face of some horror breaking the sea's surface and resting there. Within a week the outline of the whole skeleton had been sketched, as it were, into view – my own contribution the right hand and the knees upon which the scattered knuckles rested. From the edge of the tumulus, a man's height above it, the body resembled that of a foetus, legs tucked up towards the chin – except that the head was curiously swivelled towards us, staring at the sky.

Walking home one evening that week I saw a group of children running excitedly to the low wall that fronted one part of the square, and which penned in a few pigs belonging to several

of the villagers, one of which was Toller. I heard the children
chant and as I drew closer saw Toller scattering straw across the
churned mud. With a shock I recognised the words:

'Bidatome, bidatome, bidatome!'

Toller appeared to be taking no notice, checking the sow's ears
or slapping another as its great bulk lumbered away with that
intelligent grin. I confess that I shouted at the children, and
they scattered, one of them throwing a pebble vaguely in my
direction, but which the force of gravity sufficiently enfeebled
to close its parabola with a *ping* on the handle of the pump,
well short.

Toller merely touched his cap and continued his work. I
walked on.

I did not know it then but 'Wipers' had begun a day previously,
and that afternoon Trevick's young wife received the news that he
had fallen in action. The unit he had been a part of had been raked
by machine-gun fire and almost wiped out in the time it took me
to cross the square. It was from that day the nickname stuck,
but 'Bidatome' himself appeared to remain untouched, growing
only more solitary and silent by the week, confining himself to
the barest of greetings.

That was a terrible time; my nightmares increased, and for the
duration of the month and well into November Ypres claimed
man after man who had stood shoulder to shoulder on that
August evening. It was as if Ulverton had been deliberately
placed in the front line. Up on the downs, brushing in silence
at the burial, we would hear the bell tolling out in long, slow
arcs of sound, and the Squire would whiten as we paused,
wondering who.

One afternoon a lad came running up the track towards us,
soon after we had heard the bell once more. He panted on
the rim.

'Well?' snapped the Squire. His eyes, I noticed, were full of
fear.

The lad took a deep breath.

'It's Mr Allun, sir.'

'Allun?'

'He's back.'

'They've sent him back? Was that the tolling?'

'Reverend asks as to make an apology, sir. 'E's not dead,
sir.'

The Squire closed his eyes.

'Thank God,' he said. 'I will go and see him.'

The boy shifted from foot to foot. I asked him if there was anything else he wanted to say. He stared for a moment at the skeleton, although he had seen it some days before. The Squire was climbing the side, and Lock was looking slightly piqued, as if Allun was likely to slip on his chauffeur's gloves immediately.

I think I guessed what the boy was going to say.

'E's got no arms, sir.'

The Squire paused on the rim, feet still on the clay steps, hands ready to push him onto the level. I remember his back against the sky, his shoulders, his bowed head. He looked colossal, the very figure of utter weariness. Dart laughed.

Allun, however, put a brave face on it. He had been handling a grenade, a German stick type, attempting to pick it up and hurl it back. He lost one arm immediately and, as he put it, 'thought as how it would miss the gear-stick, look.' His other arm developed gangrene in the flesh-wound. He was terribly thin, stranded amongst his automobile mementoes in the estate cottage, his prostheses leaning against the wall while his stumps 'took a rest.'

Soon afterwards we spent our last afternoon on the downs: the weather was blowing cold and the soil was hardening with early frost. We had dug right round the skeleton and it was lifted by means of a pulley and hands onto the side. Wrapped in canvas, the body of the ancient was placed on cushions in a cart, and then, at a nod, taken slowly down the track, the great iron-tyred rims circling through the ruts and over flints so cautiously we could count the spokes. The Squire followed.

As I watched them go, preparing to clear the site of our implements, Ernest came up with the wooden box in which he had placed the smaller finds. I asked to see them, perhaps for the last time, before they were assigned to some glass case. Like a boy with his stone collection, he handed them to me one by one: the bronze dagger, and the iron hair-pin; a polished greenstone wristguard (or so we guessed), with nine holes at each end capped with sheet-gold, and broken – probably as part of a ritual; and a bone pendant, stained by the corroding dagger, found beside the ribs, carved into the form of a leaping animal, and crude. Hardly a treasure, but each, as it lay in my hand, had an extra weight; of silence, perhaps, and of the value of silence, that had lain undisturbed under tussocks and cloud for four thousand years, until the Squire smote through the turf with his spade.

Habits

What is it keeps some married couples together long after their Best Before date – you know, when they're no longer compatible, when they don't even like each other any more, and when divorce has lost its stigma and is relatively painless to achieve? You can never guess, can you, which of your married friends will break up and which will stick it out; in fact haven't you noticed that very often it's the most unlikely ones, the obviously miserable ones, who stay the course, whereas the marriages that always seemed to you to've been made in heaven blow apart? And why should that be?

It was a stranger at a party who asked these questions of Nessa (they'd both had a fair amount to drink at the time). He didn't wait for her reply. Instead, he told her his theory, which was that unhappiness is a stronger bond than happiness. That would account, wouldn't it, for all those henpecked husbands and battered wives you read about, who find it impossible to break away?

The stranger leaned towards Nessa and smiled at her with the intimacy only a stranger can afford. He tapped her empty glass and asked her, how would it be if he were to go and get them both a refill?

This encounter took place a few days ago. At the time, Nessa had felt got at. The stranger couldn't have known anything about her marriage – he and Nessa hadn't been introduced and hadn't even bothered to swap names – nevertheless she felt he'd somehow, perhaps with the special, specious intuition of the inebriated, decided she was a battered wife, or Otto a henpecked husband. It was only afterwards that she considered the questions themselves, in particular the first one, the one about what it is keeps people together long after their Best Before date, as the stranger had put it. What was it kept her and Otto together, then? Could it be they were bonded by unhappiness merely? What a terrible thought! What a throat-cutting idea!

'Was he right? Is that all we've got going for us?' Nessa asked her best friend Lindsey, via the telephone. (It was Lindsey's call, a Christmas call, ten days early because she and Duncan were off to Spain for the holiday, the first time ever they'd done such a thing.) Nessa and Lindsey talk a lot on the telephone. There was a time when they wrote letters to each other, long ones at regular intervals, but they haven't for years – no one Nessa knows writes letters any more. They do send each other postcards and they talk on the telephone, once every ten days or so, taking it in turns to foot the bill – for their husbands to foot the bill. In these calls they discuss Lindsey's children, the books they're reading, the films they've been to see or want to see, the television programme they've watched or missed, people they both know. Sometimes, in a frivolous mood, whole conversations will be conducted in French, in school textbook French:

'*Eh bien, mon brave, qu'est-ce que tu as fait ce matin?*'

'*Alors, je suis allée au marché acheter des legumes. J'ai envie de preparer une bonne soupe pour mon mari.*'

'*De bons legumes? Pour faire cette bonne soupe?*'

'*Mais bien sûr, de bons legumes!*'

'*Quels sorts de legumes as tu acheté, dis donc.*'

'*J'ai acheté un kilo de carottes, et puis –*'

'*De bonnes carottes?*'

'*Assurement, de bonnes carottes!*'

'You and Lindsey were made for each other. I can't think why you didn't get married' – Otto, jokey but sharp, coming in on the end of one of these exchanges.

Nessa and Lindsey talk seriously about serious things, they discuss their worries and their fears. Cancer, for example. They are both in their forties now, the age when breasts and wombs and cervixes become vulnerable, the time when X rays and smear tests are advisable. Lindsey believes in preventative medicine and regular checkups, but Nessa has a theory about cancer which is that if it hasn't been diagnosed it doesn't exist. Should you discover a small hard lump in your armpit, say (Nessa's theory goes), do nothing and it'll turn out the lump was only a boil. See your doctor, spill the beans, and before you know it you'll be under the scanner or being force-fed barium meal. And after that? Operations, radiotherapy, chemotherapy and downhill all the way. – Which was superstitious nonsense, in Lindsey's view. Dangerous nonsense. 'Jonnie would have been dead years ago if my mother'd gone along with your theory.' (Lindsey's younger brother Jonnie developed cancer of the femur when he was twelve. They'd had to amputate the leg, but Jonnie'd been OK. He was still OK, alive and kicking his umpteenth artificial limb, at thirty-four).

'D'you think unhappiness really is our only bond?' Nessa asked Lindsey, in the course of Lindsey's Christmas call.

Lindsey said no, no she didn't think it was as dire as that. Marriage was complicated. Just as you couldn't tell, from the outside, what kept seemingly incompatible people together, so you probably couldn't tell from the inside, either. Also, habit came into it. It was often habit kept people together when they shouldn't be. Habits were hard to break. 'I mean, look at you and Otto, you've neither of you given up smoking for all your talk. You refer to your "cancer tubes", you make jokes about iron lungs and respirators, but you don't give it up.'

Nessa said she thought that was quite a neat analogy, though not comforting. And she did not tell Lindsey that Otto had cut down recently, from two packets to less than one a day.

Lindsey said that, strangely enough, it was habit, habits rather, she'd missed most when she and Mike split up. (Mike was Lindsey's first husband, and the father of her two children, Angus and Elaine). She'd never thought about the habits, she'd never imagined she'd miss them, but then when they split up she did.

'What sort of habits?' Nessa wanted to know.

'I can't remember them all now. But I do remember missing Mike saying things like "I don't believe you've met my wife" to office colleagues and so on, and I missed my being able to say: "I think you'd better consult my husband on that one!" That habit – the habit of belonging, I suppose you could call it.'

Nessa stared at the stoneware jug on the table beside her that Otto's first wife had made and considered this habit, one she was familiar with. She thought: Do I enjoy it? At some level or other? Would I miss it? And decided that yes, she would. Unfortunately, she would. Yes.

Another thing she'd missed, Lindsey remembered, was being a unit, a hyphenated sounding unit, Mike-and-Lindsey, on Christmas cards and invitations, 'a sound and shape our friends all knew, that they recognised as being us.' She'd imagined, she told Nessa, that being just Lindsey again after she and Mike parted would feel like freedom, would restore her pre-marital sense of identity, but it hadn't. Rather the reverse. And wasn't that odd? Wasn't that an odd thing for a good feminist to feel?

That was the snare of being a woman, Nessa suggested, a woman of their age and class. (Nessa and Lindsey liked to imagine that they, or at least their roots, were working class. Which was crap, according to Otto. No corner street tobacconist – Nessa's father – and no railway clerk – Lindsey's – was ever working class. Anyway, what about their grammar school education? Lower middle was their roots, middle was what they had become. Sorry, lassies.) 'Working class women of our age were brought up to believe that marriage is the be all and end all.'

'How's your best friend Marion, lovey?' Lindsey asked. 'Seen anything of her lately?'

This question, which anyone listening in would have been likely to consider innocent and genuine, for that is how Lindsey made it sound, was nothing of the sort. It was a tease. The truth was, Nessa did not like Marion, who was a neighbour of hers, and had never considered her a friend, merely as another – irritating and younger – woman, down the road. One thing Nessa didn't like about Marion was the habit she had of calling Nessa 'lovey', and of prefacing remarks with 'If you don't mind my saying.' Nessa usually did mind. 'If you don't mind my saying, lovey, blue is not your colour' – Marion, having watched Nessa lug the dustbin down the steps and onto the pavement, had sidled up and tapped her on the shoulder of her ultramarine sweater, first new garment in months.

'Funny you should ask,' Nessa said, 'I've been seeing a lot of her lately. We've really got a lot going for each other. I'm currently, at this moment in time, into a book she lent me. It's called *Uncoupling*, it's about wanting out and letting go, and it really engages with the issues, believe you me.'

It was true that Marion had lent Nessa a book called *Uncoupling*. Nessa hadn't asked to read it. Marion had got the book out of the library, and told Nessa it was an instructive, in many ways, corroborative, read. Nessa ought to read it, Marion said. 'If you don't mind my saying so, lovey, it would concentrate your mind.' (Not long before this, she'd told Nessa that it was high time Nessa stopped playing a walk-on role to Otto's starring one. Nessa should leave Otto, Marion said, so that she could find herself and get to know herself and get to like herself, and use her talents and regain her self-respect and start living. Marion, who often looked careworn; who had mortgage problems and problems with her children – Barney was bedwetting, Natalie had

been caught telling lies at school – was not a good advertisement
for the manless life she advocated.)

'Is this your call or mine, by the by?' Lindsey said. 'Ye gods,
it's mine! Duncan will murder me. He's threatening to make me
pay the whole of the last bill. "You made the calls, you pick up
the tab" was how he charmingly put it.'

There was another habit, one that women shared (Nessa
thought after Lindsey had rung off) which was to mention their
husbands in what sounded like a derogatory way, a putting down
way, when all they were really doing was expressing pride in being
owned by a man.

Most evenings after supper, if they were alone Otto and Nessa sat
in the sitting room and listened to music – to classical orchestral,
Mozart opera, jazz. They listened in silence. Nessa sipped a glass
of red wine and stitched away – she'd been making a patchwork
quilt for three years now; the 'bitbags' beside her chair had
become permanent fixtures. Her eyesight had got weaker since
she started out, her magnifiers stronger; even so her fingers were
pincushions, and she had to work right under the lamp, peering
and blinking, crick in the neck, ache in the back, pain in the heart.
And Otto?

Otto would lie back in his arm chair, black leather and steel,
his eyes closed, his hands stuck to the frosted whisky glass in
his lap. Every so often he would push himself up and transport
his empty glass to the bookcase where the whisky bottle and the
water jug and the ice bucket were. Every so often, when an
uncompanionable silence fell, he would spur himself to change the
tape or the record. When they were first married, and for several
years afterwards, Otto's travels within a room had been achieved
by little sprints and leaps and pirouettes, the floor beneath him
elastic as a trampoline; but for some time now his controlled
exuberance had for the most part been replaced by a meandering
stumble, a preoccupied shamble. Not that age and whisky must
have been wholly to blame. In congenial company, Otto could still
perform in his old manner, no matter how much whisky he'd sunk;
and in his studio, where Nessa was rarely welcome, he would still
bound from canvas to paintpot. Once, arriving at his studio with
an urgent message, Nessa had surprised Otto conducting the
overture to *Figaro*, playing on the tape deck. From the doorway
she watched as he brought the violins in and then banished

them, nodded his furious head, pointed an accusing finger at the woodwind, flung both arms wide, embraced himself.

Television bored Otto. Any programme Nessa wanted to see she watched by herself in the kitchen, bolt upright on a hard chair, her face within inches of the Sony portable's small face. Come and see this, Otto! It would really interest you! For years, Nessa, who believed she wanted to share everything, whatever it was, with her husband, had run to the living room with her enthusiasms and offered them up like presents, although for an equal number of years since, she had not.

It's evening, a Tuesday, ten days before Christmas. Otto and Nessa are in the living room of their Hammersmith house. John Coltrane is playing on the Bang & Olufsen. Nessa is seated at a table in the window, writing Christmas cards. On the table is a pile of cards and another one of envelopes, plus the address book Nessa is working from. Working through.

Nessa's writing her cards, getting on with it, but her mind is elsewhere. This morning something momentous and terrible happened. This morning she learned something about Otto that she must tackle him with. She doesn't want to, but she must. She doesn't want to think about any of it. She can't stop thinking about it.

From time to time Nessa looks across to Otto, asleep in his armchair. No, not asleep; although his eyes are closed, he can't be: his right hand is still gripping the whisky glass in his lap. She gives him quick, surreptitious glances and long hard stares. In her head she's asking him: Is it true? and Who are you, Otto? WHO ARE YOU?

Out loud she asks him: 'Do you want me to send a card to the Donaldsons?' She feels she has to ask this because eighteen months or so ago Otto and Jim Donaldson fell out, a serious falling out that hasn't been repaired. Nessa still doesn't know what it was about because Otto's stonewalled her each time she's asked. The Donaldsons are, or were, old friends, perhaps their best 'married couple' friends. Otto and Nessa used to go on holiday with the Donaldsons. Christmasses were spent with them, at the weekend cottage they own in Suffolk. Nessa regrets the loss of this friendship, the discussions and arguments and jokes, the horseplay which could sometimes go too far, the freezing walks along Minsmere Cliffs. She regrets the loss of the

Donaldsons' two boys, Danny and Sam, in particular Sam, the youngest, with whom she'd always had a rapport. She misses the evenings of rummy and Oh Hell, and the steady wine drinking that had accompanied these. Most, she misses Maura, Jim's wife, her accomplice in holiday kitchens and on holiday shopping expeditions, her ally in the ongoing war against the menfolk (this was the term, enclosed by invisible inverted commas, they used for Otto and Jim and Danny and Sam). 'What's up with the menfolk then?' 'Can it be the menfolk have gone dahn the boozer?' 'Well, that's the menfolk for you!' A lot of giggling accompanied the menfolk talk. A lot of fooling around went on while they were preparing the menfolk's breakfasts and lunches and teas. A lot of drinking was done while they concocted the menfolk's suppers. Oddly, and hurtfully – for it wasn't their quarrel – Maura hasn't been in touch since Otto and Jim's bust-up, although Nessa has written two postcards to her. Sending the Donaldsons a Christmas card this year might (Nessa thought this at breakfast this morning; now she thinks what does it matter? What the hell does any of this matter?) go some way to healing the rift.

'You can send the Donaldsons anything you like.' Otto takes a swig of whisky that nearly empties the glass. 'So long as you don't put my name to it.'

This Christmas will be the first nobody has asked them over for, not the Donaldsons of course, not Otto's three married sisters in the home counties, not Nessa's weirdo Cousin Alec, not her mother and younger brother in Arbroath. For the first time in twenty years of marriage, Otto and Nessa will, barring a last-minute reprieve, be spending Christmas in London. Alone.

Neither of them has ever rated Christmas, mind you. Every October, when tinsel and coloured lights take over her local stationers and supermarket, Nessa says she'd abolish Christmas if she could, that Christmas is a farce. She won't be sending cards this year, she says, or presents. Perhaps she doesn't mean this: she always does. She buys presents for her relations and for Otto's, she chooses them for Otto's godchildren as well as her own. When the presents are wrapped, Otto writes his name on the label. He writes Otto, or Uncle Otto, or Your Favourite Brother-in-Law in the space Nesa points to on the tag. She always tells him what the parcel contains so that he knows, so that he has no excuse for not knowing, so that he won't be caught out. What a waste of time! Otto never remembers, or pretends not to, and he's usually plastered by noon on Christmas Day. When a nephew runs at him with a novelty pen or a radio-controlled police landrover and cries 'Thank you Uncle Otto, it's just what I wanted!' Otto looks amazed. 'Did I give you that? Don't thank me! Thank your Aunt Nessa – she chose it, she bought it, she wrapped it up – all I did was pay for it!' Why does Otto do this? What makes him want to show himself in such an unendearing light always?

'I am me,' Otto says grandly, 'I am how I am. If you don't like it, too bad.'

Some people don't like it. Too bad for them. Once, years ago, at a supper party at friends, Otto (who'd had three double whiskies before leaving home) announced over the vichyssoise: 'What a bourgeois collection! What witless conversation! What dull pointless lives!' In the silence that followed, while shocked eyebrows were being raised and wounded looks exchanged, Otto picked up his spoon and carried on with his soup. The following day Nessa asked him, shouldn't he write to Harry and Joanie and apologise? For all those things he'd said? Why should he, replied Otto, when he hadn't said them? He had no memory of saying them, therefore he hadn't said them, therefore Nessa was making it up. When Nessa told him, exactly, precisely, what he had said, he was very amused. Or he pretended to be. He said he wished he was guilty because the remarks were true. Weren't they, weren't they? Come on now, didn't she agree?

Not surprisingly, Harry and Joanie did not forgive him. Not really. They weren't asked there to supper again. Nessa still saw Joanie – they'd known each other since before they were married – occasionally; she'd call in for a moment on the way to collect her girls from school, but there was a constraint between them, an edgy politeness they neither of them knew what to do with, although Joannie did try, because they were old friends and because Nessa was godmother to her youngest, Marianne, to make it easier. To find excuses and explanations. Otto, she supposed, was what you might call a larger than life character. She supposed all artists were. There was a price to be paid for that, she supposed.

Well yes there was, Nessa thought, though she did not say so.

But Nessa had a problem, not revealed to Joanie then or later. A part of her could admire Otto for his refusal to compromise, and even for his rudeness which seemed to her an aspect, merely,

of his energy and masculinity. Otto was his own man, he didn't
curry favour, he didn't care what people thought. When she was
not being embarrassed or hurt by his behaviour, when she was
not cut to the heart by it, she could, in a way, admire it.

'Stop staring at me!' Otto erupts from the depths of his gloom
and his armchair. 'Leave an old man in peace!'

Nessa was not staring at him, as it happens, not this time. She
doesn't think she was. She'd merely looked up for a minute and
there he was, blocking her view of life, getting in the way of it,
no chance of avoiding him.

And what was this nonsense about Otto being an old man?
Otto wasn't old, he was young, he'd be fifty-two in March. He
looked forty. He had drive, he was someone who, when not drunk,
could get a lot done. He got a lot done in his studio – not unusual
for him to complete four large canvases in a fortnight – and he
got a lot done at home. The bathroom in their first, rented, flat
was plumbed by Otto; the tongue and groove panelling of their
present kitchen had been sawed and planed and fitted by him.
Even now, when they could afford to have someone, a team of
professionals, to do the repairs and improvements that need doing
in houses from time to time, Otto was not above putting in a new
set of bookshelves or reinventing a cupboard.

Otto was not old, and he did not look old, yet reaching
fifty affected him badly. It really got to him. Nessa couldn't
understand it. Why should he care? In her view, most men
didn't begin to be attractive until they were forty at least. It
was the most unfair difference between men and women, that
just as a woman was losing her looks and having to work
harder and harder with exercise bikes and nourishing night
cream to keep a semblance of them, a man was finding his.
Without any effort at all. Yet for months before his fiftieth
birthday, and for months afterwards, Otto complained about
his age. He peered into the shaving mirror, he made faces at
himself, he pulled his eyelids down, he tugged the corners of his
mouth this way and that, looking for trouble. His eyebrows were
going grey – *see that, Nessa?* – he had old man's whiskers in his
nose! In his ears! There was more hair in his hairbrush than on
his head!

All nonsense. Otto still had a lot of hair on his head, much of
it dark. He had more hair, and shinier hair, than many women
of his age. Unfairly, given his drinking and his smoking and

his preference for high-fat, high-cholesterol foods – the tubs of polyunsaturate in the fridge grew green fur coats unless Nessa ate the stuff herself – Otto seemed in pretty good, trim shape. On the outside, anyway. Who could say what minute changes might be taking place in arteries and organs and bloodcells? Changes which one day, perhaps tomorrow, could become significant and serious?

Otto's preoccupation with age and ageing was not just tactless. It was cruel. Reaching forty had far more implication for Nessa than reaching fifty had for him. On her fortieth birthday, after fifteen years of trying, after almost as many years of humiliating tests and consultations, Nessa finally gave up hope of ever having a baby.

'Goodbye, baby;' Nessa, in the dank back garden of the Hammersmith house, said this aloud. 'Goodbye, darling one' – rocking backwards and forwards in a crusty iron chair – 'Goodbye, my sweetheart.' (She'd had a lot to drink by this time, in celebration of her own birth, in recognition of her child's refusal – she saw it as that, a positive decision – to be conceived and born.) It was nine in the evening. Otto, who had forgotten it was her birthday, was late home from his studio. When he did get back, he was sorry for his neglect and took her out to the Tandoori round the corner. She didn't tell him it was the baby that had caused her to drink and then weep. The non-baby. The death of hope.

Nessa's best friend Lindsey, the only person from school Nessa kept up with, once wrote to her à propos of her own indecisive boyfriend Alan, who at that time kept moving in and out of her flat: 'There's always hope – unfortunately.' (This must have been twenty years ago or more; Lindsey's been married twice since then, and neither time to Alan.) Nessa understood this assessment of hope as a destructive force, a poison, a monster. 'Goodbye, baby', repeated over and over in her dank back garden, killed the monster off. Almost.

There was no biological reason why Nessa and Otto had not managed to have children. No blocked fallopian tubes, no uterine or ovarian, no penile or testicular, malfunction; no premature ejaculation, no poor sperm count.

'You and your husband are perfectly normal and fertile. Relax. Take a weekend break. Lie in the sun. Get drunk.' Stress and anxiety were the enemies of conception, the experts agreed.

How many times had she had to listen to that? How many unrelaxed, scorching or sodden, increasingly sexless weekend breaks had they had to take?

Nessa knew Otto long before she married him. Before he married her. They first met when Nessa was at Art School and Otto one of the tutors. Being taught by practising painters and sculptors, some of whom, not much older than the students, were beginning to make a name for themselves and to show their work in London galleries, was exciting to Nessa. London was exciting. She'd never been south of Edinburgh until then.

In her second week at the school, during a Life class (this was 1965, before the Seventies ban, and when Life drawing was still considered a relevant subject of study for Art students), Otto came up and stood beside her easel. Nessa had spotted him earlier, talking to a student on the top floor, outside the Litho room. She'd thought: What an attractive man! And then, almost immediately: How odd, he's not my type. As most people seem to, Nessa had made up her mind early about what her type was and thereafter was reluctant to alter her decision, no matter how often events, and men, proved it fallible. Nessa would have said that her type was thin and tall and fair. Blue, or, at a pinch, green eyed. Pale and interesting. Haggard and poetic. Whereas Otto was on the small side, five foot six or seven, not much taller than herself. A dark man. His skin was dark, his hair was dark and cut short into a soft, curly brush; he had brown, dark eyes, black eyebrows that met in the middle – 'Murderer's eyebrows,' Nessa's mother said when Nessa told her she was thinking of marrying Otto – thick, dark, curly eye lashes, the sort that are often described as 'sooty'. His chin was dark, but that was because in those days he was economising on razor blades. And he was not thin at all, he was chunky and muscular.

Otto came and stood beside Nessa's easel, hands behind his back, pencil between his teeth. He was wearing a dirty-green corduroy jacket, black corduroys, a black polo neck – a sort of uniform then, worn by anyone in the Arts, anyone who considered himself an intellectual, trying to look like Harold Pinter.

Nessa waited for him to say something rude. She'd heard about his rudeness, had been warned by the second years how rude he could be. She was not sure whether she should carry on with her drawing, or step back out of his way.

'Budge over a minute.' The pencil was still in Otto's mouth. He regarded her drawing, and then the model, and then her drawing. Then he leant forward and scribbled on a corner of her paper.

'See that' – the marks Otto had made were very pale – 'Use a hard pencil like this one. Any old rubbish looks effective if you use charcoal or a 6b.' And that was all.

'Yeah, he's attractive,' Sandra Davis said. They were hanging around the female students' wash room, wasting time before a Litho class. 'But you want to watch out. Hard pencil. I'll say. He screws anything that moves. Once. Screw and dump, that's what he does.'

'I thought he was married.' Nessa was shocked by all of this. Shocked and disillusioned. Sorry for Otto's wife and for all betrayed wives. Scandalised. Excited.

Sandra Davis gave her a pitying look. She chased a splinter of black-grooved soap around the basin. She pulled the roller towel out and down, searching for a clean patch; there wasn't one. She shook her hands in the air to dry them, and then wiped them on her jeans. She left the cloakroom.

Nessa was a virgin when this conversation took place. Not a wise thing to be at Art School she discovered, where the students' talk, when it was not about work, was about sex. She'd had several near misses (or were they near-successes?) with boys her own age back home, and thought of her virginity as a technical rather than an actual thing. Now it seemed to her actual, and a problem. The other students knew about it. Not from anything she let slip, but from what she did not; from all the gaps, the omissions, the silences her end of the table in the coffee bars they frequented – The Black Toenail and the Kandinsky. Conversations in these seemed aimed at her, at finding her out.

'Size is important, don' you think, Scottie dog?' Angeline turned to Nessa on a thin grey elbow. 'One fellar I went with had a dick no bigger'n this.' She held up her little finger and jiggled it unpleasantly. 'Honest, no kiddin'. Couldn' feel a *thing*.' And she upturned a bowl of sugar and demonstrated, with a matchstick in the spilt demerara, on the red-mottled formica table top, what dimensions a dick had to have to be of any use to anyone.

Watching this, Nessa's curiosity was mixed with some other, not quite identifiable, emotion. According to Sandra Davis, Angeline had been to bed with Otto. What's more, Sandra Davis said, Otto had broken his once-only rule for Angeline. He'd had her twice.

Angeline's dirt-ingrained hands – it was not just the paint stains they all had – her black-polished yet bitten nails, her waist length hair (backcombed on top and all the colours of the paintbox), her chalk lips and kohl-rimmed eyes, Nessa would see clearly when other images of Art School life had smudged and faded. Angeline personified every resentful taxpayer's understanding of the words 'Art' and 'student'. Nessa said as much to Otto in 1989 when they were lamenting the school's proposed closure, but Otto said he had no memory of Angeline at all.

Angeline was a grotesque, an attenuated clown. She reeked of rush hour tube trains and midnight ashtrays. Why did all the boys fancy her?

Because she was dirty. Because dirt was sexy. Sandra Walters – there were three Sandras in Nessa's year – told her this over coffee in the students' common room.

Still, even though she had a bath whenever the hot water in her bed-sit allowed, and rolled Odorono over her armpits before setting off in the mornings, several of the boys at the school found Nessa sufficiently fanciable to try to get her into bed. Or onto the back seats of borrowed cars. Or, on one occasion, onto the sculpture department floor. (This was Roy, who had green teeth.) But Nessa, who wanted to do it, or at least to get it done and over with, couldn't. Confronted by a slobbering mouth, a trespassing finger, an excited trouser front, she froze. (Once to her horror, she laughed out loud.) The boy, whoever it was, would roll off her and sit up. He would say she was a cock-tease, a ball breaker. Frigid. A lesbian.

'I hear you're a lesbian,' Angeline announced in The Black Toenail. 'What do lesbians do? D'ya fancy me?' She unbuttoned her shirt and revealed her bosom which was small and grey. She wriggled her shoulders provocatively. She put her arms round Roy's neck, leaning into him, and from this vantage point blew Nessa a pouting, noisy kiss.

The following term, her second, Nessa went to bed with Otto.

He had begun to flirt with her when he criticised her work. Not obvious flirting. A light touch on her shoulder, a comment, usually satirical, on her clothes or her red hair or her accent. He would mimic this, as she discovered English people often did, although in his case perhaps mimic was not the right word. 'Adopt' probably came nearer to describing the way he picked up her rhythms and

cadences, and then handed them back, recognisable but altered.
He would peer at her work, moving in close, then stand back with
crossed arms, eventually turning to give her a furrowed, quizzical
look. He said little. 'Huh.' 'Uh-huh.' 'Getting there.' 'So-so.' 'So
far as it goes.' 'Dishonest.' 'Crap.' 'Work work work, fame fame
fame.' (This last chanted in a sort of sing-song.) He would take
her pencil or paintbrush from her in such way that she could feel
a slight, only just detectible pressure from his hand.

His hand; his hands: broad palms, small narrow fingers, a
ring on the wedding finger. The backs – and his wrists – were
hairy. The merest glimpse of his hands, of the black hair on the
pale brown skin, triggered a dissolving weakness in her stomach,
low down. Another unsettling aspect of him was his smell. No,
not smell. Not scent or odour either. This emanation had more
to do with temperature than any olfactory sense. It had to do
with heat.

One morning he said to her: 'If you're not busy in the lunch
break, come and have a jar.'

It was not unheard of for a student to have a drink with a tutor
in the lunch hour, but it was not that usual either. Not for a first
year. Nessa imagined they'd go to the pub the tutors habitually
patronised, the Unicorn it was called. It didn't occur to her they'd
be going anywhere in Otto's car. But Otto had to collect some
notes and slides from home, 'and then afterwards we'll have a
wee bevvy, hen.' Was this true? Or a seducer's fiction? It might be
true, it could be: Otto taught Art History to the second years.

Otto's car turned out to be a souped-up Morris Traveller. He
drove it as though it were a racing car. He pushed it through the
gears and through the traffic. Once, when they were stuck behind
a van delivering in the Old Brompton Road, he pulled out left
onto the kerb, and then drove a few yards along the pavement to
overtake the van on the inside. Nessa wasn't frightened – Otto's
driving was too confident and authoritative to induce fear – but
there were other worries. The glove pocket on the passenger side
held a spiral bound notebook with a shopping list on it in writing
that was not Otto's. It held an emery board and a bottle of
nail polish remover. Otto's wife sits in this seat, these objects
reminded Nessa, the seat you're sitting on is hers. How do you
feel about this? How would Otto's wife feel about your sitting
here, in her seat?

In Otto's flat, in the living room, Otto stood behind Nessa and

laid his head on her shoulder. He lifted the collar of her jacket and
blew softly on the back of her neck. Then he kissed her neck.

'No,' Nessa said, wanting to move; not moving.

'Yes,' Otto said 'Yes.'

'No.' This second 'no' must have carried more conviction, for
he released her.

'Let's have a drink. Wotcha fancy?'

'I don't need a drink.'

'I think you do. I know I do.'

While Otto was getting the drinks, Nessa examined the room,
sitting room she supposed it to be. The room where Otto and Janet
sat in the evenings and discussed the happenings of their day.
Where they had tea, no, supper, on trays in front of the television.
Where they made love on that settee. (It was grey wide-ribbed
corduroy and large enough, if it did not look comfortable.)
Examining the room, making a conscientious study of its colours
and furniture and objects, was a way of dealing with a mix of
feelings – with lust and resentment, nervousness and guilt. Nessa
saw sludge-coloured walls, a curtainless bay window, a square
of rust carpet on black painted floorboards. There were only
four pictures in the room and these, a series of drawings of a
standing female nude, backview, and recognisably Otto's work,
were grouped together on the fireplace wall. The mantelpiece,
the windowsill, the bookshelves, were supporters of stones or
stone-like sculptures, stone-coloured jugs and bowls, and vases
with wide bases and thin necks and runny glazes. An earthenware
pot, large enough to house forty thieves, stood in the fireplace and
contained ornamental grasses, feathery and grey. Otto's wife was a
potter. Nessa remembered Sandra Davis telling her this. Not just a
wife, not just a mother – as Nessa's own mother had been, as all the
women in her childhood were and were expected to be: cooks and
floor scrubbers, fanatical table polishers and chairback starchers,
nest builders. These pots and jugs, on the face of it domestic items,
described an independence unheard of in the marriages she knew.
Their presence on ledges and shelves seemed to Nessa evidence of
marital equality, and a real, punchy competitiveness.

The drink Otto brought her was gin and tonic, ice and lemon,
only the second time she'd tasted this.

'Sit down, sweetie,' Otto said, 'take your coat off, I'm just going
to make a phone call.'

It was hot in the room, but Nessa kept her jacket on. She

perched on the corduroy sofa, stiffly upright, her knees together, her hands round the freezing tumbler, while Otto made his call.

'Halloo there,' an unfamiliar Otto cooed into the receiver, 'hallooo, it's me. No, I'm at home. Can't remember whether you wanted me to do anything else about supper? Yeah, I've got the booze, and the salad stuff. I've made the ice. Yes. Yes, OK. Mischa's going to be very late.' Otto swung round in his chair, and while he was listening to what his wife had to say about this news, he gave Nessa a severe, investigative stare. With his free hand he groped behind him on the architect's desk for his cigarettes, shook a cigarette from the packet, lit up and threw first the packet and then the lighter to Nessa.

'Fine. OK. No, no one. No, I just came home for some Art History slides. Did you say you'd be back about four? Yus. Yus I will. Yus. Promise. Love you.'

How could Otto do this? How was he able to? What shocked Nessa was not so much that he should lie to his wife, by omission, in that cooing, intimate voice, but that he should do it in front of her. How could he bear to show himself up in such a way to someone he hardly knew, to one of his students? What sort of person did he think she was?

'Would your wife mind if she knew I was here?' Nessa pulled hard on her cigarette. Her question was not a real one, because she had no doubts that Janet would mind. She had asked it deliberately, to disconcert Otto.

Otto was not disconcerted. Of course his wife wouldn't mind, he assured Nessa. Of course not! Why should she? Theirs was not that sort of relationship, the sort that cared about such things. They were both creators, creative people had needs, they both understood those needs. Seeing separate friends separately was one. They had no secrets from each other, as it happened, if Nessa really wanted to know. So she needn't worry about that one! What was worrying him was that Nessa hadn't had anything to eat. He was going to go and concoct a sandwich now. Could she eat cheese and something? Cucumber?

Nessa hadn't remembered Otto taking his shoes off, but in the kitchen he wasn't wearing any. He sprung about the room in thick socks, from fridge to bread bin to table, where he buttered and chopped and sliced and sprinkled. Deft and efficient; lithe like a cat, or a ballet dancer. He reminded Nessa of all the photographs she'd ever seen of Nijinsky.

'Who are Ben and Dom?' The mugs they were drinking their coffee out of had these names painted on them. Ben on Nessa's mug, Dom on Otto's.

Ben and Dom were his step-children, Otto said, Janet's sons from her first marriage. Janet was eight years older than him, he explained, leaving this information to hang in the air above their heads, where it gathered weight and significance.

Did he like them, Ben and Dom? Nessa wanted to know, did he get on with them?

Well yes, of course he did! Why wouldn't he? They were good lads, they were very nice kids.

(Of course? Why of course? Nessa felt she might have believed him if he hadn't said of course.) She asked him if he wanted children of his own, and Otto said No, no he didn't, he'd never wanted children, and Janet didn't want any more, so that was all right.

'I do,' Nessa said, 'I want a lot of children. Four or five, mebbe.'

Otto said he'd got it into his head that she wanted to paint.

'I do. I want to paint and have babies.' (Why should this surprise him, when he was married to Janet?) 'I want both. Is there a toilet anywhere round here?'

The toilet was on a little half landing between the basement and the hall. When she came out, Otto was sitting at the foot of the stairs, his head on one side, his thumb in his mouth. Little boy lost. Wouldn't she like to do a little tour of the house before they left? Little Boy Otto asked engagingly. Wouldn't she like to admire the fruits of his amazing, innovative, masterly, do-it-yourself labours?

No no no no no! But Nessa did not say this, and afterwards she blamed her failure on the gin. Instead she allowed Otto to take her hand and lead her up the stairs, which he did on tiptoe, as if there might be children sleeping on the floor above whom they must be careful not to wake.

Nessa lost her virginity in Ben's room, after she'd inspected shelves and cupboards about the house that Otto said he'd made. He'd even carpentered Ben's bed, he'd cut it down from an old worm-eaten fourposter that came originally from his grandmother's house in Galway.

Nessa hadn't wanted to go into Ben's room. Pinned to the door was a notice in red felt pen: BEN'S ROOM. ADMITENCE TO TICKET HOLDERS ONLY.

'We cannae go in there. We have nae got tickets.'

But Otto said not to worry, he had a season ticket, he'd paid over the odds for it, it allowed him entrance any time night or day, she mustn't worry about it at all. He was standing behind her as he said this, and now he put his arms round her in a protective, consoling way, as to one who had suffered a punishing bereavement; and blew on her neck, and murmured into her ear.

'A little lie down is what we need after that climb,' Otto's voice said inside her ear, 'a little, little, lie down. My sleepy Agnes.' His hands, sleepy-seeming themselves yet inexorable, travelled from her waist to her breasts as he spoke, robbing her of protest. (What Otto's hands were doing to her breasts, her nipples, was affecting another part of her body altogether. This was new. No one else's hands had achieved this.)

'You smell delicious.' Otto inched her, slow but very sure, nearer Ben's narrow bed. The bed that he had made.

But the worry over the lack of tickets remained. It inhabited a part of Nessa's mind all the time Otto was undressing her, and while he was undressing himself, and while he lowered himself onto her – the narrowness of the bed did not allow for two adult humans to lie side by side – and while he explored her person, and while he, methodically and devastatingly, occupied her person. The lack of tickets for Ben's room, plus the fact of doing it in Ben's bed, would haunt her with guilt and shame whenever she thought of that first time with Otto, the iniquitousness of her crime intensifying through the years so that in her forties Nessa would tell Lindsey that she believed, she really believed, it accounted for her failure to conceive a child. Not having babies was a punishment, she told Lindsey. (Lindsey said she'd never heard such nonsense, such dangerous nonsense.)

Afterwards they didn't light cigarettes, or lie still with their arms around each other. On the contrary, things speeded up. Otto looked at his watch and leapt into his clothes and threw Nessa hers. Dazed, and sleepy from the gin, Nessa followed the speeding, speeded up Otto. Down the stairs. To the living room, where he removed the ashtrays and the glasses. To the kitchen, where he washed these and the lunch things, and dried them and put them away. Back – taking the stairs three at a time – to Ben's room, where he shunted the bed back to the position it had travelled from; and punched the pillows, and sniffed and smoothed the bedclothes, and withdrew the towel he'd thought it wise to fetch when Nessa – rather late in proceedings – had mentioned it was the first time she'd done this.

The towel went into the twin tub in the kitchen, along with some socks and shirts and a bri-nylon babydoll nightdress Otto extracted from the bathroom on his flight down the stairs.

'Work work work, fame fame fame,' Otto encouraged himself cheerfully as he put on his shoes.

'What about the Art History notes?' Nessa felt she had to remind him of these. It seemed strange he should forget them, when he'd remembered everything else.

In the car going back to the college, Otto took his hand from the gear lever and placed it on Nessa's thigh. He ran his forefinger the length of her thigh, pressing down firmly, drawing it along, cutting a groove. A knife through butter. (She would be able to feel that pressure on her thigh for always.)

'Bonnie wee Nessa,' he said, 'bonnie wee Agnes. You were lovely. You are lovely. We must do this again. Soonest.'

They didn't do it again. Not for years. (Not until after Janet had left Otto, not until Nessa met him, by chance, one January morning, at the Tate). Having screwed Nessa, Otto dumped her.

Why did none of the dumped students betray Otto? Why didn't she betray him? Nessa asked herself this then and later. An anonymous telephone call to his wife, or an anonymous letter, would have done it. Or she could have – any of them could have – reported him to the principal. No one reported Otto. At the time, Nessa asked Sandra Davis why not.

'You could have said no, mate,' Sandra Davis said. 'We can all say no, y'know. Anyway, Otto's good at it, and he's useful – if he likes your work. Andrea Watkins was a student of his.' Andrea Watkins was having her first one-man show at the Ariel Gallery just then. Her work had received a lot of critical attention. Nessa had been to see Andrea's show and had decided it was OK, nothing special, but OK.

'Anyway,' Sandra Davis said, 'look on the bright side. No one calls you a lesbian anymore, so that's something.'

When men, in the Middle Life Crisis much written about these days, lose interest in their wives, it's invariably to do with sex, with unsatisfactory or boring sex. That's what the women's magazines say, that's what the health pages of national newspapers suggest.

Nessa read a great many of these articles, the ones that tell you
how to be inventive in bed, the ones with jokey headings like How
to Keep your Man's End Up through Forty Years of Marriage.
What the message of these usually boils down to is this: that men
being men (polygamous; natural philanderers), it is up to women
(monogamous; natural homemakers) to keep the sexual interest,
and thereby the marriage, going. 'Day after day there are girls at
the office, and men will always be men; if you send him off with
your hair still in curlers, you may not see him again.' That line of
singing and thinking, thrown out in the feminist Seventies, shelved
in the Eighties, seems to be being dusted down and polished up
for the Nineties. Perhaps AIDS has something to do with it. Nessa
thought so. AIDS, spelt out, or euphemised, came into the articles
she read more and more.

Nessa and Otto's sex life wasn't satisfactory – well, it couldn't
be, it hardly existed. It only ever existed if Otto initiated it, and
nowadays he seldom did. Not that Nessa had ever been much
of a leader, although for a time she was a keen follower. During
those years she followed Otto anywhere his fantasies led him. Take
underwear. She wore the black underwear Otto used to insist on
when he wanted her to be naughty, and the white underwear he
insisted on when he wanted her to be nice – that is, virginal; a
schoolgirl. He would not allow her to wear a coloured bra and
pants ever. No flower patterns or psychedelic sworls or dayglo
spots – a turn-off, he said. This was a problem in the Seventies,
when brilliant flower power hipster briefs were all you could buy.
In those days Nessa bought her white pants in the girls' school
outfitters departments of large stores: knicker linings they were
called. In the mid-Eighties, when plain underwear came back in
fashion, Nessa didn't have to make a trip to Debenhams, she could
buy all the white pants she wanted in her local Marks and Spencer.
But Otto didn't mention her nether garments any more. If he had
a preference for lacy, strapless bras, if he had sudden and urgent
desires to see her in camiknicks or open-crotch panties, he never
said so. Nessa knew this was her fault, that it was she who was
to blame for Those Old Bedroom Blues (the expression used in
one article she read to describe ordinary, uninventive, infrequent,
marital sex) she and Otto were suffering from. Otto was suffering
from. For the truth was, once she'd convinced herself there would
be no baby, she lost all interest in sex. What could be done about
it? None of the pieces she read made the connexion between sex

and babies. Sex for pleasure was what they were concerned with. Sex for warmth, sex for comfort, sex for health. Sex as cement for crumbling relationships. Nessa wasn't against any of these, she could see the value of them. If asked, she would have said that most of them had been contained, to some extent, within her and Otto's lovemaking. Desirable in themselves, they had been part of desire, and of its aftermath, of sweat cooling on exhausted bodies, of a shared glass of whisky or of wine.

It was a shock then, to discover at forty that none of these aspects of sex counted. That all that energy and lust and concentration had had for her one purpose only.

'Have an affair with him if you must, but don't, for God's sake, marry him,' Lindsey said when Nessa was talking about moving in with Otto. 'He willnae be faithful to you for more than five minutes, and he doesnae want children.'

But Otto wasn't interested in screwing around any more, he was only interested in Nessa. He loved her. He needed her, and probably always had (he saw this now). His open marriage to Janet had been – a hard thing to have to admit, but true – a disaster. Commitment was what he was ready for. Also, he'd changed his mind about having children.

'Having babies with you would be delicious,' Otto murmured into Nessa's ear as they were making love.

Nessa was teaching Art full-time in a boys' grammar school when she married Otto, a job she saw as a stopgap, not a career. She was going to be a painter, she was going to be a mother. These were certainties. Teaching had not left her much time or energy to paint, and the school holidays were somehow taken up with other things, with visits home to her mother, with visits to Lindsey, newly married and with a baby on the way; but now Otto's drive and ambition was going to rub off on her. Otto told her it was so, and she believed it. And he took practical steps to encourage her: he whitewashed the back bedroom of their Putney home, he set her up with lighting and materials. He would do everything he could to help her, he had the contacts, there wouldn't be a problem when it came to showing her work – when she'd done the work. But she'd never get anywhere if she taught full-time.

So Nessa gave up the grammar school and got herself a two-day-a-week job at a comprehensive. Then she waited for inspiration and for babies to arrive.

Throughout Nessa's life with Otto there were mornings when she'd wake and think: Today is the day. Today it will happen. These were the mornings when she believed, from the first moment of consciousness, that she held the key to an enduring energy, a graspable vision, an attainable truth; that as soon as breakfast was over and Otto out of the house, she would climb the stairs to her studio – the room that Otto had whitewashed for that purpose – and paint the paintings, beautiful and true, beautiful because true, it had always been her destiny to paint.

Pie in the sky. Some demon in Nessa had other ideas. This demon kept her busy in the kitchen, washing up, drying up, putting away; wiping surfaces over and over, scrubbing the floor. He sent her into the utility room to wash a bundle of dirt- and polish-clogged dusters by hand, for God's sake (there was a perfectly adequate washing machine under the worktop). He decided it was the ideal day for airing the kelims on the garden line and once they were there, for mugging them with a broom. (She would have to wash her hair afterwards.) He insisted that the lavatory seats were overdue for disinfecting, and the fridge for defrosting. He pointed out that there were mouse – or were they rat? – droppings in the larder, and water rings on the living room furniture. And how come she hadn't noticed until today how filthy, how stomach-turningly sticky and fluffy, the stair treads and the skirting boards were?

Only when she was exhausted would the demon let her go; only when she was quite safe from any obligation and responsibility to her vision. After that she was free.

There was one consolation Nessa hung onto. The bare walls of her studio, the near-empty sketchbooks and blank canvases that littered its floor, contained, didn't they, a paradox: somewhere in all this vacuity the truth remained intact. White hot. Inviolable.

Whereas Otto. Whereas, who was to say that Otto, in his quest for fame fame fame, on a journey that had taken him from vapid Fifties Figurative, through Kitchen Sink realism, some Constructivist stuff ('motorway cones' one phase Nessa remembers), a fling with the Minimal and the Conceptual, to the paint-laden Abstract Expressionism of his latest work, had come any nearer to the truth than she had? Who had done nothing? Mightn't he even, with his mania for reinventing and making it new, have profaned the truth, or lost sight of it altogether?

There were times when Nessa could console herself with this

hypothesis; moments when she knew her apathy and lack of achievement were not her fault. In one household there can't be room, can there, for two burning ambitions, two artistic temperaments, two super egos.

(What about Otto's encouragement of her, though? She wasn't going to deny that, was she? – It was Lindsey who asked this. He'd always encouraged her, hadn't he? No. Not really. Not unless you called years of head-patting patronisation encouragement. Not unless you did.)

Other times Nessa told herself that Otto was a gifted, courageous man. That looking after the needs of such a man, or indeed of any man, was a valid mission, and what she was for. What all women were for. That doing it well implied a talent not to be despised.

This morning after breakfast, Nessa went round to Marion, next door neighbour but one, to return the book, *Uncoupling*, that Marion had lent her. Nessa hadn't read it all. *Uncoupling* hadn't concentrated her mind as Marion had predicted, only depressed it. Also, she'd noticed the book was three weeks overdue at the library, a fact which made her feel a criminal. Then there was the embarrassment of having something with so unambiguous a title on the table by her bed, and of reading it in bed while lying alongside Otto. Not that Otto often noticed what she read any more. It was years since they'd discussed the books they were reading, swapped them, read passages out to each other, laughed over or at them. Even so, she'd felt awkward reading *Uncoupling* within an inch of Otto's nose. And he had noticed it. He'd stopped her side of the bed on his way to the bathroom one morning, and picked up the book from her table and scrutinised its jacket.

'Uncoupling presupposes coupling – you have to couple first,' Otto said slowly. 'Or is this a book about trains? What a dark iron horse you are, Nessa, to be sure.'

Marion was doing her washing when Nessa called in with the book. She offered Nessa a cup of coffee. Marion used to be married to a university lecturer, an archaeologist, but divorced him three years ago. She has two children, Natalie who's eleven, Barney who's five. In her kitchen was evidence of this fruitfulness: messily pasted paper chains looped the ceiling; a red felt pen message on the pinboard reminded that Natalie's ballet class is on Fridays at six now, not Wednesdays at six thirty; a magnetic Mickey Mouse clung to the fridge door. And the kitchen itself was an art gallery, a part retrospective two-man show of Natalie's and Barney's work. Most of Nessa's friends' kitchens had looked like this at one time or another. Maura Donaldson's had. Lindsey's had, for years. Alienating years, Nessa had found them.

'Well, apart from anything else, Otto couldn't manage without me,' Nessa said, on the defensive, in Marion's chaotic kitchen. Marion had just quizzed her on *Uncoupling*; she'd just asked if it hadn't helped Nessa make up her mind to leave Otto, once and for all. Nessa had often considered leaving Otto. She was constantly wondering how it was she'd wasted her life on Mr Wrong all these years, but in the same way that she could become a loonie leftie when in a room full of fascists, and Hitler when in a room full of loonie lefties, so she felt a need, in the face of Marion's impertinent certainties, to defend Otto, and herself, and their sad marriage.

'Otto would go to pieces if I left him. His work would suffer. I know.'

Which was balls, according to Marion. Behind her, the washing-machine, up to that moment a moaning depressive, turned suddenly manic: screamed hysterically, worked itself up into a complete spin, and went off its rocker.

'No, not balls!' Nessa had to shout above the din.

It was, Marion insisted. Nessa deceived herself, it was a form of conceit to imagine one's spouse couldn't manage without one. Otto had been married before Nessa came along, hadn't he? He'd found himself a new wife then; well, he'd do so again. Anyway, it wasn't Otto she was concerned with, it was Nessa. By turning the argument round to Otto and his needs, Nessa was refusing to engage with the real issue.

'Otto is a difficult man, OK,' Nessa said, 'but he's wrapped up in his work, he's not interested in women any more, not in that way. He can't be bothered. I doubt any woman would take him on. Also' – Nessa added a little, plausible, lie – 'he depends on me for critical judgement. There are enough sycophants in his life –'

Marion snorted at this, and wrinkled her nose in an unpleasant way. On her otherwise pale cheeks two round spots of high colour glowed. The spots reminded Nessa of a Dutch doll she'd been given one Christmas when she was five, and never liked.

'No man welcomes criticism,' said Marion, whose fund of wise saws was perhaps surprising in one of only thirty-three, 'not from a woman. What men want from women is to have them sitting at

their feet, praising them, bringing them sherbet.' She paused here
to let a probable literary allusion sink in. 'Otto is no exception.'
Marion was silent again while she spooned instant coffee into two
mugs, the insides of which were stained a dark rusty brown. 'What
beats me is why you've stayed with Otto so long, when there was
nothing – no children – to keep you.'

Nessa took the mug Marion handed her. She said it was quite
likely that it was not having any children that had kept her and
Otto together. That if they had had them, they might well have
landed up in the divorce courts years ago.

She was not sure why she said this, but she saw at once that it
was true – it was contrary enough to be true.

Marion cleared a space in the leftover breakfast things for her
own mug, and sat down opposite Nessa at the table. Then, leaning
towards Nessa with a concerned and caring expression on her face,
one that somehow managed to involve her eyes and her eyebrows
and her mouth and the attitude of her little sharp chin, she said:
'Nessa lovey, if you don't mind my asking, what gives you the idea
– what proof have you got – that Otto isn't interested in women
anymore?'

What an intolerable question! Nessa wasn't going to answer it.
She shouldn't have, but she did.

'Well, I'd know, wouldn't I? I don't need proof. I live with the
man. I know.'

'I wasn't going to tell you this, lovey. I'd hoped you were going
to take some sort of initiative yourself, but now I think you should
be warned –' Marion made breaking off to sip her coffee, and then
stretching an arm for the sugar bowl, an excuse for a significant
pause. She was wearing a white and dirty crocheted jumper with
sleeves pushed up to the elbows. Her forearms displayed the black
moles and wiry black hairs that are characteristic of a certain type
of white skin, the type that never tans in sunshine, only reddens
and burns. Otto had told Nessa more than once that he disliked
that combination very much indeed, and that he found Marion
physically repulsive.

'– When you went home to see your mother last Easter –
remember? – Otto came round here, and tried to get me into bed,
tried to get into my bed. He came round twice, he tried twice.'
Marion paused again, presumably to allow time for her words to
have effect, then she said: 'I had to turn him out because he was
drunk. And also because he didn't want me – though he wanted

my body of course. What he really wanted was a confessional, a convenient ear for his troubles. Otto may not be interested in women, lovey, as you say, but he's interested in *a woman*. He's been in love with a woman, a married woman, for years. They have a child. Her husband thinks it's his, but it isn't, it's Otto's.'

Not a quick screw and dump then, or a series of these, but a long-standing affair. A commitment, a loving commitment. With a child.

It wasn't true. Marion was a liar, anyone could see that, she always had been, the truth was not in her.

It was true.

What an extraordinary thing, Nessa thought from a long cold distance, from the uninhabited planet she'd just landed on, that it should be Marion to impart this news. To rain these blows. Blow after blow after blow. What an extraordinary thing.

'. . . Otto told me he's felt for a long time that you aren't really interested in him,' said Marion, who had yet more blows up her sleeve, 'and that you don't really like men. If you don't mind my telling you this, he's convinced you prefer women. "In every way," was how he put it.'

A picture presented itself in Nessa's head, a picture of herself and Maura Donaldson in Maura's cottage kitchen. They were concocting supper for the menfolk. They were giggling; they were adding, between swigs from a bottle of wine on the worktop, increasingly bizarre ingredients to what they'd feared was a dullish stew. And then, somehow – crossing the room? – rummaging for crême de menthe or peanut butter or caraway seeds? – they'd collided, collapsed into each other's arms, and stayed there. Hung in, hung on, and stayed there. Relaxed against each other and breathed in the scent of the other's neck, and stayed there. Stayed there too long. 'Well, this won't buy the menfolk a new pair of hiking boots,' Maura had said eventually, releasing herself.

That was all. After that, they'd got on with the supper, as though nothing had happened. Well, nothing had happened. And Otto couldn't know about it because of course Nessa had never told him. No one knew. Lindsey didn't know. No one.

But afterwards, when Nessa was at home in Hammersmith and thought about it, she'd come to the conclusion: 'If Maura and I had been alone in the cottage, and if there'd been a bed in the kitchen, we'd have landed up in it.' She knew this with certainty. What she could never be certain about was whether she was glad or sorry they had not been alone, and that there'd been no convenient bed for them to fall into.

'. . . Otto stays with you because he thinks you're helpless without him, he says he can't leave you . . .' Marion's parting shots followed Nessa from the kitchen table and out of the house, chased her down the steps. 'He's convinced you aren't capable of earning your own bread. He says . . .'

On Nessa's desk, the pile of dealt-with Christmas cards is taller now than the untouched pile. She's got as far as the Ts in her address book. She's written cards to the Trevillions and Ira Tredgett and Bill Thorpe and the Templetons, and next she's going to do one for the Tuckwells.

Nessa is on her own in the living room. Half an hour or so ago, John Coltrane stopped playing his sax, and when he did Otto put his empty whisky glass on the floor and lay back in his chair and fell asleep.

It is true? Is it TRUE? Nessa, in her head, asked the unconscious Otto. Is any of it true? When he wakes I'll confront him, she told herself. But when, some minutes later, he did wake, abruptly and noisily as he always did, groping his way to the door (like a blind man, or a sleepwalker, or a *drunk*) as he always did, she said nothing.

'Happy Christmas to John and Suzy', Nessa writes inside her card to the Tuckwells, 'Love from Otto and Nessa.' John Tuckwell is a sculptor, an old friend, an old sparring partner, of Otto's. Suzy is his second wife. (The Tuckwells used to be John and Alannah, but back in the Seventies Alannah left John and their three children and went off into the sunset with a male model, a boy of twenty.) John and Suzy are in Canada this winter because Suzy, an Art historian, has a lectureship in Montreal.

'No news from the frozen North, you so-and-sos,' Nessa writes to the Tuckwells in her version of the italic script she and Lindsey learned at high school in Arbroath, 'How goes it? Otto's retrospective is end of Feb – any chance you'll be back in England by then?'

Biographical Notes on the Authors

Dannie Abse was born and educated in South Wales and later studied medicine in London. While he was still a student Hutchinson published his first book of poems. His most recent volume, *Remembrance of Crimes Past*, appeared in 1990. This was preceded by *White Coat, Purple Coat: Collected Poems 1948–1988*. Amongst his prose works are *Ash on a Young Man's Sleeve* (Penguin) and most recently its companion volume, *There Was a Young Man From Cardiff* (Hutchinson). Dr Abse has been President of the British Poetry Society since 1979 and is a Fellow of the Royal Society of Literature.

Gilbert Adair is the author of *The Holy Innocents*, which won the Author's Club First Novel Award in 1989; *Myths and Memories*, a collection of essays on British culture; *Hollywood's Vietnam*, which analysed the American cinema's treatment of the Vietnam war; and two sequels to classics of children's literature, *Alice Through the Needle's Eye* and *Peter Pan and the Only Children*. He lives in London.

Fred D'Aguair, poet and playwright, was born in 1960 and was brought up in Guyana. He trained and worked as a psychiatric nurse and read English at the University of Kent and the University of Warwick. His first collection of poems, *Mamma Dot*, was published in 1985. He has won several awards for his poetry.

Martin Amis was born in Oxford in 1949. He was educated in Britain, Spain and the USA and gained a first class degree in English at Exeter College, Oxford. His first novel, *The Rachel Papers* (1973) won the Somerset Maugham Award. His other novels are *Dead Babies* (1975), *Success* (1978), *Other People* (1981), *Money* (1984), *London Fields* (1990) and *Time's Arrow* (1991). He has also published a collection of short stories, *Einstein's Monsters* (1987), and a collection of essays, *The Moronic Inferno* (1986).

Paul Bailey was born in 1937 in Balham, the setting for his highly eloquent memoir *An Immaculate Mistake* (1990). He was a professional actor for eight years and has also worked as a journalist, a publisher's reader and a university teacher. Twice listed for the Booker Prize, he has been the recipient of the E.M. Forster Award and the Somerset Maugham Award. His first novel, *At The Jerusalem* was published in

1967. Other novels include *Peter Smart's Confessions* (1977) and *Gabriel's Lament* (1986).

Christopher Bigsby was educated at the University of Sheffield and is now Professor of American Studies at the University of East Anglia. He has delivered papers at numerous national and international conferences, has toured extensively for the British Council and edits several literary periodicals. His publications include *Confrontation and Commitment: A Study of Contemporary American Drama* (1967), *The Black American Writer* (1971), *Approaches to Popular Culture* (1976), *The Second Black Renaissance* (1980), *A Critical Introduction to 20th-century American Drama* 1900–1940 (1982); *Vol 2*: Williams, Miller, Albee (1984) and *Vol 3: Broadway and Beyond* (1985).

A S Byatt studied at Cambridge and taught at the Central School of Art and Design before moving to University College London to teach English and American literature. She is now a full-time freelance writer. Her first novel, *Shadow of a Sun*, appeared in 1964, and was followed by *The Game* (1967), *The Virgin in the Garden* (1978), *Still life* (1985) and *Possession* (1990), which won that year's Booker Prize for fiction. Her collection of short stories (*Sugar and Other Stories*) appeared in 1987, and a volume of critical essays, *Passions of the Mind*, in 1991. In 1990, she was Chairman of judges of the European Literary Prize. She reviews regularly for *The Times Literary Supplement* and other journals and for radio and television.

Mel Calman is an artist, writer, cartoonist for *The Times* and others. He was educated at Perse School, Cambridge and St Martin's School of Art. He founded the Cartoon Gallery, 44 Museum Street, London WC1. His books include *Couples, My God, How About a Little Quarrel Before Bed* (1981), *The Big Novel* (1983, dramatised for radio 1986), *What Else Do You Do?* (autobiography, 1986) and *Calman at the Movies* (1990).

Angela Carter was born in London, where she still lives, though she has spent time in Japan, America and Australia. She is a short story writer, journalist and novelist. Her novels include *Heroes and Villains* (1969), *The Infernal Desire Machines of Dr Hoffman* (1972) and *Nights at the Circus* (1984). Her short story collections are *Fireworks* (1974), *The Bloody Chamber* (1979) and *Black Venus* (1985). *Wise Children*, her latest novel, was published in 1991.

Wendy Cope was born in Kent in 1945, read history at Oxford, and taught in London primary schools for fifteen years. She began writing in her late twenties. Her first collection of poems, *Making*

Cocoa for Kingsley Amis (Faber 1986), reached the bestseller lists. In 1987 she received a Cholmondeley Award for poetry. Her most recent publication is a narrative poem, *The River Girl* (Faber 1991).

Paul Cox studied illustration at Camberwell School of Art and then at the Royal College of Art. He is involved in all kinds of publishing and design work. Among the books he has illustrated are Dylan Thomas's *The Outing* and *Three Men in a Boat* by Jerome K. Jerome. He illustrates for numerous newspapers and magazines including the *Observer* and the *Sunday Times*. His new book, *Honourable Estates*, is published by Pavilion this year.

Valentine Cunningham was born in 1944 and educated at Keble College, Oxford, where he was also a graduate student. He is Tutor in English Literature at Corpus Christi College and Dean of Corpus Christi. He has published numerous critical books, of which the most recent was his study of *British Writers of the Thirties* (1988). He has reviewed fiction for *The Listener*, the *Times Literary Supplement*, the *New Statesman* and the *Observer* and has talked about books on a number of BBC radio programmes, including *Kaleidoscope* and *Meridian*. He has travelled widely, lecturing for the British Council.

Carol Ann Duffy was born in Glasgow in 1955 and studied philosophy at the University of Liverpool. She was awarded the C. Day Lewis Fellowship in 1983 and 1984; received a Gregory Award in 1984, the Somerset Maugham Award in 1987 and the Dylan Thomas Award in 1989. Her first collection, *Standing Female Nude* (Anvil Press, 1985) received a Scottish Arts Council Award and her second, *Selling Manhattan* (Anvil 1987), received the Somerset Maugham Award. *The Other Country*, Duffy's third collection, was published by Anvil in 1990 and received a Scottish Arts Council Award. It was the Poetry Book Society's Spring Recommendation and was short-listed for the Whitbread Prize. Carol Ann Duffy lives in London.

Suzannah Dunn was born in 1963. Her first book, *Darker Days Than Usual*, a collection of short stories, was published by Serpent's Tail in 1990 to launch their Nineties series of new writing. In 1991 her first novel, *Quite Contrary*, was published by Sinclair-Stevenson. She is currently writing another novel and evaluating a pilot scheme by Hospice Arts to place three writers in residence in three hospices for six months.

Geoff Dyer was born in 1958. He is the author of three books: *Ways of Telling* (1986), a critical study of John Berger; *The Colour of Memory* (1989), a novel; and *But Beautiful* (1991), a book about jazz.

Lucy Ellmann was born in 1956 and educated at Falmouth and Canterbury art schools, the Courtauld Institute of Art and Essex University. Her first novel, *Sweet Desserts*, was published by Virago in 1988 and won the *Guardian* award for the best first novel. She lives near Oxford with her small daughter.

Penelope Fitzgerald was born in 1916 and spent her childhood in Sussex and Hampstead. She was educated at Somerville College, Oxford. Her first novel, *The Golden Child* (1977), was followed by *The Bookshop*, which was shortlisted for the Booker Prize in 1978. She went on to win the Booker the following year with *Offshore*, based on her experiences living on a houseboat on the Thames during the 1960s. Other novels include *Human Voices* (1980), based on her wartime experience at the BBC, *At Freddie's* (1985), *Innocence* (1987), *The Beginning of Spring* (1988), also shortlisted for the Booker Prize, and *Gate of Angels* (1990), which appeared on the shortlist the same year.

Lesley Glaister was born in Wellingborough, Northamptonshire, in 1956. She completed part of a B.Ed degree at Stockwell College of Education and then worked for a year as a clerical officer with the DHSS. She married in 1976 and began studying for a degree with the Open University in 1979, shortly after the birth of her first son, Joe. She completed her first-class honours degree in English Literature in 1986. Soon after the birth of her second son, Joshua, she moved to Sheffield and worked as a part-time adult education tutor. She was divorced in 1984 and decided to concentrate on her writing, completing two as yet unpublished novels. In 1988 she completed a Master's degree in Socio-Legal studies at Sheffield University. Her novel, *Honour Thy Father*, was published by Secker and Warburg in 1990 and received a Betty Trask Award and a Somerset Maugham Award in 1991. Her second novel, *Trick or Treat*, was published in 1991.

Alasdair Gray was born in Glasgow in 1934, studied at Glasgow Art School and has since lived by painting, book design and writing. For the past six years he has been working on *The Anthology of Prefaces*, a collection of introductions to great books in vernacular English arranged chronologically from Caedmon to Vonnegut with historical, biographical and critical marginal commentaries. He expects to finish this work before the end of the 20th century, and meanwhile supports himself by the enjoyable exercise of writing popular fiction.

Georgina Hammick's first collection of stories, *People For Lunch*, was published by Methuen and Abacus. A new collection will appear in 1992. She is currently editing an anthology of stories for Virago, on the theme of love and loss. She lives in West Wiltshire, and has three children.

Michael Ignatieff was born in Toronto in 1947, educated at the University of Toronto and worked for the *Toronto Globe & Mail*. He went to Harvard in 1969 and completed his PhD in history in 1975. Until 1984 he was a Fellow of King's College, Cambridge and since then has worked as a presenter of BBC2's *The Late Show* and as a columnist for the *Observer*. His books include *The Needs of Strangers*, *The Russian Album* and a novel, *Asya*. He lives in London with his wife and two children.

Peter Kemp has published two critical books, *Muriel Spark* (1974) and *H.G. Wells and the Culminating Ape* (1982). He is currently writing a book for Faber & Faber on fiction in English from 1970. He works as a freelance reviewer and broadcaster. He reviews regularly for the *Times Literary Supplement* and occasionally for the *Independent* (for which he was theatre reviewer from 1986 to 1990). He has been lead fiction reviewer for the *Sunday Times* since 1987.

James Lasdun is the author of a collection of stories, *The Silver Age*, and one of poems, *A Jump Start*. He was born in London in 1958. At the moment he lives and works in New York. A new collection of his stories will be published in 1992.

Doris Lessing was born in Iran of British parents and grew up in Southern Rhodesia, now Zimbabwe. She came to England in 1949 with the manuscript of her first novel, *The Grass is Singing* (1950). Her publications since then include *The Golden Notebook* (1962), the tetralogy *Children of Violence* (1952–69) and the *Canopus in Argus Archives* sequence which began in 1979. Her short stories include *A Man and Two Women* (1965) and *The Story of a Non-Marrying Man* (1972). They were collected in *Collected African Stories* (2 vols, 1973) and *Collected Stories* (2 vols, 1978).

David Lodge is Honorary Professor of Modern English Literature at the University of Birmingham, where he taught from 1960 to 1987. He is the author of several works of literary criticism, the most recent of which is *After Bakhtin* (1990), and has published nine novels, including *Changing Places* (1975), *Small World* (1984), *Nice Work* (1988) and *Paradise News* (1991). He adapted *Nice Work* as a TV series for the BBC, broadcast in 1989, and his first stage play, *The Writing Game*, was produced at the Birmingham Rep in 1990.

Hilary Mantel was born in Derbyshire in 1952. She lived for some years in Africa and the Middle East and was the first winner (1987) of the Shiva Naipaul Memorial Prize for travel writing. Her books are *Every Day Is Mother's Day* (1985), *Vacant Possession* (1986), *Eight Months on Ghazza Street* (1988) and *Fludd* (1989), which received the Winifred Holtby Prize, the Cheltenham Festival Prize and the Southern Arts Literature Prize. She is married, lives in Berkshire and is working on a fifth novel.

Philip MacCann recently graduated from Trinity College, Dublin, and is working towards a collection of short stories.

Glyn Maxwell was born and educated in Welwyn Garden City, Hertfordshire. He took a first-class degree in English at Worcester College, Oxford and his first collection of poems was published in 1986. He has appeared at several festivals and took part in the Poetry Society's New British Poets tour in 1990. Bloodaxe published his *Tales of the Mayor's Son* in 1990 and will publish his second collection, *Out of the Rain* in 1992. *Tales of the Mayor's Son* was shortlisted for the John Llewellyn Memorial Prize and was a Poetry Book Society Choice in 1990. In 1991 he received an Eric Gregory Award for his poetry.

Clare Morgan has published a novel with Gollancz, and a number of short stories. She also writes reviews and critical pieces, and is working on a study of 1950s literature and visual art. She lives in London, Oxford and Snowdonia.

Ben Okri is a Nigerian writer resident in London. He has published four books including two volumes of stories, *Incidents at the Shrine* and *Stars of the New Curfew*. Ben Okri has won several prizes, including the *Paris Review* Aga Khan prize for fiction. A volume of his poetry was published in 1991 and a novel, *The Famished Road*, appeared the same year.

Craig Raine was born in Shildon, Co. Durham in 1944. He was educated at Exeter College, Oxford and, after graduate work, taught there and at Lincoln College and Christ Church. He has been books editor of the *New Review*, editor of *Quarto* and poetry editor of the *New Statesman*, as well as contributing to a wide variety of journals, including the *New Statesman* and the *Times Literary Supplement*. He was poetry editor at Faber & Faber, a post he held for many years. His books include *The Onion, Memory* (1987), *A Martian Sends a Postcard Home* (1979), *A Free Translation* (1981), *Rich* (1984), *The Electrification of the Soviet Union* (1986) and '*1953*', a version of Racine's *Andromaque* (1990). He has also published a collection of essays, *Haydn & the Valve Trumpet* (1990) and has edited a selection of Kipling's prose for Faber in 1987. He is married and lives in Oxford.

Peter Reading was born in 1946 and trained as a painter at Liverpool College of Art. He has lived in Shropshire and worked at an agricultural feed-mill for over twenty years. Reading received the Cholmondeley Award for Poetry in 1978 and has published fifteen books, including *Diplopic*, which won the first Dylan Thomas Award in 1983, and *Stet*, which was awarded the 1986 Whitbread Prize for Poetry. In 1990 he was the recipient of a major award from the Lannan Foundation.

Lorna Sage teaches literature at the University of East Anglia in Norwich, and has written on Milton, Peacock, Hardy, Meredith, Virginia Woolf, Christina Stead and Doris Lessing, among others. She also writes for the *Observer*, the *Guardian* and the *Times Literary Supplement*. Her latest book, *Women in the House of Fiction*, is published by Macmillan this year, and includes an essay on Angela Carter, whom she first met – and interviewed – in the mid-1970s.

Graham Swift was born in London in 1949. He read English at Cambridge and began a PhD on Dickens at York. His first novel, *The Sweet Shop Owner* (1980) was followed by *Shuttlecock* (1981), which was awarded the Geoffrey Faber Memorial Prize in 1983. A collection of stories, *Learning to Swim* (1982) was followed by *Waterland* (1983), which was shortlisted for the Booker Prize, and by *Out of This World* (1988). He has also published *The Magic Wheel: An Anthology of Fishing in Literature* (1986) together with David Profumo. His novel *Ever After* is to be published in Spring 1992. He lives and works in London.

Adam Thorpe was born in Paris in 1956, and brought up in India, Cameroon, and England. He has had two collections of poetry published by Secker & Warburg: *Mornings In the Baltic* (1988) and *Meeting Montaigne* (1990). The story which appears here is one of twelve that make up *Ulverton* (Secker 1992), a sequence spanning three centuries of a fictional English village. He now lives in France with his wife and two children.

Anthony Thwaite was born in 1930. He spent his childhood in Yorkshire, four wartime years in the United States and after army service was at Christ Church, Oxford. Since then he has been a visiting lecturer at Tokyo University, a BBC radio producer, literary editor of *The Listener*, assistant professor of literature at the University of Libya, literary editor of the *New Statesman* and from 1973–85 co-editor of *Encounter*. His first book, *Home Truths* (1957) was followed by many others, including *The Owl in the Tree* (1963), *The Stones of Emptiness* (1967), *Inscriptions* (1973), *A Portion for Foxes* (1977), *Victorian Voices* (1980) and *Letter from Tokyo* (1987). His *Collected Poems 1953–88* appeared in 1989. He lives in Norfolk with his wife, the biographer and author Ann Thwaite.

Rose Tremain was born in 1943 and was educated at the Sorbonne and the University of East Anglia. Her first novel, *Sadler's Birthday* (1976) was followed by *Letter to Sister Benedicta* (1981), *The Cupboard* (1983) and *The Swimming Pool Season* (1985). A collection of short stories, *The Colonel's Daughter*, also appeared in 1983, when she was listed among the best young British novelists by the Book Marketing Council. She has also written extensively for radio and the stage. In 1989 her novel *Restoration* was shortlisted for the Booker Prize.

Marina Warner was born in 1946 and brought up in Egypt, Belgium and Cambridge. Her father was a bookseller, her mother teaches Italian in London. Her books include *Alone of All Her Sex* (1976), *Joan of Arc* (1981) and *Monuments and Maidens* (1985). Her third novel, *The Lost Father*, was on the Booker Prize shortlist in 1988. In 1987–88 she was a Visiting Scholar at the Getty Center for the History of Art.

Hugo Williams has published several books of poems, the most recent being *Writing Home* (1985), *Selected Poems* (1989) and *Self-Portrait With a Slide* (1990). He has written two travel books, *All the Time in the World* and *No Particular Place to Go*, and made a film about the Pan-American Highway in the BBC *Great Journeys* series 1989–90. He was theatre critic of the ill-fated *Sunday Correspondent*. He is poetry editor of the *New Statesman* and writes a regular column in the *Times Literary Supplement*.

Adam Zameenzad was brought up in Nairobi where his Pakistani parents were teaching, and in Pakistan. As a young man he travelled widely before settling in England. His first novel, *The Thirteenth House* won the David Higham Award in 1987. His next three books, *My Friend Matt and Hena the Whore* (1988); *Love, Bones and Water* (1989) and *Cyrus, Cyrus* (1990) won consistently high praise from critics, enabling him to give up his teaching job and write full-time.

Acknowledgements

The editors are grateful for advice and suggestions from Harriet Harvey Wood, Jonathan Barker and Christina Koning.

Acknowledgements are due to the following for permission to include the stories and poems which appear in this book:

'Ever After' copyright © Graham Swift Limited 1992 reprinted with permission from *Ever After* by Graham Swift, published in the UK by Picador, in the USA by Alfred A. Knopf Inc., and in Canada by Random House of Canada Limited.

'D H S S' copyright © Doris Lessing, was first published in by Jonathan Cape in *London Observed*, 1991 and is reprinted by permission of the author and Jonathan Clowes Ltd.

'Over' copyright © Rose Tremain, was first published by Bloomsbury in *Soho Square III* and is reprinted by permission of the author and Richard Scott Simon Ltd.

Clare Morgan's 'L'Hotel Des Grands Hommes' was first published in the Canadian magazine *Prism*.

'Poem Composed in Santa Barbara' by Wendy Cope was first published in *Poetry Review*'; Wendy Cope's 'Reflections on a Royalty Statement' was first published in *The Author*.

Glyn Maxwell's 'Poem in Blank Rhyme' was first published in *Atlantic Monthly*.

'Art Work' by A.S. Byatt was first published in *The New Yorker*.

'Of Poets and Their Antagonists', by Ben Okri, was inspired by the deaths of three poets: Christopher Okigbo, in 1967 during the Nigerian Civil War; Michael Smith, who was stoned to death in Jamaica; and Dambudzo Marechera, in Zimbabwe. It was first read in 1988 at the P.E.N. International English Centre.

The British Council would like to thank Booker PLC, Whitbread PLC and Waterstone's Booksellers for their sponsorship of this publication.

1742 1992

WHITBREAD PLC

*'Committed to quality
for another 250 years'*

Booker
Prize

FROM ONE SUCCESS

TO ANOTHER......

BOOKER WELCOMES

NEW WRITING

AS A VALUABLE STIMULUS

TO LITERATURE

BOOKER

KEY LINKS IN THE FOOD CHAIN

SPONSORS OF THE BOOKER PRIZE
FOR FICTION ESTABLISHED 1968

A Selected List of Titles Available from Minerva

While every effort is made to keep prices low, it is sometimes necessary to increase prices at short notice. Mandarin Paperbacks reserves the right to show new retail prices on covers which may differ from those previously advertised in the text or elsewhere.

The prices shown below were correct at the time of going to press.

Fiction

☐ 7493 9026 3	**I Pass Like Night**	Jonathan Ames	£3.99	BX
☐ 7493 9006 9	**The Tidewater Tales**	John Bath	£4.99	BX
☐ 7493 9004 2	**A Casual Brutality**	Neil Blessondath	£4.50	BX
☐ 7493 9028 2	**Interior**	Justin Cartwright	£3.99	BC
☐ 7493 9002 6	**No Telephone to Heaven**	Michelle Cliff	£3.99	BX
☐ 7493 9028 X	**Not Not While the Giro**	James Kelman	£4.50	BX
☐ 7493 9011 5	**Parable of the Blind**	Gert Hofmann	£3.99	BC
☐ 7493 9010 7	**The Inventor**	Jakov Lind	£3.99	BC
☐ 7493 9003 4	**Fall of the Imam**	Nawal El Saadewi	£3.99	BC

Non-Fiction

☐ 7493 9012 3	**Days in the Life**	Jonathon Green	£4.99	BC
☐ 7493 9019 0	**In Search of J D Salinger**	Ian Hamilton	£4.99	BX
☐ 7493 9023 9	**Stealing from a Deep Place**	Brian Hall	£3.99	BX
☐ 7493 9005 0	**The Orton Diaries**	John Lahr	£5.99	BC
☐ 7493 9014 X	**Nora**	Brenda Maddox	£6.99	BC

All these books are available at your bookshop or newsagent, or can be ordered direct from the publisher. Just tick the titles you want and fill in the form below. Available in:
BX: British Commonwealth excluding Canada
BC: British Commonwealth including Canada

Mandarin Paperbacks, Cash Sales Department, PO Box 11, Falmouth, Cornwall TR10 9EN.

Please send cheque or postal order, no currency, for purchase price quoted and allow the following for postage and packing:

UK   80p for the first book, 20p for each additional book ordered to a maximum charge of £2.00.

BFPO   80p for the first book, 20p for each additional book.

Overseas   £1.50 for the first book, £1.00 for the second and 30p for each additional book
including Eire   thereafter.

NAME (Block letters) ....

ADDRESS ....

....

....